MW01156752

COLONIZING HAWAI'I

EDITORS

Sherry B. Ortner, Nicholas B. Dirks, Geoff Eley

A LIST OF TITLES

IN THIS SERIES APPEARS

AT THE BACK OF

THE BOOK

PRINCETON STUDIES IN

CULTURE / POWER / HISTORY

COLONIZING HAWAI'I

THE CULTURAL POWER OF LAW

Sally Engle Merry

PRINCETON UNIVERSITY PRESS

PRINCETON, NEW JERSEY

COPYRIGHT © 2000 BY PRINCETON UNIVERSITY PRESS

PUBLISHED BY PRINCETON UNIVERSITY PRESS, 41 WILLIAM STREET,

PRINCETON, NEW JERSEY 08540

IN THE UNITED KINGDOM: PRINCETON UNIVERSITY PRESS, CHICHESTER, WEST SUSSEX

ALL RIGHTS RESERVED

LIBRARY OF CONGRESS CATALOGING-IN-PUBLICATION DATA

MERRY, SALLY ENGLE, 1944–

COLONIZING HAWAI'I : THE CULTURAL POWER OF LAW / SALLY ENGLE MERRY.

P. CM. — (PRINCETON STUDIES IN CULTURE/POWER/HISTORY)

INCLUDES BIBLIOGRAPHICAL REFERENCES AND INDEX.

ISBN 0-691-00931-7 (CL. : ALK. PAPER). — ISBN 0-691-00932-5 (PB. : ALK. PAPER)

1. HAWAIIANS—GOVERNMENT RELATIONS.   2. HAWAIIANS—LEGAL STATUS, LAWS, ETC.

3. HAWAIIANS—POLITICS AND GOVERNMENT.   4. CUSTOMARY LAW—HAWAII.

5. UNITED STATES—FOREIGN RELATIONS—HAWAII.   6. HAWAII—FOREIGN RELATIONS—

UNITED STATES.   I. TITLE.   II. SERIES.

DU624.65.M47   2000   996.9—DC21   99-30345

THIS BOOK HAS BEEN COMPOSED IN TIMES ROMAN

THE PAPER USED IN THIS PUBLICATION MEETS THE MINIMUM REQUIREMENTS OF ANSI/NISO

Z39.48-1992 (R 1997) (*PERMANENCE OF PAPER*)

HTTP://PUP.PRINCETON.EDU

PRINTED IN THE UNITED STATES OF AMERICA

1   3   5   7   9   10   8   6   4   2

3   5   7   9   10   8   6   4   2

(PBK.)

To

Murry Engle Lauser

Patricia Lee Engle

Sarah Elizabeth Merry

CONTENTS

CONTENTS

ILLUSTRATIONS

Figures

Charts

Tables

ACKNOWLEDGMENTS

THIS WORK has been generously supported by several grants. The Cultural Anthropology Program and the Law and Social Sciences Program of the National Science Foundation provided two grants to support the research. The National Endowment for the Humanities and the Canadian Institute for Advanced Research also supported me during the period of this research. The Bunting Institute at Radcliffe College provided a congenial and stimulating atmosphere for a year of research and writing. Wellesley College contributed generously to my research through research support to my chair, the Class of 1949 Professorship in Ethics.

My colleagues and friends in Hawai'i have always given most generous support and encouragement, particularly Rikki Amano and Neal Milner. Harry Ball provided the initial inspiration for doing this project, sharing with me his vast body of knowledge on nineteenth-century Hawaiian social and legal change as well as the data from his nineteenth-century court study, which served as the basis for my subsequent data collection. Jane Silverman, the principle investigator of that study and an eminent historian of Hawai'i was also a continuous help. The Hawai'i Judiciary History Center was a center of inspiration and help. I am particularly grateful for the support of T. Lani Ma'a Lapilio, the director. Esther Mookini was a continual inspiration as well as a great contributor in her translation of the nineteenth-century court records, an enormous task. Her translations and the Hawaiian original are available at the Hawai'i Judiciary History Center in Honolulu. Charlene Dahlquist at the Lyman House Memorial Museum in Hilo, Hawai'i was a great resource for archival materials and enthusiasm. I also learned a great deal from Williamson Chang, Ben Gaddis, Sue Heftel-Liquido, June Gutmanis, Ka'ohulani MacGuire, Pua Brown, Yuklin Aluli, Manu Meyer, and many other people in Hilo and Honolulu. Unfortunately, I did not discover Jonathan Osorio's fine dissertation (1996) on the constitutional transformation of nineteenth-century Hawai'i until I had completed drafting this book.

Several colleagues read and commented on drafts of this book and I have benefitted enormously from their insights: Jane Collier, Malcolm Feeley, Lidwein Kapteijns, Manu Meyer, Neal Milner, and Austin Sarat. Their comments were provocative and helpful and I am most grateful for their thoughtfulness. Several research assistants, most of them students at Wellesley College, contributed greatly to the project: Marilyn Brown, Joy Adapon, Erin Campbell, Nancy Hayes, Madelaine Adelman, and Tami Miller all worked hard. My colleagues at Wellesley College contributed to a supportive and positive working environment. My children became teenagers and then left home for school during this project, adding the challenge and excitement of those years to my writing. My husband has been, as always, supportive of my work but also mindful that there are mountains to climb and seas to sail. I dedicate this book to the strong, supportive women in my family: my mother, Murry, my sister, Patricia, and my daughter, Sarah.

Wellesley, Massachusetts
December 1998

A NOTE ON LANGUAGE AND TERMINOLOGY

HAWAIIAN WORDS are not italicized as foreign words in this text because, following the usage adopted by the editors of the 1997 issue of *Social Process in Hawai'i* (vol. 38), I recognize the Hawaiian language as indigenous to the place I am writing about rather than the language of a foreign country. As Kahulu Palmeira notes in the beginning of that issue of *Social Process*, this approach reflects a new consciousness about sovereignty and the place of Kanaka Maoli language and culture in the islands.

I adopt modern Hawaiian orthography in this book, using the macron and 'okina (glottal stop), but I have not added these markers to quotations from historical texts and nineteenth-century court records that did not use them. Where these early texts used hyphens to separate syllables, I have kept this usage. Although the term *Kanaka Maoli* is increasingly the preferred term for people of Polynesian Hawaiian ancestry, I have used this term primarily in modern contexts and elsewhere have adopted the terminology used by the writers at the time, including *Hawaiian*, *Native Hawaiian*, and *Kanaka Maoli*. I have followed the spelling and orthography of Lilikalā Kame'ele-ihiwa, a prominent Native Hawaiian scholar. I have also consulted Noenoe Silva, who has endeavored to correct my mistakes in spelling and orthography of Hawaiian words. The responsibility for errors remains mine.

COLONIZING HAWAI'I

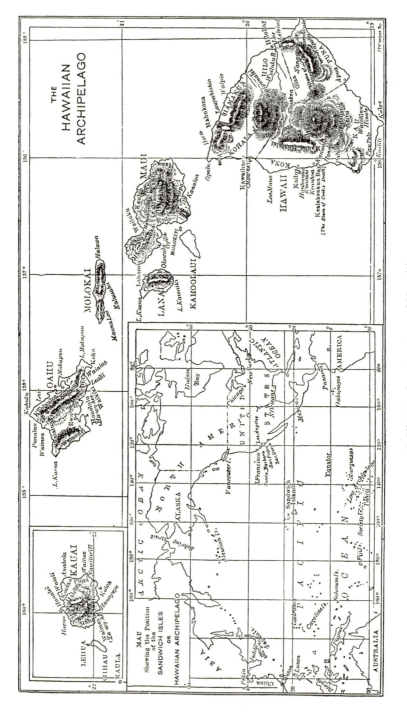

1. Nineteenth-century map of Hawai'i

1

INTRODUCTION

IN OCTOBER 1846 William Little Lee arrived in Hawai'i after a long and arduous sea passage around Cape Horn. Driven from upstate New York by his search for a more healthful climate, he was en route to Oregon Territory with his friend Charles R. Bishop. Lee was twenty-five years old and a lawyer. Trained in law at Harvard University under Judge Joseph Story and Professor Simon Greenleaf, Lee had practiced law in Troy, New York, for a year and had been admitted to practice before the Supreme Court of the State of New York. Scarcely a month and a half after his ship docked in Honolulu, Kamehameha III, the king of Hawai'i, had persuaded Lee to stay on in the independent Kingdom of Hawai'i and become a judge in the Honolulu court (Dutton 1953). By 1847 he had helped to draft legislation creating a new Superior Court of Law and Equity; he was immediately elected its chief justice. In the same year he was appointed to the Privy Council and appointed president of the Board of Commissioners to Quiet Land Titles. In 1849 Lee brought a wife from Albany, New York, to Honolulu and invested in one of the earliest sugar plantations with his friend Bishop. In 1850 he became the first president of the Royal Hawaiian Agricultural Society, an organization dedicated to improving the commercial agricultural production of the islands. This society became a major promoter of the sugar industry. By 1850 Lee had penned a new criminal code for the islands, modeled after a Massachusetts prototype, and by 1852 a new constitution.

In 1852 Lee celebrated the creation of the architecture of modernity in the streets of Honolulu. Delivering an address at the opening of the new Superior Court building in Honolulu, Lee, then chief justice of the Supreme Court of Hawai'i, began with lyrical praise for the rule of law and concluded with applause for the changes in the architecture of the courthouse:

> In England and the United States, I may say perhaps without contradiction, the two freest and best governed countries on the face of the earth, the law is respected most, and the people bow to its supremacy, from the force of deep settled public opinion, without the aid of cannon and bayonets to keep them in subjection. Their doctrine is, to obey the law while it is the law, so long as it accords with the constitution, and when wrong, to reform it through the legal channel of the Legislature.
>
> (Dutton 1953)

He continued in a curious vein, considering his Polynesian constituency: "Let that deep reverence for the law which dwells in the lands of our fathers animate us here." He concluded this speech with a reference to the architecture of the building itself, a metaphor for the relationship between American law and the Hawaiian state of the nineteenth century:

> I well remember when I landed on these shores, now nearly six years ago, the court met in an old grass house, floored with mats, without benches, seats, or comforts of any kind, with one corner partitioned off with calico, for judge's office, clerk's office, police court, and jury room, standing on the very ground where now stands this substantial edifice erected at a cost of upwards of forty thousand dollars, and which would do credit to any land. Justice in a grass house is as precious as justice in one of coral, but no one can fail to agree with me, that the latter with all its comforts and conveniences is greatly to be preferred, inasmuch as it tends to promote that dignity and propriety of manners so essential to secure a proper respect for the law and its administration. May this Hall ever be the temple of Justice—may its walls ever echo with the accents of truth—may its high roof ever look down upon us in the faithful discharge of our duties—and may the blessing of Him who built the Heavens and whose throne is the fountain of all justice ever rest upon us.
>
>   (Dutton 1953)

This speech encapsulates the contradictory position of the ali'i (chiefs) at this time: to make claims to "civilization," to "dignity and propriety of manners," required a massive displacement of systems of governance and ordering based on Hawaiian law in favor of those of European states. In the metaphoric replay of this transformation, the grass house was replaced by the coral house just as Lee celebrated the change in the architecture of law itself.

Lee had arrived in Hawai'i at a critical time. Caught in the crosscurrents of global mercantile trade involving Europe, the United States, and China and at the center of the burgeoning Pacific whale fishery, the Kingdom of Hawai'i had become home to a large and fractious group of foreign merchants and sailors. As Britain, France, and the United States vied for power and influence in the Pacific, each sent warships to the islands demanding special treatment for its resident citizens and threatening to take over the kingdom. In response to these pressures, Kamehameha III and the high-ranking chiefs were engaged in transforming the Hawaiian system of law and governance into an Anglo-American political system under the rule of law. Their strategy was to create a "civilized" nation, in European terms, to induce those European and American powers whose recognition defined sovereign status to acknowledge the kingdom's independence. A trained lawyer from New England seemed a rare find to the beleaguered king and his American missionary advisors. Even though the Hawaiian public complained bitterly about the number of foreigners employed by the government, deluging the king with petitions of protest, Kamehameha III felt he had no choice (Kamakau 1961).

By his death in 1857, Lee had contributed in significant ways to changing the Hawaiian system of law and governance to one resembling that of his native New England. He had spearheaded the reshaping of governance and land ownership that propelled the islands from a system of chiefly control over land occupied by a chief's followers to a regime of fee simple, individual landownership. The opportunity for private landownership, soon made available to foreigners, proved a boon to the nascent sugar plantation economy. This economy, resting largely in foreign hands, ultimately displaced the vast majority of Hawaiian commoners from their lands.

Yet, despite his prominence in facilitating these changes, it is not clear how much Lee knew of the Hawaiian language or legal system. Obviously, he was actively involved in changing the legal system almost as soon as he arrived. According to an article in the *Polynesian*, the official government newspaper, on the occasion of his death, he had a "fair degree of proficiency" in the Hawaiian language and corresponded with natives in their own language (May 30, 1857: 10). In his private letters, Lee expressed a paternalistic concern for the Hawaiians, prefiguring the infantilization of Hawaiian people that became the dominant trope in the late nineteenth century. In a letter to Joel Turrill on October 11, 1851, following a seven-week tour of the island of Hawai'i, he said he had visited Hawaiians, listened to their grievances, redressed their wrongs, and settled their quarrels.

> Certainly they are a kind and peaceable people, with a superabundance of generous hospitality; but with all their good traits, they lack the elements necessary to perpetuate their existence. Living without exertion, & contented with enough to eat and drink, they give themselves no care for the future, and mope away life, without spirit, ambition, or hope. Now & then we meet an enterprising native, climbing up in the world, and I feel like crying bravo! my good fellow! bravo! but the *mass* of the people, where are they? I consider the doom of this nation as sealed, though I will labor on without ceasing, hoping for the blessing of heaven to bring some change. I am just now engaged in revising the Constitution, and I trust I shall have wisdom given me to frame it in such a manner, as to secure to the people of these islands for all time to come, the blessings of liberty and justice.
>
> (Turrill Collection 1957: 47)

Despite the widespread praise of Lee by whites living in Honolulu at the time, others were more critical. Kamakau, a Native Hawaiian historian writing in the 1860s, was probably referring to Lee in the following discussion, although he does not mention him by name. After praising the choice of John Young (Keoni Ana) as premier (1845–1846), Kamakau continues:

A learned man had arrived with knowledge of the law, and the foreigners who were holding office in the government hastened to put him forward by saying how clever and learned he was and what good laws he would make for the Hawaiian people. The truth was, they were laws to change the old laws of the natives of the land and cause them to lick ti leaves like the dogs and gnaw bones thrown at the feet of strangers, while the strangers became their lords, and the hands and voices of strangers were raised over those of the native race. The commoners knew this and one and all expressed their disapproval and asked the king not to place foreigners in the office of government lest the native race become a footstool for the foreigners.

(Kamakau 1961: 399)

From the perspective of the late twentieth century, Kamakau was chillingly prophetic.

William Little Lee's actions in Hawai'i reflect both serendipity and world historical processes. Colonialism is made up of both: chance conjunctures of particular individuals and broad economic, political, and cultural forces. The colonial transformation of Hawai'i was a fragment of global processes of imperialism, capitalist expansion, and transition to modernity but it was also the product of the actions of particular people who found themselves there at the time: bodies cast up on distant shores carrying with them the civilizing mission. It was Massachusetts prototypes that formed the basis of Hawaiian criminal law, for example, because these law books happened to be in Honolulu. But it was global trade networks that brought the ships that carried the books from New England to Hawai'i.

Nor did the foreigners see eye to eye about the colonizing process, the long struggle for economic, political, and cultural transformation that involved the "civilizing" of the heart, the soul, and the body of non-European peoples. An ongoing battle raged between proponents of commerce and proponents of conversion about the optimum approach to the civilizing process. The Protestant New England missionaries in Hawai'i struggled to control the sexual behavior of sailors on American and European ships while many American and British merchants and ship captains tolerated grog shops and prostitution. Ordinary seamen and sailors, often from many parts of the world, had little interest in the stern prohibitions of the missionaries. Lee himself was inspired by complex motives: paternalistic concern for Hawaiians seen only as children; moral commitment to the rule of law; capitalist desires for wealth. Lee thought he was doing good for the Native Hawaiian people by his expansion of sugar plantations, his promotion of private property ownership, and his support for constitutional monarchy as a form of government.

For individual agents of the civilizing process at the heart of colonialism, the magnitude of the challenge and the inadequacy of the resources at hand were often overwhelming. Resistance was all too evident, as it was to Kipling in his classic imperialist poem from 1899, "The White Man's Burden."[1] The "fluttered folk and wild" were sullen, unappreciative, and uncooperative. For Kipling, the audience that would applaud the struggle to tame, to domesticate—his vision of colonialism—were not the subjects of this effort but the peers of the colonizer.[2] Kipling's poem points to the need to construct a rationale for this process beyond the gratitude of its objects (which evidently was not forthcoming). The title of his famous poem uses the language of duty, the sense of "burden."[3] But this is not a universal human duty: it is the *white man's* burden. This is not a duty for women or for children. It is a thankless task that defines manhood. And of course it is not for all men, but only for white men.[4] As this poem signals, the cultural transformation of the colonial project was a raced and gendered one played for a European audience.

The targets of colonial transformation also received widely varying treatment. While viewing the chiefly class of Hawaiians with some respect and supporting their political authority during much of the nineteenth century, the Americans and Europeans helped to displace the Hawaiian commoners from lands held often by ancient grants from chiefs. As the demand for sugar plantation labor escalated, American and European landowners imported vast numbers of immigrant sugar workers from Europe and Asia. These groups were largely labor units in the imagination of the dominant groups, both white and Native Hawaiian, never the targets of a reformist gaze. They remained an alien "other" while the Native Hawaiians were assimilated into a category of "us" by the economically and politically dominant whites. Even so, the Native Hawaiian population was ousted from political power in 1893 in a coup engineered by Americans living in Hawai'i with the energetic support of the U.S. consul and U.S. troops.

Thus, as vastly different understandings of the body and sexuality, race and citizenship, and work and capital were juxtaposed in the colonial situation, serendipity and struggle were part of the process. This was a process developing over time, in which decisions had to be made under conditions of uncertainty and ambiguity. From a distance, the changes appear predictable and inevitable, but close at hand the process was an uncertain groping toward a dimly perceived future. Reexamining these decisions in hindsight, with far greater knowledge of their consequences, it is difficult to appreciate the very different conditions under which these decisions were made in the first place. In this rapidly shifting and culturally complex terrain, individuals such as Kamehameha III and William Little Lee sought to read the signs of the future, to anticipate the shape of the coming institutions and the transformations they would wreak, wondering where to find a place in the new order. Although the Hawaiians confronted European nations vastly greater in military and economic power, they constructed some space for autonomous action by playing on European competition and the exigencies of physical and cultural distance.

The law was one of the core institutions of colonial control, serving the needs of commerce and capitalism by producing free labor and privatized land (see Wolf 1992). But it was also an ideological cornerstone of the civilizing process. European imperialists felt that they were giving the rude peoples of the rest of the world who had suffered under despotic rule the benefits of the rule of law (Fitzpatrick 1992). Law became a marker of the seductive idea of "civilization," that complex set of signs, practices, and forms of bodily management that could confer sovereignty even upon a female monarch with brown skin when white masculinity seemed the essential badge of rule. From time to time, the law provided ways of resisting the capitalist appropriation of land and labor, but only for those who had mastered its forms and language, who were already incorporated within the system of "civilization." The law was simultaneously a means of change and a sign of progress.

One way to understand the complexities of the colonial process is to take a magnifying glass to one small place and at the same time to deploy a wide-angle lens to view the larger processes that envelop that place. To explore the dynamics of colonialism from microscopic and telescopic perspectives simultaneously, this book analyses the way Western law came to Hawai'i in the nineteenth century and the changes it wrought in one community. It uses the vantage point of a town on the rainy side of the largest island. Here, among the vivid green of sugar cane fields, the deep blue of a relentless sea, and the intense black of recent lava flows, a distinctive colonizing process traced the lineaments of the religious and legal culture of New England onto an ancient Hawaiian civilization and a new mosaic of peoples brought to work the sugar or to manage the plantations. Economically, the region shifted from mercantile activities centered on the whaling trade to the expansion of capitalist plantation agriculture throughout the nineteenth century.

Sixty years of records of the lower court in the town of Hilo provide a window into the legal system's regulation of everyday family, community, and work life. These cases concern work, marriage, sex, drugs, violence, and public order. In the 1850s and 1860s, many cases concerned adultery or lewd and lascivious behavior. By the 1870s and 1880s, violations of contract labor regulations dominated court activity as planters struggled to force contracted laborers to stay on the job using penal sanctions. By the turn of the century, the courts increasingly focused on gambling, drinking, or riding horses too fast after the penal contract labor system was dismantled. This is law at its bottom fringes, where it intersects the social life of ordinary people rather than where legal doctrines are created. The court records reveal who is in court, for what kinds of problems, and with what results. They also provide stories of ordinary people and their problems during a period of dramatic social change. Most of the cases are criminal cases, since my focus is on the transformation of family, gender, and community. The social networks of judges, attorneys, and constables shaped local legal processes. I found intimate links among the judiciary, the missionary community, and Hawaiian elites and deep fault lines separating these groups from Hawaiian commoners and immigrant sugar workers.

Court records provide a special lens on everyday life, but they are mediated by the language of the law and the perspective of their writers. These texts do not reveal the smells, sights, feelings, and noise in the courtroom, yet they are full of ordinary people describing their lives. In these courts judges were required to produce a record of proceedings, but the level of detail, the choice of facts, and the presentation of the story was up to the judge. Fleeting references in judges' private letters indicate that they did not always write these records on the spot, but sometimes a few days after the cases. Moreover, there were frequently two or more different languages in use in these courts, so accounts were translated. During the mid nineteenth century, testimony was generally in Hawaiian and the judges spoke Hawaiian but wrote their notes in English. Beginning in the 1880s, the judge in Hilo wrote notes in Hawaiian, but an increasing proportion of the cases involved interpreters who translated into either Hawaiian or English from many other languages. Thus, the stories of the litigants emerge through an interpretive screen. Understanding who the judges were and what perspectives they brought to their task is important in interpreting the case records they produced. Nonetheless, these case records provide a rare opportunity to glimpse the tensions and conflicts of everyday life, to hear the stories of ordinary people who were not otherwise producing archival texts, and to understand the complex role of legal institutions in the dramatic social changes that preceded and facilitated the American colonial takeover of the islands in 1898.

This project began in the late 1980s when Harry Ball, professor of sociology at the University of Hawai'i, told me that he had rescued sixty years of minute books from the Hilo District Court that were headed for destruction. They were now safely ensconced in the Hawai'i State Archives in downtown Honolulu. Intrigued, I looked at these books, fascinated by the detailed descriptions they included that were written laboriously in longhand, sometimes in Hawaiian, more often in English. They were an intimate slice of everyday life, like the cases I had already studied in New England courts (Merry 1990). Clearly, here was detailed evidence of the way the law intersected with the everyday lives of people in a small town during a period of immense change. The cases showed the courts in operation, but they also told the stories of ordinary people and their problems. I immediately noticed an 1874 case of a worker convicted of refusing to work, who was required to pay a fine. Because he had no money, he was sent to work off his fine on a plantation of one of the attorneys in the case. This seemed odd to me—a strange joining of judicial and economic interests. But these records, although tantalizing in their detail and their stories, were also very opaque. Who were the people? How did these cases fit into the context of the social organization of the town? How were they part of larger economic, social, and legal changes? What did they reveal about the legal consciousness of ordinary people? To what extent did the courts support the structure of power relations in town and to what extent were they autonomous from that structure?

Understanding these cases became the core project of this book. As I studied them, I had to constantly expand the context I considered. I began by looking at the texts of the cases themselves, then at the patterns of cases over time. Then I explored the social organization of the town, focusing in particular on the judges and attorneys and their relationships with each other. This led to an analysis of the economic and social transformations of the region during the period and of the conceptions of race and difference that underlay the plantation system itself. Although I had hoped that this was a wide enough context, it soon became clear that I had to ask still broader questions: How did this legal system come to Hawai'i in the first place? And how was it different from the legal system that governed Native Hawaiians before this law arrived? These questions are at the heart of the analysis of colonialism.

This book follows my exploration in the opposite direction. It begins in Part One from the broader question of how Hawai'i adopted Anglo-American law and how it transformed Hawaiian law. It then moves in Part Two to a discussion of the social organization of the town and the plantation hierarchy so fundamental to it. Chapter 5 presents this background. Only with this broader context is it possible to explore the case records themselves, and this information provides the frame for chapters 6, 7, and 8. Appendix A includes the texts of many of the cases. In addition to examining the particular cases and the personnel who managed the courts, I have charted changes in the types of cases and the nature of defendants over time, based on a one-year sample every decade. This material is presented in charts, but for those who wish to see the underlying numbers, tables are included in appendix B. Thus, I have examined these cases both as individual stories and in terms of patterns of change over time.

As an ethnographer making her first foray into archival work, I found the archives both fascinating and frustrating. I finally felt able to ask questions about change over time and to get some sense of historical processes. Only this historical approach can appreciate the complexities of the colonial process. On the other hand, this is a slow and fragmentary way of doing ethnography. I wanted to observe, to ask questions, to find ways to fill in the gaps. My archival work has been very substantially supplemented by ethnographic research in Hawai'i, mostly in Hilo, over the last ten years. Interviews with people who remember the plantation system and worked in it, those who managed it, and those who served as attorneys for it expanded my perspective. I was able to interview a county attorney who worked in the town in the 1930s and a prominent attorney who worked for the plantations in the 1920s to 1950s, as well as several judges who have worked in town since the 1950s. Many of the current judges and attorneys in town grew up on the plantations. I interviewed a labor activist who was wounded in a 1938 labor conflict and a Japanese-American judge who was told by his teachers in the early part of the twentieth century that he could not aspire to be an attorney. I have also made many visits to plantation camps and mills, talking to plantation managers—including one family that had been in the business of running sugar plantations for five generations—and plantation workers. I have had tours of various plantation camps and talked about the system with elderly Filipino workers who remember the 1920s and 1930s, as well as with descendants of Portuguese lunas. I have also discussed the transformations in Hawai'i with descendants of prominent white families in the nineteenth century. I have traveled extensively around the Hilo region, as well as other parts of Hawai'i, talking to people from a range of backgrounds.

I have been studying the lower courts during this period, focusing on an analysis of the way the courts today are managing family and gender conflicts, particularly violence against women, but I have also explored the issues in the contemporary Kanaka Maoli cultural renaissance and political movement. The contemporary Hawaiian sovereignty movement is deeply engaged in reexamining Hawaiian history, producing a great deal of new scholarship and material for discussion, and I have read and talked with many of the leaders of this movement. I have visited museums of Hilo, of the plantation system, of Native Hawaiian culture. This ethnography has contributed in significant ways to my historical analysis, although it is not extensively discussed here. Much of it will appear in a book on the 1990s mobilization of the law to contain gender violence, currently in process.

Colonialism and Postcolonial Theory

The last decades of the twentieth century have witnessed a florescence of literature on the postcolonial, seen simultaneously as an era and a condition of social life. Inspired in large part by the work of Frantz Fanon, Michel Foucault, and Edward Said, this work has examined how the relations of power and culture forged during the colonial era have shaped the present. One legacy is Orientalism, another our contemporary conceptions of race, gender, and sexuality.

Yet the postcolonial can only be understood through a detailed analysis of the colonial: the forms of imposition of rule, the extent and nature of resistance, and the ambiguous and contradictory position of colonized elites. Although the colonial process meant taking political control over a remote region, the transformation was deeply cultural and economic as well as political (Comaroff and Comaroff 1997: 16). Major changes often predated actual political takeover, as occurred in Hawai'i. Although connected to global movements of capitalist expansion and imperial competition, colonizers arrived with a wide range of interests in addition to those of profit and empire. Those targeted for reform and rule responded with varying degrees of complicity, resistance, and accommodation. Understanding the legacy of colonialism requires a thorough understanding of its complexities: its uncertainty, accident, and serendipity; its deep engagement with various forms of moral reform, including temperance and abolitionism; and the complex responses of mimicry, appropriation, and warfare by the objects of colonial transformation. As Darian-Smith points out, despite Said's enormous contribution to postcolonial studies, his approach tends to see the discourses of the East as always subject to negotiation through the discourses of the more powerful West, instead of attending to the "transgressive potentiality of mutual dependency between Europe and its Others" (Darian-Smith 1996: 293).

This book seeks to avoid the binaries that have characterized this field: colonial/postcolonial, colonizer/colonized—binaries, as McClintock points out, that recreate the oppositions that postcolonial theory has sought to destabilize (McClintock 1995: 10). Postcolonial theory, she argues, tends to see the postcolonial as a singular, ahistorical, and generic abstraction located on a linear time frame where it represents the end of the colonial (pp. 11–13). There are important geographical, political, and historical distinctions in the ways and times in which various places became postcolonial as well as many places still involved in colonial relationships, such as Hawai'i. And the patterns and practices of colonialism persist into the present era of postcolonialism. For example, definitions of gender and sexuality produced by the colonial project are abiding features of the postcolonial period, revealed in films that exoticize and eroticize Asian women for Euro-American male audiences and feed the booming Asian sex trade (Manderson and Jolly 1997). Thus, by providing a detailed analysis of processes of colonialism attentive to agency and historical change, this book aspires to provide a perspective on the postcolonial period.

A major concern in the contemporary reanalysis of colonialism is the extent of resistance by colonized populations and the degree and extent of complicity of colonized elites. As Fanon and Bhabha point out in different ways, some colonial elites adopted the values and way of life of their colonizers, imitating the Europeans but never achieving identity with them. Fanon points to the complicity of these groups of colonial elites with European values but notes how, in the context of a war against colonial control, "a colonized intellectual, dusted over by colonial culture, will in the same way discover the substance of village assemblies, the cohesion of people's committees, and the extraordinary fruitfulness of local meetings and group-ments" (Fanon 1963: 47). He looks to the peasantry, far removed from the colonial elites and caught in the rigidly divided world of colonialism, as the location of an authentic consciousness. Fanon eloquently warns the Algerian people of the dangers of adopting European ideologies such as the rights of man as the ideological frame of the colonial world (pp. 311–316).

Homi Bhabha develops a more complex analysis of colonized subjects living in the divided colonial world. He sees colonial mimicry as "the desire for a reformed, recognizable Other, as *a subject of a difference that is almost the same, but not quite.* Which is to say that the discourse of mimicry is constructed around an *ambivalence*; in order to be effective, mimicry must continually produce its slippage, its excess, its difference" (Bhabha 1997: 153; emphasis in original). The effect of such mimicry on the authority of colonial discourse is, he argues, profound and ambivalent. Examples of colo-nial imitation "all share . . . a discursive process by which the excess or slippage produced by the <u>*ambivalence* of mimicry</u> (almost the same *but not quite*) does not merely 'rupture' the discourse, but becomes transformed into an uncertainty which fixes the colonial subject as a 'partial' presence" (pp. 153–154). <u>Mimicry is both resemblance and menace.</u> Occupying such an in-between position, the same and yet different, generates deep anxiety (Bhabha 1998).

Bhabha's analysis of the complexity and ambivalence of the social posi-tion of intellectuals and elites caught up in the civilizing process offers a framework for understanding the actions of Hawaiian chiefs and intellectuals during the nineteenth century. Their adoption of Anglo-American law and the number of advisors this required appeared to Hawaiian commoners to be a betrayal. But it is also possible to view their actions as a part of a struggle for sovereignty: an attempt to purchase independence with the coin of civili-zation. Constructing a society that appeared "civilized" to the Europeans in nineteenth-century terms clearly helped to win acceptance from those Euro-pean powers whose recognition conferred sovereignty. Under the Westphalia system of international relations, European powers had a particular capacity to confer sovereign status. Elites engaging in "civilizing" their nations did so because they saw this as a form of resistance to imperialism. In Hawai'i, they were rewarded by a temporary postponement of colonial annexation by the United States, an autonomy guaranteed by European competition as much as by the creation of a "civilized" nation under the rule of law (see chapter 4). Yet, as the Kingdom of Hawai'i reconstructed its social and legal system, its leaders necessarily drew Europeans into the heart of the opera-tion. They were hired to provide technical knowledge for the project but ultimately undermined and destroyed the conditions for independence. At the same time, although Hawaiian elites endeavored to appear the same as Ameri-cans, they never escaped their racially inscribed difference.

Whatever the ambiguous position of Christianized, educated elites under colonizing conditions, there is a considerable literature that argues that at least peasants retained a resistant consciousness. The Subaltern Studies group has engaged in a reassessment of peasant resistance movements, which it reinterprets as politically significant rather than disorderly and chaotic (Otto 1996; Guha 1997). In its reexamination of Indian historiography, the group emphasizes the extent to which peasants and elites resisted the cultural forms and ideologies of colonialism, revealing the limits of hegemonic control despite political and economic dominance. In Ranajit Guha's view, Indians never accepted the superiority of British culture even though they submitted to its power (Guha 1997). Similarly, James Scott's analysis of subordinated groups, particularly peasants, argues that they retain their capacity to critique systems that control them even as they are forced to comply with their demands (Scott 1985; 1990). Scott's peasant conforms in behavior but not consciousness, like the image of the peasant Fanon presents.[5]

Mitchell offers a cogent critique of these arguments, however, noting that they are based on a sharp division between persuasion and coercion, between behavior and culture, and between material and ideological forms of power (Mitchell 1990). They posit an autonomous subject and a form of power that coerces the body without controlling the mind. Mitchell argues that this notion of power replicates the mind/body dichotomy by creating a self whose body is controlled but whose mind remains untrammeled, a dichotomy whose production is in fact an aspect of systems of power. In contrast, Gramsci's concept of hegemony refers not only to the power of ideology but also to the nonviolent forms of control exercised by a wide range of institutions and social practices (Mitchell 1988; 1990).[6]

The Hawaiian ali'i's appropriation of Anglo-American law and the Hawaiian people's subsequent acceptance of the new law reflects both material relations of power and new ideological commitments to civilization and Christianity. This transition was not simply a matter of outward behavioral compliance and inner spiritual resistance. Clearly there was economic and military pressure on the Hawaiian leaders to change their system of law and governance but there was also enthusiasm for the trappings of civilization and the values of Christianity and the rule of law. The Hawaiians resisted American political and economic control but were open to new ideas and institutions. In the mid nineteenth century, courses in the new system of law were popular and provided a solid income to the haole (white) judges who taught them, while law books sold like hotcakes in Hawaiian villages and towns. Many lower courts were staffed by Hawaiian judges (see chapter 4). In Honolulu in the 1840s, the lower courts did a brisk business with Hawaiians bringing their personal problems to the law (Matsuda 1988a). At the same time, many objected to the introduction of foreigners into the government. But at the time, none could foresee clearly what the consequences of the change would be, neither those bringing the new forms nor those appropriating them. Chapter 2 develops a theory of social transformation that recognizes the agency of actors struggling to make sense of a complex and changing situation without presuming an authentic consciousness of resistance despite bodily compliance.

The court records in Hilo reveal both resistance to law in the forms of evasion and violence and, over time, a new form of resistance using the authority of law itself to contest abusive treatment and unlawful arrests (chapters 6 and 7). Thus, as colonial subjects were incorporated into the legal ordering of social relationships, they themselves incorporated law within their techniques for resisting injustice within these relationships.

Gender and Sexuality

Some of the most creative work in postcolonialism has focused on gender and sexuality: on the ways in which the colonizing process entailed new ways of managing the body, of presenting and displaying it, and of regulating sexuality. Ann Stoler's pathbreaking work on sexuality and race revealed the centrality of gender to creating the borders and boundaries of colonialism (Stoler 1989; 1991; 1995; 1997). Interracial mating with its legacy of racially mixed children seemed to threaten metropolitan authority by blurring crucial social boundaries between ruler and ruled (Stoler 1997). Jolly and Macintyre (1989) pioneered the analysis of the impact of colonialism on domestic life in the Pacific, focusing in particular on the effect of the Christian mission on the organization of the family and the meanings of sexuality. An explosion of creative work has explored the ways in which sexuality was inextricably bound up with the expansion of empire and the construction of the nation (Kelly 1994; McClintock 1995; Ong and Peletz 1995; Comaroff 1997; Cooper and Stoler 1997; Alexander and Mohanty 1997; Manderson and Jolly 1997). Comaroff and Comaroff explore the process of civilizing the body by draping it with clothing, which preoccupied the South African Christian missions while enriching the British textile market (Comaroff and Comaroff 1997).

The creation of empire depended on the construction of a domestic space and retraining the colonized in techniques of motherhood, cleanliness, and domestic duty (e.g., Jolly and Macintyre 1989; McClintock 1995; Davin 1997; Hunt 1997). As McClintock suggests, "the mass-marketing of empire as a global system was intimately wedded to the Western reinvention of domesticity, so that imperialism cannot be understood without a theory of domestic space and its relation to the market" (McClintock 1995: 17). Building on Walter Benjamin's insights, McClintock claims that the creation of nationalism is a product of the juxtaposition of an archaic tradition, cabined and preserved by women, and a progressive modernity, spearheaded by men thrusting forward in time (p. 359). According to her analysis of the 1938 centennial reenactment of the Boer Great Trek in South Africa, a gender politics was deeply embedded in the spectacle, presenting as it did patriarchal authority penetrating the interior accompanied by invisible, incorporated women who supported the national identity through their sacrifices and labor for husband and family (pp. 371–372).

Women's bodies were central to the civilizing project in Hawai'i as well, but through everyday, invisible processes of regulation and correction rather than transformative spectacles. Creating a new form of marriage in which women's sexuality was lodged firmly in the sphere of patriarchal control was a central project of the political and legal leadership of nineteenth-century Hawai'i (see chapter 8). Early in the nineteenth century, leadership was exercised by both men and women of rank who were endowed with spiritual and political power through descent from powerful ancestors. By the end of the century, leadership was in the hands of men of property, selected by the popular vote of males, while women were folded under the authority of husbands and fathers in family units. The civilizing process meant reallocating control over women's bodies to their husbands and incorporating all women, not just a small group of high-ranking women, into a regime of controlled sexuality (see Ralston 1989).

The struggle to control sexuality and reshape marriage through law was driven by Christian demands for conversion rather than capitalist demands for labor. It is surprising that the effort to change the family life of Hawaiians long preceded the significant use of Hawaiians as laborers in the sugar plantations. Moreover, the project of reforming sexuality and marriage did not encompass the imported plantation laborers from Europe and Asia. As new workers arrived from China, Portugal, Japan, Korea, and Puerto Rico, no equivalent pattern of prosecution for marriage violations ensued. The targets of transformation were the Native Hawaiian converts, not the whole population of the islands. Thus, although the body was a central terrain for "civilizing," this effort targeted the laboring body and the sexual body in different ways. Christian concerns focused on the management of eating, cleanliness, sleeping, and sexuality. Capitalism zeroed in on punctuality and discipline.

Law and the Postcolonial

Postcolonial scholarship has focused extensively on the cultural meanings produced by the colonial experience. The exposure of the discourses by which the West understood the rest of the world constitutes one of its key intellectual contributions. Following Said's analysis of Orientalism as a literary as well as institutional system of knowledge (Said 1978), postcolonial scholars have explored the creation of the "Other" in travel writing (Pratt 1992), popular culture (McClintock 1995), and ideologies of race and the mission endeavor (Comaroff and Comaroff 1991; 1997). In the Pacific, Thomas (1997) charts the construction of meaning through the voyages of Cook and Manderson and Jolly (1997) examine the construction of otherness in popular culture and film. While the Europeans were making their exotic "others," indigenous groups were constructing their own images of the intruders (Pratt 1992). Another stream of scholarship explores the effects of the expanding European capitalist system on the rest of the world. Wolf's is one of the most encompassing studies of the transformations in relations of land and labor and forms of social organization wrought by capitalism (Wolf 1992; see also Cooper 1980; 1987; 1989; 1997; Mintz 1985; Stoler 1985; Fitzpatrick 1987).

Law stands at the cusp of these two approaches to understanding the colonial and postcolonial. It is both a system of meaning and an institutional structure backed by the political power of the state. Laws define persons and relationships, which create, if they do not already reflect, popular consciousness. The vast majority of law-abiding behavior occurs without sanction and is the product of general acceptance of a legal regime and its system of meaning (see Ewick and Silbey 1998). At the same time, the state engages in a continual process of surveillance, judgment, and punishment in order to produce compliance with its laws and categories. As new systems of rules are introduced or new institutions for enforcement are adopted, a gradual process of transformation takes place in which the force of the state is brought to bear on ordinary people to induce them to go along. The subjects of surveillance and correction learn to comply or to conceal their behavior from the law. Thus, law plays a critical cultural role in defining meanings and relationships, but it does so in the context of state power and violence. The power of law to transform sociocultural systems is two-sided: it depends both on the direct imposition of sanctions and on the production of cultural meanings in an authoritative arena.

The anthropology of law has increasingly focused on the cultural significance of law: on the intimate linkages between legal conceptions and the surrounding cultural fabric (Geertz 1983; Greenhouse 1986; Rosen 1989). This cultural approach foregrounds the importance of discourse and meaning-making within courts and other legal arenas (Mather and Yngvesson 1980/81; Yngvesson 1988, 1993; Conley and O'Barr 1990; Merry 1990; Starr 1992; Sarat and Kearns 1993; Greenhouse, Yngvesson, and Engel 1994; Sarat and Felstiner 1995; Brigham 1996; Philips 1998). As litigants, lawyers, judges, and other legal personnel talk about problems in courts, probation offices, and police stations, they create the meanings by which individuals understand their problems and themselves. At the same time,

these local practices define what the law is and shape local legal consciousness. As Ewick and Silbey (1998) point out, ordinary people share a complex set of conceptions about what the law is, which affects the way they
understand it and relate to its demands. The discursive construction of truth
through lower-court case processing is more difficult to examine through
archival court records than ethnographically, but contemporary ethnographic
research provides clues for interpreting the mediated texts available for historical analysis.

Work on law in colonial situations and other culturally and legally plural
contexts emphasizes the role of law in furthering cultural transformations
(Burman and Harrell-Bond 1979; Chanock 1985; Moore 1986; Merry 1988,
1991; Nader 1990; Messick 1992; Starr 1992). Such work moves the anthropology of law away from its earlier preoccupation with defining the law of
colonized subjects as "primitive law" toward understanding how colonial
law transformed and controlled these subjects and how those subjects have
mobilized the imposed legal system in resistance. Theoretical models of plural legalities emphasize the way different systems of law intersect within
fields of power relationships linked to conceptions of race, nationalism, and
gender (Starr and Collier 1989; Merry 1991; Fitzpatrick 1992; Santos 1995;
Darian-Smith 1996). Early efforts to analyze the imposition of law found
that the complexities of the process required a more nuanced model and that
the term itself was inadequate (Burman and Harrell-Bond 1979; Kidder
1979). Ethnographies of the transformation of law under colonial conditions
revealed the tensions between new systems of law and transformations in
kinship and economics that determined how the law operates in practice
(Comaroff and Roberts 1981; Chanock 1985; Moore 1986; Rafael 1988).
Moore and others critiqued the tradition in British social anthropology that
ignores the colonial context and treats law as if it were a product of an
isolated social order (e.g., Evans-Pritchard 1940; Gluckman 1955; Gulliver
1963). Studies of disputing, although succeeding in moving away from a
sterile idea of law as rules, failed to theorize multiplicities of law within
single social fields even though ethnographic accounts of disputing are shot
through with evidence of this situation (e.g., Nader and Todd 1978).

Work on legal pluralism is attentive to the mutually constitutive nature of
law and the social relations of colonialism as well as the way law constitutes
family and gender (Lazarus-Black 1994; Lazarus-Black and Hirsch 1994),
citizenship and national identity (Maurer 1997), labor and recreational life
(Cooper 1989), and the modern subject (Fitzpatrick 1992). Darian-Smith
(1995; 1999) links law to conceptions of landscape and nation, holistic entities pierced by transnational influences such as the Channel Tunnel opening
in the heart of the English countryside and bringing with it new multina-
tional legalities. Law was one aspect of the contested systems of signs and
meanings that shaped the colonizing process the Comaroffs describe among
the Tswana in South Africa (Comaroff and Comaroff 1997).

Modern law itself is a creature of colonialism, developed during an era of mercantilism and imperial expansion and shaped by those conditions. Fitzpatrick (1992) shows how the creation of modern law is grounded in relations of imperialism, distinctions of race, and the opposition of savage and civilized. Anghie (1996) argues that the system of international law originated in efforts to construct a legal framework for the relations between the Spanish and the Indians that would justify Spanish intervention and war. As Otto notes in her analysis of international law, "international law, like all European institutions, is founded on the violence of imperialism and, more recently, governmentality" (Otto 1996: 359). And modern law, as we have seen, has come to define the "civilized" society.

The Civilizing Process

A fundamental feature of the colonizing process was the claim to be "civilizing" a "barbaric" or "savage" people. In *The Civilizing Process* (1994 [1939]) Norbert Elias describes changes in manners and ways of handling bodily functions in Europe from 1400 to the present. In the progressive transformation of manners, actions that were permitted in public in the 1400s, such as spitting, blowing the nose, eating with the hands, smacking the lips at table, sleeping in the same bed with strangers, nakedness in front of others, or defecation and urination, were gradually redefined as behaviors surrounded with shame and disgust unless carried out in secrecy or in private settings.[7] By the nineteenth century, sexuality was transformed from an everyday, open activity knowable to children as well as adults to a covert, secret, undiscussed form of behavior, strictly relegated to the domestic bed or to private areas of "ill repute." The frontier of shame and repugnance continually expanded, redefining the meaning of these bodily functions and placing them progressively backstage, out of the sight of nonintimates and, increasingly, of anyone. Aroma also took on changing meanings over this period, as smell came to define the underclasses rather than constituting a universal feature of social life (Classen, Howes, and Synnott 1994; see also Hunt 1995). Similarly, aggressiveness shifted from a general source of pleasure to an activity tolerated only in certain restricted spheres. Elias quotes medieval knights describing their pleasure in the pain and suffering of enemies on the battlefield and the pleasures of mutilating prisoners (Elias 1994: 158).[8] Clearly aggression continues into the twentieth century but it is increasingly monopolized by the state, with only a few enclaves for belligerence such as wars. Even these have become more impersonal (p. 165).

As new standards of shame and disgust, new restraints and inhibitions emerged, pleasures were driven into private, behind-the-scenes spaces where individuals engaged in them under strictly controlled circumstances. These standards became deeply entrenched in the growing child so that they came to seem natural and their violation evoked repugnance and disgust (Elias 1994: 156–178). In colonial encounters, such differences in manners and management of the body become the stuff of critique and exclusion, the basis for the infantilization of the subjugated.

As this book demonstrates, during the nineteenth century the Hawaiian king and chiefs adopted aspects of "civilized" society in an effort to claim an autonomous space in the world of nations. Adopting the rule of law—a declaration of rights, a constitution, an independent judiciary, and written law codes—was a central part of this strategy. Paradoxically, as Hawai'i sought to claim sovereign status as a nation, it was mocked by other nations because of its mimicry of the ceremonial forms of European nationalism. One writer labeled it a "pygmy kingdom" (Fitch 1888), for example, and after his 1866 visit, Mark Twain called it a place where the grown folk "play empire," mocking both the Hawaiians and the society they imitated:

> There is his royal Majesty the King, with a New York detective's income of thirty or thirty-five thousand a year from the "royal civil list" and the "royal domain." He lives in a two-story frame "palace."
>
> And there is the "royal family"—the customary hive of royal brothers, sisters, cousins, and other noble drones and vagrants usual to monarchy,—all with a spoon in the national pap-dish, and all bearing such titles as his or her Royal Highness the Prince or Princess So-and-so. Few of them can carry their royal splendors far enough to ride in carriages, however; they sport the economical Kanaka horse or "hoof it" with the plebeians.
>
> (Twain 1990: 31)

Twain lists a long series of officials, concluding, "Imagine all this grandeur in a play-house 'kingdom' whose population falls absolutely short of sixty-thousand souls!" After mockingly describing the elegant and ornate gold-laced uniforms of these officials, he remarks, "Behold what religion and civilization have wrought!" (Twain 1990: 31–34). The Hawaiian effort to Christianize and civilize collided with the European inability to recognize the likeness of its nationalism among peoples of a darker hue.

The colonial project of the nineteenth century was founded on the European conviction that other ways of life were wrong and needed reform or, in the term of the times, "civilizing." But the precise shape of reform changed over time. The eighteenth- and early-nineteenth-century concern that other forms of culture and religious life were evil and immoral was gradually replaced by the late-nineteenth- and twentieth-century view that individuals themselves needed reform. The transformative desire shifted from the culture that needed to advance to the individual who needed to be taught sexual self-discipline, punctuality, enterprise, and saving. At the same time, Europeans shifted from viewing the differences between themselves and the peoples of Asia, Africa, and the Pacific as cultural and religious to viewing them as biological, based on skin shade, hair contour, eyelid configuration, all understood as signs of innate character. There was, in other words, a shift in concern from the soul to the body as the marker of difference. The body was not only more visible, but it was also immutable. In place of seventeenth- and eighteenth-century views that markers of difference could be changed through learning a new language, manners, or religion grew the nineteenth- and twentieth-century notion that these markers represented permanent disfigurement. A person might adopt the new cultural practices but could never cross the border of this bodily-inscribed difference.

Gender was integral to the new language of racial hierarchy, essentialized identities, and white supremacy. Plantation masters were both white and male. Subordinate "races" were feminized in the discourse of dominant groups, viewed as passive, emotional, and childlike. The colonial plantation defined tasks by race and gender, and plantation hierarchies depended on women's subordination to the authority of their husbands at all levels. Ironically, the missionaries in Hawai'i, along with so many other agents of colonial transformation, imagined themselves freeing Native Hawaiian women from their alleged degraded status through the salvation of housework, domestic responsibility, and the benefits of an enduring bourgeois marriage (Grimshaw 1989). Civilization required laws establishing the nuclear family and punishing sexual relations outside of marriage, a process explored in chapter 8.

American Colonialism in Hawai'i

This is a study of American overseas colonialism. Just as British colonialism reflected debates about class, race, and religion taking place at home, so American colonialism was shaped by U.S. concerns. Republicanism and the opposition to the privileges of aristocracy, abolitionism, temperance movements, the Christian mission, and anti-Chinese sentiment and Chinese exclusion all powerfully shaped the colonizing process in Hawai'i. The annexation of the Hawaiian Islands closely followed the conquest and displacement of Native Americans. Policies toward Native Hawaiians were sometimes modeled after Native American prototypes, such as the emphasis on blood quantum to entitle a person to collective resources. There was widespread resistance in the United States to the takeover of the islands, in part because of resistance to becoming an overseas colonial power and in part because of the racial composition of the islands. Beliefs in the inferiority of barbarian societies and the alleged innate incapacity of nonwhite "races" rendered the incorporation of the islands deeply questionable.

Ironically, I am studying colonialism in a society that has been culturally constructed as a paradise of harmony, free sexuality, and open feelings. Two contradictory images have dominated public discussion of Hawai'i on the U.S. mainland: one portrays Hawai'i as a paradise endowed with great racial harmony, the other as a place with deep racial troubles and divisions. Under the massaging of the tourist industry, the first has assumed dominance and the second receded. Yet the second speaks more closely to the history of racial and cultural subjugation that this book describes.

The colonization of Hawai'i was a century-long project driven first by merchants and missionaries, then by the demands of the whale fishery, and ultimately and most powerfully by the expansion of capitalist agriculture in the plantation production of sugar. It joined, in often bizarre ways, the search for wealth and the desire for moral reform. The New England missionaries who fought to protect the rights of Hawaiian commoners against the despotic power of Hawaiian chiefs, for example, produced children who gradually converted the independent kingdom into a sugar plantation economy in which many of the Hawaiian commoners became landless peasants and destitute urbanites.

During the period between 1778 and 1820, the Hawaiian Islands became increasingly involved with a global mercantile economy, serving as the stopping place for an international network of American, British, French, Russian, and Spanish ships engaged in trade with then-Spanish America, the fur trade on the Northwest Coast and Alaska, and the China trade. The islands became an important source of sandalwood until the 1830s. After 1819 the fur trade declined, but the extent of foreign shipping was greatly augmented by the arrival of whaling ships, primarily from New England but also from Britain and France, which spent the fall and spring seasons refitting and reprovisioning in the ports of Lāhainā and Honolulu. A resident merchant community slowly emerged during the 1820s and 1830s, which handled ship refitting and transshipment of goods to the United States and Britain, traveling around Cape Horn or the Cape of Good Hope. These outside influences precipitated a drastic decline in the Native Hawaiian population during the first hundred years after contact (Stannard 1989). By the middle of the nineteenth century, many leaders feared that the Hawaiian population would disappear altogether.

By the 1860s the mercantile era was ending as whale stocks diminished, the sandalwood trees were cut down, fur was hard to obtain, and petroleum replaced whale oil. Hawai'i embarked on plantation agriculture, primarily sugar, as its economic mainstay, and the mercantile community was replaced by a new social order modeled after industrial capitalism in the form of large sugar plantations attached to sugar mills. American economic influence and landholding increased throughout the late nineteenth century. In 1893 a consortium of white Americans, primarily sugar planters, supported by American troops, ousted the sovereign Queen Lili'uokalani and established a republic, then turned to the United States requesting annexation. Annexation would reinstate the privileged position of Hawaiian sugar in the U.S. market. The United States refused, leaving the "Provisional Government" and its sequel, the "Republic," in a difficult position. Five years later, after a major political battle in the United States and a change of administration in Washington, Hawai'i was annexed. The presence in the act of annexation of provisions for protecting the Hawaiians and providing for them out of Crown Lands suggests some concern about the propriety of usurping the lands of a sovereign nation.

The vote for statehood in 1959 technically ended Hawai'i's colonial status. For many residents statehood ushered in a new era of self-government, incorporation into the United States as full citizens, and the end of marginalization. But for the Native Hawaiian descendants of the once-sovereign Hawaiian nation, a numerical minority at the time of the plebiscite, statehood exacerbated a long-term slide into political powerlessness, economic fragility, and cultural dispossession. The story of Native Hawaiians (Kanaka Maoli) is still one of colonialism and loss. The story of many of the other arrivals in the islands is more like that of the immigrants to the northeastern United States: immigration and adjustment to desperate and difficult circumstances, sacrifice for future generations, and upward social mobility and access to political power.

American colonialism differed strikingly from British colonialism in the willingness of the early missionaries and the government they created to welcome all peoples who were willing to transform their bodies and their lives—their cultural selves—in accordance with principles of Christian piety and comportment into the community of the "civilized." Of course, this pattern was established while the Hawaiian elites ruled the kingdom, and it applied only to Hawaiians and whites, not to Asians. Over time, notions of race undermined the willingness to incorporate at the same time that Native Hawaiians became more resistant to the project. Yet the openness to incorporation on condition of assimilation contrasted with dominant British colonial practices, which came increasingly, especially in Africa, to depend on creating separate tribally based units of governance within which "tribal" culture would theoretically be preserved (Mamdani 1996). This notion of institutional separation to protect the culture of tribal peoples instead of a regime of civilization in which those who adopted European culture could be considered citizens, regardless of their race, gradually came to dominate British colonial policy in Africa (Mamdani 1996) as well as parts of the Pacific such as Fiji (Kelly 1994). Its consequence was the creation of plural legal systems designed for distinctive tribal groups, with a separate system for Europeans under the overarching regime of indirect rule. In Hawai'i, however, missionaries argued that Hawaiians were capable of conversion and civilization and insisted on extending the new legal order to all Hawaiian citizens. The Hawaiian kingdom accepted as citizens all who would swear an oath of loyalty. Thus, in Mamdani's terms, Hawaiians were always understood as citizens. By the late nineteenth century, however, white elites pressed to exclude Asian immigrants from citizenship.

Hawai'i is not an obvious place to study the dynamics of power and resistance or the role of law in the colonization process. But as an Americanist who has studied the courts and legal system of New England (Merry 1981; 1990) I was intrigued by the dearth of work on American overseas colonialism in comparison to work on British, French, and Dutch colonialism. The overseas empire model came relatively late and hesitantly to the American scene, with worries that the United States should not stretch beyond its (already conquered or purchased) territory and fears about annexing nonwhite areas (Godkin 1893; Daws 1968). Direct colonial control of Hawai'i lasted only about sixty years, contemporaneous with British control in Africa, and was preceded in both regions by a long period of mission endeavor, land alienation, and capitalist development.

I decided to study the American colonization of Hawai'i after a conference in 1987 took me there. As I drove around the islands, I was struck by the disparities in wealth, the class differences among the residents, the persistence of the plantation hierarchies, and the colonial architecture. I began to read the history of Hawai'i and became so depressed I almost abandoned the project. My mythic understanding of Hawai'i as a vacation spot, based on tourism's constructions of it as a primitive, sexual, and out-of-time-and-place location against a backdrop of overbuilt beaches and excessively luxurious hotels, had blinded me to the extent of the tragedy that had occurred on the islands. The death of a vast proportion of the Kanaka Maoli population, the appropriation of the lands of the common people, which left the dwindling remnant of the Native commoners living in subsistence plots overrun by the cattle of indifferent chiefs and foreigners, the continuous pressure to abandon the social and cultural life of music, dance, crafts, surfing, sports, and powerful family ties that had severely undermined Hawaiian language and cultural practices by the 1950s and 1960s, the bitter struggle of immigrant Japanese and Filipino sugar workers to unionize and improve their working conditions against a powerful and entrenched American and British planter elite, and the current heedless expansion of hotels, golf courses, and roads over a lush and beautiful land were all harsh realities within this alleged paradise. Ironically, this tragic history was juxtaposed with commonplace notions of Hawai'i as paradise.

Hawai'i represents, I think, a space of denial in the consciousness of American history. I thought back on my history texts and talked to other people about what they had read about the relationship between the United States and Hawai'i. The subject typically received very fleeting attention or focused on an image of a barbaric Queen Lili'uokalani, often portrayed as indifferent to constitutional government, replaced by a committee of Americans resident on the islands. But on the U.S. East Coast nobody seemed to know much about how it happened or what was taking place in Hawai'i now beyond too much hotel building in an otherwise warm and idyllic spot. American consciousness now acknowledges massive dispossession of the Native Americans but not the dispossession of the Kanaka Maoli or the discrimination against newcomers from Asia. The history of the transformation of Hawaiian political, legal, and economic institutions is typically told as one of gradualism and invitation: the Hawaiian chiefs and king asked for help, gradually reshaping their society into a modern European nation. There was no apparent violence, confrontation, or resistance, only easy accommodation. Classic histories such as the massive three-volume work by Kuykendall (1938; 1953; 1967) and even subsequent histories such as those by Daws (1968) and, much less, Fuchs (1961) adopt this position, while others, inspired by Marxist and Kanaka Maoli perspectives, such as Kent (1983), Beechert (1985), Kame'eleihiwa (1992), and Silva (1997), are more critical. In many of the older histories, the violence has been subtracted, the pressures to change ignored, the frequent attempts at takeover by European nations neglected, the pain of the Kanaka Maoli people and of the immigrant Asian plantation workers silenced. As I read deeper into the history, explored the texts of court cases, and read letters and diaries, the arrogance of the Americans and their certainty of their cultural and, by the end of the nineteenth century, biological superiority became unmistakable.

But I was also struck by the difficulty of this American colonial project, the amount of quarreling and contention among the various groups engaged in colonizing, and the extent to which this was a patriarchal project in which lines of gender tended to reinforce those of race and nation. Women were the object of colonial transformation and the prize to be seized by the colonizers. This is a complicated story, with nobility, cupidity, uncertainty, frustration and despair, humanistic desires for reform, and dogged persistence in the face of continuing and successful resistance to the message of change.

As I began to look more closely, the story was not all depressing. A vibrant political movement of Kanaka Maoli is demanding sovereignty from the United States and labeling the takeover an act of war (see Trask 1993; Hasager and Friedman 1994). There is currently a powerful cultural renaissance in Hawai'i, shared by local people of Kanaka Maoli and other ancestries, focused on resurrecting crafts, dance, music, canoe paddling, navigation, sea voyaging, language, spiritual life, and history. Although it gets relatively little play on the East Coast of the United States, it is flourishing in the islands. Although some feeds into the tourist industry, much of it is separate from tourism. Some groups are demanding reparations, insisting on a reexamination of the takeover in the past (see Merry 1997). Although there is no agreement about the shape of a new political and social arrangement in which the dispossession of the Hawaiian lands and culture is addressed, it is seriously debated.

So I decided to go forward. I quickly discovered that there was a strong link between New England, where I had previously done research, and Hawai'i, particularly in the first half of the nineteenth century. Much of the shape of the political and legal institutions of the islands was the result of a combination of New England merchants, whalers, missionaries, and lawyers who arrived in the islands and contributed their knowledge, skills, and interests to the reshaping of Hawaiian society. Although their influence waned in comparison to California's by the close of the century, the New Englanders had already set their stamp on the islands.

Since this book is an ethnography of the colonizing project in Hawai'i, it focuses on these New Englanders, examining what they did and what they thought as they struggled to transform Hawaiian society into an idealized version of New England. I have included the perspectives of Kanaka Maoli and immigrant Europeans and Asians on this process as much as possible. But I write as a New Englander, not as a Kanaka Maoli, and I am aware of the limitations this imposes on my work. Although I have spent considerable time in Hawai'i over the last nine years, my primary purpose is to understand the colonial project as the New Englanders saw it and as it unfolded in local courts. There is a rich body of scholarship by Kanaka Maoli that provides a Hawaiian perspective on these events, both historically and in the present, scholarship I have relied on extensively in my work. Much of this work is exploring Hawaiian-language archives and expanding our knowledge of Hawaiian resistance to the U.S. takeover (e.g., Kame'eleihiwa 1992; Hasager and Friedman 1994; Osorio 1996; Silva 1997).

Some of the New Englanders came to do good, others to do well for themselves, and some to do both. But such lines are hard to draw clearly. Consequences were rarely foreseen by those who tried to make changes, and things that now seem self-evident were hardly clear to these people. Many left their homes and traveled thousands of miles in small, leaky boats in rough weather to try to change a people that appeared to accept change yet held on to its own culture in ways that they found surprisingly determined and frustrating.

In many ways, understanding those who came to do good is more challenging than those who came to get rich. The indifference of the latter group to other ways of life, their arrogance about making changes, their callous disregard of appropriations of land and resources, seems more comprehensible, if reprehensible. It was those who thought they were helping whom I find most intriguing. The missionaries and lawyers often arrived with ideals of bringing civilization and improving the lot of the Hawaiians, including protecting commoners from the power of the chiefly class. Yet their doing good was premised on categories of personhood, on ideas about the meanings of race and culture, that denigrated those they came to help and their culture. They knew that releasing commoners from the control of chiefs and providing them with their own lands would throw them onto the mercies of the market but expected that this would develop habits of industry and self-reliance rather than marginalization and despair.

With the passage of time these notions appear more transparent, more open to contest. But the situation was not as simple as it appears to us looking back. The missionaries arriving in 1820 entered a field of great turmoil and exploitation. Sailors cast up on the shores of Honolulu and Lāhainā had left God on the other side of Cape Horn, as the saying goes, and rampaged through the streets in orgies of violence, drinking, and sex. In the early postcontact years chiefs competed for lands and followers through increasingly destructive wars with cannons and muskets imported from Europe and America while the consumption of rum spread to remote rural villages. In competition with one another for a "civilized" way of life and the silks and porcelains it required, chiefs ratcheted up the taxes they demanded from common farmers. As introduced diseases decimated the population, people were intrigued by the Christian doctrine that promised everlasting life. Yet they were also anxious about the loss of land they heard about on the Marqueses and elsewhere. Commoners and chiefs alike were eager for the material wealth that the newcomers assured them existed in their home countries and could be theirs if they would follow the European way.

With what notions do we now construct the world, notions that prevent us from understanding the consequences of our actions? It is far easier to see the blindness of the past than that of the present; and it is to help us better discover these assumptions, these ideas that have gone unnoticed except by those who suffer their consequences, that we study the past. What can we learn about what we are doing now from looking at these early pioneers, these missionaries of Christianity, of industrial capitalism, of the values of self-governing and self-disciplined selves? What hegemonic frames do we live in now? What will be so clear to those who follow us in one or two centuries? What do our current legitimating ideologies such as development, democratization, the rule of law, religious fundamentalism, and nationalism conceal? Although there has been an extensive critique of development and nationalism (e.g., Gellner 1983; Ferguson 1994; Escobar 1995) there has been far less critique of the recent enthusiasm for the expansion of democracy and the rule of law. It is important to use this history to interrogate the present, to challenge ideas of virtue and reform that now seem unquestionable.

As I write this in the late 1990s, I hear echoes of the same ideology of self-management and self-responsibility, of the privileging of the family over the autonomy of the woman, that dominated missionary and legal thinking. Perhaps this is the missionary movement in postmodernity. One must worry anew about maintaining respect for difference, about containing the calls for cultural purity and family values, now armed with the far greater strength of the regulatory, disciplinary society. The missionaries and lawyers and judges

of mid-nineteenth-century Hawai'i may have sought to transform the social
and sexual order of the Hawaiian people, but there was more opportunity to
slip through the cracks, to evade and avoid, to benefit from space and isolation, than we experience now. Calls for work instead of welfare, the end of
teen pregnancy, control of illegal immigration, and a war on drugs and crime
suggest a social agenda backed by a far more powerful and pervasive system
of discipline and control than was available in the nineteenth century. We
still live in a contact zone of peoples and values, but the possibilities of
resistance and retreat by individuals and groups are much diminished.

The Colonial Field and the Concept of Culture

As I worked on understanding the historical process of colonizing Hawai'i, I
became increasingly aware of the inadequacy of the anthropological concept
of culture. In the past, social situations such as colonialism were described
as acculturation or social change, deploying a fundamentally static, systemic
notion of culture. Constructing a definition of anthropology's core concept
has always been difficult, but at no time more so than the present. Culture is
everywhere a topic of concern and analysis, from cultural studies to literature to all the social sciences. At the same time, classic conceptions
of bounded, coherent, stable, and integrated systems clearly are inadequate.
Although the difficulties posed by the concept of culture in the analysis of
cultural change have been widely discussed, it is less clear what concept can
replace the totalizing, coherent, normative idea of culture that developed in
the natural history approach to cultural difference. Historically, culture was a
concept developed when there were moderns and "primitives" who lived
unchanging and utterly different although internally coherent lives, which
had to be tolerated, not because they conformed to the values of the observer
but because they were, in a sense, off the edge of her moral universe.

The process of colonization produces deeply fractured cultural fields. The
violence and disruptions of this field has increasingly received anthropological attention (e.g., Stoler 1985, 1991, 1995; Taussig 1987; Comaroff and
Comaroff 1991, 1997; Keesing 1992; Pratt 1992; Cohn 1996). Colonialism
creates fields with competing cultural logics, rooted in particular structures
of power. Nineteenth-century Hawai'i, for example, was a field containing
the distinctive cultural worlds of Hawaiian ali'i (chiefs) and maka'āinana
(commoners), British and American whaleship owners and crews, European
and Chinese sugar planters, American Protestant missionaries, French Catholic priests, resident American and British merchants, and roving fortune
seekers from around the globe. Pratt describes such fields as contact zones:
"social spaces where disparate cultures meet, clash, and grapple with each
other, often in highly asymmetrical relations of domination and subordina-

tion—like colonialism, slavery, or their aftermaths as they are lived out across the globe today" (Pratt 1992: 4). Unlike the term *frontier*, which privileges a center and an edge, the term *contact zone* focuses on intersections among equally centered entities.

Culture in contact zones consists of contested and shifting signs and practices. Comaroff and Comaroff take culture to be "a historically situated, historically unfolding ensemble of signifiers-in-action, signifiers at once material and symbolic, social and aesthetic. Some of these, at any moment in time, will be woven into more or less tightly integrated, relatively explicit world views; others may be heavily contested, the stuff of counterideologies and 'subcultures'; yet others may become more or less unfixed, relatively free floating, and indeterminate in their value and meaning" (Comaroff and Comaroff 1992: 27). Nicholas Thomas advocates the study of "colonial projects" rather than a totality such as a culture. A colonial project is "a socially transformative endeavor that is localized, politicized and partial, yet also engendered by longer historical developments and ways of narrating them" (Thomas 1994: 105). The term *project* emphasizes orientations toward transformation and innovation rather than stasis. In contact zones, concepts of cultural production and appropriation are more valuable than a singular notion of culture as a system of shared values held by a social collectivity.[9]

Ironically, the problems in the anthropological concept of culture are the result of its anticolonial project of explicating difference in ways of thinking and acting for an intolerant European imperialist audience. This perspective builds, in part, on a natural history approach to delineating difference that emerged during the colonial period. Ironically, that approach becomes exoticization in the postcolonial world: an unwillingness to accord respect or equality, even if the terms of that respect—rationality, in particular—are local European cultural terms now part of a global hegemony.

The older concept of culture has historical roots in a politics of national distinctiveness. As Elias (1994) notes, the concept as used in anthropology emerged from the German notion of *Kultur*, which was juxtaposed with civilization. Civilization referred to the manners and practices shared across national boundaries that joined the French, the British, and other "civilized" peoples in a global society. *Kultur*, on the other hand, emphasized difference: it was the category through which the German bourgeoisie claimed a distinctive peoplehood—their own manners and customs. They celebrated German *Kultur*, he argues, because they were excluded from European civilization by the marginality of their aristocracy. *Kultur* was, in fact, the way that the bourgeoisie emphasized to themselves that they were better than the aristocrats of other nations. They celebrated their own values and work ethic rather than aping the manners of "civilization." Thus, *Kultur* became a way of claiming separateness and superiority against a globalizing aristocracy of learning, language, and custom.

It is understandable that anthropologists, searching for a language to cele-brate the divergent yet legitimate way of life of those generally labeled savages, would turn to the concept of *Kultur* already in use to emphasize difference and legitimacy in a world of globalizing civilization. Just as the Germans had *Kultur*, so did the Nuer and the Tallensi. Boundedness and coherence are therefore fundamental political features of this concept, as well as a militant assertion of separateness and superiority. The concept that served so well in the context of nineteenth- and early-twentieth-century imperialism, however, now carries with it far different implications. It fixes and separates just as national, cultural, and ethnic boundaries become more fluid and identities more hybrid and as anthropology turns to the analysis of contact zones, colonial projects, and borderlands rather than "societies." Despite the obvious exceptions where war, nationalism, or exclusion has rigidified cultural boundaries, the combined impact of technology, tourism, global capitalism, and migration are blurring and redrawing cultural boundaries at a rapid rate.

Ironically, as contemporary anthropology is discarding this older concept of culture, it is being vigorously reappropriated by indigenous peoples and ethnonational movements searching for sovereignty and self-determination (Comaroff 1995). For example, Jackson notes that the tendency to essential-ize culture within anthropology has been adopted by Indian movements in Colombia as well as other indigenous societies (Jackson 1995: 18).[10] The Hawaiian Sovereignty Movement and Native American peoples make claims on the basis of their "traditional" cultures, addressing a legal order that can hear arguments about cultural authenticity and tradition but not consider rep-arations for acts of conquest and violation in the past.

Instead of culture and cultural change, therefore, I use concepts of cultural production and cultural appropriation. Cultural production draws on "a stock of already existing *cultural* elements drawn from the reservoirs of lived cul-ture or from the already public fields of discourse" (Johnson 1986/87: 55). Cultural appropriation means adopting a cultural product in terms of local meanings and practices. Cultural appropriation can be a form of resistance since it means taking an existing cultural form and replaying it with different meanings or practices: perhaps taking the tune and playing it in a different key or at a different speed so it becomes something different, although also the same. The game of Trobriand cricket captured in a well-known eth-nographic film provides a dramatic illustration of such subversive appropria-tion.[11] The Hawaiians appropriated the New England legal system in order to be civilized, and the New England missionaries appropriated Hawaiians as dark savages against which they saw themselves as the light. The concepts of production and appropriation incorporate agency and power since they define culture as contested, historically changing, and subject to redefinition in multiple and overlapping social fields. This book examines how cultural forms of law are produced, appropriated, and redefined in historically changing social fields, and examines the relationship between these forms and the practices that gave them life.

The book is based on both archival and ethnographic research. In addition to the court records and government documents in the Hawai'i State Archives, I have consulted archives of the Lyman Memorial Museum in Hilo, the University of Hawai'i at Hilo and Mānoa, the Hawaiian Mission Children's Society in Honolulu, and the Hawaiian Sugar Planters Association as well as archives in New England including the American Antiquarian Society in Worcester, Massachusetts, the Houghton Library at Harvard University, the Harvard Law Library, and the Essex/Peabody Museum in Salem, Massachusetts. I have also spent considerable time doing ethnographic research in Hawai'i, making one or two trips for a few weeks to a few months every year from 1991 to 1999. I have interviewed many older residents of Hilo about the past and studied contemporary legal life in Hilo and the legal management of family problems (see Merry 1995). I have been ably assisted by several research assistants who have spent considerable time in Hawai'i, principally Marilyn Brown, Nancy Hayes, and Erin Campbell.

The first part of the book examines the intricacies of the process by which the Anglo-American legal system was appropriated by the sovereign Kingdom of Hawai'i in the early nineteenth century. Its canvas is the Kingdom of Hawai'i as a whole during the middle of the nineteenth century. Chapter 2 offers a theory of cultural transformation and delineates the two transitions through which Western law was appropriated in nineteenth-century Hawai'i. It discusses the nature of the Hawaiian system of law that had developed before the nineteenth century and locates the Kingdom of Hawai'i in a process of historical change. Chapter 3 describes the first transition, the shift from a Hawaiian legal order premised on divine authority to a Protestant Christian one premised on the authority of Jehovah. Chapter 4 describes the second transition, the rapid transformation of the legal system to an Anglo-American one that replaced Jehovah with a sovereign populace. William Little Lee puts in a return appearance in this chapter.

The second part of the book examines the consequences of the legal changes outlined in Part One for everyday life in one port town. It provides a detailed historical study of the caseloads of the Hilo district and circuit courts between 1850 and 1985 and analyzes the new cultural meanings of gender, sexuality, work, and the family produced by the operation of the court. It focuses on criminal cases, particularly those concerned with the regulation of family and community life. Chapter 5 delineates the social composition of Hilo and the nature of the racialized hierarchy produced by the plantation system. Chapter 6 examines changes in court caseloads over time. An analysis of economic changes and the social identities of the judges indicates that caseloads reflect differing prosecutorial strategies and judicial concerns, principally the moral reform agendas of judges and the economic demands of local elites. The judges, although closely tied to local economic hierarchies, exercise a some-what autonomous form of power and serve as intermediaries between local people and the state. Chapter 7 describes how the law was used to control plantation workers and how some workers mobilized the language of the law to contest the conditions of their subordination. Chapter 8 focuses on changes in the way the courts reshaped marriage, family, and gender relations through the prosecution of adultery and fornication cases. Chapter 9 concludes with an analysis of the contradictory role of law in processes of social change such as colonial projects.

PART ONE

ENCOUNTERS IN A CONTACT ZONE:

NEW ENGLAND MISSIONARIES, LAWYERS, AND

THE APPROPRIATION OF

ANGLO-AMERICAN LAW, 1820–1852

2

THE PROCESS OF LEGAL TRANSFORMATION

THE KINGDOM OF HAWAI'I, sovereign until the coup of 1893, adopted a fundamentally Anglo-American legal system with extraordinary rapidity during the second quarter of the nineteenth century. During the brief period from 1825 to 1850 the Kingdom of Hawai'i was transformed from a system of governance based on sacred laws, hereditary rank, and religious authority to one based on Anglo-American common law, a written constitution, and an elected legislature. Sovereignty shifted from the high chiefs (ali'i nui) and king (mō'ī) to the people as a whole. The shift to popular sovereignty was mostly in theory, since in practice power was increasingly vested in the hands of men of property, often resident and naturalized foreigners. At the beginning of this period the mō'ī and the ali'i exercised power under a fundamentally Hawaiian conception of law: a system of kapus (tabus) under the authority of the gods, or Akua. But by 1850 the mō'ī and ali'i ruled through a structure of government, courts, and laws derived from American and British models.

But it was far easier to transfer the texts of law than the practices that gave them life. The new laws entered a field already rich with legal rules and practices developed in the hierarchical Hawaiian society. One form of law defined the hierarchical relations of chiefship while another governed the daily life of local communities. Moreover, resident foreign nationals from Europe, the United States, and China brought their own laws. Visiting European dignitaries proposed their systems as models. The legal transformation was not a simple substitution of one form of law for another but a negotiation of the meaning and practices of law in various local places over time. The practices of the old shaped the practices of the new, particularly in rural areas but also in the growing towns of Honolulu, Lāhainā, and Hilo. The choice of the new depended on some congruence with the structure of the old. This was a dynamic legal pluralism in which coexisting but distinct legal orders continually penetrated and redefined one another. The texts of laws changed before the practices by which they were enacted and enforced were transformed.

To a large extent the new system was managed by foreigners who already understood the minutiae of its practices. Unlike many of the colonized states of Africa, Hawai'i did not adopt a dual legal system for foreigners and natives but created a unitary system modeled on the West. Yet under this new legal order, people were arrested, convicted, and sentenced for social and sexual practices that had previously been acceptable within Hawaiian communities. How did this happen?

The mōʻī and aliʻi were engaged in a search for sovereignty in Euro-American terms. In order to maintain their independence in an era of imperialism, they created a nation that would be recognized as sovereign by other civilized nations. Allegedly "primitive" societies were being annexed by European nations throughout the Pacific in the mid nineteenth century, including closely related Polynesian societies in New Zealand, Tahiti, and the Marquesas. There were serious assaults on the sovereignty of Hawaiʻi as well in the late 1830s and 1840s. Consequently, the Hawaiian aliʻi appropriated the practices and institutions of civilization for themselves and for the makaʻāinana, the common people who worked the land. They sought to form a "civilized" society as that concept was understood in the nineteenth century by the European powers that created it.

One of the fundamental characteristics of such a "civilized" society was the rule of law: a written system of law codes enforced by an independent judiciary and backed by a system of constables and prisons. In order to be "civilized" in the global moral economy of the nineteenth century, a country had to present itself as a society governed by law. Even eighteenth-century efforts to classify the populations of the world frequently relied on the rule of law, along with an incoherent combination of physical and social characteristics, to distinguish different groups. For example, within the Linnaean scheme of natural history, a classification from 1758 divided humanity into six groups, each characterized by a distinctive relationship to law:

> a. Wild Man. Four-footed, mute, hairy.
>
> b. American. Copper-colored, choleric, erect. Hair black, straight, thick; nostrils wide; face harsh; beard scanty; obstinate, content, free. Paints himself with fine red lines. Regulated by customs.
>
> c. European. Fair, sanguine, brawny; hair yellow, brown, flowing; eyes blue; gentle, acute, inventive. Covered with close vestments. Governed by laws.
>
> d. Asiatic. Sooty, melancholy, rigid. Hair black, eyes dark; severe, haughty, covetous. Covered with loose garments. Governed by opinions.
>
> e. African. Black, phlegmatic, relaxed. Hair black, frizzled; skin silky; nose flat, lips tumid; crafty, indolent, negligent. Anoints himself with grease. Governed by caprice.
>
> (Burke 1972: 266–267)

Not surprisingly, this European-authored model associates intellectual and social superiority with government by law or religious custom. The original Latin term *Ritibus* in Linneaus's 1758 classification of the mode of governance of Europeans meant religious custom.

The superiority of the rule of law framed the great nineteenth-century evolutionary models of social development as well. The stages of savagery, barbarism, and civilization, for example, were defined by the form of social regulation in each (see Rouland 1994: 28–34). In Sir Henry Maine's theory of law and social development, every man lived under patriarchal despotism in ancient society and was controlled by a regime of caprice rather than law (Maine 1917 [1861]: 5). With social evolution, individuals became capable of making contracts for themselves outside of this structure of family control. Law shifted from status to contract as rights and obligations based on the individual's status in society gave way in modern society to rights and obligations based on contracts (Rouland 1994: 21–22).

Lewis Henry Morgan's influential *Ancient Society* (1964 [1877]), based in part on his work with Native Americans, described three stages of society: savagery (hunting and gathering), barbarism (domestication of animals, agriculture, tribal or clan ownership), and civilization (invention of writing, paper, steam, electricity, monogamous family, private property, and the state). Morgan optimistically thought that private property was the engine that would promote progress among savage and barbaric societies and encourage the development of government and laws. His ideas were very influential in U.S. policy toward Native Americans in the 1870s and 1880s, encouraging the dissolution of reservations in favor of individual allotment of land (Hoxie 1989 [1984]: 17–20).

Evolutionary models provided a framework through which nineteenth-century Europeans and Americans interpreted cultural differences and developed policies for change. For example, a British traveler to the islands in 1849 justifies his travel account as a picture of an isolated portion of the "great human family, in a stage of progress of peculiar interest, since it is that which, at one period or other, has in every Christian state, formed the first step from barbarism towards those degrees of refinement which older nations have severally attained" (Hill 1856: v–vi). He compares the Sandwich Islanders (the European name for the Hawaiian islanders) when they first met Europeans to the early Britons when the Romans arrived. Now, seventy-five years later, he likens them to the Britons when most of their barbarous customs were changing along the lines of Roman refinement. Thus, he maps Hawaiian history onto British history as an earlier and more primitive stage of the same process. The Kingdom of Hawai'i is interpreted as primitive rather than different.

The emphasis on the acquisition of law as a measure of progress is echoed by a missionary writing in 1847 to the kingdom's minister of foreign relations on the state of the kingdom. He writes from O'ahu:

The improvement of this people as a whole in the advance of civilization is still going forward, and more rapidly during the few years since the first publishing [*sic*] a code of laws than before. These improvements consist, particularly, in facilities for acquiring property, such as cattle, horses, &c, and in the possession of considerable money. Their dress is also considerably improved. Many of them have also built houses on an improved model. Chairs, tables, and some table furniture, are also found in many of their dwellings.

(Bishop, in Kingdom of Hawai'i 1846: 90)

Bishop describes the Hawaiian people in a state of transition from barbarism to civilization. An article from a Honolulu newspaper from 1865 compares the level of "civilization" of the Hawaiians to that of other Polynesians and finds them much superior, having benefited from Christianity and the effects of foreign travelers and trade, whose influence on the whole has been "upward."[1] The article refers to "the herculean labor of elevating a heathen people and giving them a standing among the civilized nations of the earth."

The adoption of a "civilized" system of law provided the kingdom with an important mechanism for "advancing" within this scheme and for enhancing its global respectability and power. At the same time, it protected the Kingdom of Hawai'i against internal complaints, particularly from foreigners who resisted the authority of what they viewed as primitive law and demanded that they be judged only by their own nation's laws and by juries of their compatriots (Nelligan and Ball 1992). Establishing the rule of law on an American model made it easier for the Hawaiian state to exercise legal authority over these individuals.

Moreover, visiting Europeans always insisted to the Hawaiian people that "civilization" was connected with wealth and prosperity. Foreign visitors repeatedly assured the Hawaiians that if they wanted to become as rich and powerful as Europeans, they had to adopt their way of life. For example, the British missionary William Ellis, touring the kingdom in 1822, reports a conversation with some of the people attached to the king. He assured them that they could be as wealthy and powerful as the European nations if they would only change their ways, learn to read and write, and work harder (Ellis 1969: 87). He asked several servants working in the king's storehouse in Lāhainā what they did with their time. They said they worked in the plantations (wet kalo fields, probably) three or four days in a week, sometimes from daylight till nine or ten in the morning. Preparing an oven of food took an hour. When they went for sandalwood, which was not very often, they were gone three or four days, or sometimes three or four weeks. They said they worked less than people who occupy and cultivate lands. He asked what they did the rest of their time, and they said they ate poi, slept, and "kamailio no" (just talked for amusement). Ellis asked, what would be most advantageous to them: learning to read and seeking the favor of Jehovah and Jesus Christ that they might live forever, or wasting their time

in eating, sleeping, or foolish talking, and remaining ignorant in this world, and liable to wretchedness in that which is to come? They immediately endeavored to give a different turn to the conversation, by saying, "What a fine country yours must be, compared with this! What large bales of cloth come from thence, while the clothing of Hawaii is small in quantity and very bad. The soil there must be very prolific, and property easily obtained, or so much of it would not have been brought here."

(Ellis 1969: 87)

Ellis replied that the difference is not in the countries but in the people. Since they had become enlightened and industrious and had embraced Christianity, the people of his country had been wise and rich and, they hoped, after death they went to a state of happiness in another world. They owed all their present wealth and enjoyment to their intelligence and industry, he said, but if the people of his country were to neglect education and religion and spend much of their time in eating, sleeping, and jesting, "they would soon become as poor and as ignorant as the Sandwich Islanders." He reports that the Hawaiians said perhaps it was so, perhaps industry and instruction would make them better and happier, and if the chiefs wished it, they would attend to both. Clearly, Ellis linked the rewards of material wealth and eternal life with education and the emerging capitalist virtues of industry and discipline. These were all measures of "civilization." The Hawaiians seemed skeptical.

The abiding irony of the historical process of "civilizing" is that in order to acquire the status of a civilized society, Hawai'i had to adopt a set of laws that differed from everyday practices in many ways. The definition of "civilization" required the containment of the body and the restriction of its emissions to private and secluded spaces (Elias 1994). Sex was a central sphere for the construction of the "civilized" self. In practice, this meant urging Hawaiians to don clothing, build partitions in houses, eat with forks instead of fingers, abandon surfboarding—which was done naked and in mixed sex groupings—and restrict all sexual congress to the marriage bed. Laws even redefined as crimes some aspects of the familial, recreational, and sexual lives of the people. Adultery, fornication, prostitution, and "lewd" behavior were particularly targeted as well as the production and consumption of alcohol. Those who violated these laws were prosecuted and punished, often by imprisonment and hard labor on the roads. Chapter 6 examines the effects of the new laws on everyday life in Hilo and chapter 8 focuses on the criminalization of sexuality outside marriage.

Economic and Social Transition, 1780–1850

A small community of traders grew up in Honolulu beginning in 1780, as merchant shippers plied the trade routes between China, the fur sources on the northwest coast of the United States and Canada, and New England (Sahlins 1992: 37). The firearms and ships introduced by these merchants enabled one chief, Kamehameha, to conquer all the islands in a series of devastating wars. By 1795 all the islands except Kaua'i were under Kamehameha's control and in 1810 that island peacefully acquiesced to his control, forging the chain of islands into a single kingdom. Merchant shipping increased in the 1810s and 1820s, fueled by the discovery that Hawaiian sandalwood was considered desirable by the Chinese, who spurned so many other European goods. The ali'i monopolized the sandalwood trade, sending maka'āinana into the mountains to harvest the precious wood in exchange for a burgeoning supply of European and Chinese textiles, porcelains, and furniture, signs of a new system of hierarchy defined by the goods of civilization (Sahlins 1992: 57–82). But the population of Hawaiians declined precipitously as a result of introduced diseases, food shortages from warfare and sandalwood collection, the depredations of cattle, and other disruptions in the local economy. During the 1830s sandalwood became far scarcer and the pressure of the ali'i on the maka'āinana to produce surplus food and wealth ever greater.

The mercantile economy shifted the relations between ali'i and maka'āinana in fundamental ways. The chiefs turned to the mercantile capitalists as a new source of wealth and mana, exchanging sandalwood for imported Chinese and European luxury goods. Taxes were increased to pay the debts of the ali'i, furthering the economic hardships of commoners. In some areas commoners faced an ever-increasing population of free-roaming cattle (introduced in 1793) owned by chiefs and foreigners and interference in kalo (taro) fields from introduced plants that overran their plots. Although chiefs attempted to control external trade, commoners managed to bypass the blockade of the chiefs by trading foodstuffs, working as seamen, and providing sexual services (see Ralston 1989). Thus, the commoners themselves became less dependent on chiefs for trade goods. Mercantile capitalism, dominant until the 1860s, did not fundamentally disrupt notions of selfhood or family, but it did radically transform the relationship between chiefs and commoners.

In 1820 the first missionaries from the United States arrived, bringing a particularly strict and harsh version of Protestant Christianity rooted in rural New England culture. In 1823 the highest ranking ali'i in the kingdom, Keōpūolani, the mother of the king, Liholiho, was baptized on her deathbed (Grimshaw 1989: 40). In the same year, Hoapili, governor of Maui, had a Christian marriage (Schmitt 1967) and Liholiho embarked on his tragic trip to England, where both he and his queen perished, leaving Ka'ahumanu, the late Kamehameha's wife, as regent. In 1825 Lord Byron returned Liholiho's body along with the notables who had accompanied him, including Boki and his wife Liliha, daughter of Hoapili, and Kekūanao'a and Manuia. Within a month of Liholiho's funeral in 1825 the young Kauikeaouli became king. But effective power was in the hands of Ka'ahumanu and her powerful kin group. Ka'ahumanu and her brothers Hoapili and Kuakini were descendants of the Kona chiefs who had supported Kamehameha in his earlier drive to conquer the islands (Kamakau 1961: 286).

Ka'ahumanu saw the possibilities of the new Christian priests, both religious and political, and in 1825 converted to the new religion, along with several other high-ranking ali'i. Until her death in 1832 she retained her loyalty to the new priesthood, relying on its skills of literacy and its knowledge of foreigners. The agency sponsoring the missionaries, the American Board of Commissioners of Foreign Missions (ABCFM), founded in 1810 and located in Boston, wrested a stunning triumph from this conversion, the first major missionary endeavor of the new nation (Hutchinson 1987; Grimshaw 1989: xiv). The missionaries were required to marry before they left New England and almost never married Hawaiians, in marked contrast with the early merchants, who usually mated or married Hawaiian women.

Opposed to Ka'ahumanu and her American missionary supporters were those who had been to England with Liholiho in 1824, the resident merchants, and the British and American consuls (Kamakau 1961: 273–276). The American missionaries' puritanical approach to drinking and the sex trade particularly infuriated the merchants and their ali'i allies. Thus global political rivalries between the United States and Britain fed into local rivalries between ali'i reaching back a generation or more.

With Ka'ahumanu's death in 1832, the young king Kauikeaouli rebelled against the Christian strictures, turning to ali'i who favored the British and renouncing the strict laws of the Protestant priesthood (Sahlins 1992: 120–122). But his rebellion in 1833–1834 was fairly quickly suppressed by Ka'ahumanu's successor, Kīna'u (1832–1839), and the Christian regime of law and governance was reinstated. In 1838 the ali'i began their efforts to adopt a Western system of governance and law under the leadership of Hoapili and the missionary William Richards on Maui.

By the 1840s the sandalwood was gone, the peasantry was alienated and shrinking, revenues to the ali'i were being strangled by a hierarchy of konohiki (land stewards) each taking his share of a dwindling land product, and the ali'i were willing to divest themselves of their vast tracts in exchange for smaller parcels more clearly under their control (Sahlins 1992). The missionaries pushed for individual land ownership in the 1840s to promote industriousness and the emergence of the bourgeois family (Kingdom of Hawai'i 1846). The land division of 1848–1855, the Māhele, officially severed the relationship between the konohiki and the tenants. This was an event of enormous importance for the organization of Hawaiian society, substituting individual private land ownership for the elaborate hierarchy of tenants and haku, lords of the land. Although the intention of the Māhele was to give the ali'i and mō'ī their own lands and to provide firm title to the maka'āinana, the people on the land, very few commoners actually acquired land in their own names (Bradley 1968; Sahlins 1992). Instead, large tracts of the land passed into the hands of naturalized foreigners and, after 1850, non-naturalized foreigners.

Meanwhile, a new trade quickened the streets of Honolulu and Lāhainā and brought new forms of revenue to the islands—the whale fishery in the Pacific. Starting in 1819 and mushrooming during the 1830s, 1840s, and 1850s, the whaling business brought thousands of sailors to Hawaiian ports between seasons of whale hunting. As the length of trips increased to three and four years, the towns of Honolulu and Lāhainā, in particular, became centers for provisioning ships and, by 1850, for transshipping whale products back to New England, where most of the whalers originated. In 1844 R. C. Wyllie commented: "It is obvious that the prosperity of these islands has depended, and does depend, mainly upon the whale-ships that annually flock to their ports" (Kuykendall 1938: 310). Between 1843 and 1854, 419 whaling ships arrived every year, on average (Kuykendall 1938: 305). In 1846, nearly six hundred ships entered Hawaiian ports (Daws 1968: 169). Ships typically stayed a few weeks in the spring and fall.

Supplying the needs of the ships provided opportunities for farmers and sex workers, while the deserters and riotous sailors posed new challenges to police and prison systems. Daws estimates the return to Hawaiian women from prostitution at $100,000 a year in the 1850s (Daws 1968: 167). The growing merchant community provided repair and merchandise services for ships and sent whale products back to the United States around Cape Horn in faster merchant ships. At this point the Americans almost completely controlled the trade of the islands, which were an important distribution point for the entire Pacific (Griffin 1938: 20). By the 1860s, however, the fishery was in decline: whale stocks were depleted, the Civil War disrupted the fleet, and the discovery of petroleum in 1859 provided an alternative to whale oil (Daws 1968: 171).

In 1850 the sugar plantation economy was in its infancy. The legal groundwork for this system, however—private ownership of land, masters and servants legislation, and a system of government and law that protected private property in American terms—was in place. Missionary children and grandchildren were prime movers in the transition to agricultural capitalism, founding the sugar plantation economy and related enterprises in shipping and railroad construction. By the end of the nineteenth century, the missionary descendants had forged a union with the merchants through marriage, ownership of property, and political power, although many of the smaller planters had lost control to larger companies that provided credit and shipping services.

The American missionaries were deeply opposed to the merchants and mercantile capitalism, already well established when they arrived in 1820.

Yet the schools, religious values, conceptions of marriage and personal responsibility, and legal system introduced by the missionaries created a fertile ground for the expansion of industrial capitalism. In 1825 Hiram Bingham, the most prominent missionary in Honolulu, tried to persuade Kalanimōkū, the premier, to let him install a large bell and clock (King 1989: 103). This was, of course, the technology not only for regularizing religious attendance but also for creating the time discipline of capitalist labor. The American merchant Stephen Reynolds reports that Kalanimōkū walked out on Bingham (King 1989: 103).

The transformation in economic, social, and legal systems in nineteenth-century Hawai'i has sometimes been portrayed as gradual and voluntary (for a variety of historical accounts of this transformation, see Frear 1894; Daws 1968; Kuykendall 1938; Silverman 1982; Nelligan 1983; Kame'eleihiwa 1992; Nelligan and Ball 1992; Sahlins 1992). It appears that the Hawaiian government simply invited New England missionaries and jurists to transform the legal system of the sovereign nation. Many facts support this story. In 1838 Hoapili, governor of Maui, along with the mō'ī and the the kuhina nui (premier), Kīna'u, invited William Richards, a New England missionary resident on the islands since 1823 with no legal training, to teach the ali'i political economy and government. He was released by the American missionary society and initiated instruction in the summer of 1838 (Ii 1959; Kamakau 1961). Under Richards's direction, and probably with his help, a bill of rights was passed in 1839 and a constitution in 1840, followed by a succession of laws in the early 1840s. In 1842 the ali'i hired Gerrit Judd, a missionary doctor from New York state who had arrived in 1828, to help manage the finances of the kingdom. In 1844 a trained American lawyer, John Ricord, arrived in Honolulu on his way elsewhere and was quickly hired by Judd to serve as attorney general. He stayed in the islands only three years but during this period he prepared two organic acts that fundamentally restructured the government. He departed in 1847 but was replaced by William Little Lee who, as we saw in chapter 1, was the chief legal advisor until his death in 1857.

This history presents the Hawaiian government as voluntarily asking Americans for help in adopting a Western legal system. But this narrative ignores the devastating consequences of the infusion of European guns, ships, and military technology into Hawaiian society. Wars for supremacy between rival chiefs during the late eighteenth and early nineteenth centuries contributed to the rapid depopulation of the islands. Mounting small cannons on the bows of war canoes, for example, dramatically transformed sea battles. Introduced diseases devastated the population. Recent estimates suggest that the population declined from as many as 800,000 people in 1778 (although it is impossible to know the population at the time precisely) to about 40,000 in 1893, a little more than one hundred years later (Stannard 1989;

Kameʻeleihiwa 1992: 20).[2] Some estimate that diseases such as cholera killed 150,000 people in 1804, perhaps half the population at contact if one uses the lower estimate of 200,000–300,000 (Native Hawaiians Study Commission 1983: 49). By 1839 prominent Hawaiian scholars such as David Malo were deeply concerned about the catastrophic population collapse and predicted the death of the kingdom (Malo 1839: 130).

Early confrontations between Hawaiians and Europeans were often violent, beginning with Captain Cook's death in 1779 and the extensive retaliatory killing by the British. In 1790 one hundred Hawaiians were massacred in retaliation for the killing of a single European guarding a boat stolen for its coveted nails (Kuykendall 1938: 24). During the first half of the nineteenth century, warships bristling with guns from the United States, France, and Britain repeatedly arrived in the islands making demands on the government, threatening to fire or flatten the small seaside town of Honolulu if they were not accepted. The aliʻi and mōʻī were constantly pressured by major European powers to repay debts to resident foreign merchants, to accept the countries' demands for trade privileges, and to provide a separate legal system for their subjects. The French insisted that the Hawaiian government allow Catholics to evangelize while the Protestant Americans told them it would be terrible to do so.

Meanwhile, economic forces pulled the aliʻi, mōʻī, and even makaʻāinana ever deeper into the web of the capitalist economy. Sahlins (1992) documents the increasing dependence of the aliʻi on European traders during this period as they indulged their desires for foreign goods in exchange for a dwindling supply of sandalwood gathered by a dwindling population of tenants. It was the muslins and silks of the European merchants rather than the feathers and tapas of the makaʻāinana that provided the prestige goods marking rank and power in the 1820s and 1830s. In the 1820s, during the height of the sandalwood boom, the aliʻi nui acquired crystal chandeliers, Chinese brocades, and American pleasure yachts in exchange for sandalwood harvested in the forests by commoners. Ordinary Hawaiians had very little of even simple iron or cotton goods (Ralston 1985: 316). Despite their continuing love for the aliʻi (Kameʻeleiheiwa 1992), the dislocation of makaʻāinana from farming and fishing as well as the population decline resulting from introduced diseases led to periodic food shortages. Deepening involvement in the mercantile economy drove the chiefs to ever greater demands for labor and tribute, gradually alienating the makaʻāinana (Sahlins 1992).

The Two Transitions

Although the appropriation of Anglo-American law by the Kingdom of Hawaiʻi is a complex historical story, it can be understood as two major transitions: first from Hawaiian law to a theocratic Hawaiian and Christian law and second to a secular law based on American models. In each, there were complementarities and contradictions in the underlying cultural logics of the systems in play. Apparent similarities induced acceptance while differences pushed social change into new and unanticipated directions. In the first transition the ali'i appropriated a sacred system of law from their priestly advisors, the American missionaries. Like the Hawaiian kapu system, this Protestant law came from the deities via their emissaries on earth and supported their authority as representatives of divine power. In the second transition the ali'i adopted a secular system of law and popular sovereignty based on New England prototypes of law and governance. At least in theory, this was a system based on the will of the populace. By the time of the second transition, the ali'i were rapidly losing control of the economy and political system to the whites, the haoles. The move to secular law represented a desperate effort to retain control of their country and to assert sovereignty over the fractious and increasingly numerous resident foreigners.

In the first transition, from 1825 to 1844, the ali'i turned to Christianity and adopted the laws proposed by the missionaries as state law. The missionaries urged the ali'i and mō'ī to pass laws based on religious authority such as the Ten Commandments. The ultimate authority for the new law was God, as it was in the Hawaiian conception of law. As Sahlins points out, the missionaries offered the ali'i connected with Ka'ahumanu an alternative legitimation of their rule that was consistent with the political functions that had always been performed by the priesthood (Sahlins 1992: 68). When the converted Christian ali'i imposed the Christian regulations, in effect they ended the period of disorder that typically followed the death of an ali'i nui, or paramount chief, by establishing a new kapu system based on Christianity. In doing so, they followed the traditional practice by which a new king recreated the social order dissolved by his predecessor's death. But the god was now Jehovah, Ka'ahumanu and her siblings were the kings, and the society was governed by the tabus of Calvinist Christianity (Sahlins 1992: 69). "Seen, then, from the Hawaiian perspective, what the Ka'ahumanu *ma* and the American clergy were doing was reinstating the tabu (kapu) system. The word was explicitly adopted in this context, and Christianity thus received as a Polynesian ritual order—which in European terms would be a politico-religious order" (Sahlins 1992: 72).

But the missionaries' law differed in important ways from the kapu system. Laws were written rather than oral. Executions were public affairs carried out after a public judicial procedure. And the objective of the laws was the creation of a self charged with making itself through discipline and self-control rather than defending the order of distinction and rank or maintaining connections within local communities. When the Hawaiian people appeared frustratingly slow to subject themselves to the Protestant regime of self-governance and self-entrepreneurship, missionaries turned to practices of exclusion and punishment. Church members were suspended and expelled in large numbers for violations that often involved sexual conduct, while prisoner ranks swelled with new offenders. Those incapable of making themselves through self-discipline were expelled from the society of the saved and punished in order to induce moral reform through habituation. Many were sent to prison to be taught discipline. And throughout the 1830s and 1840s Europeans complained about lax prisons and the failure to enforce laws severely. Chapter 3 describes the first transition in more detail.

The second transition, from 1845 to 1852, was a shift from a sacred Christian-Hawaiian law to a secular New England law. It continued the "civilizing process" by implementing a rule of law based on borrowed American law codes and American and European constitutional forms. But this further implicated the Hawaiian people in a system of discipline administered by the state through constables, courts, and prisons that was unprecedented in Hawaiian law. The second transition implied a substantial transfer of power from the aliʻi and the Akua (the gods) to the people, represented by a legislative body. The public was the ultimate source of authority. The authority of the aliʻi over the people was substantially diminished by laws that circumscribed the duties of the makaʻāinana to the aliʻi, gave rights to lands to the commoners and foreigners, and placed judicial power in the hands of an independent judiciary rather than the aliʻi themselves. During this period, the land arrangements that constituted the basis for the Hawaiian state were radically transformed: land was no longer held through the delegation of use rights by ruling chiefs but by permanent tenancy under the legal regime of fee-simple. Relations of inequality based on kinship and clientage were replaced by those based on the market.

This second transition was far more radical in its redefinition of legal institutions and law codes than the first. Within the space of five or six years, enormous changes in the statutory law transformed the legal system of the Kingdom of Hawaiʻi into one similar to European nations of the mid nineteenth century. The kingdom acquired individual land tenure, taxes by cash payments rather than goods or labor, the right of foreigners to hold land, masters and servants' legislation specifying the conditions of hiring labor, coverture in marriage, and a penal code based largely on a Massachusetts prototype.

The mōʻī and aliʻi, battered by demands of resident foreigners for special privileges as well as demands of European nations that their subjects be tried only by juries of their countrymen and that their products and their religious teachers be allowed access to the kingdom, turned increasingly to foreign advisors to help them construct a government and legal system that would be recognized by the leaders of European and American nation-states as sovereign. This meant creating a nation that was viewed by European and American powers as capable of governing itself and those inhabiting its borders. Through these advisors, the apparatus of a state and legal system understandable to Europeans was created. Ironically, although these institutions permitted claims of sovereignty in the nineteenth-century global order, they also deepened dependence on foreigners to run them. As many observers noted, few Hawaiians understood the intricacies and practices of European mechanisms of government and law sufficiently, at least in the early nineteenth century, to run them in ways the Europeans found acceptable. Chapter 4 presents the second transition in detail.

Agency, Consciousness, and Change

Did the ali'i understand the transformative power of the new system of law they adopted? It is impossible to answer this question, but it is possible to see the extent of their agency by examining a similar phenomenon: the creation of chiefly indebtedness and the consciousness of the ali'i concerning this debt. This question provides some insight into the related process of legal appropriation. During the years of the sandalwood trade (1809–1842, peaking in 1810–1818 [Levin 1968: 421]), many of the chiefs became enormously indebted to foreign merchants, largely American, from whom they purchased ships and luxuries such as silks and porcelain in exchange for the promise of sandalwood collected from the mountains (Sahlins 1992: 57–82). Did the chiefs fail to understand the enormous debt obligations they were creating? Or did they simply seek to delay and distract the importunate merchants under the assumption that debts required active intervention by creditors? It is often assumed that the ali'i did not understand these debts. But Stephen Reynolds, a native of Massachusetts who worked as a merchant in Honolulu from 1823 to 1855, made regular visits to his debtors to remind them of their obligations to him during the 1820s, according to his private journal (King 1989). He even included the text of an agreement to pay signed by Boki, the ruling ali'i of O'ahu. One wonders how the chiefs could fail to understand the concept of debt in the face of his regular pleas for money and sandalwood.

It appears that they did understand debts, although not as Reynolds did. The difference is in the notion of repayment. According to an account of the Hawaiian legal system written by a mission-educated Hawaiian who lived in this period, if a person suffered from great robbery or had a large debt owed him, it was only by the goodwill of the debtor that he was repaid (Malo 1951: 58). Thus, the person who lends takes a chance. The ali'i were probably acting in ways familiar to them in managing debts. Reynolds apparently followed a different strategy of managing debt, but one oddly complementary to that of the ali'i. He frequently visited the ali'i who owed him money and asked for payment. The chiefs put him off, making some efforts to pay a bit but never the full amount they owed. Meanwhile, Reynolds extended more and more credit to them despite their failure to pay previous debts (King 1989: 110). He was, of course, in competition with other merchants for sandalwood. They apparently vied with each other to create indebtedness among the chiefs. Reynolds was unhappy whenever another merchant managed to acquire some sandalwood. Apparently the merchants created debts, then pestered the chiefs for repayment. Meanwhile the chiefs acquired goods, then resisted paying for them as long as possible in accordance with Hawaiian conceptions of debt and repayment.

But despite the apparent congruence in these approaches to debt, the differences in underlying cultural logics created difficulties. One can imagine the merchants, fresh from Benjamin Franklin's equation of moral virtue with the reliable repayment of debt, interpreting the failure to repay quickly and willingly as a moral flaw. Meanwhile the ali'i, finding themselves capable of a continuing extension of credit without firm demands for repayment, felt no reason not to escalate their obligations. The ali'i did not misunderstand the concept of debt, but rather interpreted it through their own cultural terms and the permissive behavior of the merchants themselves. In the long run they were forced at gunpoint to pay and to extract the resources from a diminishing population on the land. In 1826 the first of several gunboats arrived, this one an American ship demanding repayment of debts to the American merchants. This example suggests the idiosyncratic and even erratic nature of local processes embedded in similar global trajectories of mercantile capitalism and military power.

In these processes of transition, similarities in underlying cultural logics led to cultural appropriation, while embedded differences in meaning and practice produced a dizzy spin of unanticipated consequences. The religious basis of the law advocated by missionary advisors made sense to the ali'i, but as they began to enact the missionaries' laws, they confronted new ideas about printing and fixing laws, about applying them universally regardless of rank, about determining guilt through a public trial by jury, and about enforcing laws through systems of imprisonment rather than death or banishment. The ali'i were eager to construct a nation-state recognizable as "civilized" and therefore sovereign in the European global order but found themselves at the same time transforming commoners into modern, self-disciplining bourgeois subjects through the new apparatus of courts and prisons.

Transplanting Practices

Law's operation is a consequence of practices embedded in local courts, police units, lawyers' groups, judicial social networks, and law schools. These practices are informed by cultural understandings and routine ways of doing things that often are not articulated. Foreign laws can be introduced without adopting the practices with which they were interpreted, administered, and enforced in their home territory. New laws do not necessarily bring new practices in tow. In nineteenth-century Hawai'i, the foreigners constantly fretted about how to introduce desirable practices along with newly transplanted institutions. This problem plagued mission, school, and court alike. As Hawaiians took over these institutions, they shaped them to their own purposes and adopted practices familiar to them. Euro-American missionaries were reluctant to let go, recognizing that if they did, these institutions would not be run exactly as they thought they should be. The same problem emerged as the government became more European and bureaucratic. Who was to run the new systems?

This was an enduring problem for the mission as well as the law. Rufus Anderson, long-term secretary of the American Board of Commissioners of Foreign Missions, struggled with this problem as he tried to persuade the missionaries he sent throughout the world to let go of the churches they had founded. He tried to persuade the missionaries to turn their churches over to local converts and leave the field, but all over the world they resisted (Hutchinson 1987). They seem to have recognized that it was not possible to have a foreign institution run according to foreign practices unless foreigners were doing it. The New England missionaries in Hawai'i strongly resisted leaving the field, fearing that if they turned their churches over to Hawaiian ministers, they could no longer control the way these ministers interpreted the Christian message or guarded moral conduct within the church. They pointed to the number of converts suspended or excommunicated for failure to uphold the strict codes of conduct. Anderson describes this dilemma clearly, drawing the parallel between management of the government and management of the churches:

> What I fear is, that the foreign members of [the Hawaiian] government will imperceptibly be so multiplied, that the young chiefs now in school, will never be able to rise to consideration and influence. . . .[Foreigners] deem themselves more competent to fill the offices than the natives, and would fain believe that the natives are incompetent to fill them. . . .[Natives] cannot, indeed, perform the duties as well as foreigners, *if the duties must be performed just as they are in foreign courts and governments;* but at the same time, it is better for the islanders, and it is essential to the continuance of their institutions as a nation, that the offices should be filled by natives. Better have the duties performed imperfectly, than not be done by them.
>
> (Hutchinson 1987: 88–89, quoted from Anderson, Sandwich Islands Mission, pp. 126, 125. Italics in original.)

In an 1846 letter to the Sandwich Islands (Hawai'i) mission he says: "I feel bound to call your attention to the subject because I believe that if the churches are officered by foreigners, the offices of the government will continue to have foreign occupants. Nothing will save the native government but a native ministry placed over the native churches" (Hutchinson 1987: 89, quoted from Anderson, Sandwich Islands Mission, p. 126). Anderson's argument applies to law as well as churches: if the institution is to be run exactly as it is at home, it cannot be run by Hawaiians. As Kamakau said of the legislature, "The stranger has no more skill with the axe than the worn-out hewers of Hawaii, but not ten Hawaiians combined have the skill and wit to equal that of the stranger in the legislature" (Kamakau 1961: 377). Those who did not know the practices of the new institutions were often barred from participating in them lest they transform them.

It was relatively easy to build a new edifice for the court, celebrated in William Little Lee's speech in front of the courthouse. Yet the practices required to produce decisions and punish offenders on a daily basis were far more difficult to transfer. Well into the 1840s, twenty years after the passage of laws against adultery, male and female adulterers were imprisoned together, apparently without regard to the danger of unbridled sexuality that loomed so large in the missionaries' view. The enforcement of laws of sexual morality and sobriety fluctuated during the 1820s, 1830s, and 1840s depending on the enthusiasm of particular ali'i. Boki, the ruling chief of O'ahu from 1819 to 1830, for example, did not share Ka'ahumanu's or Hoapili's enthusiasm for regulating prostitution and rum-selling, (Boehlen 1988: 104), and Kauikeaouli (Kamehameha III) abrogated most of these laws in 1833–1834 in his period of protest against the Calvinist regime of Ka'ahumanu (Sahlins 1992: 120). On the other hand, Kapi'olani and Nāihe imposed strict laws against drinking, adultery, prostitution, idolatry, and other sins committed on their lands (Kamakau 1961: 382). Local chiefs had very extensive authority over their lands and could determine whether they wanted to enforce the laws severely or not. Authority rested with the chiefs rather than a legislature or judiciary or any concept of a sovereign "people."

As the number of foreign residents in Hawai'i grew in the early nineteenth century, there was tremendous pressure on the government to create a system of law to which the unruly and resistant resident foreign merchants and visiting captains and crews would submit. The issue of whether foreigners could assert the right to be judged by juries of their countrymen was an ongoing struggle throughout the nineteenth century (Nelligan and Ball 1992). Yet, once created, these legal and governmental institutions required new social practices and skills, which the foreigners felt they could perform better than Hawaiians. Foreigners became increasingly central to running these new institutions. At the same time, those parts of the legal system left in Hawaiian hands were subjected to a constant barrage of complaints by foreigners who claimed that they were not being run correctly.

This contact zone is not a place where one system is collapsing in favor of another but a place of intersections located within unequal and shifting power relations. The ali‘i, the maka‘āinana, the American Protestant missionaries, the foreign residents, the British consul, and the New England whalers are all navigating a complex field without full knowledge of the larger consequences of the cultural paths they are choosing. As various groups attempt to make sense of one another over time and negotiate this uncertain field, they continually constitute and reconstitute culture. The law stands out as a more sedimented and less easily changed cultural form than many others. Consequently, it takes on particular importance under conditions of such dramatic confrontation and change.

Hawaiian Law in the 1820s

How did this new spiritual and political order change the legal system? To answer this question requires an exploration of the nature of the system of law before 1820. Law was always changing, of course, but, as John Papa ‘I‘ī, an early-nineteenth-century Hawaiian government leader and jurist writes, "Knowing right from wrong has existed from ancient times" (Ii 1959: 19). There are many accounts of the government and legal system in the early nineteenth century but most are framed by Protestant missionary views. Some of the most reliable accounts come from educated Hawaiians who were born in the late eighteenth century and were trained by the mission school, Lāhaināluna, such as David Malo, John Papa ‘I‘ī and Samuel Kamakau. But these writers often shared the missionaries' critique of Hawaiian religious ideas and social practices. Another source is early travelers, one of the most observant of whom was William Ellis, the British missionary who toured the islands in 1822 and 1823. Unlike most of the early missionaries, he spoke the language well since he had already spent several years in Tahiti and had mastered that similar language, and he traveled with Tahitian Christian converts. Yet he viewed Hawai‘i through a Tahitian lens, to some extent, and his account shifts between relatively straightforward descriptions of institutions and customs and harsh condemnation of heathen practices. Kame‘eleihiwa's book (1992) takes a contemporary Native Hawaiian perspective and relies on Hawaiian-language sources in addition to the more conventional missionary accounts. Sahlin's study of a valley on O‘ahu uses both archeological data and an extensive analysis of archival data, largely from government and merchant documents, to reconstruct Hawaiian society between 1800 and the 1840s (Sahlins 1992). There is a wealth of archeological evidence (Kirch 1985) and ethnographic work on early Hawaiian political and social organization and myth, which I have not attempted to incorporate here beyond some key works (e.g., Sahlins 1958; 1995; Goldman 1970; Handy and Pukui 1972 [1958]; Linnekin 1990) and some comparative studies of Polynesian peoples (e.g., Firth 1936; Gailey 1987).

These sources indicate that the social organization of Hawai'i has continually changed since its earliest settlement early in the first millennium. The earliest settlers came from central East Polynesia sometime in the first two or three centuries A.D. After a long period of growth and development of fishing techniques and of agriculture in the fertile windward valleys, the islands experienced a period of rapid population growth and social differentiation starting in 1100 A.D. (Kirch 1985: 303). Between 1300 and 1650, irrigation systems expanded and intensified in the wet windward valleys, leeward areas were converted into vast dryfield taro farming areas, and fish farming was expanded with the construction of numerous fish ponds (Kirch 1985: 305). By the seventeenth century, the ahupua'a system, in which chiefs rather than kin groups controlled territory, was established and an elaborate system of ranking was emerging along with sporadic warfare between chiefs and the redistribution of lands at conquest. High-ranking chiefesses became the main transmitters of rank and mana and were much sought after. There were a number of marriages of high-ranking women with Hawai'i Island chiefs.

The period from 1650 to 1795 was one of intense rivalry and warfare accompanied by the rise of the Kū cult, the construction of increasingly massive luakini heiau (temples connected with human sacrifice) such as Pu'ukoholā, and the further elaboration of the kapu system, especially the kapu surrounding the high chiefs (Kirch 1985). Beneath the new power and status of the ali'i, the maka'āinana continued to engage in a sophisticated system of wetland kalo farming, fishing, fish farming, dryland kalo and sweet potato farming, gathering, and rearing of pigs and dogs as they had done for centuries. Thus, the kapu system protecting ali'i power and rank was a relatively recent development, whereas the religious beliefs and kapu system of the maka'āinana are far older. They have endured far better in the face of change.

By the time Captain Cook arrived in 1778 there had been considerable political consolidation. The largest island, Hawai'i, still had several competing chiefs. The infusion of European weapons, ships, and techniques of war radically escalated warfare and increased the death toll. It was not until 1795 that Kamehameha united all the islands except Kaua'i under his rule. Although it is debated whether or not there was a state in existence before this unification, most agree that Kamehameha consolidated the islands into a state structure with regularized tribute and appointed an ali'i nui on each island responsible to him. Thus, the political and social organization of Hawai'i changed over time, building on previous practices but developing new forms of centralization and power (Kirch 1985). Accounts of Hawaiian law and government in the early nineteenth century describe not a static phenomenon but a society in dramatic transformation that had recently become centralized in significant new ways.

The system of government and law in the early nineteenth century, after consolidation into a state but before the transition to a Western government and legal system, was a hierarchical system in which power depended on connection with the Akua, on rank and kapu status, on control over lands, and on linkages with the new mercantile economy. Hawaiian society, like other Polynesian systems, was fundamentally hierarchical, with differences in status related to ritual rank. Lower ranks owed tribute and military service to higher ranks in exchange for use of land (Frear 1894: 1; Chinen 1958; Goldman 1970; Sahlins 1992: 182). As Gailey notes of the similar system in Tonga, processes of state formation entailed a struggle between elites and local kin-based groupings over the control of labor, goods, and social continuity (Gailey 1987: 27). Elites attempted to restrict the rights of the people on the land to use subsistence resources. A similar situation prevailed in Hawai'i as the relationship between the producing communities—local groups of kindred with some claims to land—and the ruling elites gradually changed from one based on putative kin connections to one organized around political control over territory (see Goldman 1970; Sahlins 1992).

In the early 1820s Ellis described four ranks, although others note that the system had a gradation of ranks (Ellis 1969: 412–413; Goldman 1970: 228–233; Kame'eleihiwa 1992: 45). These ranks were based on descent, but individuals could move through ranks over time on the basis of political power and strategic marriages. Mana was distributed along this hierarchy, with those at the bottom possessing little or none. Status was generally determined at birth, so that the only way for a man to maintain or improve mana was to mate with or marry a high-ranking woman or to achieve mana through warfare (Kame'eleihiwa 1992: 46–47). The highest ranking chiefs or ali'i were the intermediaries between the people and the Akua (Kame'eleihiwa 1992: 45). Those with high genealogical rank claimed a variety of kapu observances from subordinates, such as the kapu moe, which demanded full prostration from subordinates of a lower rank, or the kapu wohi, which required subordinates to kneel when the holder of the kapu was eating and to appear before him or her only if the subordinate was clean and properly attired (Goldman 1970: 217). Violations of kapu moe and kapu wohi subjected the offender to the death penalty. "Kumu Kānāwai" is the name given to the first major body of Western law passed in 1840–1842, indicating that Western law was understood as similar to the system of restrictions and punishments that supported the political/religious hierarchy of the kapu system. Chapter 3 discusses the new system of law in more detail.

In Ellis's day, the second rank were governors of the different islands and chiefs of large land divisions. The third and most numerous rank, called kaukau ali'i, were holders of districts or villages cultivated by their dependents or let out to tenants. Most priests were of the third rank. All ali'i were proprietors of the land, haku 'āina. The land was managed by konohiki (land stewards)—ali'i of various ranks, but usually kaukau ali'i. They were responsible for managing land, collecting tribute, and directing the daily activities of cultivation and fishing (Ellis 1969: 412–413; Kame'eleihiwa 1992: 29). Ralston estimates that not more than one-tenth of the population was chiefly persons removed from subsistence labor (Ralston 1989: 51).

The maka'āinana were the fourth rank and by far the largest. Most were small farmers working ten to thirty acres, canoe and house builders, fishermen, musicians and dancers, and general laborers. Some attached themselves to a chief or ali'i and worked on his or her land for their food and clothing. These people showed respect to chiefs according to their rank or office and, Ellis says, regarded the sacred chiefs almost with adoration, prostrating themselves before them. They could not touch the sacred chiefs or enter their houses without permission (Ellis 1969: 412–41). In Kame'eleihiwa's view, despite their economically and socially subordinated status they had great love for their chiefs and this love persisted throughout the nineteenth century (Kame'eleihiwa 1992: 46).

In every island, the mō'ī (a single paramount) was acknowledged as the lord and proprietor of the soil by hereditary right or the laws of conquest. When Kamehameha had subdued most of islands in 1795, he distributed them among his favorite chiefs and warriors on condition of their rendering him military service and a certain proportion of the produce of their lands. This was common practice, as a division of land among the victors invariably followed the conquest of a district or island (Ellis 1969: 414; Sahlins 1992). When Ellis toured the islands, each was under a high chief who paid rent or tax to the king and followed his orders. There were six divisions on the island of Hawai'i, each governed by a chief or two appointed by the king or by the governor and approved by the king. Large divisions or moku were divided into districts and villages. The basic division, the ahupua'a, was a pie-shaped piece of land extending from a wide end at the sea to a narrow point on the mountain. This was the basic unit for tax collection into the monarchy period. A headman, nominated by the governor, usually presided over villages, which were again subdivided into a number of small farms or plantations (Handy and Pukui 1972 [1958]). In the 1820s the king personally held a number of districts on most of the islands, and several of the principal chiefs received districts directly from the king independent of the governor of the island where they were situated (Ellis 1959: 414).

Sahlins's detailed study of one valley indicates the coexistence of two kinds of land rights for maka'āinana in the early nineteenth century, one based on several generations' residence in the same place and the other on conquest and redistribution to victorious ali'i. Land could be acquired by inheritance or by a grant from an ali'i. Inherited land had fewer obligations, whereas land granted by a konohiki/chief reduced the recipient to a more servile form of dependence and higher tributes (Sahlins 1992: 178–180). A person receiving land in tribute might become an kama'āina in time, a person of long tenure who acquires inherited rights to land. Security of tenure depended on a gradual process of becoming a kama'āina as a person stayed in the same place over generations. Redistribution after conquest or death of the mō'ī did not generally displace the producing people on the land, only the konohikis (see Wise 1933: 82). Maka'āinana were generally free to move but were permitted to stay if they wished. Some displaced konohikis remained on the land as maka'āinanas, claiming kama'āina status over time and serving as local leaders even though their ali'i patrons were no longer in control of the land. Thus, the composition of local communities was a complex joining of kinship and clientship relationships.[4]

The local kin unit was a loose collection of affinal and consanguineal kinsmen joined by common descent from kupuna (grandparents) as well as by ascent from a shared child.[5] Handy and Pukui, in their twentieth-century ethnography of Hawaiian kinship in Ka'ū, a rural area of the island of Hawai'i, describe the 'ohana as a kindred under the leadership of an elder male from the senior branch of the 'ohana designated haku, leader (Handy and Pukui 1972 [1958]: 6–7). The 'ohana engaged in reciprocal exchange of goods from mountain to sea among its members. It does not appear to be a corporate group, although it was collectively responsible for tribute during the Makahiki (Pukui and Handy 1972 [1958]: 6).

The Kapu System of Hierarchy and Distinction

There are several accounts of the nature of law and regulation in the 1820s, all more or less shaped by missionary influences. Ellis says there were no records and no written laws, but there was a traditional code consisting of regulations promulgated by former kings or followed by general consent, which governed the tenure of lands, the right to property, personal security, and exchange or barter. This code was well understood and usually acted upon. The portion of personal labor due from a tenant to his chief was fixed by custom and a chief would be justified in banishing the person who refused to perform it, but if a chief banished a man who had performed labor and paid the required rent, this would be contrary to right. If the man complained to the governor or the king and there were no other charge against him, he would probably be reinstated. Irrigation of plantations was very important in most areas, and there was a law that every plantation should have water twice a week in general and once a week during the dry season (Ellis 1969: 420).

The kapu system of law regulated relations between maka'āinana and ali'i. The hierarchy of rank was maintained by kapu systems. David Malo, born in 1795, describes the tabus (kapus) of the great chiefs and the system of punishment for their violations, writing retrospectively but from his own experience in the 1820s (Malo 1951: 56–57).[6] The great chiefs had many tabus, and a large number of people were slain for breaking or infringing them, according to Malo. Both Malo and Kamakau think the system of kapu and punishment is fairly recent, Kamakau estimating that it is no more than three hundred years old (Kamakau 1961: 223). Malo describes the tabus surrounding the chiefs as very strict and severe (Malo 1951: 56–57). If the shadow of a man falls on the house of a tabu chief, the man must be put to death, or if his shadow falls on the back of the chief, or his robe or malo (loin cloth), or any of his belongings, or if anyone climbs over the stockade or enters the private doorway of a tabu chief, he would be put to death. When an ali'i with kapu moe, the prostrating kapu, went out in the daytime, a person went ahead calling out "Kapu! Moe!" and everyone prostrated themselves. The kapu a noho, the sitting kapu, required sitting when the holder of the kapu or his possessions moved along the road. A person who remained standing was put to death. These kapus were personally attached to particular individuals of rank and acquired through inheritance. Those who violated the tabu of the chiefs were burned, strangled, or stoned to death. "Thus it was that the tabus of the chiefs oppressed the whole people," concludes Malo (1951: 57).

But fundamental to this system of majestic power was mercy. The king could have a chief or commoner put to death, or spare his or her life. The guilty could always seek to escape to a pu'uhonua or place of refuge. Persons of high rank could grant pardons either in person or by establishing pu'uhonua (Nelligan and Ball 1992: 116).

Malo describes the system as arbitrary rather than merciful: "Everything went according to the will or whim of the king, whether it concerned land, or people, or anything else—not according to the law" (Malo 1951: 58). His criticism seems influenced by the missionary critique of Hawaiian rule as arbitrary and despotic, and as denying rights to commoners. His account of the law is quite different from Ellis's. Whereas Ellis argues that the system governing land and water was well regulated, Malo says: "The king, however, had no laws regarding property, or land, regarding the payment or collection of debts, regulating affairs and transactions among the common people, not to mention a great many other things" (Malo 1951: 57). In ancient times, Malo says, retaliation with violence and murder was the rule, and the only recourse for an offender was to run away and hide. Those who wanted help turned to the chiefs for assistance. The king had the right to select for himself fleet runners, men to paddle his canoes, canoe makers, "and spies to keep watch of the law breakers and criminals in all parts of the land" (Malo 1951: 195). The ubiquitous constable of the 1850s apparently had a Hawaiian as well as a New England ancestry.

Judicial practices were embedded within this political hierarchy (Ellis

1969: 422). The mōʻī as chief magistrate over all the islands, the governors over their islands, and chiefs of districts all served as arbitrators in quarrels among their own people. A person dissatisfied with the decision of his or her chief could appeal to the governor and to the king. There was no regular police, but the king relied on those chiefs in attendance on him who, with the assistance of their own dependents, executed his orders. The house or front yard of the king or governor was usually the court of justice. Judgment was seldom given till both parties were heard face to face. "They have several ordeals for trying those accused of different crimes. One of the most singular is the *wai haruru*, shaking water" (Ellis 1969: 422–423). In the wai haruru, a large calabash of water is placed in the middle of a circle, prayer is offered by the priest, and the suspect holds his hands over the water. When the person who is guilty holds his hand over the water, it trembles. There was no system of separating the act of managing a trial (judge) and rendering a verdict (jury) in Cook's time and probably not before 1820 (Nelligan and Ball 1992: 116).

There were no unnecessary delays in the administration of justice. For example, Ellis was once sitting with Kāraimoku (Kālaimoku) when a poor woman came to complain that the chief in her district kept water running through his own plantation for several days while potatoes and taro in hers were parched. He sent one of his favorite chiefs with her to see if the chief had kept back the water, and if he had, to let it flow over her field immediately. Ellis notes that no lawyers were employed to conduct public trials. Each puts forward his or her own cause, usually sitting cross-legged before the judge, and parties express their own interests (Ellis 1969: 423).

Thus in the 1820s legality was inextricably joined with the institutions of chiefship and religion, with conceptions of mana, and with the link between the aliʻi nui and the Akua. Religion functioned to maintain chiefly authority, not merely the rule of a particular dynasty but political authority in general (Linnekin 1990: 35). The chiefly and priestly kapus served to protect and enhance the spiritual/religious power of the chiefs, much as the eating kapu protected masculine power. They maintained the elaborate system of distinctions in rank and dramatically and severely punished those who violated the system. Commoner men were put to death for violating tabus of chiefly women, whereas chiefly women were generally impervious to punishment for infractions of kapu (Linnekin 1990: 35). In the highest ranks, adultery was punished by death (Ellis 1969: 421) but this severity was restricted to the first matings of high-ranking women.

The system of law regulating relations between aliʻi and makaʻāinana defined the prerogatives and power of chiefship. The focus was not on the correction of everyday offenses but on the dramatic and vivid display of the awesome power of the aliʻi and the reinforcement of hierarchy and rank. This was a symbolic economy of punishment whose severe rules tinged with

mercy dramatized the power and majesty of the aliʻi and marked them as
different.

The Regime of Community Control

Everyday offenses among makaʻāinana were handled within local communities in a different regime of law and punishment. The system was more
compensatory and conciliatory and included collective decision making directed to restoring harmony (the process of hoʻoponopono) and imposing
punishments (Nelligan and Ball 1992: 116). Since the makaʻāinana tended to
stay on the land while the chiefs moved from place to place, these were
relatively stable communities (Malo 1951: 61). Mutual assistance, hospitality, and other forms of reciprocity were fundamental parts of the ordering
of local communities, and those who failed to abide by these principles were
excluded (Handy and Pukui 1972 [1958]: 49–51). In the event of a very
serious offense, such as helping a sorcerer to destroy a member of another
person's family or cruelty to another's child, the offended person could declare that love was cut off between them and mutual aid and obligations
would cease. But if the offender went to an older relative, preferably a religious leader or kahuna, with a pig, and the two brought the pig for sacrifice
to the family deities (ʻaumakua) to ask forgiveness, the relative had to for-
give the offender or risk rejection by the ʻaumakua (ibid.).

Rules of morality within local communities focused on the quality of interpersonal relationships and feelings. Malo lists as things understood to be
very wrong coveting, theft, thrusting oneself on the hospitality of one's
neighbor, deceit and lying, finding fault with others, and having evil
thoughts against others such as anger or jealousy, as well as scowling, intim-
idation, and killing an innocent person (Malo 1951: 72–74). Morality meant
not desiring other people's things, not finding fault, not lying or deceiving or
having bad thoughts about others, and not living off the work of others. The
virtuous person did not shift from one chief to another, change wives frequently, or run into debt. The good person took a wife, brought up children
properly, dealt squarely with neighbors and landlords, worshipped the gods,
and engaged in some industry such as farming, fishing, housebuilding, ca-
noemaking, or raising swine, dogs, and fowls rather than indulging in sports
(Malo 1951: 75). Thus, controlling feelings toward others within intimate
relationships, supporting oneself and sharing with others, and maintaining
stable relationships were highly valued.

Vengeance was an important aspect of local justice between people of the
same social rank. According to Ellis (1969: 420–421), in case of assault or
murder, except when their own chief was the culprit, the family and friends
of the injured party were justified in retaliating. When they were too weak to

attack the offender, they sought the aid of their neighbors or appealed to the chief of the district or the king, who seldom inflicted a heavier punishment than banishment even for murder. In disputes with people of higher rank, the injured party would appeal for justice to the king or the chief where the accused lived (Frear 1894: 2). Ellis notes that murder was very rare, an observation echoed in 1846 (Kingdom of Hawai'i 1846). Theft was severely punished. In the past, when a house or garden was robbed, the victims went to the house or garden of the offenders and seized whatever they could find. The guilty party would not dare resist the retaliation because of the general support for punishing individuals who steal.

There were kapus within the family—known as kapu 'ili ("skin kapu")—but their punishment was less draconian (Handy and Pukui 1972 [1958]: 48; Levin 1968: 413). For example, women were prohibited from using any article of clothing used by males. Among the maka'āinana, transgression of any kapus and/or any misdemeanors could be atoned for at the Pōhaku o Kāne (stone of Kāne) that belonged to the family. In the morning, the family went to this place early, bringing a pig, kūmū fish, 'awa, and tapa as offerings, and offered prayers for forgiveness and repentance for the wrong committed by the family (Levin 1968: 413). Then the family drank the 'awa or ate the pig. Thus, within the local community the legal process focused on apology and forgiveness rather than punishment or death, restoration and reparation rather than pain and correction. When these mechanisms failed, the common approach was vengeance and seizing back stolen property or, if the offender was stronger than the victim, recourse to the assistance of an ali'i.

Offenses by maka'āinana against ali'i were handled more severely: if the victim was a high chief, in some islands the thief was tied and put in an old canoe, towed out to sea and left adrift to sink. If a maka'āinana was discovered wearing the malo of an ali'i, he/she was sacrificed to the personal god of that ali'i. The only recourse available for a maka'āinana was to flee to a pu'uhonua (Levin 1968: 414).

Although the kapu system was destroyed by the transformations sweeping Hawai'i in the nineteenth century, the regulation of community life has proved far more durable. Remnants of this system of law persisted in rural pockets of Hawai'i long after the system of chiefship and kapu disappeared (Handy and Pukui 1972 [1958]: 16–17). This is a morality that focuses on the self-in-relation, whose virtues are those of being in a group, staying in it and contributing to its maintenance through sharing and negotiation.

The End of the Eating Kapu

In 1819, soon after Kamehameha's death, the new mō'ī, Liholiho (Kamehameha II), under pressure from the powerful ali'i Keōpūolani, the most sacred chiefess and his mother, and Ka'ahumanu, the kuhina nui or premier, declared the end of the 'aikapu, or men and women eating separately, in favor of free eating or 'ainoa. This signaled a major change in the kapu system, the political/religious order that underlay Hawaiian society (Kame'eleihiwa 1992: 74–78). 'Aikapu separated the sacred male element from the dangerous female one, thus creating order in the world (Kame'eleihiwa 1992: 25). By separating men's and women's eating into different houses, the 'aikapu prevented the "unclean" nature of women from defiling male sanctity. The foods forbidden to women were phallic symbols and also forms of the major male Akua or gods: the pig, coconut, banana, and certain red fish (Kame'eleihiwa 1992: 33). If women ate these foods, it would encourage them to devour male sexual prowess, including the sexual prowess of the Akua Lono (fertility and agriculture), Kū (war and wood carving), Kanaloa (ocean and ocean travel), and Kū'ula (deep sea fishing). As Kame'eleihiwa describes it, 'ai means to eat, to devour, and also to rule and to control, so if women ate the forms of these Akua, they would get the mana to rule the domains represented by men and men would have nothing left to do (Kame'eleihiwa 1992: 34).

For society to function properly, ali'i nui had to observe 'aikapu restrictions on eating together (Kame'eleihiwa 1992: 39). The ali'i were responsible for protecting themselves and for maintaining pono for the people, which they did by following the patterns of the ancestors. According to the concept of pono, when Hawaiians care for the land, the land will care for them, producing a perfect harmony, or pono. The pono ali'i nui was one who kept order upon the 'āina, the land (Kame'eleihiwa 1992: 26). The ali'i nui were mediators between divine and human; they had the role of protecting the maka'āinana from terrible unseen forces by proper ritual and pious behavior, thus avoiding a famine or calamity. If one occurred, the ali'i nui were held responsible and were deposed. If the ali'i were stingy and cruel to the maka'āinana, they would cease to be pono, lose favor with the Akua, and be struck down, usually by the people.

Kame'eleihiwa argues that Ka'ahumanu ended 'aikapu because this powerful chiefess thought that the Akua had failed the people. She faced an enormously high death rate in the years after Cook arrived. The first missionary census in 1823 reported only 134,925 people (Schmitt 1968), a loss of perhaps 80 percent of the population (Kame'eleihiwa 1992: 81). Ellis's informants in the same year reported a three-fourths drop in population during the previous forty years (Ellis 1969: 319–320). This horrendous death rate, despite the pono behavior of Kamehameha, suggested that the ali'i nui needed to 'imihaku (to search for a chief), to search for a new source of mana. The 'aikapu religion was apparently no longer pono. Besides, white men had criticized this religion for a long time and were not dying, despite their defiance of its restrictions. Somehow they held the secret of long life.

Kame'eleihiwa argues that Ka'ahumanu and the ali'i nui may have thought that 'ainoa (free eating) was the white men's secret to life (Kame'eleihiwa 1992: 82). As kuhina nui, an administrative post newly created by Kameha-meha, and a leader of the powerful Maui-Hilo ali'i who had loyally sup-ported Kamehameha, Ka'ahumanu was very powerful (Levin 1968: 423). She was joined in her effort to end the 'aikapu by most of the ali'i nui in high administrative positions: Ke'eaumoku, Kuakini, Kalanimōkū, and Hoapili. It was this group that subsequently adopted Christianity as well. Kame'eleihiwa argues that Ka'ahumanu maneuvered Liholiho into the posi-tion of either adopting 'ainoa or killing his mother, brother, and adopted mother for their violations of the 'aikapu (Kame'eleihiwa 1992: 78).

The reasons for this major transformation have been much debated (Ka-makau 1961: 219–231; Webb 1965; Levin 1968; Davenport 1969; Kame'el-eihiwa 1992: 74–78) but it seems clear that it reflected the effects of forty years of economic and social change. The kapu system required that the mandate to rule be established through religious ritual, so eliminating it meant a major redefinition of the spiritual power of the chiefs and a change in the power of the priestly class. The abolition of the 'aikapu also illustrates Ka'ahumanu's readiness to appropriate new sources of power and authority, a pattern she continued when the first American missionaries arrived six months later.

The missionaries heard the joyous news of the ending of the 'aikapu as they put into harbor in 1820. They interpreted this change on the eve of their arrival as an act of God (*Missionary Herald* 1821: 111). They were imme-diately impressed with the dress and decorum of the first Hawaiians they encountered. A collective journal, published in the *Missionary Herald*, de-scribes their first visit from a Hawaiian ali'i, Krimakoo (Kalanimōkū), and his wife and two widows of Kamehameha (unnamed). The missionaries noted that these people sat down to dine with them "and behaved with much decorum" (*Missionary Herald* 1821: 115).[7] The journal describes the chief's dress as unexpected: "a neat white dimity jacket, black silk vest, nankeen pantaloons, white cotton stockings, shoes, plaid cravat, and a neat English hat" (*Missionary Herald* 1821: 115). Yet when they petitioned the mō'ī, Liholiho, for permission to stay, he was reluctant. He had apparently heard that missionaries at Otaheite (Tahiti) and Eimeo had monopolized the trade and government of the Society Islands (*Missionary Herald* 1821: 117). They observed that the king worried that the Americans intended to take posses-sion of the islands and therefore hesitated to allow the missionaries to settle (*Missionary Herald* 1821: 119). Future events prove the wisdom of the king's concern.

In their first service at the islands, Hiram Bingham preached from Isaiah xlii, 4, "The Isles shall wait for his law." He talked about the character of the Law-giver, the law waited for, those who wait for it, the evidence that the isles do wait for it, and the consequences of receiving it (*Missionary Herald* 1821: 116). The missionaries noted that most of the islanders did not understand the precepts of the law of Christ, but listened to the sound of Bingham's voice. The moment was prophetic. It revealed the centrality of law to the missionaries' vision and the inability of both the ali'i and the missionaries to hear one another and understand what that might mean for the future.

3

THE FIRST TRANSITION: RELIGIOUS LAW

Christianity and Conversion: The 1820s

THE ADOPTION of Anglo-American law was inextricably joined with the adoption of Christianity, a severe Calvinist version of Protestant Christianity brought by stern, impassioned, and ethnocentric missionaries from New England. Once the ali'i had converted to Protestant Christianity, they were expected to adopt the rules of the new religion. Although not restricted to any denomination, most of the missionaries were Congregationalists and a smaller number were Presbyterians. A large proportion came from more rural parts of New England and upstate New York. Many were trained in colleges and seminaries in the area. In contrast with the British missionaries in South Africa, many of those who came to Hawai'i had advanced educational degrees in theology (see Comaroff and Comaroff 1997). Between 1820 and 1848 the missionary agency, the ABCFM, sent a total of 153 men and women to Hawai'i. They were joined by another forty independent missionaries (Piercy 1992: 201; see also Grimshaw 1989: xv). This was an extraordinarily large missionary contingent for the population of the islands. One missionary, writing in 1880, estimated that churches in the United States contributed about 1.5 million dollars to the mission in Hawai'i and supported a total of 170 people there (Coan 1882: 248). The ABCFM supported the mission until 1863, when missionaries were required to find support from their local congregations.

To the ali'i, the missionaries spoke for a new and powerful god, Jehovah. It was common practice for a chief or king to take a new god from the pantheon of thousands of deities as his or her personal god, to build temples to that god and make offerings in the hope of support in his or her endeavors. Kamehameha chose Kū as his personal deity and was favored by Kū in his military and political exploits. Conversion to Christianity was, then, consonant with existing politico-religious practices. Moreover, when Ka'ahumanu successfully put down the 1824 rebellion in Kaua'i with the help of Hoapili and Kalanimōkū using Christian prayers, she decided this was the new source of mana she needed and she became a devout Christian (Kame'eleihiwa 1992: 152–153). The new religion offered a way to return the troubled kingdom to a state of pono (Kame'eleihiwa 1992).

The missionaries offered the ali'i something else of great importance, in addition to a new god who might counter the massive and frightening de-

population. This was the palapala, the written word. The palapala was desired both for its strategic usefulness and for its transcendent power. It is
clear that the initial enthusiasm of the chiefs for the new religion was intimately linked to their desire for palapala. All the chiefs wanted to be able to
read and write and they quickly started writing letters to each other
(Kameʻeleihiwa 1992). Once they had acquired this magical skill, they urged
the missionaries to teach the makaʻāinana and encouraged the expansion of
schools for the purposes of literacy. Keōpūolani, the most sacred aliʻi and
the first convert, quickly saw the advantages of reading and writing and had
her children trained by the missionaries, while Liholiho also saw that this
was a skill valuable for governing the nation (Sinclair 1969: 5).[1]

The famous story of Kapiʻolani's confrontation with Pele, told and retold
throughout the nineteenth century, illustrates the spiritual power attributed to
writing. The confrontation was a contest fought in Hawaiian cultural terms,
in which the transcendent power of writing measured the spiritual power of a
deity. An early convert to Christianity, Chiefess Kapiʻolani visited the volcano on December 22, 1824, in order to confront the deity Pele (Piercy
1992: 204). A private letter from Levi Chamberlain, the business manager of
the Sandwich Islands Mission, written to Jeremiah Everts, the secretary of
the ABCFM at the Mission Rooms in Boston on March 26, 1825, includes
an eyewitness account Chamberlain heard while he was in Hilo. Goodrich,
the Hilo missionary, was at the volcano with Kapiʻolani and recounted the
story to Chamberlain when he arrived in Hilo.[2] Chamberlain's story reveals
the spiritual meaning of writing:

> In Dec., they heard that Kapiolani, wife of Naihe, the interesting chief of Ker-
> eakekua [Keleakekua], was on her way to make them a visit. Mr. Goodrich met
> her at the volcano, and was welcomed by her with the most friendly salutations.
>
> With her he descended the crater, and viewed its fires, and smoke, and run-
> ning lava. None of her countrymen had probably ever viewed the tremendous
> scene with feelings like those which filled her breast. *They* had always ap-
> proached with trembling awe, as to the feet of a god of terrible prowess, whose
> wrath must be appeased with offerings. *She* approached feeling that what she
> beheld was a display of the power and majesty of that God who made heaven
> and earth, and who sustains and controls, directly all things; and all whose works
> praise him, and in all is to be adored. While standing on the ledge, which bounds
> the crater at the distance of more than 500 feet from the top, with those materials
> of destruction before their eyes, which had often spread terror and dismay
> among the inhabitants of the Eastern and Southern divisions of that island, she
> directed one of her attendants to engage in prayer, in which service, she and her
> whole company with much solemnity united.
>
> Before her arrival at the volcano, she was met by a priestess of Pele, who
> warned her not to proceed as, in case she did, the god would come out and

destroy her. Kapiolani demanded who she was that thus addressed her. The reply was, "One in whom the god dwells." "Then," said Kapiolani, "you are wise, and can teach me, come and sit down." She seemed loath to obey but Kapiolani insisting on her compliance, she yielded. Food was offered her, but she said she was a god and did not eat. She held a piece of tapa in her hand which she said was a *palapala* [a writing or letter] from *Pele*. She was requested to read it, but was reluctant, and when forced to comply, she muttered over a medley of nonsense. Kapiolani then produced her spelling books and hymns and said, you have pretended to deliver a message from your god, but we have not understood it. I will now read you a message from the true God which you can understand: for I too have a *palapala*. She then read sentences from the spelling book and some of the hymns, and spoke to the imposter concerning Jehovah the true God, who made all things,—of Jesus Christ the only Savior, of repentance, and a new heart. During the confrontation the woman held down her head, and was silent, and when Kapiolani had finished her address, she said, the god had left her, and she could make no reply. Being afterwards invited to eat she partook without ceremony.

Writing was clearly a source of spiritual power to the Hawaiian priestess and chiefess as it was to the missionaries. Hawaiian chiefs enthusiastically supported the missionaries' efforts to teach reading and writing to their followers and later to the maka'āinana. They wanted the palapala for themselves and their followers. But the Hawaiian chiefs appear to have reinterpreted writing in their own cultural terms, as a form of spiritual power with which to contest the power of the deity Pele. They saw its mana just as the missionaries did, but in a different way. For the missionaries, the ability to read the Bible was fundamental to religious life, to access to the spiritual world. The words of Scripture took on extraordinary importance as guides to moral living, appearing constantly in their writings. For the Hawaiians, writing also was related to spiritual power, but apparently as a sign of the deity's power to speak.

Books also possessed a power transcending secular/spiritual distinctions. Books were constantly in demand, more people desiring books than were able to read them. In a letter in 1827, Levi Chamberlain reports that there have been lots of books distributed, many of whose recipients cannot read but regard the book as a talisman—mea ola—a thing of salvation.[3] The term *palapala* itself refers to Scripture, to writing, and popularly to the education offered by the missionaries (Kuykendall 1938). Many of the books used in the early schools were based on the Bible. Moreover, the ali'i were aware of the power writing gave them to communicate readily among themselves on different islands, a power they initially took to be almost magical. In 1822 Ellis noted: "Supposing it beyond the powers of man to invent the plan of communicating words by marks on paper, they have sometimes asked us, if, in the first instance, the knowledge of it were not communicated to mankind by God himself" (Ellis 1969: 434).

Palapala was linked to political as well as spiritual power. After he returned from England in 1825, Boki assured the ali'i that what impressed him most was the great importance given to the word of God in the great cathedrals and churches of London and the importance accorded those who were educated and learned in letters. The commoners who could not read were like dust under their feet. He said the king of England lived like a tabu chief of old. Kamakau says that these words made an immense impression on the chiefs, who redoubled their efforts in the study of letters and the word of God (Kamakau 1961: 273). Indeed, foreigners complained about the sense of authority that the ability to read and write gave the ali'i and later the maka'āinana.[4]

Ellis reports a conversation with three priests that again reveals the power of palapala: "They said they thought their tao (traditions) respecting Tu, Tanaroa, Rono, or Orono, and Tairi, were as authentic as the accounts in our book, though ours, from the circumstance of their being written, or, as they expressed it, *hana paia i ka palapala* (made fast on the paper), were better preserved, and more *akaaka*, clear, or generally intelligible. To this we replied at some length, after which the old men ceased to object, but withheld their assent" (Ellis 1969: 296–297).

Yet, despite the obvious power and appeal of palapala, there are indications of resistance to the missionary project. In the following extraordinary account, Ellis lays out the entire theory of civilization and nationalism to a group of maka'āinana in the Hilo area, who express a sophisticated skepticism about the effect of missionaries (Ellis 1969: 318).

They said, they had heard that in several countries, where foreigners had intermingled with the original natives, the latter had soon disappeared; and should Missionaries come to live at Waiākea, perhaps the land would ultimately become theirs, and the kanaka maore (aborigines) cease to be its occupiers. I told them, that had been the case in some countries; but that the residence of Missionaries among them, so far from producing it, was designed, and eminently calculated, to prevent a consequence so melancholy. At the same time I remarked, that their sanguinary wars, their extensive and cruel practice of infanticide, their frequent intoxication, and their numerous diseases, partly gendered by vicious habits, had, according to their own account, diminished the population of the island three-fourths within the last forty years; and from the destructive operation of these causes, there was every reason to fear the Hawaiian people would soon be annihilated, unless some remedy was applied. No remedy, I added, was so efficacious as instruction and civilization; and, above all, the principles and doctrines of the Bible, which they could not become acquainted with, but by the residence of Missionaries among them. Such, I informed them, was the opinion of the friends of Missions, who, anxious to ameliorate their wretched condition, preserve from oblivion the remnant of the people, place them among the nations of the earth, and direct them to the enjoyment of civilized life, and the participation of immortality and happiness in another world, had sent them the word of God, and Missionaries to unfold to them, in their own language, its divine and invaluable truths. At the close of this interview, some again repeated, that it would be a good thing for Missionaries to come; others expressed doubt and hesitation.

(Ellis 1969: 319–320)

Here Ellis lays out succinctly the missionary arguments in favor of conversion that ultimately persuaded some of the ali'i to become Christians and to accept the new god Jehovah and the missionaries as their priesthood. The Hawaiians expressed realistic fears of dispossession.

Introducing Christian Law

New law followed close on the heels of the new religion. One of the first ideas was to adopt the Ten Commandments as the law of the land. In a speech in 1825 the boy mō'ī Kauikeaouli exhorted the people to follow the Ten Commandments because the nation belonged to Jehovah (Kamakau 1961: 319). In December 1825 many high-ranking ali'i converted and the idea of making the Ten Commandments the basis for the law was discussed seriously (King 1989: 114).[5] Exactly who was responsible for this idea was disputed at the time. The merchants were furious about the proposal, contending that the missionaries put the chiefs up to it, while the missionaries claimed it was the idea of the chiefs. Hiram Bingham, the most powerful missionary on the islands in the 1820s, denied responsibility for the idea of making the Ten Commandments law (Bingham 1981). He claimed he simply translated the Decalogue in 1825 and showed it to the chiefs but did not force them to make it into law (Bingham 1981: 282).[6] But he clearly thought that promulgating new laws was critical to establishing the Christian religion. Bingham described this law to the chiefs as "the Law of Jehovah, which we desired all might regard as a holy rule of life. They were grateful to see that portion of God's Word fairly rendered in their own language, and ready for publication" (Bingham 1981:282).

The ali'i may have been attracted to a set of laws that would give them greater control over the unruly sailors and resident foreigners in the booming port towns. Bingham's account of the lawmaking process indicates how central the law was to the struggles between the merchant, missionary, and Hawaiian segments of the population:

But he and the queen seeing in God's law how plainly and forcibly certain
crimes cognizable by civil rulers, were prohibited, and concerned to see how far
the people of the realm and strangers who visited their shores came short of
obedience, and how many there were who violated their laws, called a meeting
at Honolulu with a view to urge forward the work of reform, which they had
taken up in a special manner in the spring of 1824, and in the summer of 1825;
and to secure the co-operation of other chiefs and the people in the suppression
of evils, which their orders and tabus had not wholly restrained. It was rumored,
that further regulations were about to be made for restraining crimes forbidden
in the Word of God. Had this been strictly true, it afforded no just ground of
alarm to honest men. But scarcely had the chiefs and people convened, when a
number of foreigners intruded, and showed their indignation that the chiefs
should attempt further restraints, or receive laws from the missionaries. To remove the impression, if indeed it existed among influential foreigners, that the
missionaries were dictating laws to the rulers, I disclaimed it in the name of the
mission, but freely admitted that I had translated for them the Divine commands
which prohibited existing evils.

(Bingham 1981: 282)

Stephen Reynolds, the American merchant, placed responsibility for the
Ten Commandments law squarely on the missionaries. He wrote in his journal on December 10, 1825, that Bingham was at Pitts's (Kalanimōkū) with
Ka'ahumanu "trying to have laws of his own making put in force. Boki
opposed him[,] told him he would not let him (B) have any thing to say
about the laws. Ka'ahumanu said she was a lone woman of course she could
do nothing" (King 1989: 115).[7] Because the resident merchants and Boki
objected strenuously to the proposal of Kalanimōkū to adopt the Ten Commandments as law, the measure was not passed in toto (Kuykendall 1938:
124). But the desire for a new law code that included provisions from the
Christian law continued.[8]

Printed Laws

One of the major transitions in the 1820s was to a written rather than an oral
system of law. There are differences between oral and written codes in their
flexibility and adaptability to particular situations, although the boundary is
not firm. The locus of authority shifts to a text, although written words are
always interpreted.[9] Indeed, the production of written texts can be a pro-
foundly oral process (see Riles 1999). Moreover, law may be embodied in
persons as well as texts (Messick 1992). Oral systems of law are consistent
and stable as well as written ones. However, the shift to a printed system
fosters universalism at the expense of local particularism.

Until the arrival of the missionaries in 1820, Hawaiian laws were proclaimed orally and enforced by ali'i within their own districts. The first time laws were printed—fixed in writing—was in 1822, when they were directed at the disruptive and violent behavior of seamen stopping off ships in the port towns (Kuykendall 1938: 121). Even Christian-inspired regulations were mostly proclaimed orally until the end of the 1820s. Laws were enacted through verbal proclamation in local places by ruling chiefs through criers at large gatherings and during tours around the islands. On June 5, 1824, in Lāhainā, Ka'ahumanu, as regent, orally proclaimed five laws to be in effect: laws against murder, theft, and boxing or fighting, to regard the Sabbath as a sacred day, and to enjoin the people to learn to read and write (Kuykendall 1938: 118; King 1989: n. 33). In August 1825, Chamberlain reports that for two or three nights a crier was sent out in Honolulu to proclaim an edict from the chiefs that prohibited several games, encouraged people to turn to the palapala, urged husbands not to forsake their wives (or vice versa) or be guilty of lewdness, and told people to observe the Sabbath and go to meeting (Kuykendall 1938: 122).

The first printed code of laws for Hawaiians was enacted December 8, 1827. These laws prohibited murder, theft, and adultery (moe kolohe). Three other laws, prohibiting rum selling, prostitution, and gambling, had been proposed but because of the strenuous opposition of the merchants, were listed as laws to be taught to the people but not to be enforced (Kuykendall 1938: 126; King 1989). Kauikeaouli, Ka'ahumanu, and Boki also proclaimed these laws orally at a large gathering in a coconut grove in Honolulu on December 14, 1827, and exhorted both the Hawaiian people and foreigners to obey them (Kuykendall 1938: 126). It seems, in Bingham's account of his participation in the proclamation of these laws, that Ka'ahumanu was using him to emphasize her attachment to this new priesthood. In a private letter to the mission board in Boston, Bingham writes that the chiefs have assembled "in the face of opposition from some 'official' or officious foreigners" to adopt and publish laws for the prevention of crimes: "The chiefs and a great concourse of people assembled under a grove of cocoanuts near the sea, to hear the three primary laws of the nation promulgated. The chiefs invited me to attend and offer a prayer *if I were not afraid the foreigners would be angry with me for it*."[10] When Bingham arrived, Boki offered him a chair and Ka'ahumanu put a hymn book into his hand. He sang a few verses and offered a prayer and left without staying to hear the laws. Although Bingham argues that these laws were the ideas of the chiefs, not his, the chiefs clearly wanted him situated in a prominent public location.[11]

The hostility between the resident merchants and the missionaries over the law was deep and long-lasting.[12] Many of the laws the missionaries advocated criminalized activities tolerated by the mercantile community, such as drinking, prostitution, working on the Sabbath, sexual relations outside of marriage, and gambling. The struggle over the Christian law also tended to

polarize Americans and Britons and to divide the ali'i supporting each nationality. Boki and Liliha, for example, favored the British and the merchants
while Ka'ahumanu and Kalanimōkū favored the Americans and the missionaries. There was only a small French community, but the French government
was very anxious for French Catholic priests to evangelize in the islands
while Ka'ahumanu refused to let Catholic priests stay and persecuted Catholic converts. Thus, while the missionaries were trying to manipulate the ali'i
to promote education and the passage of laws, the ali'i were viewing the
laws as a valuable resource to deal with the contentious and demanding
foreign residents and competing ali'i. Ka'ahumanu's strategy was to return
religion to the center of law and chiefly power, with herself as the delineator
of law and of hewa (sin)—refashioning Christianity to meet her Hawaiian
ends (see Silverman 1987: 61–67).[13]

Public Trials and Hangings

A second major change in the system of law and legal procedure in the
1820s was the use of public trials by jury and public hangings. Before this
time, infractions of the kapu system were punished by secret killings, usually
at night and without public trials or sentences (Sahlins and Barrere 1973:
28). William Richards, a missionary, describes a class of servants, called
ilāmuku, whose task was to kill those who had displeased the king or committed offenses. They usually went in the night and killed their victims with
clubs or stones. Those who violated religious kapu were seized by officers of
the priests and taken to the heiau (religious edifice) where they were stoned,
strangled, or beaten to death and placed on the sacrificial altar. Richards
notes that there were "comparatively few" executions for violations of religious tabus. The last secret beheading with the ax at night took place in
1822, and there was a midnight killing of a treasonous officer in 1824. The
first public hanging, held in a public place and witnessed by multitudes,
occurred in 1826 (Sahlins and Barrere 1973: 29).
    A Dutch merchant captain, Jacobus Boehlen, en route from Latin America
to Canton with a load of Hawaiian sandalwood, describes in his journal what
he claims is the first hanging in the kingdom, on February 23, 1828 (Boehlen
1988: 70); but Nelligan and Ball as well as Richards refer to a case in 1826
(Nelligan and Ball 1992: 119). The man had killed a woman, but it was said
that the killing was not intentional but occurred in a fit of insanity. Boehlen
questioned whether all the circumstances had been investigated and all the
available evidence weighed before such a sentence was given and executed.
In reply, merchants told him that the ruling chiefs in such cases generally
followed the opinion of the missionaries. "Nevertheless, it appeared that the
kind-hearted Indians [as he termed the Hawaiian people] were favorably

disposed toward the condemned, for I was told repeatedly that the prisoner would be released soon. And thus for all of them it was an unexpected event when it was announced that the unfortunate would really be hanged the next day—near a pair of coconut trees at the side of Diamond-head" (Boehlen 1988: 70). This account not only suggests some ambivalence about the new regime of punishment among Hawaiians, but also reflects the merchants' view that the missionaries dominated the chiefs.

Public hanging represents one appropriation of what the missionaries and the ali'i called "civilized" modes of conviction and punishment. Trial by jury was another. Foreigners constantly demanded trial by jury rather than by a king or high ali'i (Kuykendall 1938: 127). This was one of Lord Byron's few recommendations to the ali'i in 1825 when they asked his help in forming a new legal system (see note 8). Thus, by the mid 1820s the ali'i were moving to adopt a novel judicial form promoted by many respected foreigners. According to Chamberlain, in the late 1820s three chiefs called on the missionaries to find out how murderers were executed in "civilized countries" (Kuykendall 1938: 127). They were told that the means of execution was not important but that the regularity of the trial and the certainty of the condemned's guilt were. Under this advice, Ka'ahumanu named twelve Hawaiian men to a jury and held a trial. Kuykendall, relying on missionary sources, says that Boki thought the prisoner should die but the jury would not pronounce the crime murder because they were uncertain whether the intent was to kill. Nevertheless, the man was hanged publicly on March 18, 1828 (Kuykendall 1938: 127).[14] Clearly, the ali'i were appropriating these new practices from their missionary advisors.[15]

Trial by jury and public hangings mark a major transition in modes of determining guilt and punishment: from secret killings by ilāmuku on the basis of a private determination of guilt by an ali'i nui for kapu violations to public hangings on the basis of a public trial in front of a jury. One striking feature of these changes is the remarkable willingness of the ali'i to ask and experiment. The changes were obviously made in the name of "civilization" as well as Christianity. But the new practices of trial by jury, public killings, and printed laws displaced power from the hands of the ali'i. The use of printed rather than oral laws diminished the localism by which laws were declared and enforced by particular ali'i. These changes were part of a gradual process of replacing the sovereignty of the ali'i as embodiments of the will of the Akua with the sovereignty of the people (at least in theory) expressed through procedures of representative government.

But in many ways the new system of law shared the cultural logic of the kapu system. Both the missionaries and the Hawaiians envisioned law as descending from a divine source through earthly intermediaries. The kapu system was largely focused on maintaining the status and authority of the chiefs, the earthly representatives of the Akua, by guarding their persons from contact and intimacy with lower-status individuals and by protecting their privileged access to valuable resources such as certain kinds of fish, feathers, and other fine goods. The missionaries hoped that God's law would create the kingdom of God on earth, a social order in which God's power reigned supreme. But the new system of law provided the ali'i the same transcendent authority to articulate and enforce the law as the kapu system, now descending from Jehovah rather than the Akua.

As the ali'i gradually adopted a form of law based on printed texts using new procedures such as trial by jury, new problems emerged as missionaries and other foreigners insisted on uniform enforcement of these laws (Kuyken-dall 1938: 127). The ruling ali'i had appropriated a new system of law under the spiritual guidance of Jehovah, but they had also, perhaps inadvertently, acquired a new system of discipline.

The Struggle over Discipline and Punishment

There were significant differences between the missionary and the Hawaiian conceptions of punishment. The Calvinist vision of Christianity brought with it an emphasis on self-governance and self-regulation of conduct, the importance of constant vigilance against the seductions of evil, and intense self-scrutiny and evaluation. Indeed, Peter Fitzpatrick argues that the Calvinism of the sixteenth century was a pastoral precursor to modern forms of disciplinary power relying on normalization, the production of personhood, and the discipline of the body (Fitzpatrick 1992: 128). These new forms of discipline, as Foucault argues, operate through microtechnologies of power rather than through repression and constraint (Foucault 1979). With modern law came a new demand for self-responsibility, a capacity for self-governance, and a new subject whose efforts at self-subjection in disciplinary, civilizing, religious, legal, or other spheres were private and voluntary (Fitzpatrick 1992: 128–136).

Discipline and punishment under the kapu law was quite different: an occasional, repressive intervention by the sovereign in response to transgressions of the sovereign's prohibitions. The chiefly law was designed to enhance the awesome power and distinctiveness of the chiefs, its majesty tempered by the mercy of pardons and places of refuge. There is no indication that chiefly authority was engaged in policing and controlling the everyday life of commoners beyond enforcing kapus and deciding conflicts brought by maka'āinana. There was no prison, no concept of correction through punishment. Within maka'āinana communities, of course, a distinct legal regime emphasized interdependence and reciprocity as well as vengeance and ostracism when these failed.

Yet the discipline of everyday life was fundamental to the Christian law.

Membership in the churches was contingent on successful self-discipline. Mission reports from the 1820s and 1830s record large numbers of people suspended or excommunicated for violations of conduct. The missionaries themselves had been grilled about their own conduct before they were allowed to depart for Hawai'i (Grimshaw 1989). Appropriate conduct ranged from a clothed body, church-going, and journal-writing to approved practices of marriage and sexuality. In many ways, marriage and the control of sexuality was at the core of the mission project, the bedrock of virtue. By 1827 the kingdom had adopted laws condemning adultery and fornication and establishing a new model of indissoluble marriage. All sexual encounters outside marriage were prohibited. The Christian law defined the family as a private realm, not subject to the intervention of the state in its internal affairs but under the sovereignty and protection of the father. Only men were capable of self-governance, of acting as fully empowered legal persons (Collier, Maurer, and Suarez-Navaz 1995). Chapter 8 discusses the transformation in the family and the regulation of sexuality in more detail.

The transition in disciplinary systems was rocky and uneven. A few chiefs enforced the new laws stringently in their own districts, as Kapi'olani did on the island of Hawai'i and Hoapili did on Maui, while others ignored the laws, as Boki did while governor of O'ahu. Hoapili was particularly active, proclaiming many laws against adultery, prostitution, liquor drinking, stealing, and the taking of life, as well as judging offenders, pronouncing sentences, and subjecting chiefs and commoners alike to punishment (Kamakau 1961: 353–354).[16] Even a chief caught breaking the marriage law might be sentenced to stone breaking on the roads. Summoned to O'ahu during the breakdown of the Christian law in 1834, Hoapili stopped liquor drinking and distilling and tried to restore husbands and wives to their legal spouses on other islands. Some lesser chiefs and prominent citizens as well as maka'āinana were arrested and sent back to Kaua'i, Maui, and Hawai'i (Kamakau 1961: 340).

But in most places, lax enforcement earned constant complaining by the missionaries. In 1826 Levi Chamberlain, writing back to Boston, offered an explanation for the lack of enforcement that was deeply shaped by the language of civilization and nationalism:

Neither the Chiefs nor the people are yet sufficiently enlightened to adopt on rational principles a code of civil regulations to be enforced by severe penalties. The pleasure of the king and of the chiefs has heretofore been the only law and it would be easy to see that the dark minds and depraved hearts of despots who hold the common people in the most absolute subjection, would lead them to institute rules of duty for their subjects at variance with the plainest rules of right. It will be difficult for the chiefs to free themselves from their old notions and propositions; and if they should concede that their former principles were wrong, they could not easily be made to feel the force of new principles and to act with promptness and energy in enforcing them. Savages do not view crimes in the light that civilized nations view them. And as this people have not been in the habit of viewing murder, adultery, incest, sorcery, theft, treachery, and numerous other acts allied to them, as crimes, in the light in which Christians view them, it would not be a matter of surprise if persons acting in the new capacity of magistrates should be lax in enforcing penalties against such crimes.

Much has been said with respect to the *kau ana o ka kanawai* (establishing of the law) but I think little will be done for a long time yet to come, more than recommending justice and mercy to the people and threatening those who violate the regulations with the displeasure of the chiefs. Some punishments may be inflicted, and daring offenders will be intimidated.

It would be a very happy circumstance if the chiefs should unite with energy to suppress vice and immorality, but the imbecility manifested on former occasions, when opposed in their measures for effecting reformation, has fully satisfied me, that little can be hoped, at present, from their firmness in carrying into effect any great plan. As knowledge increases among them, and correct principle gains ground, they will grow in energy, and eventually be able to enforce laws for the general good and the promotion of virtue and true religion. The nation is apparently making rapid advances in civilization and knowledge and towards a character as a nation. Surely the Lord has done great things for us. The aspect of things may however soon change for the worse and our bright prospects be clouded.

Whatever is said of the improvement and the interesting state of this people is to be understood comparatively. If this island were to be visited by a person from a civilized land who had never before seen a heathen people, had never thought much upon the subject of their salvation, and had never seen a nation emerging from heathenism and wretchedness, he would be likely to enquire where is the civilization, the boasted improvement, where are all these things which have been so much talked of in the social circles of Christians in America. We see ignorance and vice of every kind, and so much degradation and misery that we think the missionaries must be infatuated or have intentionally misrepresented things.[17]

Resistance to the new disciplinary order is attributed here to savagery, irrationality, and imbecility. There is also a strong critique of the "despotic" power of the chiefs. Their apparently unconstrained power was particularly repugnant to these antimonarchical Americans, only forty years removed from their own revolution against the British crown. The French revolution against aristocratic power was also not far behind them. Indeed, the change in modes of discipline in Hawai'i occurred only slightly later than the similar transformation Foucault (1979) describes in France.

This passage also reflects a discourse on undisciplined savagery widespread in Europe and the United States. Fitzpatrick argues that the modern subject was constituted in opposition to the savage, the criminal, the child, and the insane. Modern self-governance was juxtaposed with lawless, ungoverned savagery located far away in other lands and close at home within every person (Fitzpatrick 1992: 132). The constant overcoming of the savage in oneself as well as out there required discipline. The image of the savage within embodying the savage without was vividly captured by Joseph Conrad in *The Heart of Darkness*, as Kurtz's inner evil mirrored the savagery of the African interior and the darkness of primeval time. Failure to change conduct thus becomes a sign of the inability to achieve self-governance, to conquer the savage within.

Overcoming the "savage" within is made more difficult if one is surrounded by others who are not engaged in this kind of self-repression and self-discipline. If humans are imagined to have a core of unrestrained feeling and sexuality constrained only by the bonds of civilized society, then persons who are not so constrained are inherently dangerous. This was the dilemma for the missionary mothers raising their children in Hawai'i. As they struggled to place the veneer of civilized laws and self-restraint over their "savage" children, their children played happily with Hawaiian children and quickly learned to speak fluent Hawaiian. But along with this easy sociability came an open attitude toward sexuality and sexual pleasure, particularly among young people. The missionaries found this intolerable. Many attempted to separate their children from Hawaiian children, although few followed the extreme measures of seclusion adopted by the Thurstons, who erected a high wall around their compound and prohibited their children from leaving it. Many sent them home, thousands of miles away, at an early age (Grimshaw 1989: 47–48; Piercy 1992: 44–45).

Hawaiian people, like Euro-American women and children, were thought to require constant supervision from adult white males since they were thought unable to acquire the self-restraint characteristic of the liberal subject. This is the only kind of person who can exist without the control of law because the minute systems of disciplinary power have induced him to engage in such control himself (indeed, this is often a gendered self). Racially coded understandings of Hawaiians as incapable of self-control were emerging during the 1820s and 1830s. Thus, European images of Hawaiian "nature" and the tendencies of "savages" shaped the way foreigners interpreted Hawaiian resistance to the new disciplinary order.

Although the late 1820s were years of triumph and victory for the missionaries as the ali'i nui converted to Christianity and then threw their enormous political and religious authority behind attending school and church, by the 1830s missionaries began to report a distressing failure to change conduct, particularly in family and sexual relationships. By the late 1830s Lorrin Andrews, a missionary fluent in Hawaiian, attributed this failure to cognitive deficiencies of the Hawaiians and their inability to think abstractly (Andrews 1836; see chapter 8). By the 1840s theories of the licentious, indolent, and childlike "nature" of the Hawaiians were pervasive among missionaries (Kingdom of Hawai'i 1846). Throughout the 1830s and 1840s they complained about the laxness of prison discipline, the prevalence of sexual encounters between prisoners being disciplined for adultery, the miserable condition of the Fort—the space used as a prison in Honolulu—and the ease with which the prisoners there, including women sentenced for prostitution, could escape and ply their trade (Kingdom of Hawai'i 1846; Kuykendall 1938: 126–132).

Systems of imprisonment were rarely secure or designed to foster repentance. For example, during the time Kekāuluohi was premier, 1839 to 1845, she converted the dry islands of Kaho'olawe and Lāna'i into penal settlements for lawbreakers to punish people for such crimes as rebellion, theft, divorce, breaking marriage vows, murder, and prostitution (Kamakau 1961: 356–357). There was no protection for the people there, however, and although the government provided food, some starved, some died in the sea, and many suffered from hunger. Some swam at night, stole a canoe, paddled elsewhere and stole food, then went back again to Kaho'olawe. Some of the men being punished for adultery landed at Ka'ena, where women were being held for adultery, and took their women and ran away with them to the mountains of Maui. Even some petty chiefs were sentenced to Kaho'olawe. One was pardoned by Kuakini and one, by Hoapili's written command, was sent to Kaho'olawe for ten years as a rebel, but was pardoned after seven years. This and other stories suggest that the use of pardons was common in the earlier years, but that under the influence of the missionaries, chiefly pardons became less acceptable and perhaps less available, thus making the entire system more severe. In an epitaph for the law in this period, Kamakau concludes: "The law in those days was never very clear and left one to grope in the dark" (Kamakau 1961: 357). Chapter 4 returns to the problem of discipline, highlighting the particular situation of Hilo.

Kumu Kānāwai: The Constitution and Laws of 1840–1842

Although religious fervor and the search for a pono way to govern was important in the adoption of the missionaries' law in the 1820s, by the 1830s and early 1840s two other problems suggested the need for a more extensive adoption of Western law. One was the crisis caused by the substantial debts of the ali'i to resident merchants and consequent threats to take over the islands. As we have seen, the ali'i deferred debt payment as much as possible while the merchants continued to extend credit on the promise of future sandalwood harvests. As the sandalwood disappeared, the debt problem grew. As early as 1826 an American warship arrived to enforce payments of the aliʻi debts to the merchants, most of whom were Americans. During the 1830s foreign governments continued to press for debt repayment and special privileges in trade relations. According to Kamakau, during this battle over debts to American merchants, there was a rumor that the kingdom was to be taken over by the United States (Kamakau 1961: 285). Indeed, he says, this might have happened if the mōʻī had not declared a constitutional form of government and found ways to use government revenues to repay the debts. "Certain of the foreign teachers who loved the Hawaiian people, the chiefs, and the whole nation, were taken into the government, and it became an easy thing to pay these debts and deal with other abuses that had been heaped upon the government" (Kamakau 1961: 285).

The second problem was that foreign governments demanded special legal treatment for their subjects such as trial by a jury of their conationals rather than by Hawaiians (Nelligan and Ball 1992). Between 1836 and 1839 the British and French acquired special privileges for their subjects through a series of treaties and conventions (Kuykendall 1938: 167). In 1839, threatening war, a French warship demanded concessions such as the entrance of Catholic priests, the importation at lower duties of French wine and brandy, and the right of French citizens to trial by a jury selected by the French consul from the foreign community, guaranteed by a payment of twenty thousand dollars (Kuykendall 1938: 165–167). In 1844 the British formed a treaty with the kingdom guaranteeing British subjects trial by a jury of foreigners and in 1849 the United States negotiated a similar treaty (Cheever 1856: 124–125). In the early 1840s Cheever complained that foreign demands to be governed only by national compatriots were unreasonable because the government was more competent to try and punish crimes than most of the republics of South America:

> Why, then should it not be permitted to administer its laws like other independent nations, without the arrogance of protests on the part of foreign consuls and commissioners, or the interference of navy captains? It has a written code of laws, which are singularly simple and direct: they are translated into English and all foreigners may know them. Why, then should they not be tried and dealt with for crimes committed, according to the laws of the land?
>
> (Cheever 1856: 126)

The right to govern foreign subjects under national laws was clearly a critical and contested aspect of sovereignty.

In response to this increasingly difficult international situation in which the threat of a colonial takeover was very real and immediate, the Hawaiian leaders began to search for a new legal and governmental structure. They asked William Richards to look for a legal advisor during his trip to the United States in 1837 (Damon 1857: 5; Williston 1938), but when he failed to find such a person, the ali'i hired Richards himself as chaplain, interpreter, and teacher of political economy, law, and the science of government. In 1838 he resigned from the ABCFM and took on the task of advising the chiefs, although he was not a lawyer. In the summer of 1838 he lectured the ali'i on political economy and the relationship between industry and happiness. He urged them to pass a body of laws that would govern all the people equally. He "almost certainly" had a large share in writing the Declaration of Rights of 1839 and the Constitution of 1840 (Dutton 1953). But the kingdom still wanted the advice of a legally trained person. In 1840, on a trip back to the United States Bingham again tried and failed to recruit a legally trained advisor, as did Richards on a trip in 1842 (Dutton 1953).

The 1839 Declaration of Rights, the 1840 Constitution, and an extensive body of laws passed between 1840 and 1842 constituted a new legal foundation for the nation. It was called Kumu Kānāwai—"foundation of law," using a term for law based on the kapu system. These documents were published in a small book of two hundred pages in Hawaiian followed by a translation of two hundred pages in English. Because it had a blue cover, as did the legal codes of New England at the time, these became known as the Blue Laws, as they were in New England (Kingdom of Hawaii 1894).

The laws were originally written and published in Hawaiian and only later translated into English and published in a local newspaper. The English version was not published in book form until the blue English/Hawaiian version appeared in 1842. In his introduction to the English version, the translator (probably Richards) ([Thurston 1904: viii]; Kamakau 1961) notes that the original Hawaiian, not the English version, will be the basis for all judicial proceedings. He emphasizes the plurality of the legal landscape these laws represent. The document incorporates recent laws passed since 1823 as well as a kind of common law system that consists of ancient tabus, the practices of celebrated chiefs as the history of their actions has been handed down, and the principles of the Bible (Thurston 1904: vii). "The established customs of civilized nations have also in most cases the force of law in these Islands provided that custom is known. This little volume, therefore, must not be considered as containing the whole system of Hawaiian law, although it contains most of the printed statutes" (Thurston 1904: viii).

The translator then describes the process by which these laws were created. Some were suggested by foreign visitors, commanders of warships, foreign residents, and foreign consuls, but the greatest proportion were not. Some were written by David Malo, some by John Papa 'I'ī and other Hawaiians. All were fully discussed and modified by the House of Nobles and the House of Representatives at their annual council and approved unanimously before being signed by the king and the premier, the kuhina nui (Thurston 1904: viii). Thus the Declaration of Rights, the 1840 Constitution, and the laws of 1841 and 1842, although Anglo-American in some of their inspiration, were joined with Hawaiian systems of law and the interpretations of Christian-educated Hawaiians and the Hawaiian-speaking missionary Richards. The result was a system of laws far closer to Hawaiian law than subsequent legislation beginning in 1845.

This set of laws is very eclectic. Unlike subsequent laws (the 1850 Penal Code and 1852 Constitution), Kumu Kānāwai incorporates significant amounts of Hawaiian customary law and practice. Of fifty-three pages of text dating from 1840 (in Thurston's edition, 1904), twenty-two pages (Chapter III, An Act to Regulate the Taxes) delineate the relationship between konohiki and makaʻāinana, specifying tax and labor obligations, water rights, fishing tabus, and the proper behavior of men and women on the land. On the other hand, some sections, such as quarantine laws and harbor regulations, are clearly of foreign origin. The weights and measures are those of Massachusetts. And many of these laws cover new problems: for example, fast riding of horses, roaming cattle, the hire of servants, debts, vagrancy, partnerships, and forgery.

The other significant source of the constitution and laws was the Protestant Christian tradition. As Kamakau says, the "chiefs and commoners rejoiced because they had a constitution based upon the Holy Scripture" (Kamakau 1961: 370). Hiram Bingham considered the passage of the laws an accomplishment for the mission. "The mission rejoicing in every effort of the rulers to secure the just rights of the people, to encourage industry and thrift, to restrain vice and punish crime, took encouragement from this evidence of progress probably more than the mass of the people themselves" (Bingham 1981: 561). The religious inspiration is clear in the beginning of the Declaration of Rights:

> God has made of one blood all the nations of men, that they might alike dwell upon the earth in peace and prosperity. And he has given certain equal rights to all people and chiefs of all countries. These are the rights or gifts which he has granted to every man and chief of correct deportment,—life, the members of the body, freedom in dwelling and acting, and the rightful products of his hands and mind: but not those things which are inhibited by the laws.
>
> From God also are the office of rulers and the reign of chief magistrates for protection: but in enacting the laws of the land, it is not right to make a law protecting the magistrate only and not subjects; neither is it proper to establish laws for enriching chiefs only, without benefitting the people, and hereafter, no law shall be established in opposition to the above declarations; neither shall taxes, servitude, nor labor, be exacted without law of any man in a manner at variance with those principles.
>
> (Bingham 1981: 562)

The Constitution similarly begins with reference to the Christian God:

It is our design to regulate our Kingdom according to the above principles and thus seek the greatest prosperity, both of all the chiefs and all the people of these Hawaiian Islands. But we are aware that we cannot, ourselves alone, accomplish such an object. God must be our aid, for it is His province alone to give perfect protection and prosperity. Wherefore we first present our supplication to Him that He will guide us to right measures and sustain us in our work. It is, therefore, our fixed decree:

I. That no law shall be enacted which is at variance with the Word of the Lord Jehovah or at variance with the general spirit of His Word. All laws of the Islands shall be in consistency with the general spirit of God's law.

(Kingdom of Hawai'i 1894)

Some chapters respond to religious concerns, such as the Law for the Protection of the Sabbath (Chapter XI), and the Law Prohibiting Reviling, Swearing, and Slander (Chapter XII).

Some laws show an intriguing blend of Hawaiian law and Western law, such as Chapter XXI, the Law Respecting Parental Duties, passed in 1841. This law acknowledges the widespread practice of hānai (adoption) and allows parents to commit their child to the care of another but requires that the agreement be executed in writing in front of an officer who will witness the transaction. If there is no writing, the child cannot be transferred (sec. 2 in Thurston 1904: 73). In another example, if parents disagree in relation to a child, the father's decision stands unless the mother is the higher chief, then her decision stands (sec 6 in Thurston 1904: 73). Here, rank trumps gender, but as we will see, this Hawaiian way of thinking is soon submerged under the Western notion that gender trumps rank.

In several places, the Kumu Kānāwai emphasizes that this new law is being erected on a landscape of existing rules and practices. Chapter I, from 1840, begins, "The subjection of the people to the chiefs, from former ages down, is a subject well understood, as is also a portion of the ancient laws. That subjection and those laws are not now as a matter of course discontinued, but there are at the present time many new laws, with which, it is well that all the people should become acquainted" (Chapter I, sec. 1, in Thurston 1904: 10).

These new laws are to be made knowable through printing. Chapter I continues: "There is no way to make them thoroughly understood except by printing, wherefore in a council of the government the following acts were passed. I. Hereafter no law of the kingdom shall take effect without having been first printed and made public" (Chapter I, sec. 1 in Thurston 1904: 10). The official law is no longer oral. Yet, there are remnants of earlier practices. The law specifies that it is the duty of the governors, the konohiki, and the tax officers to read the law, frequently and on all days of public work in the presence of the tenants, that circumscribes the power of the chiefs to demand labor and property from the poor and to infringe on their businesses (Chapter III, sec. 9 in Thurston 1904: 23–24). This is followed by a statement of the guiding principles of political economy (the new hegemony), in which industry rather than rank provides wealth and happiness: "The man who does not labor enjoys little happiness. He cannot obtain any great good unless he strives for it with earnestness. He cannot make himself comfortable, not even to preserve his life unless he labor for it. If a man wish to become rich, he can do it in no way except to engage with energy in some business" (Chapter III, sec. 9 in Thurston 1904: 23–24). It is intriguing how closely this statement parallels Ellis's admonitions to the Hawaiians twenty years earlier, described in chapter 2.

These new laws are embedded within the older system of law. When crimes are not particularly defined by these laws or when a judge is not sure what statute applies, "then the judges shall reflect on the nature of the crime and the kind of punishment which would formerly have been inflicted; he shall also consider the principles of the laws now in existence, and shall pass such sentence on the criminal as in his opinion the general principles of the new system require" (Chapter XXV, sec. 1 in Thurston 1904: 78). The new texts are to be interpreted and deployed through existing meanings and practices.

The Kumu Kānāwai constructed a new political system as well. It redistributed power between king and chiefs and restricted the chiefs' power. A ruling chief could neither pass a decree nor seize the property of another chief and give it to one of his favorites. A House of Representatives, selected by the people, joined the House of Nobles—the council of aliʻi appointed by the mōʻī—as a lawmaking body. The document also enunciated the rights of makaʻāinana in relation to aliʻi. The American advisors, in tandem with the rising bourgeoisie of Europe, were eager to protect the rights of subordinates, including their right to private property, from the unconstrained power of the aristocracy (see Mehta 1997). Constitutionalism was a constraint on monarchy. The Kumu Kānāwai expressed an egalitarian social vision, reflecting American opposition to aristocracy and Enlightenment ideas of rights. The passage of the Declaration of Rights locates Hawaiʻi in the forefront of political developments of the time, since it enunciated the rights of commoners only sixty-five years after the French and American revolutions and long before many other European nations.

Yet the notion that law should serve as a constraint on the chiefs' power over commoners represented a radical break from Hawaiian conceptions of this relationship as rooted in aloha (love, regard) and service by the people to the earthly representatives of the Akua. The chiefs saw these new laws as threats to their authority (Kameʻeleihiwa 1992: 175). In Kamakau's words,

"When the constitution and the written laws were made, then the power of the chiefs was thrown down and only that of the king remained" (Kamakau 1961: 345).

In accordance with Hawaiian practice, which delegated the power to judge to the mōʻī and aliʻi, the Constitution says that the king "shall be Chief Judge of the Supreme Court and it shall be his duty to execute the laws of the land; also all decrees and treaties with other countries; all however, in accordance with the laws" (Kingdom of Hawaiʻi 1894: 5). The Constitution specifies that the king, the premier, and the four governors of the islands shall supervise tax collectors and judges, shall see sentences executed, and shall appoint judges and give them their certificates of office, subject to the king and premier. These chiefs, as we have seen, had long exercised judicial power in their districts, so this provision accords with established practice. Appeal was to the Supreme Court judges. Four of these judges were appointed by the representative body (apparently only the House of Representatives) and joined the king and premier as the Supreme Court. Their decision was final (Kingdom of Hawaii 1894: 11).

The laws defined new roles for judges and police officers as well. In the past the aliʻi had retainers who would carry out their judgments. Now constables and police officers were appointed by governors. Police were required to carry badges at all times, and without their badges were unable to forcibly seize suspects. The badge was a little stick, made round, with the name of the king at the top. The duty of the constables was defined as follows: "It shall be the duty of the police officers to watch, spy out and detect criminals, carry them to, and deliver them up to the judges, who will bring them to trial. It shall be their duty to seize all persons who violate the laws, and in case of a quarrel or a mob, it shall be their duty to restore or demand peace, and seize the guilty persons" (Kingdom of Hawaii 1894: 43). They are to be punished if they fail to report a crime. If they hear of disorder or mischief, it is their duty to investigate.

One important feature of this new disciplinary role is that police officers' pay came from fines. If a police officer seized a man for a crime and he was convicted, he received one fourth of the fine. Any person who reported a crime received one fourth of the fine. Thus the Kumu Kānāwai provided for the appointment of a set of individuals with authority to search out and arrest violators of these new laws and rewarded them for doing so.

Finally, these laws include references to the problems of discipline in prison and articulate the differential duties of male and female prisoners. An 1841 law begins: "At the present time much evil results from the laboring of a great number of criminals at the same place. Criminals are made to subserve the interests of individuals, and on account of the great number who labor at the same place, they are in high spirits, and great evils result from the practice" (Chapter XXVI in Thurston 1904: 79). The law specifies that convicts shall not work for a particular chief but for national works such as roads, fences, prisons, and forts. Further, it says that males and females should not labor together or sleep in the same house or the same yard. Females should not do labor appropriate to males but only that appropriate to females: beating tapa, braiding mats and hats, sewing, twisting fish lines, weaving nets, and such labor.

In sum, during the first transition the ali'i adopted the religion and laws of the missionaries. The missionaries' notion of law as the command of God was congruent with Hawaiian understandings of the authority of the Akua. In both systems, law was derived from God and made manifest through the actions of chiefs in declaring that law. The Ten Commandments were analogous to the commands of the Akua. But the missionaries brought with these law codes a very different set of ideas about discipline and correction. A system of judges, constables, and prisons was necessary for the new disciplinary order. The missionaries hoped that the enactment of religious law on earth would promote the transformation in social relationships they envisaged, but as we have seen, they quickly developed doubts about the chiefs' commitment to enforcing these laws. In the hopeful years of the 1820s they imagined that it was only a matter of time and habituation, but by the 1830s it became clear that such a transformation in conduct was eluding them. The Hawaiians readily went to church and adopted Western dress of various forms, but were far slower to take on the new marriage and sexual practices that the missionaries advocated. People were frequently suspended and excommunicated from membership in the church, often for sexual improprieties.

School attendance also remained sporadic and difficult to police. Although large numbers of students appeared for the periodic examinations, there were suspicions that they had memorized texts rather than learned to read them. The missionaries were engaged in a constant struggle to impose their notions of discipline while critics, both from mission backgrounds and from other perspectives, pointed to their failures. As the missionaries confronted the failure of the law to produce the self-governing subject, they decided that Hawaiians lacked the capacity to become such persons. Complaints about their fundamental character, either too close to nature or too wedded to licentiousness and indolence, appeared more and more often in missionaries' writings. Hawaiians were gradually reinterpreted as by nature unable to achieve the forms of self-governance associated with civilization. The problem of governance then shifted from elevating the Hawaiians to a state of self-governance to creating a system of governance within which these perpetual children could be adequately disciplined and controlled by those able to achieve adult status: Christian church members, but ultimately white males.

Ironically, the adoption of a disciplinary system was simultaneously the route to independence and the mechanism by which the Hawaiian people were reinterpreted as incapable of self-governance by the missionaries and their allies. From these roots sprang the military takeover of the islands in 1893.

Discipline and Civilization

The wisdom of the aliʻi in adopting a constitutional monarchy and code of laws as a route to sovereignty in the mid nineteenth century was evidenced by Bingham's account of his efforts on behalf of Hawaiian sovereignty in 1842. It is clear that a nation's state of "civilization" affected its entitlement to protection and sovereignty in the global arena. In his 1842 mission to the United States, Bingham corresponded with President John Tyler. Tyler laid before Congress this message:

> To the House of Representatives of the United States:
> The conditions of those Islands has excited a good deal of interest, which is increasing by every successive proof that their inhabitants are making progress in civilization, and becoming more and more competent to maintain regular and orderly civil government. They lie in the Pacific ocean, much nearer to this continent than the other, and have become an important place for the refitment and provisioning of American and European vessels.
> Just emerging from a state of barbarism, the Government of the Islands is as yet feeble; but its dispositions appear to be just and pacific, and it seems anxious to improve the condition of its people by the introduction of knowledge, of religious and moral institutions, means of education, and the arts of civilized life.

He concluded that the community should be respected and its rights strictly and conscientiously regarded (Bingham 1981: 586–587). In order to be recognized as an independent government, it was clearly necessary to establish a state of civilization, which means the discipline of the body, the adoption of written laws and constitutional government, Christianity, and schools.

Similarly, when Richards was sent on a mission to negotiate treaties of independence with Britain, France, and the United States at the same time, the state of "civilization" in Hawaiʻi was again of critical importance. Richards prepared a statement describing how well equipped the kingdom was to care for itself, emphasizing that the people were intelligent and Christian. "To show their progress in intelligence he described from the beginning how they had been educated and the laws that had been promulgated, 51 sections or more" (Kamakau 1961: 366–367). Richards left Hawaiʻi for Washington with the Honorable T. Haʻalilio, and on December 19, 1842, the United States agreed to Hawaiian independence. Richards and Haʻalilio sailed to England, where they talked about good government, elementary and high schools, Christian churches, the legislation the Hawaiians had enacted, and their fitness for independent government. The French government agreed at once to independence. In London on November 28, 1843, the British acknowledged the independence of Hawai'i, as did the Belgians (Kamakau 1961: 368). Thus the ability of the kingdom to negotiate treaties of independence depended on the extent to which Hawaiian society and the state conformed to the patterns of European civilization and concepts of statehood.

These efforts to achieve autonomy were fragile. In 1842 a second foreigner, Gerrit Judd, also a missionary, was hired by the Hawaiian government to cope with the debt crisis and to manage the unruly foreigners. He remained powerful until 1853. Judd was first appointed the official government translator and recorder. In May 1842 he was appointed to the Treasury Board along with Ha'alilio and John 'I'ī (Kuykendall 1938: 232). After Richards and Ha'alilio left in search of a treaty of independence in summer 1842, Judd became even more powerful. In October 1843 he was named secretary of state for foreign affairs (Kuykendall 1938: 234). Kauikeaouli (Kamehameha III) wanted a foreigner to deal with foreigners, but now he had two foreigners taking upon themselves roles formerly reserved for ali'i nui (Kame'eleihiwa 1992: 182).

In 1843 a new crisis struck. In February a British warship under Lord Paulet arrived in Honolulu making a series of demands on the government, including the return of disputed land to the British consul Richard Charlton and the freedom of British subjects from imprisonment in fetters unless they were accused of a crime that by the laws of England would be considered a felony (Kamakau 1961: 361–362). The British demanded that conflicts between British subjects and natives of the country or others residing there should be referred to juries composed half of British subjects approved by the consul (Kuykendall 1938: 214). In effect, the British government wanted British subjects to remain under the jurisdiction of British law. These demands were backed by threats of violence.

The king replied that he would comply with the demands under protest and provisionally ceded sovereignty to Britain. Some of the demands were of a nature "calculated seriously to embarrass our feeble government, by contravening the laws established for the benefit of all" (Kamakau 1961: 362). Six months later, on July 31, 1843, Rear Admiral Thomas arrived in the islands and restored the sovereignty of the king (Kuykendall 1938: 206–226). Soon after this incident, the number of haoles in the government began to increase dramatically. The stage was set for the second transition in the legal order, from a system based largely on Hawaiian and Protestant Christian law to one derived from secular Anglo-American law.

4

THE SECOND TRANSITION: SECULAR LAW

ON DECEMBER 29, 1850, William Little Lee wrote from Honolulu to his friend and a former U.S. consul in Hawai'i, Joel Turrill: "Our most prominent improvement since you left is the new town clock, which is a fine time keeper. It is on the King's Chapel" (Turrill Collection 1957: 38). Twenty-five years earlier, when Bingham asked Kalanimōkū to install a clock and a bell, the Hawaiian premier had walked out on him. The clock, finally installed prominently on the king's church, marked the turn to a new order of time, discipline, and penality. The period from 1844 to 1852 was one of extraordinary change in the law of the kingdom: eight short years in which secular Anglo-American law came to govern the spheres of family, land, and work. A series of statutes imported largely from the United States began to transform land into a privately owned commodity, women into possessions of their husbands, and the exchange of goods, services, and loyalty between land possessors and land users into cash taxes. New laws opened more ports to foreign commerce, land to foreign purchase, and laborers to penal control for failure to work. Debates about the prisons led to a new regime of isolation and habituation through the discipline of work and time paralleling that of the United States.

The implications of these legal changes for the distribution of power in Hawaiian society and between Hawaiians and foreigners were enormous. Within a few short years, foreigners controlled the vast proportion of private property and had begun the importation of substantial numbers of Asians and Europeans to work as plantation laborers under the contract labor law. As the Hawaiian population fell and these newcomers settled, stayed, and often married Hawaiian women, the Hawaiian people lost not only the land but also the plurality in their own country. As early as the 1830s there was concern that the Hawaiians would die out altogether. In 1836 Hawaiians were estimated at 99.5 percent of the total population of 107,954, and by 1850, 98 percent of the total population of 83,567 (Morgan 1948: 114). But by the census of 1884 Native Hawaiians were only half the population (40,014 of 80,578), and by 1890 they were a minority in their own land, representing only 38 percent of the population. As the Native Hawaiian population plummeted, part-Hawaiians gradually increased. Nevertheless, in the 1890 census combined Hawaiians and part-Hawaiians were still only 45 percent of the total of 89,990. The dwindling Hawaiian population was submerged by waves of newcomers from Europe, the United States, China, Japan, and Portugal, many of whom were imported as plantation laborers. At the vote for statehood in 1959 descendants of Hawaiians were vastly outnumbered. Despite the appearance of fairness and democratic process, the Hawaiian people were unable to reclaim their sovereignty through a popular election.

Conditions for the maka'āinana at the beginning of the second transition were desperate. Missionaries writing from all over the kingdom in 1846 and 1847 described the displacement of the maka'āinana, their poverty, the poor quality of their housing, and the depredations of cattle on their farms (Kingdom of Hawaii 1846). By this time there was a general pattern of maka'āinana visiting seaports during the shipping season (Linnekin 1990). The resident merchant community was strong and growing. Some looked down on the missionaries for their lack of manners and civilization and many continued to resist their influence on the government. But the influence of the missionaries and their Puritan morality was on the wane (Daws 1967).

As we saw in chapter 3, by the mid 1840s the Hawaiian kingdom had achieved a fragile independence through the negotiation of treaties with the major European powers. But there were conditions on this independence. It is clear from accounts by the negotiators that their success depended on their claims to "civilization" in the kingdom. Threats of takeover by imperial powers and challenges by resident foreigners remained strong and imminent. The kingdom's independence required maintaining "good government" and the rule of law as well as playing off the competing powers in the Pacific, particularly the Americans, British, and French. The Māori lost their sovereignty when the British annexed New Zealand in 1840. In 1842 the French conquered the Marquesas by force (Coan 1882: 163) and made Tahiti into a protectorate, annexing the latter in 1880. These were all closely related Polynesian peoples. In 1853 France annexed New Caledonia and in 1874 Britain annexed Fiji. The Pacific was being rapidly divided into imperial possessions.

Yet the new laws and institutions necessary to claim independence required foreigners to run them (Kuykendall 1938: 238). On February 27, 1844, a lawyer, John Ricord, arrived in Honolulu and on March 9, 1844, scarcely two weeks later, he was appointed attorney general of the kingdom by Gerrit Judd, then secretary for foreign relations and an influential official in the government from 1842 to 1853. Ricord worked for the next three years in Hawai'i. In May 1845 at the Legislative Assembly he advocated the enactment of three Organic Acts to organize the Executive Ministry, the Executive Department, and the Judiciary Department. The first two acts were prepared and became effective in 1846, the third became effective January 10, 1848. In March 1845 R. C. Wyllie, who had arrived in Hawai'i in 1844 from Scotland,[1] became minister of foreign relations. In September 1845 Lorrin Andrews, a missionary with no special training in law, began to substitute for Governor Kekūanao'a, who spoke very little English, as judge in cases with foreigners (Kuykendall 1938: 243). On October 29, 1845, when the mōʻī Kauikeaouli appointed his top advisors, they included Robert C. Wyllie as minister of foreign affairs and three Americans, G. P. Judd as minister of the treasury, William Richards as minister of education, and John Ricord as attorney general.

By 1845 there was strong popular protest against the number of foreigners in the government by the Hawaiian people (Kuykendall 1938: 257). Many Hawaiians were worried about the dependence on foreigners. Some wrote petitions to the government urging them to dismiss the foreigners while others urged Hawaiian parents to send their children to school and get educated so that they could serve the government (Kameʻeleihiwa 1992: 192). In a letter he wrote to Kamehameha III on July 22, 1845, Kamakau presented a chillingly prophetic vision of the impact of foreigners in the government. He constructs a dialogue between himself and "the old people" (Kamakau 1961: 399–401). The old people say, "In the time of Kamehameha the orators were the only ones who spoke before the ruling chief, those who were learned in the words spoken by the chiefs who had lived before his day" (Kamakau 1961: 399). They object to putting foreigners in the government, saying that the government will come into the hands of the foreigners and the Hawaiian people will become their servants and work for them. "We shall see that the strangers will complain of the natives of Hawaii as stupid, ignorant, and good-for-nothing, and say all such evil things of us, and this will embitter the race and degrade it and cause the chiefs to go after the stranger and cast off their own race" (Kamakau 1961: 399). Kamakau answers the old people that perhaps the chiefs cannot handle the work of the foreigners and that the powerful nations may agree to independence only if the country is governed intelligently. He continues:

> Therefore I disapprove of the people's protest against foreign officials since it is the desire of the rulers of Great Britain, France, and the United States of America to educate our government in their way of governing, as I have heard. . . .
> These rulers believe that the Hawaiian group has a government prepared to administer laws like other governments and hence it is that they allow Hawaii to remain independent. We ought therefore not to object to foreign officials if we cannot find chiefs of Hawaii learned enough for the office.

But, the old people reply, the laws of those governments will not do for our government. "They are good laws for them, our laws are for us and are good laws for us, which we have made for ourselves. We are not slaves to serve them."

Kamehameha III replied to Kamakau's letter in August 1845 (Kamakau 1961: 401–402). He says that he has appointed foreign officials because "my native helpers do not understand the laws of the great countries who are working with us. That is why I have dismissed them. I see that I must have new officials to help with the new system under which I am working for the good of the country and of the old men and women of the country." He says he has retained those who have learned the new ways, such as G. L. Kapeau, secretary of the treasury (one of the first makaʻāinana to receive a missionary education and attain a high governmental position). Among the chiefs, Leleiōhoku, Pāki, and John Young (son of a British sailor and a Hawaiian high chiefess) are capable, but they already have government offices. But young people are not speakers of foreign languages and he cannot have those who speak only Hawaiian. Thus he has refused appeals to dismiss foreigners. The king justifies the foreigners in government by the need to run the new forms of government he has created in order to deal with the foreigners.

Despite the strong protest from the Hawaiian people about the increasing numbers of foreigners employed by the kingdom in powerful positions in the 1840s, the mōʻī found it difficult to manage the foreigners without them. In 1846, for example, Kauikeaouli said that if it were not for the foreigners living under his jurisdiction he would be able to manage his own subjects very easily, but foreigners with great cunning and perseverance often involved him in difficulties so that he found that he could not get along except by appointing foreigners to cope with them (Kameʻeleihiwa 1992: 190).

This is the sovereignty paradox of the late 1840s: in order to produce a government able to deal with the foreign residents and to gain respectability in the eyes of the imperialist foreign community, the leaders adopted the forms of modern government and rule of law, but these forms required foreigners skilled in their practices to run them. And as foreigners developed and ran these new bureaucratic systems of law and government, they redefined the Hawaiian people as incapable, naturalizing this incapacity in racialized terms. This is the political and discursive context for the second transition in the law.

Threats to Sovereignty, 1845–1855

Threats to sovereignty continued in the late 1840s and early 1850s. Many of the haoles (foreigners) working for the government at this time no longer shared the passionate commitment to the independence of the kingdom felt by the first advisors, members of the mission. Gerritt Judd, for example, highly influential in the government from 1842 to 1853, was strongly opposed to any form of annexation (Sahlins 1992: 132). Although the Hawaiians were always opposed to annexation, it seems that by the early 1850s there was a grudging willingness to consider it. Laura Judd, Gerrit Judd's wife, says in her memoirs that Lee was involved in negotiating terms of annexation to the United States at the command of the king in 1853–1854 (Judd 1966: 317–318). She says the king was concerned about the recent French occupation of Tahiti and hoped annexation would protect the royal line and provide needed funds to the royal house (Judd 1966: 218–219). In his private letters to Joel Turrill in the early 1850s, Lee said he favored annexation to the United States as a protection against French threats of takeover, although he recognized the opposition of the aliʻi and mōʻī to this idea (Turrill Collection 1957). Lee wrote to Turrill on July 30, 1853: "The idea of annexation is not a pleasant one to the chiefs, and they will only take such a step as a *dernier resort*" (Turrill Collection 1957; italics in original). Nevertheless, in 1853 Lee worked with the king and chiefs on a plan of annexation to the United States and on August 29, 1854, Lee wrote to Wyllie, the Hawaiian foreign minister, emphasizing that the king and chiefs wanted to be admitted as a state and guaranteed all the rights of American citizens.

But Kauikeaouli (Kamehameha III) died in 1854 and the new king, Kamehameha IV, strongly opposed annexation. Lee wrote to Turrill on February 26, 1855: "The new King will not, of course, lay down his crown unless driven to it by necessity, and he is infinitely stronger on his throne than the late King [Kamehameha III]" (Dutton 1953). In an 1855 letter to Turrill, Charles Bishop, a good friend of Lee's and an important businessman in Honolulu, notes that annexation is now virtually dead since it is deeply opposed by Hawaiians: "the truth is, the King, Chiefs, and most of the people have been Strongly opposed to it, first and last, appearances, letters and newspaper reports to the contrary notwithstanding; and all that was done was at the advice and threats of *Americans*, and nothing has been gained" (Turrill Collection 1957: 79).

As threats of a French takeover continued in the 1850s, Kamehameha IV returned to the strategy of forming treaties guaranteeing independence with European states and the United States. In 1855 he sent Lee on a mission to get a reciprocity treaty with the United States and a tripartite treaty with the United States, Great Britain, and France. Wyllie wanted this treaty "for the preservation of the King's Sovereignty and the Independence of the Hawaiian people as a distinct nationality" (Dutton 1953). Thus the threat of takeover remained strong through both transitions, although some of the leaders of the second transition thought that annexation to the United States with dignity and some autonomy would be preferable to a takeover by France or Britain. Certainly the competition among Britain, France, and the United States impeded all of them from taking the islands.

The American Lawyers

Although Richards penned the first constitution and declaration of rights, John Ricord was the first trained lawyer to work on the Hawaiian legal system. Ricord was hired by Judd, but he did not come from the missionary tradition or from New England. Ricord was born in New Jersey of Huguenot extraction, was trained in law in Buffalo, New York, worked as private secretary for two Texas presidents, and practiced law in Florida and Texas, where he served as attorney general (Morgan in Judd 1966: 187–188). He left the government in the spring of 1847 after virtually completing the three Organic Acts and left Hawai'i in the fall of 1847 in a dispute over a romantic involvement with the Judds' daughter, according to the editor of Laura Judd's memoirs, Dale Morgan (ibid.).

Ricord rejected the missionaries' religious notion of law. Instead, he saw law as organic to a particular mode of life, probably reflecting the more evolutionary mode of thinking of the nineteenth century, in which different stages of society possessed different kinds of law. In Kamakau's view: "John Ricord's work was to use the laws of the civilized world as a foundation and adapt them to the conditions of the people in Hawaii. He was a man whom Kamehameha III trusted. He said openly that the laws of the Bible were not adapted for use by modern governments; they belonged to the people of God, a Jewish race descended from Abraham, a race begotten for everlasting life" (Kamakau 1961: 402). Moreover, Ricord said that the laws of Rome could not be used for Hawai'i, nor those of England, France, or any other country, but that the Hawaiian people must have laws adapted to their mode of living, although he thought it right to study the laws of other people and adapt those which are appropriate (Kamakau 1961: 403). In 1846 Judge Lorrin Andrews issued extensive rules of legal pleading and practice that were probably written by Ricord (Frear 1894: 12; Silverman 1982). Ricord also handled the complicated litigation with foreigners in this period.

The other major figure in the second transition was William Little Lee. As Reverend Damon said in his elegy at Lee's funeral in 1857, Lee arrived at a critical period when the old order of public affairs was passing away.[2] Reverend Damon, an American missionary who ran the Seamen's Bethel in Honolulu for many years, was careful not to blame Richards for inadequacies in the government and legal system Lee confronted in 1846: "It is not intended by these remarks to cast the least reflection upon those who had been laboring to build up a temple of justice upon the ruins of the old feudal laws, arbitrary rule and system of *tabus* which had existed, and the influence of which was still felt" (Damon 1857: 5).

Damon's perspective on pre-1820 law is much more critical than Richards's view recorded in his introduction to the translation of the Laws of 1842 (see chapter 3) and in his 1841 letter to Wilkes (Sahlins and Barerre 1973). Both were penned sixteen years earlier, toward the end of the first transition. At that point, Hawaiian law was still respected and incorporated into the law of the nation. In contrast, during the second transition Hawaiian law was reinterpreted as arbitrary and irrational. Damon notes that the Constitution and Code of 1840, which, given the circumstances of their production, were considered by men of eminent legal abilities worthy of great praise, "were not adapted to the advancing state of affairs in the Hawaiian kingdom" (Damon 1857). The time had come for an entire remodeling of the law. Ricord started the process, but it was Lee who largely carried it out.

Through Damon's encouragement and Ricord's influence, Lee was persuaded to stay in Honolulu. The second Organic Act was already in force, which provided that until the Act of 1847 to Organize the Judiciary was passed, there should be one or more judges to sit in Honolulu on cases from Oʻahu over one hundred dollars in value, with general appellate jurisdiction in all other cases from all over the kingdom. In 1846 Lorrin Andrews, a former missionary, was appointed to be one of these judges. Lee was paid $2,500 a year to be another (Dutton 1953, n.p.). At the time there was also a Supreme Court established by the Constitution of 1840, which consisted of the king, the kuhina nui, and four other judges elected by the representative body (Dutton 1953). All of its proceedings and records were in the Hawaiian language (Third Organic Act, 1847). It was designed for Native people who wished to appeal from the circuit court at chambers and to hear appeals from the Commission to Quiet Land Titles. It was under the control of the aliʻi and the mōʻī.

Lee and Andrews assisted Ricord in preparing the Third Organic Act, which created a new Superior Court of Law and Equity (Dutton 1953). The new court consisted of a chief justice and two associate justices, appointed by the legislative council and sitting in Honolulu. Judge Lee was elected as chief justice and Lorrin Andrews and John ʻĪʻī, a mission-educated Hawaiian, as associate justices. This court had appellate jurisdiction in all cases and original jurisdiction in all the more important cases. In addition, these judges went to the circuits to hold court along with the circuit judges. The Supreme Court continued in existence but, as Dutton says, its work now became "merely nominal." Thus the 1847 Organic Act created a parallel and more powerful court but did not eliminate the Hawaiian-language court.

The Third Organic Act clearly separated the executive and judicial powers, eliminating the authority of the king over judicial proceedings except for his role as chief judge of the Supreme Court and his ability to pardon or nolle pros (Kingdom of Hawaiʻi 1847). It created two kinds of courts, courts of record with original and appellate jurisdiction and courts not of record, over which governors presided. Circuit Court justices were appointed by the governor of each island with two local judges per court, to be joined by a judge from the Superior Court (Kingdom of Hawaiʻi 1847: 27). Five District Courts were established on the island of Hawaiʻi, with one for Hilo and Puna. District Courts had jurisdiction over civil cases and theft under one hundred dollars plus riot, assault, fornication, and other misdemeanors where the fine was under one hundred dollars. They also had the right to investigate other cases and, if probable guilt was determined, to commit to the Circuit

Court or Supreme Court for trial (Kingdom of Hawai'i 1847: 10–11). Police courts in Lāhainā and Honolulu had jurisdiction over maritime affairs, masters, and crews of vessels.

Thus, this act contains no significant provision for customary law, for native courts, or for a dual system of law (Silverman 1982: 57–58). The only vestige of a dual legal system was the Supreme Court, established by the Constitution of 1840, which specifically focused on serving Native Hawaiians and was mandated in the Organic Act to hold all proceedings and records in the Hawaiian language. It is the only court for which the language of operation is specifically mentioned. But this court was eliminated in 1852. Silverman argues that this act displaced the ali'i from the judiciary, stripping the role of judges from the governors (Silverman 1982: 51).

Lee was not publicly religious but Damon (1857) asserted that he was a devout and moral person. He became a member of the O'ahu Temperance Society in 1847. In August 1847 he was appointed president of the Board of Commissioners to Quiet Land Titles. This board was responsible for overseeing the division of lands that had been initiated by John Ricord in the second Organic Act. The Board of Commissioners to Quiet Land Titles was initially headed by Richards and assisted by John Ricord, J. Y. Kanehoa, John Papa'I'ī, and Z. Ka'auwai (Kame'eleihiwa 1992: 185). When Richards had a stroke, he resigned and Lee took the job. In 1847 Lee was appointed to the Privy Council. Lee spent a great deal of time between 1847 and 1855 traveling around the islands holding Circuit Court and settling the massive number of land claims arising from the Māhele, or land division (Dutton 1953). Thus, as we saw in chapter 1, in a few short years this trained lawyer dramatically reshaped the legal landscape of the kingdom.

Changes in the Substance of Law

Land Tenure

The most significant legal transformation of this period was the creation of a system of private fee-simple landownership in place of the previous system of land tenancy. Lee strongly favored this because of his commitment to democracy and his belief that private landownership by commoners would give them a sense of their rights separate from the rights of chiefs, and that it would designate something that they owned as a way of enhancing their independence, self-respect, and desire to work the land (Silverman 1982: 61). The king hoped by this land allocation to protect his lands from confiscation in the event of foreign conquest (Chinen 1958: 25). The process began with a permanent division of land in 1848 between the king and 245 chiefs called the Māhele (Kuykendall 1938: 288; Chinen 1958, Kame'eleihiwa 1992). This division was followed by the Kuleana Act of 1850, which gave the maka'āinana the right to apply for permanent titles to their lands. According to the Kuleana Act, commoners could be awarded lands in fee simple, both house lots and cultivated lands, although not waste lands or lands they had cultivated in different spots. They were guaranteed the right to gather for use firewood, house timber, aho cord, thatch, ti leaf, drinking water, and running water, and they were given the right of way on landlords' lands (Kingdom of Hawaii 1850: 202–204 quoted in Linnekin 1990: 195).

For a wide range of reasons including the unfamiliarity of this new relationship to the land to the maka'āinana, the very short time period allotted to file claims, and the difficulties of filing claims and surveying lands, relatively few maka'āinana actually acquired titles to the land (Lam 1985; Kame'eleihiwa 1992; Sahlins 1992). Few knew how to apply for titles, and some wanted to stay on lands under their chiefs. But when the chiefs leased their lands to the foreigners, the people were obliged to leave and "were left to wander in tears on the highway" (Kamakau 1961: 407). When the Land Commission ended its work in 1855, approximately one million acres were crown lands, one and a half million government lands, one and a half million chiefs' lands, and thirty thousand acres kuleana lands of the maka'āinana (Kuykendall 1938: 294). The common people had less than 1 percent of the total acreage of Hawai'i (Kame'eleihiwa 1992: 295) and only 9 percent of the population received any land in the Māhele (Kame'eleihiwa 1992: 297; see also Lam 1985).

The Māhele and Kuleana Acts were paired with a law, written by Lee and passed July 10, 1850 (while Judd, who had opposed this law, was away), enabling foreigners to buy and sell land (Kingdom of Hawaii 1850: 146–147, in Linnekin 1990: 195; Kuykendall 1938: 297). This was justified by the need for foreign capital, skill, and labor to develop the agricultural resources of the land. Lee promised that foreign ownership would mean great wealth and miraculous prosperity for the kingdom. When the new law was proposed to the House on July 10, 1850, the maka'āinana representatives objected strongly, but R. Armstrong, another New England missionary, said that foreigners had the rights to own land in all "civilized" countries and they could already own land now if they were willing to take the oath of allegiance (Kame'eleihiwa 1992: 300). The proposed law allowed any alien resident in the Hawaiian islands to acquire a fee-simple estate in the kingdom, but it required aliens to submit to judicial tribunals of the kingdom and to abide by the final decision of that tribunal without seeking foreign intervention by any foreign nation or representative. If any person refused, his estate and all his right ceased and was forfeited to the Hawaiian government (Kingdom of Hawaii 1850: 146–147). Although this law permitted alien landownership, it avoided creating a distinct legal system for those aliens by requiring them to submit to Hawaiian law.

In 1850, as soon as foreigners were allowed to buy land, Lee bought some in partnership with his friend Bishop and started the Līhu'e sugar plantation as well as buying land in Mānoa, O'ahu (Kame'eleihiwa 1992: 299). In his private correspondence with Turrill after the passage of this law, Lee is clear that he expects property values to increase after annexation (Turrill Collection 1957: 73). Thus, at the same time that commoners were given the right to own and sell their lands, foreigners were also given the right to buy land. The land fairly quickly passed out of the hands of both ali'i and maka'āinana, reducing many to the status of landless laborers. By 1896, 57 percent of the land area paying taxes belonged to whites, while Native Hawaiians owned only 14 percent of the taxable land (Morgan 1948: 139 n. 59). This pattern of privatizing the communal land of indigenous peoples and then making it available for purchase by whites paralleled but predated the similar policy of the Dawes Act of 1887, which divided up Native American reservation lands into individual homesteads and sold the "surplus" land to the federal government and to settlers (Hoxie 1989; Parker 1989: 47–48).

The transformation in land ownership broke apart the relations between maka'āinana and ali'i, substituting relations of inequality based on property ownership and the market for those based on genealogy and rank. Although the maka'āinana acquired rights, including the right to own land, their lives were considerably worsened as a result of the Māhele. They became an increasingly displaced, mobile population migrating to the towns, occasionally employed in the new sugar plantations although the long hours, arduous and repetitive labor, and strict discipline were not appealing, or struggling to survive in more remote, isolated valleys. By 1872 Hawai'i had experienced massive land alienation and was considered a worst-case scenario in the Pacific (Linnekin 1991: 221).

The Status of Women

There were several major changes in the law in this period that redefined the status of women. The common law principle of coverture, brought from England to the United States and from there to Hawai'i, redefined the relations between husband and wife and greatly increased the subordination of women to their husbands. Coverture was introduced to Hawai'i in 1845 in a law, The Marriage Contract, included in the 1846 *Laws of His Majesty Kamehameha III*, vol. 1, p. 57 (Gething 1977). As the principle of coverture was defined in Massachusetts in 1835, at marriage the husband and wife became a single legal person who was, in effect, the husband. He acquired virtually full legal responsibility for and control over his wife (Gething 1977: 192n. 22). Because he was responsible for her, he was entitled to discipline her as long as he did not kill or seriously injure her. The husband was legally responsible for the support of his children and, on divorce, got custody of the children. Women were not allowed to vote, serve on juries, or run for office. Because of a woman's inability to make contracts, she was impeded in business activities. The Massachusetts law relegated women to the private sphere of the family.

Hawai'i appropriated this law through the 1845 Hawai'i statute on marriage. This law specified that a man was to provide for and support his wife in the same manner as he supported himself (Article I, sec. iii, in Gething 1977: 202). He became the "virtual owner" of all his wife's property belonging to her before the marriage and of all her movable property acquired during marriage. In addition, he had custody and use of all her fixed property. Article I, sec. iv states that the wife "shall be deemed for all purposes, to be merged in her husband, and civilly dead." As in Massachusetts law, she could not make contracts or sell or dispose of her property without his consent. She could not sue or be sued separately from him, nor was she liable for prison in a civil action. The wife did receive a "dower" of a one-third ownership of his movable property after payment of his debts at his death. The husband was responsible for support and control of his children under age twenty. Moreover, children born out of wedlock were declared "bastards" and could not inherit from their fathers without a specific bequest.

Divorce was granted only on grounds of adultery, but separation was permitted if the husband habitually subjected the wife to ill treatment, was habitually drunk, or refused to provide necessities for the wife. At divorce, the woman forfeited her dower and alimony as well as her own property if she were guilty, although her fixed property would go to her heirs after her husband's death. If he were guilty and she received a divorce, she became a single woman entitled to buy or sell property, sue or be sued, and make contracts. But she did not receive her husband's property as he did if she were guilty (Gething 1977: 202–203).

Clearly, this new marriage law defined a position for married women vastly different from that of pre-1820 Hawaiian society, in which women of rank exercised enormous power and maka'āinana were free to leave an unsatisfactory marriage. Gething notes that the Constitution of 1840, which included a good deal of Hawaiian law, was considerably less sexist than the subsequent constitutions (Gething 1977: 197). An 1840 law on marriage and divorce specified that if one spouse attempted to take the life of the other and the judges perceived the life of the innocent person to be in danger, the innocent person could divorce and marry again but the guilty party might not (Of the Duties of Husbands and Wives, and of Divorce, 1840, Kamehameha III, in *Laws of 1842*, Chapter X, sec. 8 in Thurston 1904). If the judges perceived a woman to be in danger from the frequent assaults of her husband, he should be confined in irons (chapter X, sec. 2). Thus this law, adopted in 1840, recognizes that within a marriage, a woman who experiences frequent violence or severe threats to her life should be released from the marriage and the man should be punished.

After 1845, however, as legislation extended the coverture disabilities for women, they were increasingly treated like children and idiots in the civil law (Gething 1977: 205). In 1853 the divorce law was consolidated and restricted to adultery, willful desertion for five years' five years absence in a foreign country, or a prison sentence of five or more years. Divorce on the basis of life-threatening violence was no longer allowed. As chapter 8 indicates, the courts routinely returned women to battering husbands in this period. In 1860 women were required to adopt their husband's name (Gething 1977: 205).

Moreover, after 1845 the duties of parents to children were defined entirely by gender and the special privileges of rank were eliminated. In 1842 children were to obey the mother if she was of a higher rank than the father, but by 1845 children were to obey their fathers first and then their mothers, regardless of rank (Gething 1977: 203). As Gething says, by 1845 the legal status of women in Hawai'i and New England was very similar, except that women in Hawai'i had more political freedom (Gething 1977: 204). In 1888 the Married Women's Property Act somewhat reduced the control of men over their wives' property, again following similar legal changes in the United States in the preceding decades (Gething 1977: 211).

In 1850 a new elections law denied women the vote and excluded them from many other public activities that depended on being a qualified voter (Gething 1977: 210). Women were thus excluded from political life, in marked contrast to the situation in the 1820s and 1830s. Although women were not excluded from serving in the House of Nobles until 1892, few served after 1850 (Gething 1977: 211). Thus, laws passed after 1845 dramatically transformed gender relationships and repositioned women as legal subordinates to their husbands enclosed within the private sphere of the nuclear family where they exercised few legal rights. This was an enormous shift from the open kindred system of the 'ohana with strong brother/sister linkages and relatively easy entrance into and exit from marriage (see chapter 8).

Labor Relations

The Masters and Servants Act, probably written by Lee (Beechert 1985: 41–42) and passed quietly and with very little discussion in June 1850, established the legal basis for the contract labor system used by the plantations throughout the second half of the century (Kuykendall 1938: 330–331). One part of the law was an apprenticeship law drawn from a Massachusetts model and the other a contract labor law from another New England state. Although Kuykendall claims it was based on American shipping law (Kuykendall 1938: 330), Beechert argues that it parallels New York state law and finds it probable that texts of this law were available in Hawai'i at the time

(Beechert 1985: 44–45). Judging from a global study of masters and servants legislation by Douglas Hay in Toronto, the law is even closer to Connecticut master/servant law of the time (Martin Chanock, personal communication). This law allowed persons more than twenty years old to bind themselves by written contract to a term of service not exceeding five years (Kingdom of Hawai'i 1850 For the Government of Masters and Servants, secs. 22–29). The law provided penal sanctions for failure to appear for work and stipulated that a person could be arrested and forced to work double the time of his absence, up to one year after the end of the contract. Those who refused to work could be committed to prison at hard labor until they consented to serve. Masters had even more complete and arbitrary authority over seamen at the time (Beechert 1985: 44).

There were a few protections for workers. A district magistrate, rather than the master, had to convict for failure to work. Moreover, a master guilty of cruelty, misusage, or violation of the terms of the contract could be fined between five and one hundred dollars or be imprisoned at hard labor until it was paid. As we will see in chapter 6, however, there were an enormous number of cases concerning failure to work or refusal to work in Hilo, whereas the number of cases charging masters with violence could be counted on one hand. Indeed, leaving work to file charges in court immediately subjected a worker to criminal charges for failure to work. This appropriated law thus established the legal basis for capitalist labor relations, backed by penal sanctions. It provided a new, contractual basis for social and legal inequality in place of the earlier relations between ali'i and maka'āinana. Clearly, the second transition involved the extensive appropriation of American laws that laid the groundwork for the expansion of capitalist agriculture. These laws created the legal framework for private landownership, the bourgeois family, and penal wage labor.

Open Ports and Cash Taxes

In 1850 the ports of Hilo, Kawaihae, and Kealakekua on Hawai'i and Waimea on Kaua'i were opened to foreign commerce. Commerce had previously been restricted to Honolulu and Lāhainā but now fee collectors and port regulations were instituted as in Honolulu (Kingdom of Hawai'i 1850: 159–160; Linnekin 1990: 195). A law passed in 1850 abolished the collection of taxes in kind and required taxes remitted in the "current coin of this kingdom." This contributed to the mobility of the population as rural farmers struggled to obtain cash incomes (Kingdom of Hawai'i 1850: 168–169; Linnekin 1990: 195). Since 1846, land taxes had been payable only in currency but the person who could not pay could have the government take produce, goods, or "hereditaments" of any defaulter and sell it up to the full amount for which the person was in default. Earlier, in the laws of 1840 and 1841, payment in money was recommended but cash equivalents were established in arrowroot, cotton, turmeric, fishnets, bags, and fish. Most government revenues came from shipping dues and, until 1840, a 50 percent levy on produce bought on the Honolulu market (Linnekin 1990: 197–198).

The Criminal Code of 1850

Ricord had suggested drawing up new civil and criminal codes, and in 1847 the legislature asked Lee to prepare such codes "adapted to the wants and conditions of the Hawaiian Nation." In 1850 he presented a code based largely on a proposed penal code for Massachusetts (Phillips and Walcott 1844) as well as a code from Louisiana (Dutton 1953). This Criminal Code of 1850 became the basis of all subsequent criminal law in Hawai'i (Dutton 1953). In his introduction to the code Lee says that he borrowed heavily from the penal codes for Massachusetts and Louisiana, but "In this chrysalis state of the nation, I have thought it proper to keep an eye to the future as well as to the present." Again, the language of infancy shapes the way the relations between peoples and nations are understood. Lee says that although he has tried to conform to the principles of the ancient laws and usages of the kingdom, he has relied primarily on the principles of the English common law as the best basis for the future of the kingdom. His statement on this compromise is telling:

> To prepare a system of laws equally well adapted to the native and foreign portions of our community,—one not too refined for the limited mind of the former, and yet enough so to meet the wants and capacity of the latter, it will be evident, is no easy task. I have no confidence to believe that I have performed it successfully. My chief aim has been to be so brief, simple, clear, and direct, in thought and language, as not to confuse the native, and yet so full as to satisfy his increasing wants, together with those of the naturalized and unnaturalized foreigner.
>
> (Kingdom of Hawai'i 1850: iv)

A close comparison between the 1850 Penal Code and the 1844 proposed Massachusetts code (which Silverman [1982] says was never passed in Massachusetts) reveals that the chapters and sections are virtually the same, although in many areas the distinctions in the Massachusetts code have been collapsed in the Hawaiian version. The Massachusetts code was an effort to produce a condensed and systematic specification of crimes and punishments from the common law, taking into account the entire criminal law, rather than an effort to specify punishments or revamp the law itself (Phillips and Walcott 1844: iv–v). It is an effort at system and arrangement rather than change or improvement. "The object has been to distribute and arrange the

several titles in a perspicuous order; to give in the table of contents of each
chapter a convenient index to each subject embraced in it; and to express
each definition, doctrine and illustration, in clear, concise and exact phrase-
ology, so as to render the law, as far as practicable, intelligible to every
reader, whether learned or unlearned" (ibid.: iv). Thus, this was a work that
endeavored to create coherence and order out of the common law of Massachusetts. The Kingdom of Hawai'i also desired to create a systematic law
code, but instead of trying to systematize the existing common law in Hawai'i,
Lee used the Massachusetts organization of common law and its definitions,
concepts, and language.

The chapter headings in the two codes are almost identical, beginning
with explanations of terms, general provisions, and local jurisdiction of offenses. Offenses are listed in the same order, beginning with treason, homicide, dueling, assault and battery, kidnapping, rape, abortion, polygamy-
adultery-fornication-incest-crime against nature (sodomy in the Hawaiian
code), burglary, robbery, and larceny. The text is often identical, although
abbreviated in the Hawaiian code. For example, the proposed Massachusetts
code defines homicide as "the killing of a human being" and murder as
"homicide done with malice aforethought, without authority, justification, or
extenuation by law" (Phillips and Walcott 1844: Chap. VII, secs. 1 and 2)."[3]
First-degree murder is "Murder committed with deliberately premeditated
malice aforethought; or in the commission of, or attempt to commit any
crime punishable with death; or committed with extreme atrocity or cruelty"
(ibid., sec. 3). The Hawaiian code defines murder as "the killing of any
human being with malice aforethought, without authority, justification or extenuation by law" (Kingdom of Hawai'i 1850: Chapter VII, sec. 1). It divides murder into two degrees, the first marked by "deliberate premeditation;
or by the commission of or attempt to commit rape, robbery or burglary; or
any crime punishable with death" (ibid., sec. 2). It is clear that the Hawaiian
code borrows heavily not only the language but also the analytic categories
of Massachusetts law.

The definition of adultery and fornication is similarly parallel in the two
codes. In the Massachusetts code, adultery is "Sexual intercourse between a
man, whether married or unmarried, and a married woman not his wife."
for both men and women, and "between a married man and an unmarried
woman" for a man (Phillips and Walcott 1844: Chap. XIV, sec. 6). Apparently it is not adultery for a woman if she is unmarried but the man is. If
only one party is guilty of adultery, the other is not subject to punishment for
this offense (ibid., sec. 7) but is guilty of fornication (ibid., sec. 9). A foot-
note adds that the two crimes differ widely in the severity of punishment.
Fornication is defined as sexual intercourse between an unmarried man and
an unmarried woman (ibid., sec. 13). In the Hawaiian code, adultery is
"Sexual intercourse between a man, married or unmarried, and a married

woman not his wife" for each, while sex "between a married man and an unmarried woman, is adultery by each" (Kingdom of Hawai'i 1850: Chap. XIII, sec. 4). The penalty is a fine of thirty dollars or, in default of payment of the fine, hard labor for eight months. Thus, the Hawaiian code does not contain the provision that an unmarried woman is guilty of fornication and not adultery if the man is married. The Hawaiian code is somewhat more severe, less tolerant of women who have sex with philandering men than the Massachusetts code.

In the Hawaiian code, fornication is "sexual intercourse between an unmarried man and an unmarried woman" (ibid., sec. 7). As in Massachusetts, the penalty is much less: a fifteen-dollar fine or four months prison at hard labor. But in an intriguing contrast to the Massachusetts code, in Hawai'i if the couple chooses to marry, the penalty is not imposed. Both codes criminalize sodomy, called the "crime against nature, either with mankind or any beast" in the Massachusetts code (Phillips and Walcott 1844: sec. 15) and "sodomy, that is, the crime against nature, either with mankind or any beast," in the Hawaiian code. The penalty in the Hawaiian code is a fine up to one thousand dollars and prison at hard labor up to twenty years (Kingdom of Hawai'i 1850: sec. 9).

These examples indicate that the language of offenses and their definitions were drawn almost entirely from the Massachusetts code rather than from Hawaiian practices or laws. Many sections are repeated verbatim in the Hawaiian code and the title pages are clearly similar. But there are also some intriguing differences. Whereas the constables in Massachusetts receive rewards or part of the fine for convictions of people accused of burglary, robbery, larceny, embezzlement, receiving stolen goods, forgery and counterfeiting, purveying obscenity, or gambling (Phillips and Walcott 1844: Chap. XLIII, sec. 1–4), in the Hawaiian code constables receive half of the fine in all convictions unless the constable is paid a salary. But the constable must pay one tenth of all rewards received by him to the officer next above him (Kingdom of Hawai'i 1850: Chap. LIV, sec. 1). If a person not an officer informs and prosecutes an offense under this code, he receives one quarter of the fine paid and the constable making the arrest receives one quarter of the fine (ibid., sec. 2). Somewhat similar to the Massachusetts law, there are special provisions for rewards for convictions for counterfeiting and vagrancy (ibid., sec. 3). Thus, whereas the Massachusetts code provided rewards for a specific set of offenses in which the constable might be tempted to keep the property for him or herself or for offenses with significant moral hazards such as obscenity and gambling, the Hawaiian code created a blanket system of paying constables and prosecutors for convictions in all offenses. This system required a lower government payroll but empowered a large number of people to spy on and arrest their neighbors for a wide variety of new offenses and rewarded them for doing so.

In matters concerning public religion, the Hawaiian code was more elaborated than that of Massachusetts. A Massachusetts chapter on disturbing worship, blasphemy, profanity, and drunkenness was divided into two in Hawai'i, with a detailed discussion of violations of the Sabbath not found in the Massachusetts code. Although the language of disturbing religious worship is virtually identical, the Hawaiian code adds: "The Lord's day is *taboo*: All worldly business, amusements and recreation are forbidden on that day" (ibid., Chap. XXXVI, sec. 2). It defines a wide range of behaviors forbidden on the Sabbath such as labor, dancing, games, sport, play, drinking, and secular business (ibid., secs. 3–4). Reflecting the power of the missionaries, this law governed the Sabbath more stringently than Massachusetts law.

In sum, the 1850 Penal Code was radically different from the 1840 Constitution and Laws of 1842.[4] It was fundamentally based on Massachusetts categories and practices rather than on Hawaiian ones. Although tailored in a few places to Hawaiian practices and those of Calvinist Christianity, it was a fundamentally American common law document. Drafted first in English, it was then translated into Hawaiian. There is no statement that the Hawaiian version is binding. Thus, the laws of the first transition were largely Hawaiian translated into English but binding in Hawaiian, whereas the laws of the second transition were fundamentally Anglo-American translated into Hawaiian and, probably, binding in English.

The 1852 Constitution

The transformation in the penal code was followed by the enactment of a new constitution, drafted by people trained in Anglo-American law, and a new civil code. In 1851 the legislature asked for the appointment of three commissioners to review the Constitution of 1840 and prepare a draft of a new constitution. The three commissioners were Gerrit Judd, Judge John 'I'ī, and Judge Lee; the main work was done by Lee. In a letter to Turrill in 1851 he says he intends to abridge the powers of the governors and the Privy Council, to increase and make clear the rights and privileges of the representatives, to define and limit the action of the legislative, judicial, and executive office, and to give the legislature some voice in electing the heir to the crown, if possible (Turrill Collection 1957, October 11, 1851). Although R. C. Wyllie criticized it for being "too Republican," it was signed by the king in 1852. This liberal constitution, with its long declaration of rights and separation of legislative, executive, and judicial powers, reflected a strong American influence. Lee made no reference to traditional Hawaiian usage in this constitution (Silverman 1982: 60).

Under this constitution, the Supreme Court created by the Constitution of 1840 under the king and the kuhina nui and the Superior Court of Law and

Equity established by the third Organic Act of 1847 were both replaced by a Supreme Court composed of a chief justice and two associate justices. Lee probably eliminated the Hawaiian Supreme Court because racially separate courts violated his abolitionist convictions (Silverman 1982: 58–59). Ironically, in his commitment to democracy and opposition to slavery, he eliminated any space within which Hawaiian customary law could legitimately exist. In effect, the old Superior Court became the new Supreme Court, taking on the name but not the language or leadership of the old Supreme Court (Kuykendall 1938: 268). The new Supreme Court opened in July 1852 in the newly completed courthouse with Lee's speech quoted in chapter 1 (Dutton 1953).

Thus, the Hawaiian-language court run by the mō'ī and ali'i was swept aside, replaced by an American-style court with the same name. The high court was deftly transformed from one under the mō'ī to one under foreigners, still using the name of the old Hawaiian-controlled institution. Between 1840 and 1852 the king was the chief justice of the Supreme Court and the four associate justices were Hawaiian. But after the establishment of the Superior Court of Law and Equity with William Lee as chief justice in 1848, the all-Hawaiian Supreme Court was of symbolic significance only (Nelligan 1983: 105). The new Supreme Court was staffed almost entirely by haoles. Of the seventeen men who were justices of the Supreme Court between 1852 and 1892, fifteen were haole, one was Hawaiian, and one was part-Hawaiian. John 'I'ī (the Hawaiian) sat on the court from 1852 to 1864, and R. G. Davis (the part-Hawaiian) from 1864 to 1868 (Nelligan 1983: 104–105).

Promoting the New Disciplinary Order

The problem of producing a new disciplinary order continued and worsened through the second transition. One of the first challenges was disseminating the new laws. In Benjamin Pitman's correspondence from Hilo in the 1840s, for example, he discusses his order for fifty law books to be used by judges and citizens (see chapter 6, p. 161). D. H. Hitchcock, judge in Hilo, describes teaching law to Hawaiians in Hilo in the 1850s as a way of earning money.[5] In 1848 Lorenzo Lyons, a missionary working in Waimea, Hawai'i, reports that a law school has been opened for the purpose of imparting information to the common people concerning the statutes of the realm (*Missionary Herald* 1848: 103). The new legal system introduced new roles and terms, such as lawyer (loio) and judge (lunakānāwai) (Silverman 1982: 62). The first is an English word Hawaiianized, the second draws on the Hawaiian term for regulating relations concerning ali'i and maka'āinana (kānāwai) joined with the term for agent or leader (luna), a term that also became

central to the plantation social structure. The Hawaiians became active litigants in the district courts, judging from a study in Honolulu in the 1840s
(Matsuda 1988a) as well as from my case records from Hilo starting in the
1850s. Moreover, Hawaiians were eager to learn the law and rapidly became
trained as lawyers and judges. A listing of all 760 attorneys and judges who
appeared in civil cases in the Circuit or Supreme Courts in the kingdom
from 1845 to 1892 indicates that, based on their names, 70 percent of the
lawyers were Hawaiian and 30 percent haole. One had a Chinese name and
two had Japanese names.[6]

Along with these changes in legislation and the structure of the judiciary
came new efforts to institute a stronger system of imprisonment and discipline. This was a period of extensive experimentation and development in
prison theory in the United States. The penitentiary, with its emphasis on
repentance and correction, came to replace more physical and immediate
punishments (Rothman 1971). Complaints about prisons by haoles grew
louder in the late 1840s and 1850s. In 1846, for example, the leading businessman and magistrate of Hilo was Benjamin Pitman, a Bostonian married
to a Hawaiian aliʻi. He wrote frequently to the minister of the interior, Gerrit
Judd, to complain about lax enforcement. On January 24, 1846, Pitman
wrote about the need for a prison and promised to use "all possible dispatch"
toward its completion.

> We have been all quiet here up to this date owing probably to the extream [sic]
> laxity of the enforcing the laws for no one seems to consider himself obliged to
> punish any breach of the laws, it seems almost as though this part of His Maj-
> esty's dominions was without the pale of the laws governing other parts of the
> Kingdom; but the great cause of peace and quietness is the prohibition of Ardent
> Spirits and may the time be far very far distant ere that bane to all Happiness be
> alowed [sic] to shew [sic] itself in the Bay of Hilo.
>
> (Archives of Hawaii, Interior Dept. Misc.)

Missionaries responding to Wyllie's queries about the condition of the kingdom posed in 1846 also bemoaned the lax enforcement of laws and the poor
conditions of the prisons particularly as a check on adultery and fornication.
Armstrong argued that more and better prisons should be constructed (Kingdom of Hawaiʻi 1846: 33). Emerson advocated prisons with two yards,
one for men and one for women, and forbidding men from entering the
women's yard. "What I here suggest is something analogous to American
State prisons, which are both lucrative to the government, and exceedingly
valuable houses for correction" (Kingdom of Hawaiʻi 1846: 43).

But the missionaries also noted that the system of laws was administered
to the detriment of the common people, who did not understand them well
enough to demand their rights against the layers of konohiki who placed
kapus on the trees of the forest and the fish of the sea (Kingdom of Hawaiʻi

1846: 35–43). One missionary after another, writing from various points in the kingdom in 1847 and 1848, spoke out against the rapacious behavior of the constables, searching out crimes in order to enrich themselves; the irregular behavior of the judges, influenced by the rank and wealth of the litigants as well as the justice of their claims; and the vulnerability of the common people to this system of judges and poorly understood laws. They generally attributed the difficulties faced by the common people to the continuation of arbitrary practices of the chiefs and their willingness to accept that power. "The chiefs have been so long in the habit of having everything in their own power, that *in practice* they are inclined to retain what they have had, the law to the contrary notwithstanding. It has therefore seemed to me that an officer ought to be appointed expressly to advocate the claims of the lower classes and see that the laws in reference to them are carried out" (Armstrong in Kingdom of Hawai'i 1846: 41).

In the late 1840s the most common crimes were theft, adultery, and fornication, but many felt that the major threat to social order came from the haoles.[7] R. C. Wyllie, minister of foreign affairs from 1845 to 1865, wrote in 1846 that the king employed so many foreign officers and devoted the time of the legislature to providing laws and multiplying its tribunals for the government of a few hundred foreigners. "As for his native subjects, they are easily governed, require few laws, few courts, and no legal subtleties to adjudicate their cases."[8] Pitman and other white settlers felt that some Natives were good and some white seamen and deserters were a threat to social order.

In 1847, the minister of the interior reported a crisis in the prisons. In his report, read before his Majesty to the Hawaiian legislature on April 30, he insisted that new prisons were needed. No one had been sent to Kaho'olawe recently on account of the famine among those who lived there. More money was needed for prisons, he said, asserting that it was well known that prisoners were not confined with sufficient strictness. Many of the misdemeanors in villages were caused by prisoners both as a result of defects in the prisons and the unfaithfulness of officers. If the pay of police and prison wardens were increased so that persons of morality and distinction would accept the trust, it would be a beneficial change. At the present time, he observed, there was no suitable place for confinement of prisoners and those condemned to hard labor (Report of the Minister of the Interior, 1847: 8).

These problems were even more pervasive by 1850, according to the report of Marshal Metcalf.[9] This report was addressed to His Highness John Young, Minister of the Interior, for presentation to the legislative assembly. Metcalf said the prefects of police of Lāhainā and Hilo complained of the inefficiency of the police at these locations "owing entirely to their present miserable organization." He continued: "No Legislative Enactments, or vigilance on the part of the Police will, in any measure prevent Fornication;

neither Thieving, which is increasing at an alarming rate, unless an entire change in the Prisons and Prison-Discipline be speedily adopted." It was necessary to have places of confinement, he continued, in part because of the number of seamen discharged, passengers, and deserters, many of whom were "lawless and unprincipled characters."

> [T]here is not *one* Prison in the Islands that is worthy of the name. The whole Prison System, as it now exists is simply a means of congregating all the worst characters of both sexes, thus furnishing them facilities for concerting plans of villainy and crime, and carrying them into execution:—so little or no obstacle is placed in the way of going abroad at will. With the exception of the prisons where Foreigners have control, prisoners can purchase their liberty from the Keepers at the rate of one rial per day, which receipts, I will venture to say, are never accounted for to Government. Our Penal Laws, with the present prison system, is a mere nulity [*sic*], if not something worse.

He recommended a prison of forty-five cells built near the Fort in Honolulu and similar prisons at the place where the sheriffs lived on the other islands, "subject to their entire control." These would be lockups. He also recommended a penitentiary on O'ahu for all the islands, taking people with sentences longer than one year. Here there should be hard labor during the day and solitary confinement at night, and the superintendent should never permit prisoners to leave the enclosure or to see any of their friends or relatives from outside during the period of their sentences, nor to have any communication whatever with their fellow prisoners. They could acquire a knowledge of trades such as cabinetmaking, shoemaking, or saddlery and thus become reformed and useful if there were proper regard for their moral training, but with the present system he had never heard that this had happened.

Metcalf proposed a second penitentiary for women in order to keep them separate. He thought they were more likely to reform than men because of "their gentler and more tractable natures." Seclusion from the world outside and separation from one another inside would deter them from getting in trouble again. Now, he worried, the present place of penal confinement was a desirable home for many, where they had "perfect liberty to communicate with one another and with the opposite sex." There should be a prison on each island for women sentenced to less than a year under the immediate superintendence of the respective sheriffs. (It is notable that, at the time of this report, all of the sheriffs appear, based on their names, to be haoles. Apparently only foreigners could be entrusted with carrying out the appropriate practices of discipline, which it appears many Hawaiians resisted.)

Metcalf further discussed the problem of paying fines, implying that it had been difficult to enforce payment. Already in the 1842 laws there was a stipulation that the person who refused to comply with the sentence of the judges would be held fast with irons or a rope until he yielded to the decision. In 1850 Metcalf suggested another approach:

There should be a Law passed immediately requiring that every Convict, on receiving a penal sentence, be sent to the Sheriff of the Island where sentenced, with a Mittimus in due form, to receive punishment. Much evil arises from the present system: or rather want of a system in this respect. But a very small proportion of the fines imposed in the country District Courts is paid in Cash— and the balance, I must naturally believe is paid in work for the express benefit of the Judges imposing such fines,—as I cannot learn that the Government receives any of the avails of such labour. The Judges, therefore, become directly interested in the event of every Suit brought before them; and unless they are men of incorruptible integrity, would be likely to do great injustice to the ignorant native litigated, taught as he usually is to believe that the decision of the Judge is infallible; and that from it there can be no appeal. Were the criminals sent to the Sheriff of the Island to work out their fines it would destroy all possible interest of the Judge in the result of Suits brought before them, and thus the facilities for obtaining justice in those Courts would be much increased.

Metcalf continued:

Besides, this regulation would open a channel and perhaps the only one whereby the conduct of the Country Judges and Constables could be more effectively scrutinized: which is a sufficient reason of itself for the proposed change. I hear almost daily accounts of flagrant injustice done by these Country Magistrates in collusion with the Constables under their control. It was a sad oversight, in the first place, to suffer the present system, in this respect, to go into use; and probably more evil has resulted from it than from all other Enactments since the adoption of the Constitution. . . . There are many faults judicially at present in the disposal of criminals: but I forbear making any remarks upon this subject here, as an entire new Criminal Code is about to go into operation.

(Kingdom of Hawai'i 1850)

Finally, he recommended that the government provide clothes to prisoners because now they depended on the generosity of their friends or what they could steal.

Metcalf's complaints about practices of discipline focus on Hawaiians in particular. At this time most of the country magistrates and constables were Hawaiian, whereas the sheriffs and judges in the port towns were generally foreigners. He had higher regard for the police and penal practices in the towns, particularly in Honolulu, than in the country where Hawaiians ran the courts. For example, he noted that all sixty-eight males and fifty-one females under penal sentence on O'ahu were sentenced by the Honolulu court. Either crimes and misdemeanors occurred only in Honolulu or, as he suspected, the country judges and police were "sadly remiss" in their duty. Perhaps he had uncovered not remission of duty but resistance to the new penality.

Metcalf's concerns were reiterated a few years later by Lorenzo Lyons, a missionary working in Waimea, Hawai'i, who reported in the February 1851

Missionary Herald that although the new code of law that has just appeared (the 1850 Penal Code) had many provisions with very severe penalties, the depravity of the times called for them. The jails were particularly inadequate:

> We have places that bear the name of "jails"; but they are mere apologies for such things. Their inmates are very few, and they enjoy almost unbounded liberty. There is nothing on this island that deserves the name of a prison. Though there are culprits, their prison is the public road, on which they are working out their fines. You will sometimes fall in with these persons, as they are going to and from their work, without any one to guard them. They are so submissive that there is little fear of their running away. They are guarded while at work, however, at night, unless they are off on a visit or after food.
>
> (Missionary Herald 1851: 254)

By 1857 a set of stern rules was drawn up probably by Lorrin Andrews, replicating the new prison regimes emerging in the United States at the same time:

Prison Rules
August 24, 1857

1. No prisoner will be permitted to retain in his possession any clothing, money, or other private property, but must deliver the same to the Jailer, who will return it to the owner, upon his legal discharge from jail.
2. Every prisoner must wear the prison dress furnished him by the Jailer.
3. No prisoner will be allowed to hold any conversation with the sentries, guard, or any one else employed about the prison, nor give or receive anything to or from them, but must in all cases make known his wants to the Jailer personally.
4. Tobacco in any shape or form, opium, or intoxicating drinks or drugs, must not be used by any prisoner, unless in the opinion of the Physician of the Jail they are necessary for the preservation of health.
5. Strict cleanliness must be observed, and prisoners must not spit on the walls or floor of the cells or buildings nor deface them by writing, drawing, or otherwise.
6. Prisoners must be careful not to break or damage the night-tubs, pots, pans, spoons, or anything else used about the prison or in connection therewith; they must also avoid tearing or otherwise injuring their clothes, blankets, hammocks, &c.
7. Every noise of whatever kind or nature, whether it be talking, laughing, singing, whistling, or otherwise, is strictly prohibited.
8. At the ringing of the first bell in the morning, every prisoner must rise, put his hammock in order, and swing it up to its place. In five minutes from that time the second bell will be rung, and he will then take his night-tub and

form in line with the other prisoners of his Ward, in the passage, and at the word "March" proceed to the yard and deposit the tub in the place set apart for that purpose, after which he will wash his entire person with soap and water.

9. At the hours appointed for meals, all the prisoners not in hospital will form in line and so proceed to the dining-room, where, observing strict silence, each shall take the seat allotted him by the Jailer.

10. Every Saturday all the prisoners shall fall into line and produce for inspection their clothes, blanket, hammock, &c, and wash and mend the same, so often as in the opinion of the Jailer may seem necessary.

11. Prisoners will be shaved and have their hair cut by a person appointed for that purpose, so often as in the opinion of the Jailer may be necessary.

12. Any prisoner found gambling or stealing will be summarily punished.

13. Every prisoner when ordered by any Luna to perform any lawful work, must do so promptly, and without making any remark tending to interfere with the discipline of the prison.

Any prisoner violating the foregoing rules and regulations will be punished by a flogging, solitary confinement, placing in irons, reductions of food, shaving the head, or the pump, or shower bath, in the discretion of the Chief Warden.

The above Rules and Regulations for the New Prison were approved by His Majesty in Privy Council, August 26, 1857.

   L. Andrews, Secretary

(From the Archives of Hawai'i, Authority of His Majesty the King, *Prison Rules*, established 1857; printed in English on verso, in Hawaiian on recto; filed with Marshal's Report in Disciplinary Systems file)

These rules reflect the emphasis on the regulation of time and the body that Foucault argues is characteristic of modern penality (Foucault 1979). Yet the actual practices in prisons seem to have continued to be considerably different from the disciplinary order of these rules. The introduction of laws specifying imprisonment was not paralleled by an equal introduction of the practices of prison discipline.

This history indicates that the vast changes to the legal and governmental structure of the kingdom were not simply imposed by foreigners. They were, in some ways, desired by Hawaiian leaders, both in their search for sovereignty and in their desire to acquire the status of "civilized" people, long held out to the Hawaiian people by Europeans as a goal. Acquiring the manners and forms of civilization offered relief from the routine and repeated forms of humiliation and degradation exercised against those defined as "uncivilized." During this period "civilization" was still to some extent a matter of cultural performance and dress, but in the increasingly racialized atmosphere of the late nineteenth century, it became largely restricted to people with white skin, despite their cultural attributes (see Stoler 1997). Civilized bodies had to be white.

Henry Sheldon gives a description of the legislative session of 1850, a session whose principle business was to consider and adopt the penal code prepared by Judge Lee. His account dramatically reveals the discursive power of the concept of civilization (Sheldon 1881: 177). On April 10, 1850, the mōʻī Kauikeaouli gave a speech on the need to encourage agriculture and therefore to change the law preventing aliens from holding lands in fee simple (Sheldon 1881: 175–176, no. 28). "No nation can prosper where the interests of religion and education are disregarded. What progress we have hitherto made is mainly attributable to those two great civilizing influences. You cannot therefore neglect them, without failing in your duty to your God, to yourselves, to the whole Hawaiian people, and to me." He accepted and spoke in the language of the "civilizing process," the process of transformation achieved through changes in manners and self-presentation.

In sum, the transition of the mid 1840s to the early 1850s was very different from that of the mid 1820s to the mid 1840s. Although Lee apparently knew some Hawaiian, neither he nor Ricord had the deep understanding of the Hawaiian language and culture of the leaders of the first transition such as William Richards and Lorrin Andrews. The men who led the second transition spent far less time in Hawaiʻi before they began the complex task of forming a government and legal system than did the missionaries who guided the first transition. They saw themselves as promoting the process of "civilizing" the islands and responding to the demands of resident foreigners by introducing the rule of law and the Western system of courts, codes, and legislative rule-making.

In the second transition, sovereignty was held by the people expressed through their representatives rather than by the will of God expressed through chiefs. The Constitution and plan of government created in the second transition circumscribed the authority of the chiefs in favor of protecting the rights of commoners. Indeed, the Māhele was justified as the protection of commoners against the arbitrary authority of the chiefs. The 1852 Constitution further circumscribed the authority of the king in favor of popular sovereignty.[10]

But during the nineteenth century this authority was increasingly restricted to particular categories of persons. As the basis of government shifted from the command of the deities through the sovereign to the command of those considered capable of governing themselves, authority devolved on those with the attributes of self-governance in "civilized" societies. This meant a shift from the sovereignty of the chiefs to the sovereignty of men of property. The authority of the chiefs, which rested on their control over the land and those who worked it, disappeared as missionaries defined this authority as arbitrary and despotic and pressed for the Māhele. Inequality was gradually reconstituted on the basis of property ownership rather than birth and rank. A second attribute was maleness: only men were viewed as entitled to govern themselves. A third was racial: as more Asians arrived in Hawai'i after midcentury, they were increasingly excluded from political participation. Since 1854 the franchise had been limited to Hawaiian subjects, but this was not a racially exclusive category. But in the Bayonet Constitution of 1887, pushed on the Hawaiian sovereign by haole sugar planters, the American principle of universal suffrage was abandoned: Japanese were denied the right to vote, as were many Chinese, and only men of property were allowed to elect the members of the House of Nobles, now more powerful than the House of Representatives, the popularly elected branch of government (Fuchs 1961: 29).

There is a gendered aspect to these two transitions. The first transition was powered in part by the actions of high-ranking Hawaiian chiefesses (Silverman 1982). Even before the missionaries arrived, chiefly women spearheaded the elimination of the 'aikapu and the disabilities it created for women in their spiritual status and in their everyday lives. Ali'i women such as Ka'ahumanu, Keōpūolani, and Kīna'u seized Christianity, the palapala, and the skills of the missionaries as a new source of power. Early male converts to Christianity typically followed the conversion of wives or mothers. During the period from 1825 to 1845, Hawai'i had many powerful women rulers, particularly in the office of kuhina nui. Although there is little evidence of changes in maka'āinana gender relations in this period (see Ralston 1989; Linnekin 1990), it is probable that women's greater access to the material wealth of the newcomers through the provision of sexual services affected maka'āinana women.

The next transition reinscribed male power. Women emerged from this transition with a far more subordinate status. Under the leadership of haole men supported by male Hawaiian chiefs, male power was entrenched in a secular state rather than in a hierarchy of religious/chiefly authority. The disenfranchisement of women denied them the political roles they had previously exercised, while the new laws about marriage, divorce, and coverture locked them into enduring marriages distant from the public sphere of politics and power. The state devolved sovereign authority over this sphere to the husband/father. Laws requiring marriage and divorce to take place under the supervision of the state and establishing criminal penalties for violating these laws—against adultery, fornication, and desertion—meant that in the new order, women moved into a domestic space under the authority of husbands. As the government moved increasingly to assign sovereignty to those able to construct social contracts, women lost their ability to author such contracts. Legally they became dead, subordinated to the authority of their husbands. Nevertheless, there was substantial resistance. The missionaries complained that despite the coverture law of 1845 they had to struggle long thereafter to convert it into social practice (Gething 1977).

As the family was defined as a private legal sphere outside the control of the state, wives lost the protection from violent husbands provided in the laws of the first transition. In a law passed in 1840, women were allowed to divorce violent husbands and if a woman were in special danger from her husband's assaults, he could be confined in irons (Laws of 1842, Chapter X, secs. 2, 4, 5, 7, 8 in Thurston 1904: 49–50; see further, chapter 8). But the 1850 Penal Code dropped this provision and made no reference to violence in marriage, nor did subsequent compilations of law in the 1869 Penal Code, the 1884 Compiled Laws, or the 1897 Code. Nor were there any special provisions about violence against women in the 1844 Massachusetts code. A family-specific prohibition on violence did not reappear in Hawai'i until 1973. In court records from 1852 to 1913, domestic violence cases appear simply as assault, assault and battery, or fighting and causing injury. Moreover, throughout the second half of the nineteenth century, wives who fled their husbands in fear of their violence were routinely required to return to these husbands (see chapter 8). Outlets for battered wives were closed by coverture, by rules about divorce, and by the criminalization of wife-desertion. Women became more firmly tied to the authority of a husband and therefore more vulnerable to his violence than they had been in the Hawaiian family system, in which divorce was relatively easy, or under the laws of the 1830s and 1840, which incorporated some protection for women living with violent husbands.

Finally, the two transitions differed significantly in the alignment of the major players: Hawaiian ali'i, missionaries, and merchants. In the first transition, missionaries and the ali'i joined against foreign merchants to construct a Christian/Hawaiian legal system. In the second transition, lawyers hired by missionary advisors helped to appropriate an American legal system tailored to the needs of capitalist agriculture. Some of the missionary descendants became key players in the transition to capitalist agriculture and later pushed for the overthrow of Queen Lili'uokalani. Missionary children often felt a sense of loyalty to both the United States, where they were sent for college if possible, and Hawai'i, but many grew up with a deep disdain for the cultural practices of Hawaiian society. Many acquired vast tracts of land made available for purchase at the Māhele. After midcentury, their children and grandchildren joined with the merchants and private enterprise flourished. Only the Hawaiian people lost.

Why did the Hawaiians, leaders and commoners alike, accept the second transition? There are of course many reasons, from the constraints of global capitalism to the desire for the promises and goods of "civilization." And this was hardly an uncontested change, with continual protests in petitions and speeches in the legislature as well as more indirect protests such as separatist religious movements. Surrounding the debate was always the worry about an imperialist takeover. The fragile protection afforded by treaties depended on asserting that Hawai'i was a "civilized" nation. This was always a difficult struggle. Kamakau noted in an article published in 1869 that Hawaii was given a room in the great exposition in Paris, the only government from the Pacific so represented (Kamakau 1961: 420). But the Europeans did not see Hawaii as a civilized nation. They were astonished, he says, to see the sign outside the Hawaiian room at the exposition. "They cannot believe it. A race of man-eaters are the Hawaiian people, are they not? And do they really have a government? And have they a room here?" After touring the exhibits in the room—feather cloaks, products such as sugar and coffee, books including primers and the Bible, newspapers, books of laws, and other manuscripts, the men interested in education said, "This cannibal island is ahead in literacy; and the enlightened countries of Europe are behind it!" Kamakau noted that Hawai'i was a country with a constitution and laws while most European countries were still ruled by kings and nobles alone. Thus, on the world stage of the Paris Exposition, Hawai'i represented itself as "civilized" in the face of European assumptions of cannibalism and savagery. Civilized bodies of law and of persons were the precondition for political independence.

Dual Legal Systems

As a result of its particular history, Hawai'i never developed the dual legal system so widespread in British, French, and Dutch colonies. In these colonies, one set of laws governed foreigners and another "natives" (see Hooker 1975). In Africa, for example, both the British and French had one legal system for Europeans using European law and one for Africans based on so-called "customary law."[11] In both the French and British African colonies, some aspects of local customs were accepted. In general, legal systems were tailored to the needs of development rather than moral principles, and many aspects of family law were unaffected. Tolerance for local practices was also inspired by fear of civil disobedience (Rouland 1994: 304).[12] The British accepted "customary law" as long as it was not "repugnant to natural justice, equity, or good conscience" or British law or principles.[13]

In his study of colonialism in Africa, Mamdani argues that colonial states adopted one of two approaches to the central problem of establishing the rule of a small minority over an indigenous majority: direct or indirect rule (Mamdani 1995: 16–19). Initially, the practice was direct rule based on a single legal order defined by the "civilized" laws of Europe. Only those who were "civilized" had access to this system of law while others were excluded. This was a nonracialized regime, since segregation depended on culture rather than color, and citizenship was a privilege of the civilized. The uncivilized, however, were subject to tutelage rather than political rights. Direct rule in European settler colonies meant the dominance of market institutions, the appropriation of land, and the reintegration of "natives" into the capitalist agrarian relations. For the uncivilized, excluded from the rights of citizenship, direct rule meant a centralized despotism.

Indirect rule, by contrast, was designed to govern a "free" peasantry in which land remained communal, labor and land were only marginally incorporated into the market, and peasant communities retained some autonomy in a system of political and civil inequality. Indirect rule was characterized by legal dualism: received law coexisted with customary law that regulated nonmarket relations in land, family relationships, and community affairs. Natives were defined as tribal subjects rather than potentially civilized citizens and lived under a decentralized despotism (Mamdani 1995: 17). Mamdani notes that direct rule was first established in South Africa in the eighteenth and early nineteenth centuries and that indirect rule developed later, in the second half of the nineteenth century. The direct rule system, imagining "natives" as citizens with rights, was more characteristic of urban areas, whereas the indirect rule system, imagining "natives" as tribal subjects with tradition and community, tended to occur in rural areas. It was the latter system, however, that came to predominate in South Africa and other colonial states and provided the structure for the system of institutional segregation that became apartheid (Mamdani 1995: 19–23).

Hawai'i, to use Mamdani's formulation, developed a system of direct rule and a unitary legal system premised on the view that people of all cultural backgrounds were potential citizens. The missionaries insisted that the Hawaiians could become "civilized" and saw difference based on religion and culture rather than race, at least in the early years. The unitary legal system developed in Hawai'i at the same time as it did in Africa, reflecting global conversations about difference and rule. The single legal system virtually extinguished Hawaiian legal practices, however, while the expansion of the market, the dissolution of communal landholdings, and the disruption of relationships between ali'i and maka'āinana had disastrous consequences for the common people.

Ironically, a dual legal system maintains customary law far more effectively than an imported unitary legal system, even though the customary law that is retained is itself a product of colonial relations. Dual systems create a protected space for maintaining customary law even as they create institutional segregation and inequality. In Hawai'i, that protected space was eliminated by 1850 in the name of civilizing the body politic. Communal systems of ordering remained in remote rural valleys and within families, but the rule of kapu and distinction was virtually extinguished.

PART TWO

LOCAL PRACTICES OF POLICING AND

JUDGING IN HILO, HAWAI'I

5

THE SOCIAL HISTORY OF A PLANTATION TOWN

P ART ONE examined the appropriation of new legal texts and institutions by the Kingdom of Hawai'i up until 1852. Part Two picks up the story in 1852 and looks at what happened in one small town as a result of these massive legal changes. It considers who was empowered to enforce the new criminal laws as judge, attorney, constable, or sheriff and who ended up in court and for what reason. This section of the book examines the social organization of the court and its practices in the context of the local community. It describes the changing caseloads of the criminal side of the Hilo District Court from 1850 to 1903 and the Hilo cases from the Third Circuit Court from 1849 to 1985. The cases include stories of battered women, deserted husbands, absconding plantation workers, and adulterous couples. A small number of local judges hear these cases. Rarely do lawyers appear. The fragmentary narratives captured by the case records are supplemented by private letters, local newspaper stories, travel writings, and historical accounts of the town and its legal practitioners.

The town of Hilo changed dramatically during the nineteenth century. Chapter 5 describes Hilo and its history as a port and plantation town and delineates the racial and gendered hierarchies that emerged. Crime statistics and stories reinforced the identities these hierarchies produced, while those on the bottom of the hierarchies were typically targeted for special attention. Chapter 6 focuses on the judges and attorneys of nineteenth-century Hilo and the ties of marriage, religion, nationality, and interest in the burgeoning plantation economy that drew them together and separated them from the bulk of the defendants. Chapter 7 focuses on desertion of work cases and compares in detail two situations of conflict between plantation owners and workers, considering how the course of the conflict was affected by the differential use each group made of the law. Chapter 8 examines the relationship between sexual conduct and civilization—the mobilization of law to transform the nature of the family and sexual practices within Hawaiian society.

Local Magistrates as Intermediaries

Local practices of policing and judging translate legal texts into a stream of convictions or acquittals. As a judge hears cases and imposes sentences, she interprets the abstract texts in the context of local understandings and events. As judges and attorneys give life to the law, their backgrounds, training, and social location shape the way they impose meaning on the stream of litigants they encounter. They carry out their tasks with reference to social categories of identity. Decisions to prosecute or to let go depend to some extent on who is defined as dangerous, dissolute, or respectable. Yet the outcomes of cases themselves create identities. As courts process cases, they produce a stream of convicted criminals or acquitted innocents. Court decisions that disproportionately convict members of any group produce an identity as criminal and disreputable.

In the Marxist tradition law was originally theorized as an expression of the interests of the ruling class, but considerable research suggests that law's relationship to power is far more complex, mediated through the social processes by which laws are created and imposed (Cotterell 1995: 113–134). Law is not simply a tool of dominant classes but is a mode of regulating the exercise of power. It stands against or alongside the market, constraining its activities according to normative standards, however weakly constructed and implemented. Despite its complicity with class and economic power, law is often also one of the few constraints on that power. But its capacity to constrain the activity of the market depends in part on who is empowered to administer the law.

Thus the identities of local judges and attorneys take on particular importance, both their cultural understandings and their class, ethnic, and gender locations. All the judges, sheriffs, constables, and all but one of the attorneys were men and most were haoles, a few Hawaiians. The local attorneys and judges had close connections to the sugar planters and many were themselves planters. They generally shared the values of capitalism and work, Christian moral reformism, and hierarchical ideas of race and gender of the elites in the local community. But the judges were small planters. As the industry expanded toward the end of the century, these small growers were typically squeezed out of ownership of their plantations as control became increasingly concentrated in the hands of a small number of "factors" who extended credit to their plantations and managed the sale of the sugar and the provision of supplies (Beechert 1985: 80). By 1909 the so-called "Big Five" factors controlled 76 percent of the total Hawaiian production of sugar, and by 1920, 94 percent (Beechert 1985: 178).

Many of the judges and attorneys were also missionary descendants or mission-trained. They were to various degrees members of a respectable middle class of Christians and homeowners who had lived in Hilo for a long time. They were socially superior to the plantation workers and rural Native Hawaiian farmers whose cases occupied most of their time, and they were connected to the planter class and the educated leaders of the town. They also had strong social and religious ties to the Christian Native Hawaiians.

The immigrant sugar workers were the strangers in town. The court officials served as intermediaries between the poor and the prosperous, willing to send contract laborers back to work but refusing to prosecute on the basis of trumped-up police evidence. Although the general sweep of case decisions clearly supports the power of the planters, there are occasions in which clear evidence produced contrary decisions. At century's end, however, the courts seemed less willing or able to oppose the power of the plantations and less inclined to protect the rights of workers. Local magistrates were also intermediaries between the local community in which they lived and larger structures of governance and economic power. Ties of marriage linked some to powerful people in Honolulu, but until the last quarter of the nineteenth century Hilo was viewed as a remote and forgotten outpost.

Intermediaries such as judges and attorneys play critical roles in patterns of domination and resistance. Despite the innovativeness of James Scott's work on the meaning and processes of resistance, his work tends to dichotomize the relations between dominant and subordinate groups and to bypass the significance of such intermediaries (Scott 1985; 1990). Scott develops his model to describe the relations between rural peasants and landlords, or slaves and masters, situations of sharply unequal power. But even here there are intermediaries (e.g., Lazarus-Black 1994), and in more complex power fields intermediaries are even more important.[1]

Hilo in the 1990s

Nestled around a large bay at the foot of towering Mauna Kea, the town of Hilo faces one of the few harbors in the Hawaiian islands. It has the best harbor on the windward side of the island of Hawai'i, the farthest island to windward in the chain, and was an important district long before Cook arrived. Hilo's rainfall sometimes reaches two hundred inches a year, producing a profusion of lush vegetation. Throughout the nineteenth century, visitors commented on the beauty of the town with its intense green vegetation and sweeping black sand beach. This lush and fertile region was a center of early Hawaiian settlement. Valleys along this coast, such as Waiākea on this bay and Waipi'o and Waimanu farther north, held large populations at the time of Cook's arrival. With depopulation, some of the deeper windward valleys were gradually abandoned, in part because the rushing streams were diverted to the sugar plantations by elaborate channels and tunnels. Many Hawaiians continued to live by farming and fishing in the interstices of the plantations and in the rural regions south of the city that were too dry for sugar. Hilo in the 1990s is still a small town in the center of a large agricultural hinterland.

The island consists of two enormous volcanos almost fourteen thousand feet high, Mauna Loa and Mauna Kea, which slope gradually down to black cliffs plunging into constantly pounding surf. Hilo is in the center of a large district that lies along the base of these mountains. Stretching north of the city, the rugged Hāmākua coast is cut by numerous steep gulches that open out to the sea. After any significant rainfall upslope, roaring streams cascade down the gulches. These constituted a serious obstacle to travel in earlier periods. Hawaiians followed paths up and down the coast and daringly forded the streams but also sailed or paddled along the shore in canoes. Now a two-lane road and numerous bridges make it possible to drive up the coast in an hour. The Hāmākua coast is sparsely populated, with an estimated population of 7,300 in 1994 (Hawaii Island 1996, table 1.5).

Despite the difficulties of transportation during the nineteenth century, the heavy rainfall and rich volcanic soils proved ideal for the commercial production of sugar. In the 1860s S. L. Austin, an early district court judge, developed a system of flumes that used the abundant water to carry the cane down the steep slopes to a sugar mill at the edge of the sea. The portable flumes—long wooden troughs—were dragged from one location to another by mules as harvesting locations shifted. Similar systems, possibly Austin's prototype, were used to harvest logs in New England. Starting in the early 1880s sugar planting gradually moved up the coast so that by the turn of the century, the entire coast had a bright green mantle of sugar cane rising from the sea up the mountain as high as the cane would grow. The Hāmākua coast is dotted with plantation worker villages: dense collections of small wooden cottages arranged along a grid of dirt streets with tiny gardens. Interspersed among them are the grand houses of the plantation managers, usually surrounded by generous verandas and perched on spectacular sites above the ocean reached by sweeping drives up coconut palm–lined roads. Behind the city the ʻŌlaʻa plantation attempted to use dryer parts of the mountainside to grow coffee and then sugar. More remote regions provided timber for railroad ties.

Hilo, with a population of about forty-five thousand people in 1994 (Hawaii Island 1996, table 1.5), is the county seat for the island of Hawaiʻi, generally known as the Big Island. In addition to housing state and county offices, it has a branch campus of the University of Hawaiʻi with three thousand students, a community college of the same size, a hospital, and a daily newspaper. The town provides retail, medical, educational, and governmental services to a much wider district. Hilo's downtown is a small grid of streets sporting the raised clapboard store fronts of nineteenth-century frontier towns. A few buildings are reminiscent of early New England architecture, including a plain wooden church painted yellow, which looks as though like it came from Vermont. Across from it sits a far more elaborate pink stucco Catholic church. The downtown is surrounded by the Americana of fast-food restaurants and malls, which quickly give way to small single-family houses on generous lots. New development snakes up the mountainside behind the town, providing a substantial supply of middle-income suburban housing. At the center of the town is a large government office complex housing the court and county offices beside a park incorporating once-productive fish ponds. Beyond this park lies a curve of large tourist hotels. But this town has not been transformed by tourism as have many of the leeward communities whose perpetually sunny skies and white sand beaches are more attractive to golfers and bathers than Hilo's rain and black sand. Hilo's major tourist attraction is an active volcano in a national park forty-five minutes up the mountain.

Tucked along the shore is a small Hawaiian community located on a section of land designated in 1920 as Hawaiian Homelands for homesteading by people of 50 percent or more Hawaiian ancestry. Impinging on this neighborhood is the airport, sitting in part on Homelands lands. Farther down the road is a large shopping mall, also located on leased Hawaiian Homelands. These leases evoke a great deal of bitterness from the Native Hawaiian community, many of whose members live in poor housing in more rural areas awaiting their own awards of Homelands lots. There is an active and growing Native Hawaiian sovereignty movement in Hilo as in Honolulu.

Surrounding the town to the south and up the mountain are large areas of forest that have been laid out as potential housing developments over the last twenty years. Many of these areas are sparsely settled and stretch along long, narrow dirt roads. The Puna area has grown very rapidly in the last twenty years from a population of 11,751 in 1980 to 26,700 in 1994. During the same period, the population of Hilo has grown by only three thousand (Hawaii Island 1996, table 1.5). Many of these new areas lack water and sewage and some also lack phone service and electricity. It is not unusual to find someone living in a bus next to a shack with a blue tarp stretched between to provide protection from the incessant rains. This area, which has the least expensive land left in the state, has attracted both upwardly mobile plantation workers of Filipino, Japanese, and Portuguese ancestry and white immigrants from the mainland, largely the West Coast, seeking a counterculture lifestyle. Marijuana grows just as well as sugar cane and is a major export crop as well a continuing focus of police activity and surveillance. The police on the Big Island confiscated or destroyed $122 million worth of marijuana in 1994, down from $1.244 billion in 1987 (Hawaii Island 1996, table 4.15). It is not unusual for houses with plain exteriors to conceal expensive oak flooring and koa wood cabinets.

The first summer I worked in Hilo I rented a house in one of these housing areas in Puna, only to discover that the residents of Hilo considered this area wild and dangerous. They felt that the police blotters and court dockets were full of "Punatics." Indeed, this district does provide many of the defendants in criminal court proceedings. I no longer felt quite as safe living alone in the house, isolated in the trees from other houses. As I walked down the dirt road in front of the house, I passed other small houses with signs indicating the need to be wary of pit bull dogs. One night I was frightened by a strange sound in the underbrush next to the house and was relieved to discover the next morning that it was a small pony returning to the house of its former owners. Despite Puna's reputation, however, many of the neighborhoods are beginning to develop community centers and small gospel churches and are becoming stable communities.

People in many parts of this rural hinterland survive by a mixed strategy of hunting and fishing, occasional jobs such as construction work, and a variety of agricultural enterprises such as growing papayas, anthuriums, or house plants for export. It is transportation that demands cash: for owning a car, keeping it running, buying gas, and paying for insurance. Without a car, it is difficult to get to town or even to visit others. In earlier times, many of these areas were inhabited by small, self-sufficient Native Hawaiian communities. During his visit to the area in 1822, Ellis described a string of villages along the coast engaged in fishing and farming. Only a few of these villages remain, sandwiched between New Age retreats, nude beaches, low-cost suburbs, occasional fancy beachfront houses, recent lava flows, and a bitterly contested new geothermal energy station.

Because of its history, Hilo is an ethnically diverse community. Its early sugar plantations were developed by Chinese sugar masters who brought the skills of sugar making from China, and they and their descendants intermarried with Hawaiians to produce a Hawaiian-Chinese population. Some of these families were educated by missionaries in the nineteenth century and became prominent merchants and civic leaders. By the mid nineteenth century the plantations were largely in the hands of American and British businessmen, however (Kai 1974: 39). As the need for labor in the expanding sugar plantations became acute, the planters imported a succession of foreign laborers from China, Japan, Portugal, Puerto Rico, Korea, the Philippines, and more recently the Pacific Islands and Mexico. The population of white Americans and non-Portuguese Europeans, who tended to monopolize top managerial positions, remained small and socially separated from the largely Asian labor force.

According to the 1990 census, the racial breakdown of the district of South Hilo was 34 percent Japanese, 26 percent white, 19 percent Hawaiian, 12 percent Filipino, 3 percent Chinese, 1 percent Korean, 1 percent other Asian or Pacific Islander, 0.5 percent black, and 0.5 percent Native American. By contrast, the population of Puna has more whites and fewer Japanese Americans: the 1990 census reports 46 percent white, 19 percent Hawaiian, 15 percent Filipino, and 12 percent Japanese, with smaller populations of blacks, Native Americans, Chinese, Korean, and Pacific Islanders. These figures, based on self-report on the census form, imply that the categories of ethnic identity are unambiguous. In practice, most of the population is extensively intermarried, so ethnicity is a matter of some choice among possible alternatives and is heavily influenced by lifestyle, social class, and self-perception. The Japanese-American community is predominant in government and educational activities and largely middle-class. The white population consists of two groups, those descended from Portuguese sugar workers, who consider themselves Portuguese rather than haole (the local term for white), and whites from the mainland or other origins who are called haoles. Cross-cutting these ethnic divisions is the important distinction of local or outsider, marked largely by accent. Locals speak pidgin, a distinct version of English that immediately marks its speaker as someone who belongs on the island and separates him/her from newcomers. At the same time, speaking "standard" English is essential to upward social mobility and professional status. Those who speak only pidgin face obstacles in job advancement, particularly in the tourist industry. Older plantation workers were taught that this was a second-rate language and are often very apologetic about their "bad" English. Many professionals who grew up in Hawai'i are able to speak both pidgin and standard English and can switch easily between them.

The sugar plantation economy dominated Hilo until the 1970s, when plantations began to close. In 1948 half the laborers of the district still worked in sugar. Employment in plantations in Hawai'i began to decline in 1954 (Beechert 1985: 331). Since then, the number of sugar mills on the island of Hawai'i has declined sharply. In 1992 only three remained out of twenty-six earlier in the century, and in 1993 one of the largest remaining plantations closed down its fields and mill. By 1998 there were no longer any sugar mills in operation on the island and large stretches of sugar land lay fallow or were being converted into small truck farms, often by Vietnamese immigrants. The job market is now being sharply reoriented as plantation work gives way to employment in the burgeoning tourist industry located on the other side of the island, a two-hour drive away, and in other trade and service areas. Since Hilo provides low-cost housing but few jobs, whereas the other side of the island offers much more expensive housing plus work, many of the residents of Hilo find themselves commuting long distances to work in fairly well paid but insecure construction jobs or low-paid hotel work. A variety of new agricultural enterprises in Puna offer uncertain possibilities.

Hilo Past

Much of Hawaiian history focuses on developments in the premier city, Honolulu. This was the crossroads of world trade, the location of the government after 1845, the place where the legislature met, the powerful people conferred, the resident foreigners made demands and the mōʻī and aliʻi navigated the changing political and economic situation. The missionaries stationed here had the largest voice in influencing policy, except for a brief period when the government was in Lāhainā. Honolulu offered the best harbor for large European ships, and the harbor eventually made Honolulu the dominant city in the country. Hilo, by contrast, was a long and arduous journey of several days by sea from Honolulu in small, overcrowded, and unpredictable schooners. Not until the 1880s did steamship travel ameliorate the hardships of the journey. Unlike Honolulu, Hilo was relatively unaffected by foreign influences or shipping until the 1850s. There was a mission station at Hilo starting in 1824, with one or two mission families resident there. Two mission families devoted their lives to the town: Sarah and David Lyman, who arrived in 1832 and established the Hilo Boarding School, and Titus and Fidelia Coan, who settled in 1836 and initiated a major religious revival that temporarily drew thousands of rural Hawaiians to Hilo in the late 1830s (Piercy 1992: 110). Titus Coan described Hilo as crowded with strangers in 1837 and 1838, people from rural areas building their huts, farming, and flocking to the churches, listening to his sermons with sighs and sobs, and joining the church in large numbers (Coan 1882: 44). This revival covered much of the kingdom at the same time that it was sweeping the United States.

In the 1780s Hilo was important as a site for canoe building for the Hawaiian royalty and the seat of aliʻi powerful in the struggle to unify the islands. Between 1825 and 1860 it served as a refitting, watering, and provisioning spot for New England whalers, although always for a much smaller number than patronized Honolulu and Lāhainā (Kelly et al. 1981: 76). Even though it was the third largest port town, its lack of brothels and grog shops (reflecting the power of the local missionaries) made it less appealing to whalers than Honolulu or Lāhainā. By the 1860s the whaling fishery was disappearing. Titus Coan estimated that seventy-five warships from the United States, Great Britain, France, Russia, Germany, and Denmark as well as four thousand other ships and about forty thousand seamen visited Hilo between 1836, when he arrived, and 1880, when he wrote his memoirs (Coan 1882: 65–66). In 1868 Coan established the foreign church for English-speaking residents and seamen (Coan 1882: 135). Although when Coan was stationed in Hilo in 1835 a brother missionary "wept and condoled with us because of our banishment from civilized society," Coan reported that by the 1880s the town had a small community of "civilized" people (Coan 1882: 140).

After 1870 Hilo became a sugar town. The Reciprocity Treaty of 1876, which provided Hawaiian sugar duty-free access to the U.S. market, triggered a great expansion of sugar plantations and a concomitant search for labor. A long-term decline in Hilo's population reversed itself in the late 1870s with extensive labor importation.[2] (See chart 5.1.) Plantations, with

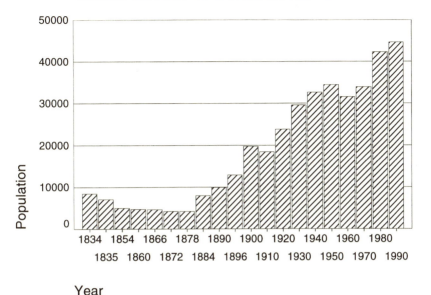

Chart 5.1. Population of Hilo

their distinctive forms of discipline and order, increasingly dominated Hilo, while the labor they imported dramatically changed its social composition. The low pay, grim working and living conditions, brutal treatment by lunas (overseers), and quasi-slave contract labor system drove each group of immigrants out of the plantations as quickly as possible. Planters constantly sought new sources of labor. During the 1860s Hawaiians did much of the arduous work of hoeing, cutting, and hauling cane, but by the 1870s the practice of importing foreign laborers under three-year contracts, after which they were expected to return home, was widespread (Beechert 1985). Despite complaints in the U.S. press that this was a quasi-slave system, it was not abolished until formal annexation to the United States in 1900 made it illegal. Chinese labor was imported beginning in 1852 and grew slowly until 1875, accelerating until public protest against Chinese immigrants induced the government to restrict this flow in 1886 (Sullivan 1923: 511). A law banning Chinese immigration, the Chinese Exclusion Act, had been passed only four years earlier in the United States. In 1893 Chinese immigrants were excluded unless they were willing to work as contract laborers and leave as soon as they had finished their contracts (George 1948: 27).

The Chinese had a distressing (to the planters) tendency to leave the plantations after their contracts expired for more remunerative work in independent rice farming or in retail or service trades in the urban centers (Takaki 1989: 147). In 1882 the Chinese were 49 percent of the plantation workforce, but only 5,037 (37 percent) of the 13,500 Chinese living in the Hawaiian kingdom worked on sugar plantations. By 1890 they were down to 25 percent of the workforce, and by 1892, 12 percent. (Okihiro 1991: 23). Planters, anxious for a white population who they imagined would make better citizens than the Chinese, imported workers and their families from Portugal between 1877 and 1913, mostly from Madeira and the Azores (Lydon 1975: 52). The major labor supply, however, was imported from Japan between 1885 and 1907.

By 1896 the population of the Hawaiian Islands was 109,020, of which 28 percent were Native Hawaiians, 22 percent Japanese, 20 percent Chinese, 14 percent Portuguese, 8 percent part-Hawaiian, 3 percent American, and 2 percent British (Thurston n.d.). In 1900 laborers were brought from Puerto Rico and Korea (George 1948: 28–29; Okihiro 1991: 24). From 1906 until 1934, large numbers came from the new U.S. colony of the Philippines (Sullivan 1923: 511; Daws 1968; Beechert 1985: 232). The proportion of Native Hawaiians to imported sugar workers continued to fall in the early twentieth century as labor immigration continued. By the 1920 census, out of a total population of 255,912, 9 percent were Native Hawaiians, 43 percent Japanese, 11 percent Portuguese, 9 percent Chinese, 8 percent Filipino, 8 percent other Caucasians, 7 percent part-Hawaiians, 2 percent Puerto Rican, 2 percent Korean, and 1 percent Spanish (Sullivan 1923: 513). By the late 1930s, however, large-scale importation of foreign labor had virtually ended. During this period, a small number of white Americans and Europeans controlled a largely Hawaiian, Portuguese, and Asian labor force.

Because the planters believed that whites were incapable of doing such grueling field work under the tropical sun for such low pay, they never envisioned the area as one for white settlement. Nor was there a substantial white working class to compete for jobs with the immigrants. The pervasive racialized hierarchy of the plantation allocated members of each nationality to a clearly defined status with the whites virtually always at the top. However, continuing patterns of intermarriage introduced complexities into this system of ethnicity, which these statistics, suggesting unambiguous, essentialized categories of identity, fail to represent. Instead, these statistics construct a certainty of identity that was only the result of an array of social mechanisms that divided the population by nationality in work, residence, pay, and social relationships. The racial hierarchy of the plantation system was a major one of these mechanisms.

Although the earliest plantations in the 1850s and 1860s in Hilo were often run by Chinese managers employing native Hawaiian workers, by the 1880s this pattern had changed. Instead, the management was largely American and British, and the workers Portuguese, Chinese, and Japanese. A list of plantations in the Hilo region in 1887 mentions eighteen plantations employing predominantly Portuguese, Chinese, and Japanese laborers and a few Hawaiian workers.[3] Native Hawaiians were often hired as camp police. A list of plantation officers on the island of Hawai'i from 1889 shows that with the exception of one plantation with a Chinese manager, all plantations were managed by Americans or Britons.[4] The 1884 census reported twenty-five thousand people living on the island of Hawai'i, with a 2:1 ratio of males to females. Of this number, there were twelve thousand Hawaiians; eight hundred "half-castes" (presumably part-Hawaiians); almost five thousand Chinese, of whom only 170 were women; five thousand Portuguese, evenly divided between males and females; four hundred Americans, of whom only one hundred were women, and about six hundred Caucasians of other nationalities (1884 census). Six thousand, or one in four, were contract laborers.

By the early twentieth century, there were some thirteen plantations along the Hāmākua coast, virtually all under Scottish managers (Leithead 1974: 53). Ownership of land and buildings was heavily concentrated in the hands of Anglo-Saxons, despite their numerical minority (George 1948: 41). Because landing cargo and loading sugar was always difficult along this coast, some plantations adopted a system of long cables to raise goods and people up the cliffs from the decks of ships anchored offshore. Hilo, with its harbor, remained the commercial and administrative center for this plantation economy as it had been for the early mercantile economy based on the whaling ships.

Immigration and Colonialism

Early contact and labor immigration in Hilo produced two distinct patterns of racial and class subordination and consequently two rather different sets of identities. These identities were intimately connected with the criminal justice process, shaping definitions of who and what was dangerous and, as court decisions were rendered, constituting evidence for alleged criminal tendencies.

First, the relationship between Euro-Americans and Native Hawaiians was a classic colonial relationship. The Europeans arrived in an overseas location seeking to transform the society of the indigenous people and subsequently wrested political control from them. Part One of this book examined the beginnings of this process in detail. Hawai'i was an American colony (territory) from 1900 to 1959. Although in the early Territory years Native Hawaiians were relatively well off, with opportunities in government and police work, plantation supervision, and ranching as well as considerable electoral power (Handy and Pukui 1972; Trask 1993), they began to lose political power and economic position by midcentury. This group now ranks at the bottom of the social hierarchy in income, educational attainment, health, and longevity and has become a largely poor, urban population (Blaisdell and

Mokuau 1994). In the last decade a powerful movement to reclaim Hawaiian language and culture and assert sovereignty has swept Hawaiian urban and rural communities, paralleling similar movements among colonized indigenous peoples in New Zealand, Canada, Australia, and the mainland United States (Trask 1993; Hasager and Friedman 1994; Merry 1997).

Second, the immigrant sugar workers had a typical immigrant relationship to the haole/Hawaiian leadership of the Hawaiian kingdom and later Territory of Hawai'i. Like other instances of immigrant labor in capitalist agriculture, after a long period of initial subordination in the workplace and community under strict paternalistic control there was some long-term upward mobility, although less than in urban areas. The sugar workers who stayed and raised families in Hawai'i managed to move out of the plantation in the next generation, by and large. Although people of Asian ancestry were denied naturalized citizenship in Hawai'i as in the United States, their U.S.–born children were able to vote and claim full citizenship as Americans.

Colonialism and the Representation of Native Hawaiians

One of the intriguing features of these two relationships is the very different images of the two groups the haole elites developed. The Native Hawaiians were regarded as "our" natives by the whites and treated as childlike but benign, lazy, irresponsible with money, and friendly, although too sensuous. When the missionaries arrived in the 1820s the dominant discourse was one of savagery and heathenism and the need to minister to souls on these dark shores. As the Hawaiians proved resistant to the enormous cultural and moral changes envisioned by the mission, the missionaries began to search for "natural" flaws in their character or intellect to account for this failure, such as their inability to think abstractly, noted by Andrews in 1836 (see chapter 8). By the middle of the nineteenth century, as haoles attempted to make Native Hawaiians into a plantation labor force, this discourse was replaced by one of childlike indolence and laziness. The frustrating efforts to transform marriage and sexual practices added a recurring complaint about licentiousness, heard loudly in the missionary reports from the field in 1846 (Kingdom of Hawai'i 1846). Looking back in the 1880s, Titus Coan, a resident of Hilo for almost fifty years, described the Hawaiians as a primitive race, claiming that "our native converts were as children, and up to this day many of them need milk rather than strong meat" (Coan 1882: 249).

Coan argues that the "natives" are not yet ready to be in charge of the churches since they are slack in church discipline and remiss in keeping track of wandering church members. Their church statistics are past remedy. He bemoans the tendency of Hawaiians to wander away from one church, to fail to take letters of dismissal and present them to the new church, and to change their names as they please (Coan 1882: 255). The frequency with which missionary reports are peppered with numbers of members, readers, writers, dismissed members, deceased members, suspended members, and the like indicates that enumerating and fixing the population was a critical part of the mission project. This was a process of rendering the Hawaiian mass known and accountable. Yet frequent movement and name changes conformed to Hawaiian kinship practices and were governed by a social geography of relatives and friends. The logic of movement seemed incoherent to those who thought in terms of fixed domiciles and permanent identity and citizenship.

Coan saw the Hawaiians as "naturally indolent," and although he granted that they were hard workers when necessary, he thought they "lack economy." "We teach them industry, economy, frugality, and generosity, but their progress in these virtues is slow. They are like children needing wise parents or guardians" (Coan 1882: 254–255). The character of this "infant race" is amorous and subject to bad influences from foreigners and from some laws that encourage licentiousness and others that, although wholesome, are unenforced (ibid. 1882: 256). They are also followers rather than leaders. They are inclined to be untruthful, speaking lies as soon as they are born, but this trait is ascribed to their racialized nature. "This is a severe charge, but it is a trait probably in all savage races" (ibid.). Coan concludes that their piety is imperfect: "Their easy and susceptible natures, their impulsive and fickle traits, need great care and faithful watching" (ibid.: 257)."

Thus, elite whites produced a Hawaiian identity that allowed them to define themselves as adults, even fathers, in relation to feminized children, while the agentic capacity of the Hawaiians themselves was progressively diminished. Writing in a missionary newspaper in 1844, Robert Wyllie praised Hawaiian seamen as both docile and competent: "I have never heard any captain of a vessel who did not speak highly of the native seamen whom he had employed. They are eminently subordinate, docile, good natured and trustworthy; and with proper training they become good efficient seamen" (Wyllie 1844: 79). In an 1864 article, along with discussions about the possibility that all Native Hawaiians would soon die out, one author describes them as "children of the Pacific; they have an aesthetic love of the beautiful beyond what is found in the most highly-cultivated circles" (Anon. 1864: 255). But, the author continues, although these people are brave, kind, and beautiful, they are disappearing, he thinks, because of infanticide. "The mothers are idle, they dislike the trouble of bringing up families, and they desire above all things to preserve their charms, which the nursing of children diminishes. They are very far from cruel." He adds, "They are very licentious" (ibid.). A missionary writer in the 1880s, retrospectively describing Hilo in 1837, evokes the childlike image as he describes the area: "15,000 natives scattered up and down the sea-belt, grouped in villages of

from 100 to 300 persons, a sensual, shameless, yet kindly and tractable people, slaves to the chiefs, and herding together almost like animals—to this
parish, occupying the eastern third of the island of Hawai'i, a strange min-
gling of crags and valleys, of beauty and barrenness, and to this interesting
people, was called the young missionary Titus Coan" (Humphrey n.d.: 2).
The same images contained in this passage—the animallike nature of the
Hawaiian people, their tractability, their sexuality, and their indolence—appear over and over in nineteenth- and twentieth-century texts.

By 1888 these traits had taken on a less benign hue, and one writer, mocking David Kalākaua, the Hawaiian king of the period, in an article titled
"The Pygmy Kingdom of a Debauchee," remarked, "The natives have the
virtue of hospitality, good nature, and honesty; but they are incorrigibly indolent and have no more care for the morrow than the American Indian. . . .Given an abundant supply of *poi*, a species of flour made from the
root of the taro plant, and the Hawaiian is content" (Fitch 1888: 126). An
1891 account furthers the infantilization and linkage with nature and animals: "Their frank open countenances, soft and flashing eyes, simple manners, and child-like deportment win the hearts of all beholders. Their sim-
plicity, easy good humor, and implicit trust in nature to provide for them are
characteristics found only in the people of the tropics" (Ingram 1891: 755).
Or, more often, in conquered peoples who have been forced to abandon their
militaristic past. These images helped to legitimate the haole-led overthrow
of Queen Lili'uokalani in 1893 and the formation of the Republic of Hawai'i. Rev. Sereno E. Bishop, a missionary descendant, reflected the view of
the leaders of the overthrow when he wrote: "The common people were not
intrusted with rule, because in their childishness and general incapacity, they
were totally unfit for such rule." Hawai'i's government, he continued, should
be in the hands of the few for the benefit of the masses, who were "babes in
character and intellect" (Fuchs 1961: 34).

The routine denigration of Hawaiians as childlike, indolent, and sensual
was so well entrenched by the turn of the century that a minister in 1908
objected to the phrase "just like a Hawaiian," which was commonly used as
a term of disparagement (Oleson 1908: 80). "It is just as much like an Anglo-Saxon as it is like a Hawaiian to do some things that are foolish, that are
disappointing, that are even at times disreputable. On the other hand, it is
just as much like a Hawaiian as it is like an Anglo-Saxon to do things that
are commendable, that evince strength of character, that reveal genuine response to high ideals" (Oleson 1908: 80). By this time the haole had constituted himself as the adult to the Hawaiian child, the energetic to the lazy, the
strong and wise to the simple and trusting in virtually hegemonic form.

The infantilization of Hawaiian people and their naturalization has persisted well into the twentieth century. Even as Hawaiians were denigrated as

inferior, sensual, and lazy, their music, dance, crafts, and foods were admired and appropriated for tourism. Haole elites from the mid nineteenth century through the 1950s felt a paternalistic concern for Native Hawaiians as the group disappeared though death and assimilation at the same time that the tourist industry increasingly relied on displays of Hawaiian cultural practices and fantasies of Hawaiian sexuality to attract business. This infantilized and sexualized image of Hawaiians is still central to the contemporary tourist industry and its portrayal of Hawai'i as a libidinous paradise distant from the disciplinary regimes of the clock and the workplace, as an oppositional world constructed to provide relief from the everyday, in which the Hawaiian becomes the sign of difference (see Trask 1993).

Immigration and the Representation of Asians

Whereas the Hawaiians were romanticized and economically marginalized, the immigrant groups from Asia were viewed as a threat by haole elites, undesirable as citizens and characterized by morally repugnant habits such as gambling, thievery, and opium smoking, attached to essentialized biological identities. These practices were seen as threatening to the fragile moral capacity of the Native Hawaiians. As the planters demanded more and more labor, they confronted local resistance to bringing in each immigrant group. During the 1860s and 1870s, the Chinese were particularly subject to public attack (Lydon 1975). Since at least the 1820s there had been Chinese inhabitants of the kingdom working as sugar masters, merchants, and rice farmers, but these individuals did not evoke comparable resistance. Between 1852 and 1875 Chinese immigration involved fewer than two thousand people, but between 1875 and 1887 25,497 entered and 10,196 left, with a net gain of fifteen thousand Chinese residents. By 1884 the kingdom was 22.2 percent Chinese. Because of the steep decline in the Native Hawaiian population, by that time there were only twice as many Native Hawaiians (44,000) as Chinese residents (18,254) living in the kingdom, and almost all of the Chinese were men (Lydon 1975: 18). By 1890 the Chinese population had dropped to 16,752, or 18.8 percent of the kingdom, as the number of Japanese workers soared. (See table 5.1.)

As early as the 1850s debates began about the Chinese workers. Planters argued that they were good laborers while long-term residents, including many Native Hawaiians, complained that they were troublesome and prone to quarrels, thefts, suicides, and other misdemeanors (Lydon 1975: 23–24). The anti-Chinese movement was fed by Native Hawaiian fears that their shrinking numbers would be engulfed by newcomers. The burgeoning anti-Chinese movement in California in the post–gold rush era was also significant, as the West Coast became the most important area for Hawai'i's con-

TABLE 5.1
Chinese Population in Hawai'i

Year	No. of Chinese	Population of Kingdom	% Chinese
1850	200 (est.)	84,165	0.2
1853	500 (est.)	73,134	0.6
1860	816	66,984	1.2
1866	1206	62,959	1.9
1872	1938	56,987	3.5
1878	5916	57,985	10.3
1884	18254	80,578	22.2
1890	16752	89,990	18.8

Sources: *Polynesian*, Aug. 28, 1858; *Advertiser* April 6, 1867, July 10, 1869, March 15, 1873, Feb 22, 1879, February 16, 1885; Kuykendall 1938: 387; Kuykendall 1953: 177; Lind 1955: 27. Table in Lydon 1975: 18.

tact and trade with the United States. The missionary element worried that the Chinese were a deleterious moral influence on the Native Hawaiian population.

Alleged Chinese criminality was at the heart of the anti-Chinese movement. Opium was a major area of contention. The Honolulu press worried that it had a bad influence on Hawaiians and caused suicides and serious riots (Lydon 1975: 27). Allegations of violence were also foci of concern. Reports in the press of violent assaults on lunas in the cane fields exacerbated the public perception that the Chinese, now envisioned as a unitary race with a fixed character, were prone to violent crimes and resistant to planter control (Lydon 1975: 29). When a Chinese employee murdered his employer, the anti-Chinese press emphasized the danger.[5] An editorial in the *Advertiser* after an 1881 incident observed that Europeans the world over had learned "to distrust him [the Chinese] as treacherous, and ready to shed human blood and take human life in revenge for the slightest provocation" (quoted in Lydon 1975: 50).

Crime statistics were also used to create an image of the Chinese people as by nature criminal and dangerous. A report published in a Honolulu newspaper in 1865 by the marshal of O'ahu indicated that between 1852 and 1864 the Chinese were 40 percent of the inmates of the O'ahu jail. Henry M. Whitney, editor of the *Advertiser,* carried on an extensive anti-Chinese editorial campaign in the late 1860s and 1870s, complaining that the Chinese (in the essentialized singular) was a pagan and had no regard for life so all who dealt with the coolie had a feeling of insecurity. He thundered from his newspaper pages that Chinese brought disease, smoked opium, and had a demoralizing effect on "the Hawaiian" (Lydon 1975: 31). Native Hawaiian opponents to Chinese immigration similarly cited crime statistics. R. G.

Davies (a part-Hawaiian lawyer), in an influential statement, articulated the opposition between the interests of the Native Hawaiians and the Asian immigrant workers, redeploying the language of civilization and race:

Our own people, the Hawaiians are dying off. Shall we import another element of destruction to hasten their extinction? The planters say that they must have more labor, and the coolies are the cheapest and best. Well, suppose they send for a thousand or two of these uncivilizable coolies. They will go on making sugar for the next ten years, and then retire with their fortunes made to travel in Europe or to enjoy their sugar-made wealth in a villa beneath the lovely skies of Italy on the banks of the lake of Como, leaving their agents to manage their plantations here, and we the people to manage the discharged coolies as best we may. We have as many coolies here as the courts can take care of. In order to resuscitate this nation, and bring prosperity to all, let us have a new infusion of good blood.

(Lydon 1975: 37, published in *Pacific Commercial Advertiser* 1869)

The imagining of the Chinese as a site of disease, gambling, opium, theft, and violence, characteristics embedded in the body and marking their undesirability, was thus substantiated by the apparently objective, scientific evidence of crime statistics.

The absence of Chinese women exacerbated the criminal image of the immigrants. In the period from 1853 to 1890 the Chinese population was only about 5–10 percent female. A petition from 1876, signed by the prime minister, Walter Murray Gibson, who used the anti-Chinese movement to increase his popularity among Native Hawaiians, says that Chinese males, "utterly unchaste in character, must aggravate still more the sterility of Hawaiian women, and so tend to increase the rate of deterioration of your Majesty's Hawaiian Subjects" (quoted from *Advertiser* 1876 in Lydon 1975: 43). When in 1874 an elderly Chinese man raped a ten-year-old Hawaiian girl and was tried and sentenced to eighteen months' hard labor, the author of the article in the *Advertiser* concluded, "These beastly low-class Chinese are doing a fearful work among the female native children" (Lydon 1975: 43). Indeed, Chinese competition for Hawaiian women may have fueled Hawaiian resistance to more Chinese immigration. An 1880 bill passed by the legislature but not signed by King Kalākaua (probably in response to planter pressure) restricted the immigration of male "Asiatics" by specifying that for each five male immigrants there should be three females (Lydon 1975: 62).

By 1877 there was considerable pressure to stop Chinese immigration altogether based on the perceived threats to public health and safety and encouraged by the growing anti-Chinese movement in California, which also focused on alleged criminality. For example, one Hawaiian who had been to California said that the California Chinese were regarded as "thieves and assassins and were looked upon as the lowest of the low" (Lydon 1975: 47).

In 1886 Chinese immigration was virtually ended, but Walter Murray Gibson, the prime minister, was able to engineer this cessation only by offering the planters a new source of labor: Japan. Between 1886 and 1894 twenty-nine thousand Japanese came and about eight thousand left, but this net increase was dwarfed by the next four years, in which private Japanese contractors brought in 64,000 more workers (Beechert 1985: 88–89). At the same time, a new law passed in 1890 allowed Chinese workers to come to Hawai'i as long as they did only agricultural labor and stayed no more than five years. Declared unconstitutional in 1892, the law was passed as a constitutional amendment in 1892 (Beechert 1985: 92–93). Between 1879 and 1898 forty-nine thousand Chinese workers arrived (Beechert 1985: 91).

But by the 1880s an anti-Japanese movement was underway, again fueled by the American movement (Takaki 1989; Okihiro 1991). In 1896 the population was 22 percent Japanese and the planters succeeded in resuming large-scale Chinese immigration for contract laborers who were required to return home (Lydon 1975: 78). The large population of Chinese and Japanese free laborers was characterized as shiftless and lazy, requiring regulation to direct their work to useful ends (Okihiro 1991: 36.)

After annexation and the elimination of the contract labor system, the planters attempted to institute a passbook system for workers and to use an old vagrancy statute to compel workers to work on public works as prisoners (Okihiro 1991: 36). Because annexation increased the possibilities of Japanese migration to the mainland, the anti-Japanese movement in the United States resulted in a 1907 executive order keeping Japanese, among others, from the mainland and produced the 1908 Gentlemen's Agreement, by which Japan agreed to restrict emigration. As a result, the flow of labor from Japan was cut off except for parents, wives, and children of Japanese residents. By 1909 new immigration from Japan had virtually stopped. However, an increase in picture brides produced a shift in gender ratios: in 1890 only 19 percent of the population was women, in 1900, 22 percent, and in 1920, 43 percent (Okihiro 1991: 38, 58). By 1902 Japanese immigrants were 73.5 percent of the plantation workforce (Okihiro 1991: 59). When the Japanese workers engineered a strike in 1909, they were seen as an alien threat, even as they began to make claims in American terms to equal pay for equal work (Okihiro 1991). By this time, perhaps 70 percent of the Japanese workers were literate, and many read one of the eleven Japanese newspapers on the islands (Beechert 1985: 169). The notion that essentialized racial identities were linked to particular patterns of disorder and criminality was virtually unquestioned among the white settlers and planter elite.

Thus, whites constructed Asians as far more threatening and different from them than Native Hawaiians. This vision of the social order emerges in an intriguing document produced by Lorrin Thurston, a leading businessman, a central figure in the overthrow, and a third-generation missionary descendant. The date is probably 1897. This "Handbook on Annexation" tries to sell an increasingly racially nativist and balky white American public fearful of the multihued population of the islands on the benefits of annexation. Thurston describes the Native Hawaiians, "only 33,000 in number," as "a conservative, peaceful and generous people" (Thurston n.d.: 27). He reminds readers that the Hawaiians are not Africans but Polynesians, brown rather than black. There is, he says, no color line between whites and Native Hawaiians in marriage or in political, social, or religious affairs. He describes the Portuguese as constructive members of society, emphasizing that they commit a smaller proportion of criminal offenses than any other nationality in the country and are "a hard-working industrious, home-creating and home-loving people who would be of advantage to any developing country. They constitute the best laboring element in Hawaii" (ibid.: 28). They were, of course, the only significant element of the work force that was white.

Asians are portrayed very differently. The Chinese and Japanese are "an undesirable population from a political standpoint, because they do not understand American principles of government" (ibid.: 28). In flagrant disregard of actual population movements, he asserts that these groups neither want to stay permanently in Hawai'i nor to migrate to the United States.[6] "The Asiatic population of Hawaii consists, however, of laborers who are temporarily in the country for what they can make out of it. As soon as they accumulate a few hundred dollars they return home. Shut off the source of supply, and in ten years there will not be Asiatics enough left in Hawaii to have any appreciable effect" (ibid.). His concluding assertion reveals how closely the racial policies of the United States shaped those of Hawai'i:

Individually, the Chinese and Japanese in Hawaii are industrious, peaceable citizens, and as long as they do not take part in the political control of the country, what danger can the comparatively small number there be to this country? They are not citizens, and by the Constitution of Hawai'i, they are not eligible to become citizens; they are aliens in America and aliens in Hawai'i; annexation will give them no rights which they do not now possess, either in Hawai'i or in the United States.

(Ibid.)

The remaining inhabitants, Thurston continues, are Americans, English, and Germans:

strong, virile men who have impressed their form of government upon the much larger population living there, and have acquired the ownership of more than three-fourths of all the property in the country. If they were able to do this against the hostility and in the face of an unfavorable monarchy, why is there any reason to believe that they will be any less strong under the fostering influence of the republican Government of the United States?

(Ibid.: 29)

This domineering population has apparently been masculinized by its racial identity and position of rule. We have seen that the process of "impressing their form of government" involved a combination of gunboats, greed, and capitalism that prevailed against determined Hawaiian resistance. Here this process is celebrated in terms of a masculinized racial supremacy. The islands are now, Thurston concludes, universally recognized as "the most American spot on earth" (ibid.: 40).

Indeed, for Thurston and others like him, the image of Hawai'i governed by a class of about four thousand Americans and other Anglo-Saxon peoples ruling more than 145,000 others of different racial/ethnic heritage seemed perfectly reasonable, legitimated by racialized and gendered conceptions of identity. Citizenship laws reiterated these conceptions. Because American laws denied naturalization to Asian immigrants, nearly 60 percent of Hawai'i's population at the time of annexation was disenfranchised (Okihiro 1991: 13). Antagonism to Chinese and Japanese had taken on the essentialized understandings of race characteristic of the United States at this time, an era of increasing nativism and exclusionism marked by the passage of laws in California in 1913 that prohibited aliens from owning land, thus denying land ownership to all nonwhite groups excluded from naturalization (Takaki 1989: 203). The early twentieth century saw the growth of racial exclusion, racially based nativist movements such as the Ku Klux Klan, and the passage of a racially based immigration law in 1924 excluding Japanese as well as many European groups (see Higham 1970; Takaki 1989: 209).

The Self-Representation of Whites

The whites defined themselves in opposition to both Hawaiian and Asian groups, again only in the masculine. In an article by a haole written in 1922 about Hilo in 1873, the author says: "Naturally by virtue of education, culture, refinement, and moral dignity, the missionaries were looked upon as the leading people in all matters of social and intellectual activities. These missionaries were: Rev. Titus Coan, Rev. D. B. Lyman and Dr. C. H. Wetmore, to which may be added the Hitchcock brothers, who were missionary descendants of the first generation, and who ranked with the missionaries themselves" (Lydgate 1922). Lyman and Hitchcock were judges and attorneys in Hilo District and Circuit Courts. Louis Sullivan comments in 1923 that "there are practically no Anglo-Saxon laborers in Hawai'i, or at least no field-laborers. The Anglo-Saxon element is of exceptional quality. The men who control the industries are largely of 'Old American,' British, German, and Scandinavian stock" (Sullivan 1923: 533).

Indeed, from annexation until 1946 a small, interrelated group of haole businessmen exerted enormous political and economic power over a numerous and heterogenous nonpropertied class (Okihiro 1991: 13). Island politics revolved around the delegate to Congress, the governor appointed by the U.S. president, and the territorial legislature. During the 1930s the so-called Big Five companies controlled thirty-six of the territory's thirty-eight sugar plantations as well as banking, insurance, transportation, utilities, and wholesale and retail merchandising. Interlocking directorates, intermarriages, and social associations bound this financial oligarchy closely together. By 1940 a dozen or so men managed the economy. During the territory period, almost half the land was owned by fewer than eighty individuals, and the government owned most of the rest, producing a concentration of wealth and power more extreme than elsewhere in the United States (Okihiro 1991: 14–15).

White power was described as paternal, both gendered and aged, and embodied. Writing a retrospective newspaper article in 1940 about his arrival in Hilo in 1898, Carl Carlsmith, one of the leading attorneys in Hilo, expresses the ideology of racialism and planter paternalism as he describes his steamer trip with frequent stops at plantation landings: "At that time the plantations ordered oriental laborers as it did any other merchandise and if 40 men were to go to John Watt at Honokaa the ship hove to and that many human beings were hoisted in a crate to the upper cliff" (*Hilo Tribune Herald*, December 30, 1940: 37). Carlsmith's account of the importance of the plantation managers to Hilo society in the 1890s indicates that the judiciary was part of this planter paternalism:

> To be a plantation manager in the 1890s was to possess not only wealth but social and political position and a right to guide the destinies and affairs of people in the district. Judges, sheriffs and all other officers were appointed by the government residing at Honolulu. A new appointment was not usually made till approved by the managers. New enterprises were not likely to succeed unless they met with the managerial sanction. At Waiakea was C. C. Kennedy and at Wainaku was John A. Scott. Both had grown old in the sugar industry and both were charitable and kindly even if strict in the conduct of all local affairs.
>
> Beyond Waiakea there was Goodale at Onomea, Deakon at Pepeekeo, Moir at Honomu, George Ross at Hakalau, McLellan at Laupahoehoe, Walker at Ookala, Albert Horner at Kukalau, Lidgate at Paauilo, Moore at Paauhau, John Watt at Honokaa and Forbes at Kukuihaele. These were all men of great dignity, tall of stature and important because of the responsibilities given into their keeping.
>
> (Ibid.)

Their height is more symbolic than physical, since at least one, John Scott, was quite short, according to one of Carlsmith's descendants whom I interviewed in the 1990s. Carlsmith also comments on the power that this social class exercised over the trial courts, again reminiscing about the 1890s:

> Every three months the circuit court had a term session. The attorney general came from Honolulu and with him Chinese, Japanese, and Portuguese interpreters, lawyers, clerks, and sometimes witnesses or litigants in important cases increased the crowd. The trial jury always had plantation managers, merchants, and the first men of the circuit and rarely did anyone ask to be excused. Crimes and civil differences were adjudicated by the men of substance and standing.
>
> (Ibid.)

Carlsmith came to Hilo to be the law partner of D. H. Hitchcock, building the firm that in 1940 was Carlsmith and Carlsmith, where Carlsmith practiced with his two sons (ibid.). Here he translates power and authority into tallness and masculinity as well as whiteness, just as in the earlier descriptions of Native Hawaiians, subordination and powerlessness were translated into soft eyes and feminine acquiescence. The same bifurcation of notions of race and virtue was replicated in Fiji, but here the indigenous Fijians were viewed by the British colonial government as childlike whereas the laborers imported from India to work the cane received the same disdain as the Chinese, Japanese, and Portuguese in Hawai'i (Kelly 1994).

The court records themselves are quite explicit about ethnicity, particularly in the nineteenth century. Of a total set of 5,628 district and circuit court cases, half (51 percent) mentioned the ethnic identity of the defendants. During the 1860s, 1870s, and 1880s, ethnicity was mentioned in about half the cases. The percentage was highest in the 1890s and 1900s, when ethnic identity was mentioned in more than three-fourths of all cases, then fell to less than 20 percent in the twentieth century. Ethnicities were inferred from names and case data for that period. In the 2,510 Hilo Circuit Court cases from 1852 to 1892, 62 percent mentioned the defendant's nationality, and in the District Court of the same period, 54 percent identified nationality, reaching a high of 89 percent in 1893. These variations reflect the fact that Puerto Ricans and Japanese are almost always identified by nationality, whereas Hawaiians are rarely so identified (20 percent of the cases) and haoles (whites) even less often (12 percent). Nineteenth-century District Court case records frequently refer to witnesses and defendants as "the Chinaman" or "Jap" rather than by name, but haoles are generally identified by name. Hawaiians are identified by name and gender—since names do not specify gender—but not by nationality. Asian defendants are identified by name and nationality but not gender, probably because the vast majority were male. In the late nineteenth century, they are also often identified by a number, presumably the "bango" number assigned by the plantation. Haole defendants are the only ones identified by name and title, such as Mr. or

Mrs. During the latter part of the nineteenth century, haoles are sometimes identified in the court record by "F," which presumably means foreign.

The practice of stating the defendant's nationality in the docket book diminished in the twentieth century, as only 9 percent of the 805 Hilo Circuit Court cases I examined between 1905 and 1985 stated the nationality of the defendant, but practices of identifying defendants by nationality occur throughout the detailed case records, probation reports, psychological examinations, and other information considered in case processing well into the 1940s. Intermarriage and cultural blending increasingly rendered these identities far more malleable and ambiguous than they were imagined to be during the late nineteenth century. Even at that time, they represented the crystallization of complex local and regional identities in their countries of origin, which became essentialized national identities within the Hawaiian context. The multiplicity of regions of China were subsumed into a single identity marker in the context of Hilo, for example. Indeed, it was processes of marking and recording these identities in official documents such as court records that helped to create the regime of essentialized national identities that came to dominate Hawaiian social life in the late nineteenth and early twentieth centuries.

Paternalistic Racism in the Plantations

As the plantations expanded in the late nineteenth century, a distinctive cultural order emerged linking social class, gender, and essentialized and homogenized conceptions of nationality. As the discourse of race flourished in the United States and in Hawai'i, difference was increasingly imagined as biological. The term *paternalistic racism* describes the position in which the dominant whites imagined themselves during the plantation era. There were, as we have seen, two different versions of paternalistic racism, one for Native Hawaiians, which envisioned them as childlike, benign, and foolish but not threatening, and one for plantation laborers, who needed authority to hold them in check because they lacked the self-restraint and self-control found among other races, such as the whites. Laborers who were Christians, as a few were, seem to have been regarded more sympathetically, as were those who were racially white. The image of the Native Hawaiians reflects the missionary past and their conversion to Christianity, which incorporated them in significant ways into haole society.

I use the term *paternalism* along with *racism* because this is an image of power that is gendered as well as raced.[7] As we have seen, white privilege is always located in a male body, often a tall or virile male body. The dominant whites imagined themselves engaged not in maternal caretaking but in paternal disciplining, exerting a benevolent but stern form of authority. Their masculinized authority drew added strength from the reformist element of Hawai'i's missionary society, since it was thought to improve the character of its subjects. The image of paternal power enabled violence to be thought of as discipline, justifying the considerable use of flogging and whips on the plantations. There were, of course, forms of violence that were thought to be excessive, just as paternal authority in the home required violence to establish and maintain discipline, but not excessive violence. Together, paternalism and racism provided a language for thinking about the violence of plantation life, tying together masculinity and whiteness. The whip was part of the necessary discipline of subordinate races, who deserved, indeed even chose, this violence when they failed to go along with the rules, just as women who fail to abide by their husbands' commands choose violence. Women choose violence by talking back to their husbands, as did workers who resisted the orders of the lunas. As with male discipline of women, the violence was envisioned as improving the subordinates.

This racism is different from that of the mainland, particularly California. Hawai'i was not envisioned as a place for white settlement, so immigrant workers did not compete with working-class whites as they did in California, raising powerful ethnic antagonisms. The immigrants to Hawai'i, Takaki argues, had ways of weaving themselves and their cultures into Hawai'i in a way not possible on the continent (Takaki 1989: 176). The white planters importing laborers were opposed largely by Native Hawaiians rather than by a white working class. Planters did have a racial preference for European workers, who were imagined as making better citizens than "coolie" labor. But Europeans were unwilling to stay on the plantations and work for such low wages. They typically complained bitterly and left. Efforts to import Germans and Norwegians failed, and even the Portuguese, who came in far greater numbers, left the plantations as soon as they could. A set of Hilo newspaper articles from the late nineteenth century describes the Portuguese as good people—industrious and helpful—but unfortunately leaving for better opportunities in California.[8]

The system of discipline created by the plantations depended on the creation of a hierarchy of racial and gendered identities. Indeed, the discourse of nationality, as it was called, was fundamental to official communications and planter journals as well as to court records, at least until the 1940s. The 1884 census counted people by gender and ethnicity as well as by place of residence. Police arrest statistics until the 1940s listed arrests by nationality. As the structure of governmentality, based on measuring and administering populations, developed, these populations were always seen as raced and gendered units. When the plantations imported laborers for the cane fields, they constructed ethnically segregated housing for them, which were generally labeled the "Japanese camp," "the Puerto Rican camp," "the Filipino camp" (Sharma 1980: 97). Supervisors, called lunas, were generally haole (white), Native Hawaiian, or Portuguese until the early twentieth century or Japanese by midcentury. They lived in special parts of the plantation housing, divided from those of other backgrounds by roads and by rules not to play with the children across the street. The plantation manager typically lived in the "big house" across the street, and although his children might sneak out to play with the workers, his social life revolved around visits with other haole manager families.

Linked to this economic hierarchy was an ideology of planter paternalism in which planters justified their extensive systems of regulation, surveillance, and control in terms of the need for a strong hand of authority against workers envisioned as "coolies." Okihiro quotes an editorial from the July 26, 1904, *Pacific Commercial Advertiser* on the psychology of the "plantation coolie:" "Yield to his demands and he thinks he is the master and makes new demands; use the strong hand and he recognizes the power to which, from immemorial times, he has abjectly bowed. There is one word which holds the lower classes of every nation in check and that is Authority." This authority was exercised through the system of contract labor and its penal sanctions for violation of the contract, local police and plantation police, a system of rules and fines, physical abuse, and fear generated by lynchings such as the 1889 murder of Goto, a well-known advocate of Japanese workers on the Hāmākua coast north of Hilo by five whites employed as foremen on nearby plantations (Case records 1889; Okihiro 1991: 35). The whites were found guilty of manslaughter but were released on bail pending an appeal and promptly left the islands (Beechert 1985: 115).

Planter paternalism incorporated missionary ideas of Christian charity and benevolence into to the old rhetoric of civilization: "A plantation is a means of civilization," says the 1886 *Planter's Monthly*. "It has come in very many instances like a mission of progress into a barbarous region and stamped its character on the neighborhood for miles around" (Okihiro 1991: 40). As Okihiro notes, plantations upheld Christianity and civilization in the wilderness, and the plantation master, through discipline and parental affection, cultivated cane and morality among his impressionable charges. An essay in the *Planter's Monthly*, "A Manager's Influence," talks about the master's burden: "Every manager has a grave responsibility in keeping up discipline and order on his plantation as well as a healthy moral tone." The plantation order was a moral order in which the manager controlled virtually all aspects of workers' lives (Okihiro 1991: 40).

Planters' paternalistic discourse toward workers was couched in the language of an essentialized racial/national identity definitive of labor capacities. For example, in 1870 E. G. Hitchcock, a judge, sugar planter, and brother of D. H. Hitchcock, also a prominent local attorney, in responding to a questionnaire from the department of finance with reference to his plantation of 65.5 acres, remarked: "Native laborers are much superior to any other laborers, if kept out of debt, well fed, and kindly but strictly treated."[9] Plantation documents described workers in categories that merged tasks with racial and gender identities. The manager's report from the 'Ōla'a Sugar Company, for example, lists its workers in 1901 and 1902, the first few years of its operation, as follows:

Labor Statement

	1901	1902
Management and office	11	13
Lunas	34	14
Mechanics	42	18
Chinese cane cultivation contractors	21	46
Japanese cane cultivation contractors	399	577
Japanese day laborers	805	424
Japanese day women	38	6
Chinese	206	2
Portuguese	100	91
Hawaiians	20	9
Puerto Ricans	220	85
Puerto Rican women	17	2
Other nationalities	19	7
Sundry clearing contracts	550	
Harvesting contracts		
Japanese	496	
Chinese	89	
Puerto Ricans	45	
Total	2,485	1,924

Source: Manager's Report, Ola'a Sugar Company, 1902, p. 23.

This curious list of employees, similar to that provided in other plantation managers' reports, blends occupation, nationality, and gender as if they all refer to the same thing. In other words, work is so deeply understood in categories of race and gender that these identities stand in for occupational identities, just as the first three categories of occupation similarly encode a racial and gender designation of haole male, although this identity is simply implicit. Race and gender to a large extent provided the categories by which haole elites talked about work and the job to which a person was assigned: there were clearly female jobs and male jobs. Top management was reserved for haoles and middle management (lunas) largely for haoles or Portuguese. In the language of H. P. Baldwin, a prominent haole planter, writing in 1894:

The field or ordinary labor on our plantations is done by Hawaiian, Portuguese, Chinese and Japanese. All these classes make good all-round plantation laborers. The Portuguese, who come from Madeira and the Azores, are the best for heavy work; the Hawaiians make good teamsters, and the Chinese and Japanese excel for factory work. The Japanese are good workers, but are not so easily managed as Chinese, and where there is a large number of them on a plantation they are apt to combine and make trouble in various ways.

(Baldwin 1894: 668)

The various groups are identified as "classes" and their essentialized identities defined by alleged shared labor capacities. Plantations often paid different nationalities different wages for the same work. For example, on one plantation in Honoka'a, north of Hilo, Portuguese workers were paid fifteen to sixteen dollars a month in 1885 whereas newly arrived Japanese were paid nine dollars (Okihiro 1991: 60). Filipino males from 1915 to 1933 were paid eighteen to twenty dollars a month whereas Filipino women were paid twelve to fourteen (Sharma 1980: 98). Such wage differentials, which were common, fueled discontent and were important grievances in the early labor movements in the twentieth century (Takaki 1989; Okihiro 1991). They impeded the formation of cross-national labor unions during the early years of the twentieth century, but as plantation workers joined across these lines, their union efforts were more successful (Beechert 1985).

Gender, race, and occupation also determined housing. The Hawaiian Sugar Planters Association developed blueprints for plantation camps in 1920 that showed how these differences in identity were reflected in the design of houses. The overall plan for the camp suggests the orderly grid of control and surveillance that Foucault (1979) sees as central to the disciplinary society. Camps were segregated by ethnicity as well as by occupational rank. As the sugar industry has declined, some of these barriers to housing have slowly and grudgingly given way. For example, the great house of the 'Ōla'a Sugar Company, a massive structure overlooking fields and the ocean, was home to its first nonhaole when a Japanese American was hired as manager to oversee the last years of the plantation's operation in 1983, just before it closed in 1984 ("Brief History of Olaa Plantation," HSPA Archives). After a few dismal years as an unsuccessful bed and breakfast hotel in the 1990s, already seedy when I toured it in the mid 1990s, the house is now in a state of decay.

Thus, the variegated identities of immigrant and settled populations were homogenized and essentialized in the social order of nineteenth- and early-twentieth-century Hilo: Japanese became a single identity, regardless of prefecture of origin, as did Filipino, despite the significant regional variations in the Philippines. Native Hawaiians also became singular, despite significant differences in rank. People are marked in court records in terms of these essentialized identities just as they are classified into such groups for purposes of disciplining and ordering a plantation labor force and reinforcing the hierarchy and the planter paternalism on which it depends. Not only subordinates become homogenized, of course, but also the haole elites who themselves took on a uniformity of identity, extending even to the body, as they all came to be "strong and virile," or "tall of stature." This identity, when it was one of authority, was also masculine.

In sum, the colonizing process in Hilo consisted of two quite different social processes—colonialism and labor importation. Each produced a distinctive set of identities and anxieties in white elites and generated oppositional elite self-representations. Law played a key role in labor importation by regulating the contract labor relationship, examined in chapter 7, and in furthering the colonial project by its focus on sexual conduct and the family, examined in chapter 8.

6

JUDGES AND CASELOADS IN HILO

MUCH OF THE CRIMINAL WORK of the District and Circuit Courts of Hilo concerned infractions that were part of everyday social life: sexual activities, hitting, drinking, entertainments such as cockfighting and gambling, and violations of work obligations. There was clearly a shift over time from a preoccupation with sex to drinking and drugs, gambling, and violations of the contract labor law. The people subjected to legal surveillance for these everyday offenses were mostly Native Hawaiians in the 1850s to 1870s and largely immigrant plantation workers in the 1880s to 1900s. Each wave of imported Asian and European laborers appeared in court in large numbers during its first decade in the Hilo region but subsequently disappeared from the dockets.

Defendants were disproportionately strangers, people new to the community and cultural outsiders to its emerging social order. In such a rapidly changing and plural cultural situation, the law served as the initial mode of cultural transformation. It was the method by which Native Hawaiians were molded into modern citizens and stranger laborers were converted into a disciplined and docile labor force. Those running the courts and police, on the other hand, were established haoles and, to a lesser extent, Christianized Hawaiians. These groups represented the old guard by the 1850s. As the century progressed, people of this background retained their control over the courts but began to lose their economic and political power in the town and in the nation. Meanwhile, the population of the town changed dramatically. The defendant population was increasingly made up of cultural "others." The courts were organized stratigraphically, with the oldest residents in charge and the more recent arrivals subject to their judicial decision making. This stratigraphic pattern has continued through the twentieth century as Japanese Americans have become the core of the judiciary and court staff, along with haoles and Hawaiians, while recent arrivals such as Tongans, Samoans, and Mexicans populate the defendant categories. Nevertheless, class cross-cuts this stratigraphy in important ways. As established populations fall into the lower socioeconomic positions, they also become the object of legal attention.

The striking feature of this pattern of court cases and defendant populations is the focus on social reform. The people running the courts tried to reform social behaviors they considered repugnant or harmful. They came from a Christian missionary tradition and brought to the judicial function a sense of responsibility to maintain marriages and prevent divorce, to control the consumption of alcohol and opium, to foster good habits of work and punctuality, to prevent violence and protect the public order, and to prohibit gambling. Their preeminent concern was the character of the Native Hawaiians, always the center of the missionary project. The moral character of the stranger populations was of less interest unless they exerted a destructive moral influence on the Hawaiians. Few were prosecuted for adultery or lewdness. The newcomers were potential workers, and as the judicial elites became more closely connected with the plantation hierarchy in the 1860s to 1880s, they energetically enforced labor discipline and protected property through larceny convictions.

Despite these abiding interests in moral reform, supporting the plantation system, and emphasizing the value of hard work, judges in this court were careful to weigh evidence. They refused to convict in its absence. However, it appears that this concern for careful evidentiary assessments began to fade at the end of the century as the plantations became stronger and the cultural and class gulf between the court and the defendants widened.

In order to examine the changing nature of the cases in the Hilo criminal courts, I tabulated all the criminal cases for a full year once a decade from 1853 to 1903 in the District Court, a total of 2,325 cases, and from 1905 through 1985 in the Circuit Court, a total of 817 cases.[1] I also analyzed data from the Third Circuit Court from 1852 to 1892 that had been tabulated in a research project under the direction of Jane Silverman with subsequent analysis by Harry Ball and Peter Nelligan.[2] I extracted the criminal Circuit Court cases from the Hilo region out of this data set, a total of 2,530 cases over the forty-year period. Taken together, these data include 5,672 District and Circuit Court criminal cases from Hilo and the surrounding region. I received generous assistance from the Hawai'i Judiciary History Center in Honolulu and from Harry Ball and Jane Silverman, who shared the data from the previous research project with me.

Judges in the Hilo District Court, as in other "police courts," were required to preserve "in written detail the minutes and proceedings of their trials, transactions, and judgments," according the Organic Acts of 1847 that established them (Kingdom of Hawai'i 1847: 12; Kingdom of Hawai'i 1884: 237). The Hilo lower court was designated a police court, reflecting the added responsibilities of managing a court in a harbor town in which cases involved foreigners and mercantile issues. For each case I recorded charge, plea, conviction, disposition, presence of an attorney, and gender and ethnicity of the defendant. I also collected the texts of all cases involving interpersonal relationships. For about half of the period from 1853 to 1903, district court records were recorded in Hawaiian; the rest were in English. These records were ably translated by Esther Mookini, an experienced translator of nineteenth-century Hawaiian court records.

During this period the court system was divided into three tiers: a lower District Court, a Circuit Court, and a Supreme Court. By 1896 there were about thirty District Courts on the islands with jurisdiction over civil matters less than three hundred dollars and misdemeanors (Thurston n.d. 25–26). These courts also could commit for trial persons accused of felonies. A person could appeal from the District Court to the Circuit Court or Supreme Court. There were four Circuit Courts that heard appeals from District Courts and had original jurisdiction over civil suits greater than three hundred dollars, persons committed for trial for felonies, and all equity, admiralty, and probate cases plus special proceedings such as habeas corpus. Each was presided over by one judge. All jury trials were held in Circuit Courts, but Circuit Courts could handle cases without jury trial as well. The Supreme Court with three judges heard appeals and had exclusive jurisdiction over some cases.

Adding together the caseload information from the Hilo District Court and the Hilo region of the Third Circuit Court between 1853 and 1985 indicates that the major categories of offense over these 150 years concerned drugs and alcohol, property, violence, public order offenses, work, and adultery and prostitution (see chart 6.1; tables for the charts are provided in appendix B).[3] However, the proportion of cases of each type changed over time, with a continual decline in the proportion of adultery cases and a rise in the drug and alcohol and property cases during the twentieth century. Moreover, throughout this period the criminal courts focused on newcomers. There are significant variations over time in the frequency with which immigrant groups such as the Japanese, Portuguese, and Filipinos were criminal defendants (chart 6.2). The rest of this chapter examines these changes in more detail, focusing in particular on the sixty-year span of District Court records from 1853 to 1903. The District Court records after this time are no longer preserved in the Hawai'i State Archives and have disappeared.

A series of charts indicates the changing caseload of the district court between 1853 and 1903, showing shifts in the types of cases and the ethnic identity of the defendants (chart 6.3). For example, adultery, fornication, and prostitution declined precipitously as a focus of court attention after the 1850s, dropping from 44 percent of all 127 cases in 1853 to 3 percent of 1,032 cases in 1903. Moreover, virtually all of the adultery and fornication defendants were Hawaiians until 1903. That year included a substantial number of Japanese defendants, but the total number of cases was quite small. The immigrant sugar workers were never the objects of a campaign for moral refashioning. Unlike the Hawaiians, these immigrants were not envisioned as the citizens of a civilized state but only as labor units. Consequently, much of the criminal sanctioning of these groups focused on work violations and very little on sexual conduct. The law focused on keeping them at work rather than keeping them at home.

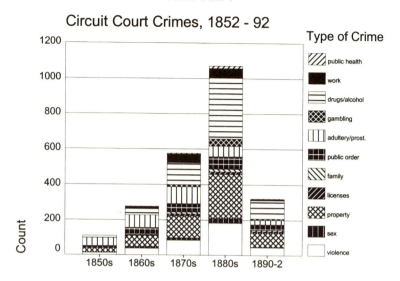

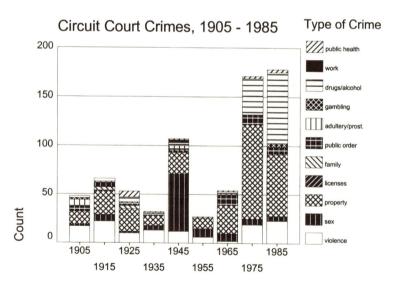

Chart 6.1. Circuit Court Cases, Hilo Region, 1852–1985. See accompanying tables in appendix B.

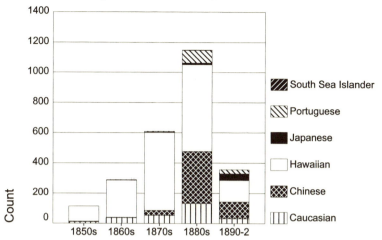

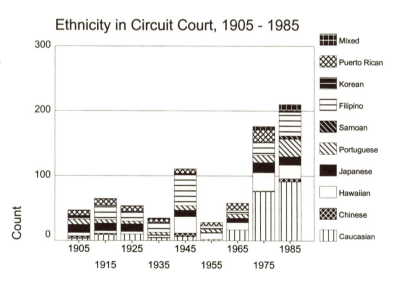

Chart 6.2. Ethnicity in Circuit Court, Hilo Region, 1852–1985. See accompanying tables in appendix B.

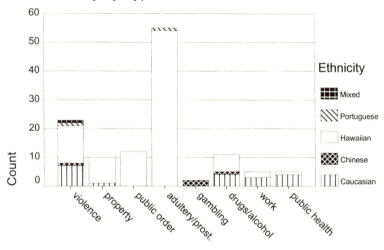

Type of Crime Categorized

Number = 124

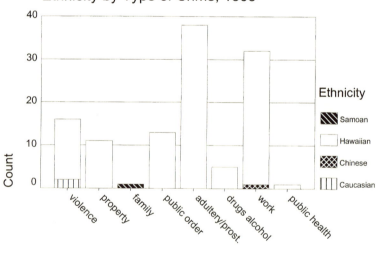

Type of Crime Categorized

Number = 137

Chart 6.3. Ethnicity by Type of Crime, Hilo District Court, 1853–1903. See accompanying tables in appendix B.

Ethnicity by Type of Crime, 1873

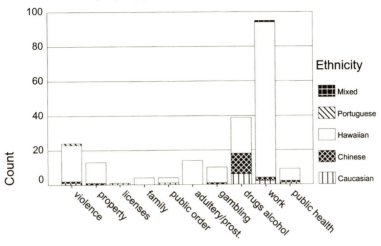

Type of Crime Categorized

Number = 240

Ethnicity by Type of Crime, 1883

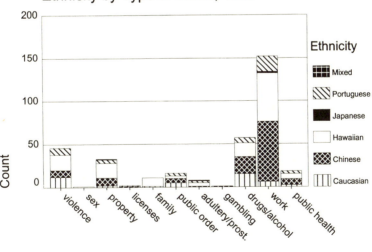

Type of Crime Categorized

Number = 409

Chart 6.3. (*cont.*)

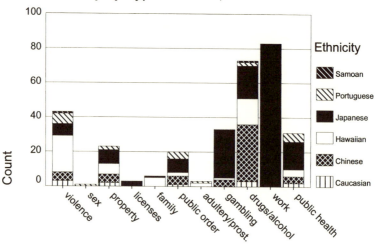

Type of Crime Categorized

Number = 379

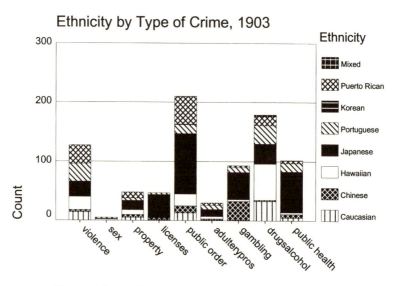

Type of Crime Categorized

Number = 992

Chart 6.3. (*cont.*)

Work violations became an increasingly significant part of the District Court caseload as the plantation economy expanded. Plantations relied on the imposition of penal sanctions for failure to work to keep laborers at their grueling tasks.[4] The ethnic composition of defendants in desertion of work cases changed dramatically as the plantation labor force itself changed, shifting from a largely Hawaiian population to half Chinese in 1883 and virtually all Japanese in 1893 (see chart 6.3).[5]

Two other areas of everyday life appeared in District Court over this time period. Drug and alcohol violations increased from a trickle in the early years to a major concern by the end of the century, largely targeting Chinese immigrants until they became fully integrated into the commercial and retail structure of the town.[6] Many of the offenses were selling liquor and opium without a license, manufacturing alcoholic beverages, and selling liquor to Native Hawaiians. Licenses to sell were expensive. These offenses reflected both state attempts to control the sale of alcohol and reformist concerns about the consumption of alcohol by Native Hawaiians. The Chinese are overrepresented in this defendant pool.[7] These statistics both reflected and produced public concern about Chinese alcohol and opium consumption. They took the public narrative about dangerous foreigners and retold it in the factual language of crime rates. But by 1903 the Chinese had disappeared as defendants in drug and alcohol violations (see chart 6.3).[8]

Gambling was part of the everyday practices of many immigrants and Hawaiians but was increasingly criminalized. Gambling was popular and well organized on the plantations. On Saturday following pay day, women and professional gamblers came to the camps. Some Chinese gamblers traveled from plantation to plantation, sometimes gambling all night and keeping laborers from work (Takaki 1989: 160–161). Cockfighting and gambling was a popular combination on the plantations. Although only 6 percent of all charges over the entire period concerned gambling, these offenses became more important by century's end and increasingly targeted Japanese.[9] Violence, on the other hand, remained a steady proportion of the caseload, 12 percent overall but varying slightly over time.[10] The small haole population was charged with criminal offenses well out of proportion to its numbers until the 1890s, particularly for violence.[11] Some violence cases were men assaulting women, usually their wives.

The object of court attention was always predominantly male. Women were a small fraction of all defendants and, as chart 6.4 indicates, were in court largely for offenses of sexual conduct such as adultery and fornication. Clearly, the major threat posed by women was their sexual activity and resistance to marriage, whereas men were far more dangerous—threatening because of their violence, drugs, and violation of contract labor obligations.[12]

By the end of the century the courts were handling primarily newcomers who could not speak Hawaiian or English. There are many more interpreters

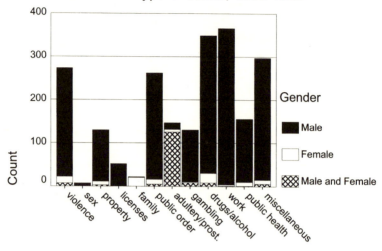

Type of Crime Categorized

Number = 2325

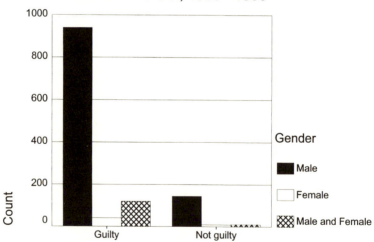

Verdict

Number = 2325

Chart 6.4. Gender, Type of Crime, and Verdict, Hilo District Court, 1853–1903

in court by century's end than at midcentury. Court records from 1853, 1863, and 1873 make little or no mention of interpreters. Most of the District Court judges could speak Hawaiian and English, and apparently these languages were adequate for the defendant population. In 1883, however, 22 cases (6 percent) had interpreters: 7 Portuguese, 19 Chinese, and 1 unknown. In 1893, 234 cases (73 percent) had interpreters: 162 Japanese, 51 Chinese, 19 Portuguese, 1 Hawaiian, and 1 English. The same names reappear frequently. It is likely that the interpreters played a critical and powerful role in helping newcomers navigate the legal system and translating its demands and requirements. Almeida Hitchcock, practicing law in the 1890s, commented that it was hard to try cases because Hawaiians, Chinese, Japanese, and Portuguese were on trial and interpreters never put a question exactly as asked (Humme 1986: 146). The merchant Goto was probably murdered partly because of his outspoken defense in court of Japanese workers (Okhiro 1991: 35).

Hilo Judges and Their Social Context

Who were the judges and how were they related to the defendants in these cases? Both District Court and Circuit Court justices came from a small, predominantly haole elite with close connections to one another through social life and marriage. Most owned plantations and worked as attorneys in addition to their judicial duties, which were not full-time until the end of the century. Many were politically active, serving in the House of Representatives. They also had close ties to the missionary community through descent, marriage, or training. Virtually all were long-term residents of Hilo. According to an 1891 map of Hilo, all owned substantial house lots and houses in town. All were Christian and belonged to the Haili Church, formerly called the "foreign" church, housed in a wood-frame building reminiscent of Vermont churches. They represented "respectable" Hilo society, predominantly haole but including a few mission-educated Native Hawaiian and Hawaiian-Chinese families.

Not all haoles in Hilo belonged to this social class. Throughout this period a substantial population of haole men in Hilo lived a drunken, violent style of life that brought them to the attention of the courts. Many had deserted from whaleships or merchant ships over the years or had drifted west following the frontier. Based on the court records, it appears that they frequently married or lived with Hawaiian women. Similarly, the Chinese community was divided by social class, principally between those Chinese residents who had arrived before 1850 and established early sugar plantations and mercantile establishments (Kai 1974) and the plantation workers imported after 1852. The early group merged with the Native Hawaiian and haole elite, acquiring Hawaiianized Chinese names such as Hapai, Aiko, and Akina and marrying Native Hawaiian women, sometimes of chiefly rank (Kai 1974: 42). Many were prominent merchants and sugar planters. Native Hawaiians retained their emphasis on rank throughout this period as well, drawing important distinctions between ali'i and maka'āinana as well as between Christian, educated Hawaiians living a European style of life and the rural poor living in thatched houses.

The 1840s and 1850s

One of the first magistrates in Hilo, and the first to leave written documents about his experiences as magistrate, was Benjamin Pitman, a trader and merchant from Salem, Massachusetts, who ran a ship chandlery in Hilo.[13] He is mentioned in Reynolds's journal as a trading partner with French in 1826 and 1828 (King 1989). Sometime in the 1830s he settled in Hilo, married a high-ranking Hawaiian woman, and acquired access to a substantial amount of land behind the town. His wife, Chiefess Kino'ole-o-Liliha, had lands extending all over 'Ōla'a and around Hilo (Pitman 1931, quoted from *Honolulu Star-Bulletin*, January 30, 1917: 18–19). Her father was the high chief Ho'olulu, an uncle of the first Kamehameha. At the time of her marriage to Pitman, Kamehameha III gave her the use of the ahupua'a of Hilo. In 1846 Pitman wrote to Kamehameha III asking permission to purchase several pieces of land (Kelly, Nakamura, and Barrere 1981: 85). At some point Stephen Reynolds became Pitman's partner in ownership of these lands and in 1859, when Reynolds died, Pitman purchased his half-interest in the estate and became sole owner of 354 ⅕ acres in Ponahawai and 367 ⅝ in Pu'u'eo, adjacent to Hilo (Kelly, Nakamura, and Barrere 1981: 85). Pitman leased some of this land to Aiko for a plantation. By 1857 Aiko is also reported to be working another plantation owned by a Chinese merchant of Honolulu (Kelly, Nakamura, and Barrere 1981: 82). Pitman built a house in Honolulu and left Hilo about 1860, but his wife died soon after and he returned to Boston with his son (Pitman 1931). A letter from D. H. Hitchcock in Hilo to his brother on January 1, 1861, reports: "Pitman has sold out, Tom Spencer is now our man here. Glad old P. is going. Others can do something now I hope." Hitchcock, who was later a judge in Hilo, had apparently borrowed money from Pitman and planned to borrow four hundred dollars from Austin to repay Pitman before he left.[14]

An English traveler visiting Hilo in 1849 described Pitman as the major figure in town (Hill 1856). Hill described the town as a missionary station, both Protestant and "Romish," with one of the best Protestant schools in the islands. Beyond that, he said it had thirty to forty scattered huts, a Protestant church, a small "Romish" chapel, the dwellings of the missionaries, a

2. Benjamin Pitman, about 1864. Courtesy of the Lyman House Memorial Museum Photo Collection.

schoolhouse, and several houses belonging to Mr. Pitman, "by whom all the proper commerce of the place is carried on" (Hill 1856: 292). Titus Coan lived in a neat house with a garden enclosed by a railing and a wicker gate (Hill 1856: 294). He described Mrs. Pitman as a very reserved and amiable Native lady. The Pitmans served him an American breakfast. Pitman had a sugar plantation and a coffee plantation with twenty-two thousand coffee trees on it (Hill 1856: 317). On a visit to Pitman's sugar plantation, Hill reported that the Chinese lease it and two Chinese supervise the boiling house while Native Hawaiians do the cutting in the field and feed the mill. Pitman told him that Chinese are better laborers than Natives and good as overseers. Already the discourse linking nationality with labor characteristics was well entrenched, but by the end of the century it acquired hegemonic status.[15]

William Lee said in 1852 that Pitman was very prosperous and had the whole business of Hilo in his hands (Letter to Joel Turrill, March 24, 1852; Turrill Collection 1957: 54–56). In 1857 he still owned one of the five stores in town (Kai 1974: 61). Henry Sheldon's account of Hilo in 1846 reiterated that the principle personage of the place was an American, Benjamin Pitman, a "dealer in ship chandlery, general merchandise and Island produce," married to a Native woman belonging to a chiefly family of secondary rank, "which gave him a sort of prestige among the natives." He kept open house for the whaling masters who got supplies through him.[16] In addition to serving as the white magistrate of Hilo, Pitman held several other government posts such as notary public and collector of customs (Hill 1856: 315). During this period, when wealth was generated largely by trade with whaling ships, Pitman was clearly a leading merchant who used his profits to invest in the fledgling sugar and coffee industry.

In his letters to government officials in the 1840s Pitman constantly complained about lax Native judges and the poor enforcement of the laws as he tried to deal with deserting seamen and rum smugglers. He had reluctantly taken on the post of magistrate and expressed frustration with the way justice was administered by the Hawaiian judges. In November 1844 he wrote to Judd, then minister of finance, saying that nothing had happened of importance

> except the recall of Puuloa our Native Judge to answer to our appeal against him before the Supreme Judges, the first intimation he got of it. . . .
>
> All I can say of him as an individual is that he tries to do the best he can but that comes far short of the Duty which devolves on him.
>
> At the request of the Governor I have combined the two offices of judges under one head for the present until Puuloa returns and shall endeavor to be guided strictly by the letter of the law but not to be rigid or over Bearing (or as Natives say Aole Hookaumalia wale, aole hoohewa wale).
>
> Since writing you in reference to the men discharged from Ship Milo, I have received a letter from His Excellency the Gov. to say I must forward them to Oahu and not allow others to stop [hole in page] grant a permit upon any condition. I cannot sense his meaning he having himself when on a visit to this Place granted permission to some of *Runaways* to reside permanently here, they paying him in Lumber once singly the amount of 60$ [*sic*] giving them in some instances 6 months others their own time to Pay without a probability of ever receiving anything from any of them.[17]

On April 6, 1845, Pitman wrote to Judd, still minister of finance, complaining about Hawaiian forms of punishment and lax enforcement:[18]

> "I find that his Excellency Gov. Pitt invariably in his communications addresses me as though I was still acting as Judge, at which I am somewhat surprised, having written both to him and likewise to you on the subject, a recapitulation is therefore unnecessary. I only took the Appointment for six months, and though I continued to act much longer, still I do not consider myself entitled to act as head in the department, nothing definite having been arranged to warrant my

doing so. . . . I wish to draw your attention to two circumstances which have come to my knowledge, through the information of Foreigners of whose veracity I have no reasons to doubt. The first is in regard to the Treatment of Prisoners (Native) a mode of Punishment is adopted which carries ones mind back to the horrors of the Spanish Inquisition; which from being diametrically in opposition of the mildness and spirit of the laws of the land as well as humanity can scarcely be credited. This punishment is not confined to any one particular crime but inflicted at the will or pleasure of the Jailor, as interest, or anger may at the time predominate. . . .[19] The other case is that the Constables are prohibited from searching or going to certain houses which are known to be the resort of the sailors for indecent purposes, because what ever is received for prostitution one half goes to the luna.

In a letter on June 29, 1845, to Judd, Pitman continued to complain about his judicial responsibilities and lax enforcement: "I trust his Excellency the Gov. will soon return and relieve me from my charge as Luna. I have got in my new store. I find I must necessarily interfere with the other business. Our Native Judges are getting somewhat *lukewarm* [underline in original] and want his Ex.'s advice."[20]

Pitman also complained about the problem of managing deserters and the problem of deserters who stay on shore. After noting that forty-seven whale ships stopped in this spring, in a letter on September 19, 1845, to Judd, Pitman complained about the disregard of instructions to keep foreign seamen from stopping on shore by the government officers empowered to issue such permits:

I have stated to Puuloa and Kaiwi [judges] and laid before them your and the Gov's express instructions not to permit foreigners to stop on shore. Letting both which they have this day granted permit to H. Tahila Martins and two foreigners. [unclear in original] I have just seen one of the permits and I do not see how it will be possible to restrict them from a permanent residence. They tell me he is to leave in some vessel but have no writing from him to that effect.

* We may expect an influx of foreigners if the luna [judges] are not restrictive in their permits.

On November 26, 1845, Pitman again writes to Judd about the ambiguity of his position as magistrate.[21] He says he has received a commission from His Excellency but it is very indefinitely worded (he provides the Hawaiian text "a e hoopauia oia e au i kou wa e manao ai e hoopauia ia ia"), which means to him that he is to do the duty to the best of his abilities but may at any time be superseded.

[H]owever either He [His Excellency] or someone having power or authority to enforce the laws are very, very much wanted here indeed, the most barefaced acts of iniquity, the most flagrant breaches of the laws are dayly and hourly commited [*sic*], without any punishment being inflicted or penalty awarded, and that in the open face of day in the precense [*sic*] of constables and natives.—In fact the scenes of immorality that have latterly occurred far surpass the olden times. The Captains and Officers are shocked and cry shame on it and we the residents have never seen any thing to equal it; in reality we are living as though there were no laws, every one following the bent of his or her own evil inclinations.

On February 20, 1846, Pitman writes to Judd to complain about the appointment of Peter Jordan as chief constable. The text of the letter is revealing of the tensions surrounding the law in this small community. Pitman writes that a transaction has caused surprise and indignation to every foreigner in Hilo, among the residents and subjects of His Majesty and also the captains and officers now in the port—the appointment of "Peter Jordan the Black-man (he who by lying to you surreptitiously procured himself to be enrolled an Hawaiian subject, and who on his return boasted of his cunning) has been at the instigation of Mr. Coan appointed a High Constable of Hilo!" Jordan got on a ship to beg, Pitman says, and, discovering women, threatened to reveal it unless he got a bribe. Getting none, he told Mr. Coan. His version of the case is that Mr. Coan, Puʻuloa, and Kaiwi made him high constable. But, Pitman goes on, Mr. Coan wrote a short time since to Mr. Paris (another missionary) that Peter Jordan is the greatest scoundrel on earth. Indeed, Pitman says, the man is

> a cunning, artfull, and deceiving liar, and common report brands him as a thief. Is such a man fit to hold so high an office? The general opinion of all here is in the negative. I know of several Natives, who would do credit to the Office, men who would do their duty conscientiously and with fidelity, but unfortunately for the community they are neither friends or relatives of those who are the rulers consequently cannot partake of the loaves and fishes. Had my opinion on the subject have been asked I should have said, I do not think you could have found in all Hilo a man in every way incapacitated [illegible] for the Office from the very worthlessness of his character.

He goes on to bemoan further the state of lawlessness in Hilo:

> My object in common with the foreign community is to pray that you would be pleased to use the power delegated in you, for the removal of so offensive and obnoxious a man from a situation which may at any time bring him in collision with us. But alas! this is only one of many evils we suffer from the maladministration of the laws. We have long hoped that something would be done for Hilo, some one appointed who would administer Justice, and enforce obedience to the Laws. We are virtually without Governor, without Judge, without Law, but to enumerate all or half of the evils we suffer would be encroaching on your

more valuable time, but I do sincerely hope you will take these things into your
ernest consideration.

He urges that the governor take up residence in Hilo.

In 1846 he begins to talk about the need for a prison and the lack of
materials to build it. He is clearly having great difficulty dealing with deserters from the now numerous whaleships. In a letter to Judd on March 5,
1846, he says there are now seven deserters somewhere in the woods and as
soon as their ships leave, they will come and either be sent to the prison

> to increase the difficulty already existing there; or be let loose on the community.
> it requires great exertion to keep what are there now in [hole in paper] and as
> their numbers increase, so of course will the difficulty; the other Evening a very
> serious tumult occurred and nothing but the most strenuous exertions, were able
> to subdue it. At the present rate of increase the prisoners will soon outnumber
> the foreign population, and I tremble for the result, for we have not an efficient
> police like Honolulu able to restrain them if they should rise and break out, and
> these are not idle fears, as the late attempt amply proves; they are a most noto-
> rious bad set and are so well known as such by the whaling captains that though
> in want of men, will not ship them. There is a most desperate fellow now se-
> creted somewhere whose captain is afraid of him, he never came on shore on
> liberty without a brace of pistols, and when his ship sails which will be in a day
> or two he comes out, is sent probably to the prison, and in all likelihood be the
> instigator of mischief. What must be done? I am something at a loss to know
> perhaps it would be best for the Government to send up a Vessel for them and
> deliver them over to their respective Consuls. Trusting however you will see the
> case in the light of a great evil, that requires prompt, speedy, and energetic
> measures to counteract its effects; and praying you may give it your very earliest
> attention is the sincere wish of your humble servant.[22]

In these stories, Pitman chronicles the creation of a poor white community.

Through the 1840s and 1850s Pitman appears frequently in the records of
the state archives distributing licenses for bowling alleys, victualling houses,
retail sales outlets, and auctions and performing a variety of other government tasks such as serving as notary public and issuing marriage licenses.
The names of individuals receiving business licenses suggest that at this time
there was a substantial group of Chinese merchants in town with Hawai-
anized names as well as a group of haole merchants. In 1846 Pitman was
responsible for distributing and selling 375 copies of the New Laws in Hawaiian, to be sold for one dollar each and given free to the five tax officers,
including Kaiwi, and the six judges, including Pu'uloa.[23] He continues to
distribute and sell law books in 1847, 1848, and 1852.

In 1852 Judd writes to Pitman asking for his assessment of native character. Although Pitman's letter has not been preserved, Wyllie writes this com-

ment back to Pitman, May 7, 1852, after receiving Pitman's letter from Mr. Judd in the House of Nobles:[24]

> The judgment you have formed of the native character corresponds very closely with that which may be gathered from the Missionary replies to my 116 queries of the 9th May 1846 [discussed in Part One as Kingdom of Hawai'i 1846]. The defects in that character, in my opinion can never be removed unless by the constant presence of a respectable clergy in all parts of the Islands, giving the natives precepts upon precept—line upon line, here a little and there a little, and above all affording them a never failing example of practical virtue and christian morality.

Thus, Pitman shares with the missionaries the view that the Hawaiian people are flawed in character and require firm discipline. The original notion that the Hawaiians were heathens who could be converted had declined by the 1840s. Instead, the haole residents concluded that the Hawaiians' failure to become New Englanders was due to inadequate character, thus reinterpreting cultural difference and practices of resistance as natural traits. From this position it was a short step to conceptualizing difference in terms of biology. In the 1840s many whites still thought that the Native Hawaiians could be reformed through stern example and insistence on discipline, but by century's end this mutability of character was submerged in the biological notion of race. The courts similarly lost some of their concern with reforming Hawaiian character and social life and devoted greater attention to labor control and public order on the streets.

The correspondence from Pitman reveals the cultural framework through which he carried out his work of judging and supervising Hawaiian judges. As the nation changed to secular law in the second transition, it was people such as Pitman who guided the development of local judicial practices. Pitman's constant complaints about the lax enforcement of laws and the lack of firmness of the magistrates and constables reveals his efforts to shape local practices. Over time, his comments and those of many others produced conceptions of Hawaiian incompetence and childlikeness and served to justify white supremacy, the political consequences of which became clear in 1893.

A letter written by a Native judge complaining about Pitman provides a different perspective on his "firmness" and "discipline." In 1848 John Hoaai was appointed district judge by the governor.[25] In the same year, he wrote to the minister of the interior, Keoni Ana, complaining that he was being oppressed by B. Pitman "through my having punished the men of his land by law. B. Pitman got very angry with me, and he has abused me on account of the law under which I passed the sentence."[26] Hoaai described the incident as follows: Three Natives on their way to cut wood drove a cart pulled by eight oxen through a taro field. They were ordered by "the Chinaman" to pay one dollar for damages if they found it difficult for the cart to pass, but the man

JUDGES AND CASELOADS IN HILO

who owned the field said he would only accept one dollar and a half. They would not go above one dollar, so they pulled the oxen right through the middle of the taro field on the way up the mountain and again on the way down. As judge, Hoaai heard the case and fined each Native one hundred dollars. So "Pikimana [Pitman's Hawaiian name] is against me. Therefore, I am troubled through this bad treatment by B. Pikimana, that I was a trouble-making Judge, very ignorant, that it was not right for children to be judges, it is not this way in my country." Pitman wanted the judge to reduce the fine.

This letter reveals the uncertainty facing Hawaiians in administering the new legal system and their vulnerability to haoles who claimed to understand it better. Clearly, Pitman expected that the letter of the law was to give way to the realities of local power, and the Hawaiians were expected to understand this slippage. Pitman asserted that things were done differently in "my country." New England, not Hawai'i, established the practices of the local courts, just as it provided the ancestors referred to by William Lee in his speech in 1852.

By 1853, however, another haole was responsible for the District Court, by then a police court, in Hilo. S. L. Austin left New York on a whaling ship in 1849 with his brother, but was forced by rheumatism to stay in Honolulu. He was born in Buffalo, New York, in 1825. Both of his brothers came to Hawai'i also: one became an associate justice on the Hawai'i Supreme Court and the other a minister of foreign affairs from 1888 to 1890 and the manager and owner of a plantation near Hilo from 1877 to 1887 (*The Friend*: [1896]; Severance Scrapbook, p. 135, "Death of Jona. Austin"). Dr. Lathrop in Honolulu referred Austin to his friend Benjamin Pitman and he worked briefly for Pitman as a clerk in a branch store.[27] After failing to make money in an Irish potato plantation, Austin was appointed police magistrate for Hilo in 1853. He had studied law and been admitted to the bar in Buffalo, according to his lifelong friend Charles Wetmore, and in 1852 he was admitted to practice law in Hawai'i by the Supreme Court.[28] He was also appointed secretary for the governess of Hawai'i Island, Ruth Ke'elikōlani.[29] He was promoted to Circuit Court judge of the Third Circuit in 1855 and appointed to the Kohala Circuit in 1887.[30]

Austin married Mary Clark, a daughter of the missionary Ephriam Clark, who came from New England in 1828. Her sister Lucinda married another Hilo notable, Luther Severance. Austin started one of the earliest sugar plantations, the Onomea Sugar Plantation, seven miles north of Hilo, about 1861, but lost it to another company in 1898, a loss that, according to his wife, broke his heart. Thus, Austin brought to his varied and extensive legal activities in Hawai'i the experience of practicing law in New York and the cultural understandings of New England. He became part of the elite haole social world of Hilo, intimately connected with the missionary community, and remained so until his death. His first interest and concern throughout his life was his sugar plantation. In the District Court of 1853, the first year for which the records are preserved in the Hawai'i State Archives, 79 percent of the defendants were Hawaiians (see chart 6.3). The small number of haole defendants (nineteen) were mostly in court for violence (37 percent). At this time, there were only four Chinese defendants and no Japanese or Portuguese, reflecting the social composition of the town, which was largely Hawaiian and haole. D. H. Hitchcock, in his reminiscences of his arrival in Hilo, says that when he got there in 1857 there were about fifteen hundred Natives and fifteen hundred others living in town (Leithhead 1974; Kelly, Nakamura, and Barrere 1981: 93).[31] The population of Hilo declined between 1853 and 1876 as the Hawaiian population continued to plummet, increasing only with the importation of labor after the Reciprocity Treaty. The haole population remained very small during this period (see chart 5.1).

S. L. Austin's caseload focused on the moral character of the Hawaiians and the control and discipline of the growing population of haole deserters and sailors. Almost a third of the cases were charges of adultery (32 percent) and almost one fifth assault and battery (18 percent). Fornication (7 percent), larceny (7 percent), drunkenness (5 percent), and common nuisance (4 percent) were the other more common offenses, and two people (2 percent) were accused of gambling. Appendix A includes four representative cases from 1853 concerning adultery, assault, selling liquor (2 percent of all cases), and drunkenness. Case 1853.1 shows the central importance of the church in monitoring and enforcing adultery cases. Case 1853.2 concerns violence between workers and lunas (bosses) in the plantation context and underscores the extent to which ethnic differences organized these conflicts. Cases 1853.3 and 1853.4 reflect the reformist concern to limit drinking by Native Hawaiians. In Case 1853.3, the court determines whether a particular brew is intoxicating or not. These cases reveal the continuing importance of the social reformist thrust of the court as it prosecutes moral offenses such as drinking and adultery. They also provide a glimpse into the nonrespectable part of Hilo society in which haoles, Hawaiians, and Chinese together participate in drinking and sexual adventures disapproved of by the haole elite. There are a few cases of serious and repeated beating of women by their husbands, often haoles or Hawaiian-haole mixes. And the cases between workers and employers indicate that violence was fundamental to this relationship in the earliest plantations.

It is not clear whether S. L. Austin spoke or understood Hawaiian at this time, but he clearly came from a very different cultural background than that of the people he supervised in court. Like Pitman, he brought understandings of legal practices from New England. Although not himself a missionary, through his wife he became part of the reformist missionary tradition in Hawai'i, which included a paternalistic concern for the moral character of the Hawaiian people and a firm belief in the moral value of industry and thrift. Like the other judges of this early period, he did not rely on his judicial role to support himself but moved early into the sugar plantation business.

Thus, as the new courts developed ways of handling cases and determining which offenses were serious and which were not, the guiding hands in Hilo applied principles and practices from New England legal practice strongly influenced by moral reformist issues such as temperance and the control of extramarital sexuality. There was far less interest in appreciating and preserving the cultural practices of the Hawaiian people. As the case records show, the courts worked closely with the churches and considered spying a reasonable strategy for apprehending wrongdoers.

The 1860s

Austin was followed briefly as District Court judge by two other haoles, R. K. Chamberlayne and L. McCully, but the next judge to hold the office for any period of time was D. H. Hitchcock. Hitchcock was the son of missionaries who had come from Massachusetts in 1831 and settled on the island of Moloka'i. He was born in Honolulu in 1832 and served as a justice of the police court in Hilo from 1857 until 1877.[32] He was named to the job at the suggestion of a missionary, Armstrong, who proposed him to Austin, at the time still clerk to the governess of Hawai'i Island, Ruth Ke'elikōlani.[33] Thus, a missionary/government network determined who staffed the new legal institutions and who developed their practices, particularly in port towns where judicial officials had to deal with foreigners.

D. H. Hitchcock grew up in Hawai'i and attended Williams College, as did his father, who graduated in 1828. He left Williams in 1853 and returned to Hawai'i, writing back to New York to bring a woman he met there to be his wife. He considered himself an Anglo-Hawaiian and spoke sufficiently good Hawaiian to work as a translator for the Circuit Court in 1857 at five dollars per day.[34] When he arrived in Hilo in 1857 to serve as police justice, Judge and Mrs. S. L. Austin took David and his new wife into their house and helped them to rent a grass house, which they inhabited until David was able to buy land from Chiefess Kapi'olani and build himself a frame house (Humme 1986).[35] Hitchcock describes Hilo at the time of his arrival in 1857 as a very small town with only thatch houses except for the lumber houses of foreigners.[36] The only foreign families living in Hilo were Fathers Lyman and Coan, Dr. Wetmore, Capt. Worth, Mr. Austin, and an employee of Mr. Pitman who lived in the old hotel buildings and was married to a Native woman. Governess Ruth lived in a fine large grass house. Mr. Coney, the sheriff, the American consul, Miller, who had an office on a lot between Worth's store and Pitman's; W. H. Reed; Mr. Rose; Mr. "Jimmy" Mill; Mr.

3. Hitchcock family group, 1896. Courtesy of the Lyman House Memorial Museum Photo Collection.

Chamberlayne; a "little Frenchman" by the name of Louis Paire, who lived at Wainaku and "who was the only white attorney in the place"; Mr. Charles E. Richardson and Mr. Williams, who were building the Haili Native church; and Father Pouzot, or Kalolo as he was generally called, constituted the rest of the small foreign population, in Hitchcock's reminiscences.[37]

There were very few "Chinamen," according to Hitchcock, but prominent among them were Hapai, John Ena, Aiko, and Akau. Hapai and Aiko had stores on Front St., along with three foreign stores: Pitman's, Worth's, and Mill's. (Of these families, Hapai and Aiko were both Roman Catholics since their Hawaiian wives had converted in 1841, while another prominent Hawaiian-Chinese family, the A'ii, were Protestant [Kai 1976: 13].) There were three plantations running or started soon after his arrival, all belonging to "Chinamen": 'Amauulu belonging to Ah Sing, Pauka'a belonging to Akau, and Pāpai'kou belonging to Aiko. The new Native church as well as the Roman Catholic church was always well filled. The 1850s were the high point of whaling ship arrivals, with as many as thirty a season, but by the late 1860s the whaling fleet had left Hilo. At that time the town was dead for business, in Hitchcock's view, since not one of the sugar plantations was paying and expenses were heavy with little sugar to export. For the next fifteen years, he says, only Native labor was used and that was all that was wanted. Wages were low at four dollars per month with food and lodgings, increasing to eleven dollars per month by the 1880s. The wages for women who worked as house servants was one dollar a week and board. The staple, preserved poi or pa'i 'ai, was selling at forty pounds for twenty-five cents, more than one man would consume in a week. In comparison to these wages and prices, the fine for adultery of thirty dollars for the man and thirty dollars for the woman was extremely high and well beyond the ability of most to pay.

Thus, this was a small town with little business or cash available except through the twice-yearly visit of the whaling fleet. In David Hitchcock's letters to his brothers in 1857 and 1858, he worries constantly about his lack of cash and his debts and his desire for more cases. At one point he hopes Circuit Court judge Austin will step down and allow him to take the generous salary.[38] He has apparently little to do as District Court judge. His wife refers to his work in 1857 as taking usually not more than two hours, and seldom more than four hours a day.[39] In 1857 he says he has a commission as "Attorney at Law" for the Hawaiian kingdom and will handle cases at the Supreme Court, mostly divorce cases for which he will earn from six dollars to ten dollars per capita as fee (ibid). In 1858 he describes teaching law school in the daytime for two days a week, which he says is a good thing, earning him eight dollars per week.[40] He writes his brother that this is hard work because: "You know how hard it is to teach kanakas." In 1858, in his first stint in the House of Representatives, he writes, "The kanakas are a lazy set and want to make the business as long as possible so as to get their $3 per day."[41]

Thus, in his private letters to his family, Hitchcock expresses the kind of paternalistic disdain toward the Hawaiian people common to missionary descendants who grew up in Hawai'i suffused by the white conceptions of Hawaiian "character" and intelligence that were developing in the 1830s and 1840s. At the same time, his letters to his brother stretching from 1857 to 1894 reveal a continuing preoccupation with business and making money.[42] He sold butter and milk, taught school, and had a butchering business in the 1850s, harvested wood and designed ditches to get it to the sea in the 1860s, worked in the sugar business in the 1870s and 1880s, and planted two thousand coffee trees in 1894. His letters indicate a detailed and careful interest in his expenses and income, with considerable concern about indebtedness and paying it off, especially in the early years. His own ideas of moral virtue clearly include working hard, trying out new ideas, turning a profit, and avoiding indebtedness.

David Hitchcock began to work in sugar in 1862. In 1876, in partner-

4. Harvey Rexford Hitchcock (*left*), Edward Griffin Hitchcock (*middle*) and Edward Northrup Hitchcock (*right*) at Pohakuloa, Ola'a, May 31, 1903. (The first two are D. H. Hitchcock's brothers, the third probably a nephew.) Courtesy of the Lyman House Memorial Museum Photo Collection.

ship with his brother E. G. Hitchcock and Charles Wetmore, he started the Pāpa'ikou Sugar Plantation.[43] In 1884 their plantation, represented by Castle and Cooke, the firm of E. G.'s father-in-law, had two thousand acres of cane land, 205 men employed at mill and plantation, nine miles of fluming, and a dependent population of six hundred men, women, and children.[44] At this time, Edward G. Hitchcock lived at Pāpa'ikou, presumably as manager, and H. Rexford (D. H. and E. G.'s brother) was head overseer. E. G. also had a house in Hilo, according to an 1891 map. In about 1881 D. H. returned to his law practice. He served in the House of Representatives from 1859 to

1884 and in the House of Nobles in 1887–1888 and was a member of the Constitutional Convention of 1894, helping to frame the constitution for the Republic of Hawaii after the overthrow (*Advertiser* 1900). His brother E. G. was marshal of the republic in 1893, just after the overthrow.

According to his letters to his brother E. G., D. H. was delighted with the 1887 change in government, which he viewed as a reform, but by the 1890s began to feel ignored and excluded by the planter community, who passed him over for a desired government post, despite his years of service to the government, in favor of Rufus Lyman, another missionary descendant.[45] Rufus was married into the Hawaiian-Chinese community of Hilo, the son-in-law of Ahung, a Chinese merchant. He worked for some time on Austin's Onomea plantation as an assistant overseer (Martin et al. 1979: 177, 144). D.H. writes bitterly that he does not understand why the Lymans have such pull with the government and complains that Lyman has not helped the government as he has, but they are friendly to the planters. In 1894 he complains that the planter crowd runs things now without opposition and it doesn't pay to buck them.[46] Earlier letters make references to differences with Luther Severance and John Scott, a prominent plantation manager. It appears that Hitchcock was no longer one with the planters, but was part of a group losing power in the face of increasing control by "factors," or agents linked to large financial interests on the mainland, as the plantation industry became increasingly centralized.

D. H. Hitchcock's daughter became the first woman attorney in Hawaiʻi after receiving a legal education at the University of Michigan in 1886 (Humme 1986: 142; Case 1992). She practiced law in Hilo with her father in the 1890s and appears frequently in the 1893 case records. In general, the missionary community sought to continue their close ties to the United States by sending their children there for an education, as they did with Almeida, a third-generation Anglo-Hawaiian.[47] D. H. Hitchcock died in 1900 (*The Friend*, 58: no. 1, [January 1900]: 6).

D. H.'s brother, E. G. Hitchcock, was primarily a plantation manager but also worked as a lawyer, sheriff, and judge. He was sheriff of the island of Hawaiʻi from 1887 until 1893, then served as marshal of the republic in 1893, and again served as sheriff of Hawaiʻi until he was appointed Circuit Court judge in 1896 at the death of S. L. Austin, a position he held until his own death in 1898.[48] It is not unusual to find a court case in which D. H. was judge and E. G. was an attorney. Born in 1837 in Hawaiʻi, E. G. was educated at Oahu College and in New York state, and in 1862 married the daughter of S. N. Castle, a prominent businessman in Hawaiʻi. In 1866 he moved to Hilo and in 1869 took charge of the Kaiwiki Sugar Plantation, a small plantation just north of Hilo with 65.5 acres planted in cane, which he managed until 1887.[49] At his death in 1898 he had accumulated considerable property in Hilo and other parts of the islands.[50] His obituary in the 1898

5. Residence of Mrs. E. G. Hitchcock and family, 1901. Courtesy of the Lyman House Memorial Museum Photo Collection.

Hawaiian Gazette reflects the typical paternalistic concern coupled with infantilization and a desire to protect subordinates' rights found in haole elites' understanding of Native Hawaiians at the time: "No man knew the native better than Judge Hitchcock and no man was more jealous of their rights than he. He tried his best to guide them as he thought for their benefit. To see one of them go astray pained him."[51]

In 1863, with D. H. Hitchcock as magistrate, there were 129 Hawaiian defendants in comparison to 98 ten years earlier. This increase occurred despite the rapid decline of the Hawaiian population and of the population of Hilo itself. Hawaiians were still 94 percent of all defendants; only four were haoles and two Chinese. Among the Hawaiian defendants, one quarter of the offenses still concerned adultery, fornication, and other sexual matters (28 percent). Overall, adultery was still 28 percent of the caseload (38 cases, compared to 39 ten years earlier) but assault fell to 9 percent and drunkenness to one case (1 percent). The new cases were desertion of service, 30 cases, or 22 percent of all cases, as Hawaiians became more involved in the expanding plantation economy. Case 1863.1 in appendix A is a suit for damages for criminal connection with a man's wife, demonstrating that the courts were used to fight over rights to women between absent Hawaiian sailors and the Chinese sugar masters. On his return after four years, the sailor sued for damages for his wife, but the court awarded him only five dollars instead of the one hundred dollars he sought. In the competition for women, the more affluent Chinese husband kept his Hawaiian wife.

Twenty-three percent of the cases with Hawaiian defendants were work offenses under the Masters and Servants law as plantations slowly developed and Hawaiians became the major source of laborers. The texts of these cases indicate that Hawaiians refused to work if the fish was not adequate (Case 1863.2) or if they had some other obligation on their time, but they were then taken to court. They also demanded higher pay. The planters interpreted the Hawaiians as lazy, indolent, and undesirable workers (Beechert 1985: 36). Although Hawaiians had worked hard on kalo fields under the chiefly system, they resisted the rigorous time discipline and continuous, grueling work required of capitalist wage labor. In case 1863.3, a worker complained about the treatment he received from his boss, charging him with grabbing him and tearing his shirt. Finding no injury, however, the court failed to convict. In this case, the worker is Chinese and the luna is haole, judging from his name. Case 1863.4, heard on the same day, suggests retaliation against the worker for this use of the court, since both the plaintiff from the previous case and his supporting witness are accused of deserting work and ordered to return to work and required to pay court costs of two dollars each. It appears that this attempt by workers to use the courts to challenge the violence of their lunas failed. D. H. Hitchcock supported the luna rather than the workers. None of the cases in appendix A for 1863 had attorneys, and attorneys were generally rare in the courts at this time.

The 1870s

By the mid 1870s, Hilo was still a small, homogenous town dominated by Christian missionary families, especially Lyman, Coan, Severance, and Wetmore. The plantations were relatively small, locally owned by Austin and Hitchcock and perhaps still by Ah Sing or Aiko, although the Chinese merchant/sugar masters gradually lost control of the plantations in this period. They relied primarily on Native Hawaiian laborers with a few Chinese workers. Society consisted of the white elites, the Hawaiian governor and other ali'i, commoner Hawaiians, and whites whom the elites considered disreputable because of their drinking and failure to work. There was class stratification within the white community as well as within the Hawaiian. The transformation of Hilo into a far more diverse place did not take place until the 1880s. Nevertheless, the caseload almost doubled from 138 in 1863 to 240 in 1873.

In 1873 D. H. Hitchcock was still the judge in the District Court. S. L. Austin occasionally appeared as judge and E. G. Hitchcock fairly often as an attorney (see Case 1873.1 and Case 1873.5 in appendix A). As the cases in appendix A indicate, all three were sometimes involved in the same case, one as plaintiff, one as defense attorney, and one as judge. The most frequent type of case was now desertion of work, 39 percent of all cases, followed by collection of debt (8 percent), drunkenness (7 percent), furnishing liquor to Hawaiians (6 percent), assault and battery (6 percent), and gambling (4 percent). Adultery, at ten cases, was a mere 4 percent of the total and the four fornication cases were 2 percent. Apparently reformist attentions had begun to shift from sexuality to liquor while the need for a disciplined labor force came to supersede all other social order demands.

The defendants included sixteen haoles, a disproportionately large number considering their small population. A third were charged with alcohol offenses. Half of the twenty-four Chinese defendants were charged with drug and alcohol violations such as possessing or selling opium or alcohol. The appearance of 193 Hawaiian defendants indicates that the population of Hawaiian defendants continued to expand as the population fell, but now they were in court for work offenses (47 percent) rather than adultery and fornication, reflecting their centrality to the plantation economy at the time. Sexual offenses declined to 7 percent of charges against Native Hawaiians. Eleven percent of the Hawaiians were charged with drug and alcohol offenses. Case 1873.4 illustrates the continuing effort to control alcohol and punish those who furnished liquor to Native Hawaiians, although the defendant was acquitted in this case, perhaps because of contradictory testimony. Case 1873.8 targets a Chinese man who is framed by the police for selling opium without a license, but the evidence is inconclusive and the defendant is acquitted. There is clearly still a strong moral reform quality to the criminal caseload as well as careful attention to evidence. These cases were probably influenced by a law that awarded a part of a fine to the constable who carried out the arrest. Yet, practices of spying continue into the 1880s and 1890s even after the elimination in 1878 of this provision in the law.

The cases in appendix A reveal continuing conflict between bosses and workers, often with strong racial overtones as in Case 1873.2 between a haole luna and a Native Hawaiian worker and the escalation of this conflict into violence in Case 1873.3. Here a worker (Native Hawaiian) takes his luna (haole) to court for assaulting him, and the luna is defended by E. G. Hitchcock. When the luna is convicted and fined ten dollars by D. H. Hitchcock, he appeals to the Circuit Court. The case is heard in front of F. S. Lyman, Rufus's brother and a descendant of the Lyman missionaries, with Severance, Austin's brother-in-law, as prosecutor and E. G. Hitchcock as defense attorney. After detailed testimony by many witnesses, the luna is again found guilty and fined ten dollars. This case reveals considerable Hawaiian/haole conflict at work—this is clearly a long-standing feud—but it also shows that the courts do not always back up the lunas. Here the evidence that an assault took place was clear and unambiguous. The underlying issue was in some ways similar to that between Pitman and Hoaai in the 1848 case: the trespass of cattle on farmland. Case 1873.6 similarly reveals the ethnic cleavages behind plantation conflicts.

In Case 1873.7 debate centers on the definition of work: is it the length of time spent at the field or the number of rows cultivated? The court serves an important function here in redefining work as time rather than task-based, in the testimony of R. A. Lyman, yet the suit is withdrawn by the plaintiff, Austin. Case 1873.9 shows the way the courts were used to discipline violence in the field since the laborer who threatened his boss was sent to prison at hard labor for fifteen days. The courts generally favored the more powerful, but were careful to examine evidence and sometimes acquitted the workers. An important aspect of labor relations of this period is that the workers were largely Christian Hawaiians and the judiciary and attorneys were missionary descendants and relatives who felt paternalistic concern for the Hawaiians and distaste for the ribald white community of this port town. Thus, class relations and religious loyalty cross-cut ethnic boundaries in significant ways.

Isabella Bird, the English travel writer, visited Hilo for several months in 1874 (Bird 1882: 63ff). Her description of the village emphasizes that it was still a small and stable community. The white population, which she says constitutes "society," is very small, including Father Coan, Father Lyman, whose large native congregation is now much shrunk although his church contributes twelve hundred dollars to foreign missions, and two of Father Lyman's sons, who are influential residents, one being the lieutenant governor of the island (Rufus Lyman.) Her host, Luther Severance, a "genial, social, intelligent American, is sheriff of Hawaii, postmaster, &c, and with his charming wife (a missionary's daughter), and some friends who live with them, make their large house a centre of kindliness, friendliness, and hospitality" (Bird 1882: 63). There are some planter's families within seven miles of Hilo who come in to sewing circles, church, and the like. But there is also a lower social class of whites. "There is a small class of reprobate white men who have ostracised themselves by means of drink and bad morals, and are a curse to the natives. The half whites, among whom 'Bill Ragsdale' is the leading spirit, are not very numerous" (ibid.: 63). There are two stores on the beach, and the men congregate there and at the courthouse. Work is light: in the morning hours she sees the governor, sheriff, and judge, with three other gentlemen, playing croquet on the courthouse lawn (ibid.: 65).

There is, she says, a large Native population along the beach and on the heights above the Wailuku river. The governess of Hawaiʻi, Princess Keʻelikōlani, has a house on the beach. The men do whatever hard work is done in cultivating kalo patches and pounding the kalo. She continues, in the dominant discourse of the white elites in this period:

one must not forget that only forty years ago the people inhabiting this strip
of land between the volcanic wilderness and the sea were a vicious, sensual,
shameless herd, that no man among them, except their chiefs, had any rights,

6. Old Courthouse in Hilo, 1863–1913. Built in Bangor, Maine, and shipped around Cape Horn, erected in 1863 and torn down 1932. Courtesy of the Lyman House Memorial Museum Photo Collection.

> that they were harried and oppressed almost to death, and had no consciousness
> of any moral obligations. Now, order and decorum at least prevail. There is not a
> locked door in Hilo, and nobody makes anybody else afraid.
>
> (Bird 1882: 67)

But after 1876 the town of Hilo and its court's business begin to change dramatically as the Reciprocity Treaty and guaranteed access to the U.S. market ushered in the sugar boom. George Washington Akao Hapai served as District Court judge for the last quarter of the century; his name's hybridity reveals his attachment to American missionaries as well as his Hawaiian and Chinese ancestors. He had the longest tenure as District Court justice, serving from 1878 until his death in 1908. He was the son of a Chinese sugar master, Lau Fai or Hapai, who was born in Canton in 1791 and died in 1874.[52] Hapai started a plantation on the other side of the island under the sponsorship of Kuakini and came to Hilo in 1845 after Kuakini's death in 1844. In 1838, at the age of forty-seven, he married Iehu, a sixteen-year-old Hawaiian woman of chiefly rank born in 1822 in North Kohala (Kai 1974: 60; Lyman House genealogy). Lau Fai/Hapai had a plantation and ran a store in Hilo for many years. G.W.A. was born in Hilo in 1840 and educated in a school run by Lucy Wetmore, the wife of Charles Wetmore, the missionary doctor (S. L. Austin's friend and business partner with the Hitchcocks), who came with her husband from New England. She started this

7. George Washington Akao Hapai. From the Hawai'i State Archives.

school in 1850 with fourteen children who had Chinese fathers and Native mothers (four from G.W.A.'s family), two who had an American father and a Native mother, including Benjamin Pitman's son, and one all-white child (Kai 1974: 60–63). The school was conducted in English rather than Hawaiian. When the Haili Church was rebuilt in 1859, the Chinese merchants contributed to the building fund and Hapai (senior) was the largest contributor (Kai 1974: 53).

Two of G.W.A.'s sisters married cousins in the Richardson family from Vermont, who owned plantations, while others married Native Hawaiians (Kai 1974: 60; Lyman House genealogy). In 1904 the daughter of Charles E. Richardson and Akana Hapai married William H. Smith, an attorney in private practice in Hilo.[53] Hapai married Harriet Rebecca Kamakanoenoe Sniffen in 1870, a haole/Hawaiian, and they had at least six children (Lyman House genealogy). One of their sons was a bookkeeper with the Hilo branch of H. Hackfeld and Co., one of the major sugar companies in the islands, at the time of Hapai's death in 1908 (*Tribune Herald*). His family genealogy indicates frequent intermarriage among haoles, Hawaiians, and Hawaiian/Chinese. Thus, the Hapai family was linked through marriage to old-timer

Native Hawaiian, Chinese, and haole families from New England and to the planter elite, although G.W.A. apparently did not own a plantation himself.

Hapai was apparently the protege of Luther Severance. He worked as a clerk in the post office and in the sheriff's office of Luther Severance starting in 1868.[54] He also served as tax assessor from 1868 until 1878. He was then appointed district magistrate for South Hilo, a position he held without interruption for thirty years. For one year he was also acting governor of the island. He had no technical legal education but was reputed to have a great deal of integrity and ability as a judge (ibid). It seems clear that he was fluent in both English and Hawaiian although more comfortable in Hawaiian, based on exchanges concerning his ability to continue as judge in Hilo after annexation (Mookini 1994). Hapai wrote his case records in Hawaiian although he used English legal terms such as *prosecution rests* and *cross-examination*, and the English names for some of the charges. He signed his first case, on February 1, 1878, Lunakānāwai Hoʻomalu o Hilo, Police Judge of Hilo (Mookini 1994: 2).

In his kinship links, his fluency in English and Hawaiian, and his religion, Hapai was in an intermediate position, closely connected to the dominant haole elite and to the Hawaiian and Chinese merchant and planter communities. He was apparently a member of the Haili Church and had been educated by missionaries. His lifelong friend and sponsor, Luther Severance, was a leading member of the dominant haole community. However, Hapai was not mentioned as an invited guest in the numerous social occasions of the haole elite described in newspaper accounts collected by Luther Severance in his scrapbook, now archived in the Lyman House Memorial Museum in Hilo. Many of these social events took place in Severance's house hosted by his wife Lu, a missionary daughter. By the end of the century these social events included plantation managers as well as missionary descendants but rarely Hawaiians or Hawaiian/Chinese. But Hapai was invited to the D. H. Hitchcocks' wedding anniversary along with his sister and F. S. Lyman, a Circuit Court judge and son of the Lyman missionaries, S. L. Austin, L. Severance, and the Wilfongs (J.A.M. [author], March 18, 1893, Severance Scrapbook). Thus, Hapai belonged to the "respectable" social world of long-term Hilo residents. He was socially quite distant from the Chinese plantation workers whose cases dominated the court in the 1880s and 1890s. There is no indication whether or not he spoke Chinese, although his father lived in Hilo until his death in 1874.

Luther Severance, on the other hand, was a prominent social and political member of the haole elite with important kinship linkages to other prominent haole families in Hilo and Honolulu. Severance's father, Luther, was a newspaper publisher in Augusta, Maine, and served as a member of Congress for four years, then was appointed U.S. minister to Hawaiʻi by President Taylor in 1850, a position he held for four years. He was succeeded in Congress by

Hon. James G. Blaine, later U.S. secretary of state. Luther Severance Sr. brought his wife and children with him to Hawai'i in 1850 but returned to Maine because of ill health in 1854 (Severance Scrapbook, p. 12). The Severance family continued to be prominent in Hawai'i politics. In 1889 Henry W. Severance, Luther's brother, was appointed U.S. consul, presumably because he was an old friend of Mr. Blaine, who had begun his business career in the newspaper office of Mr. Severance's father in Augusta, Maine (Severance Scrapbook, p. 12, *San Francisco Alta*). Henry was a Privy Council of State member during the reign of Kamehameha V and held this position during three successive kings.[55] Luther Severance's sister returned to Hawai'i in 1856 to marry William Cooper Parke, who served as marshal of the kingdom during the 1880s (Kuykendall 1967: 275).

Luther bought a plantation near Honolulu and married Lucinda Clark of

8. Luther Severance. Courtesy of the Lyman House Memorial Museum Photo Collection.

9. Lu Severance, Mrs. Luther Severance. Courtesy of the Lyman House Memorial Museum Photo Collection.

Honolulu,[56] but in 1870 he was appointed by Kamehameha V to be sheriff of the island of Hawai'i. He was also named collector of customs and port master of the port of Hilo.[57] Luther spent thirty years in Hilo, where he and his wife, the sister of S. L. Austin's wife, became prominent members of the elite haole community. A third Clark sister married Henry Lyman, a son of the Hilo missionary family of Sarah and David Lyman (Lyman journal).

In the scrapbook of newspaper clippings Luther collected during his life, the accounts of social events list who attended, indicating that the Severances were a prominent and powerful family. The Hitchcocks did not participate much in these social events, although they did in church occasions. The British travel writer Isabella Bird, who stayed with the Severances while she was in Hilo, complained in a letter to Mrs. Luther Severance written from Edinburgh, November 9–16, 1874: "I thought David Hitchcock a most

10. Picnic party at Coconut Island, Hilo, probably late nineteenth century. Closest man on left bench, Dr. Francis Wetmore. Second woman on left bench, Mrs. Lu Severance. Closest on right bench, Mr. Kennedy, a plantation manager. Second closest man on right bench, John Scott, manager of Wainaku plantation. To the right of Wetmore, Luther Severance. Others present at the picnic: Hattie Coan, Mr. Turner, Minnie Austin, Helen Severance, Mr. Wiggan, Miss McLeod. This photo suggests the friendship circle of the judicial elites of Hilo and underscores the racial exclusivity of this group in social events. Courtesy of the Lyman House Memorial Museum Photo Collection.

uppish disagreeable ungentlemanly man."[58] A photograph from the 1890s shows a picnic outing including the Wetmore descendants, Titus and Fidelia Coan, Severance, and Austin but not Hitchcock.[59]

Severance held a variety of government jobs, including postmaster general. He served as sheriff of the island of Hawai'i from 1870 until 1884 when he resigned, a job D. H. Hitchcock's daughter Almeida said was as powerful as the governor of a state in the United States (Severance Scrapbook, p. 7; Humme 1986: 145). Hapai frequently judged cases in which Severance served as prosecutor in the 1883 case records.

The 1880s

The cases in 1883, heard by Hapai and written in Hawaiian, reflect the dramatic changes in the population of the region. The number of cases has

again almost doubled from 1873, growing from 240 to 409. Desertion of
work cases continued to dominate the caseload (38 percent) followed by
debt collection (11 percent), assault and battery (8 percent), and drunkenness
(7 percent). Only five (1 percent) were accused of adultery, and none of
fornication. The number of Hawaiians was about the same, 154 cases, and
still largely for work violations (37 percent) although 12 percent were accused of some form of violence, 11 percent of property violations, 10 percent of drugs and alcohol violations, and 3 percent of adultery or fornication.
The number of Chinese defendants increased greatly from 24 in 1873 to 145.
Although 48 percent were work cases, as one might expect considering that
this was the new labor force, fully 14 percent involved drugs and alcohol.
There are fifty-four cases involving Portuguese, the newest group of laborers
at this time. Again, one third (34 percent) are charged with abandoning or
refusing work, and 15 percent involve violence. There are forty-eight
haole defendants, up from twenty-four ten years earlier, only 13 percent of
whom are charged with work violations, but 25 percent with violence and 31
percent with drug and alcohol offenses. Although it was generally assumed
by plantation managers that whites were unfit for plantation labor, there remained a white underclass in town looked down on by the mission/planter
elite. Only two Japanese defendants appeared, both charged with abandoning
work. Women appear rarely and almost exclusively for deserting their husbands or for adultery.

Eight cases involved possession of opium (2 percent), with heavy fines of
fifty dollars plus one week of prison at hard labor typically imposed. Native
Hawaiians appear as laborers, but more often for beating their wives or
drinking. The Chinese are in court for gambling and opium possession and
the Portuguese for labor contract violations. Some of the cases suggest that
the lifestyle of the Chinese newcomers was a particular target, such as a fine
of five dollars imposed for carrying baskets on a pole and selling cakes from
them, or a fine of five dollars for selling cakes on the Sabbath. As Case
1883.1 in appendix A indicates, the police were actively engaged in spying
on people suspected of opium possession or liquor sales. In this remarkable
case, a Chinese victim of the spying went to court to demand damages; he
failed to win because of a legal technicality. Several of the 1893 cases suggest that the police continued to spy on opium and liquor sellers. There are
also a number of cases of people drunk in public in the 1883 case records.

A few cases of adultery appeared in the courts in 1883. At this time, men
are fined forty dollars and women ten dollars for adultery. As Cases 1883.2
and 1883.3 in appendix A indicate, issues of sexual behavior did appear in
court, but were typically discussed in very oblique language. This discourse
of sex contrasts with that of the Hawaiian wife in Case 1893.3 in 1893, who
speaks directly about sexuality: she says her husband was angry because he

could not do his part in sexual intercourse (very soft) and he said that it was she who had weakened his genitals.

Cases of violence against women were frequently dismissed or nolle prossed by Severance, the sheriff, as they were in Case 1883.4. These were generally treated as minor violations unless the injuries were severe. Wives who deserted their husbands, regardless of the provocation that made them flee, were almost always returned to their husbands. Even wives sexually abused or neglected, as in Case 1883.2, or in fear of violence, as in Case 1883.6, were sent back to their husbands or imprisoned at hard labor if they refused. Case 1883.6, in which the woman was sentenced to two weeks hard labor for desertion, involves a couple—a Portuguese man, Joe Flores, and his Hawaiian wife, Kekuko—who appear frequently in court. Although the vast majority of labor violations resulted in the requirement that workers return to work and pay costs or a fine, there were some acquittals, particularly when defendants had attorneys (see Case 1883.5). Chapter 7 explores labor cases in more detail.

The same people are running the courts. D. H. Hitchcock appears frequently in court during this year, both for the plaintiff and for the defense. S. L. Austin is often the plaintiff in work abandonment cases, Rufus Lyman appears as tax collector, and occasionally E. G. Hitchcock and D. H. Hitchcock are both in court on the same case. Cases that are appealed are sent to the circuit judge, F. S. Lyman, Rufus's brother. Rufus Anderson Lyman married into a Hawaiian-Chinese family: his wife was the daughter of a Hawaiian chiefess and a Chinese merchant in Honolulu.[60] Joseph Nāwahī, a mission-educated Hawaiian discussed at greater length in chapter 7, is frequently attorney for the defense. Luther Severance is usually the prosecutor in criminal cases. There are many cases in which C. E. Richardson and Co. is plaintiff against workers who have abandoned work; the judge is Richardson's brother-in-law. Thus the court officials all have close ties to the plantations, the mission, and government officials in Honolulu. They are clearly interested in controlling the new labor force but at the same time are part of the Christian reformist tradition. This is a closely connected and shared cultural world quite different from that of the immigrant plantation workers who are strangers in cultural as well as economic terms.

The 1890s

In 1893 Hapai was still the judge, but the caseload and composition of court defendants was again very different. The number of cases dropped slightly to 379, of which only 22 percent were desertion of service. Assault and battery was equally frequent as in the past decade (8 percent), but gambling rose from one case to thirty-three (9 percent) and liquor selling without a license from fifteen to twenty-four cases (6 percent), possession of opium from eight to twenty-one (6 percent), while drunkenness dropped from thirty to twenty-two (6 percent). There were only two adultery cases (0.3 percent). The figures reflect the increasing surveillance of liquor selling and opium possession in the wake of the anti-Chinese movement and the expansion in gambling prosecutions following the recent immigration of Japanese workers.

The number of haoles in court dropped to seventeen, one third of the number in 1883. They were charged with violence (18 percent), drugs/alcohol (18 percent), and property crimes (12 percent). None were charged with abandoning work: they appear to be virtually absent from the labor force by this time. The number of Chinese defendants dropped to sixty-eight from 145, but they are still 18 percent of the caseload. Half (49 percent) were charged with drug and alcohol violations, reflecting continuing concerns about opium as well as struggles to control the sale of liquor. The number of Hawaiian defendants also dropped by half to seventy-four, with a sharp decline in work cases from fifty-six to none. In fact, their most common offenses are the same as those of the haoles, reflecting increasing similarities in the way of life of the two groups: 28 percent violence, 20 percent drugs and alcohol, 8 percent property, 10 percent family.

But there is an enormous increase in the number of Japanese defendants, 185 up from two a decade earlier. Japanese are now 49 percent of the defendants in court. As with other recently imported groups of laborers, half (44 percent) of the cases concern failure to work, but 15 percent concern gambling and 10 percent drugs and alcohol. Even if the eighty-three contract labor violations are subtracted from the caseload, Japanese defendants are still 34 percent of the remaining caseload. Of the thirty-three Portuguese, whose numbers have dropped from fifty-three ten years earlier when they were new arrivals, 18 percent were charged with violence, 12 percent with public order violations such as common nuisance and drinking, and 15 percent for offenses with animals such as furious riding of horses. The Portuguese no longer appear in court with contract labor violations. The Japanese are overrepresented in this defendant population, as are the Chinese. In an 1891 census of the population of Hilo and the nearby coastal region, Mr. Severance, the census agent, reported the population as:

Portuguese	1,042 (26 percent)
Japanese	1,071 (27 percent)
Chinese	466 (12 percent)
Natives, whites, and others	1,436 (36 percent)
Total	4,015[61]

11. Naikai Camp, Wainaku, north of Hilo. Charles Furneaux is identified as the pho-
tographer. This picture probably depicts the village described in a newspaper article
from about 1892, clipped from a Hilo or Honolulu newspaper by Luther Severance
and included in his scrapbook in the Lyman Memorial Museum. The *Letter from
Hilo*, by Thos. L. Gulick. (p. 91 of scrapbook), says that there is a complete Japanese
village, with its thatched roofs and bamboo walls for its houses, a mile and a half
from Hilo above the Wainaku mill. He says that many of the doors of the cottages are
shaded by luxuriant banana trees. The hamlet is swarming with rosy babes and smil-
ing young mothers. All look healthy, contented, and happy. "Mr. Furneaux has some
very artistic photographs of this Arcadian village as well as other scenes in the envi-
rons of Hilo. Few strangers know of its existence, but it is, to my eye, the most
picturesque and unique cluster of dwellings in the Hawaiian Isles." Courtesy of the
Lyman House Memorial Museum Photo Collection.

The categories used in this census reflect the deep division emerging between long-term residents and newcomers. It is largely the newcomers who
are populating the docket, whereas Native Hawaiians and whites are blended
together. There are now interpreters required for 73 percent of the entire
caseload, mostly (69 percent) into Japanese. In contrast, in 1883 only 6 percent (twenty-two cases) had interpreters, mostly (64 percent) into Chinese.

A few of those who refused to work were acquitted and two who claimed
poor food received rice, but most were returned to work with fines. Two
were convicted for being "lazy." One who abandoned work to go to Honolulu was told that he would be sent to prison at hard labor "until he agrees
to work according to the law. Then he will be discharged." He is fined $5.25.

12. Japanese house. Probably also a Furneaux photo of Naikai Camp, Wainaku. Courtesy of the Lyman House Memorial Museum Photo Collection.

13. Japanese house, Wainaku. This picture appears congruent with the physical description provided in the newspaper column, with its notable romanticization of the "grass house" and the banana tree rather than a critique of the poor quality of the housing. Courtesy of the Lyman House Memorial Museum Photo Collection.

14. Japanese man with load of cane on his back. Perhaps also in Wainaku about 1892. This is from the same series of photos in the Lyman Museum. Courtesy of the Lyman House Memorial Museum Photo Collection.

As the cases in appendix A indicate, there was considerable tension in the fields, where the power of the lunas was counterbalanced by the workers' ready access to sharp cane knives and ability to converse with coworkers in languages lunas often did not know. The court cases suggest that the bosses retaliated by taking the workers to court, as in Case 1893.1, where the worker lost. One of the witnesses against him, R. Richardson, was probably Hapai's nephew. It is significant in this case that the boss threatened to take the worker to Hilo and fine him five dollars if he did not work. Clearly, the court was a present and potent threat wielded against workers.

Workers rarely charged bosses with violence in court. Case 1893.2 represents one rare instance of this strategy; the injured worker lost in court. The evidence considered by the court was persuasive against him, as the detailed case record indicates, including the attention to the shape of the cut in his hand that he alleged was caused by the boss. The courts clearly represent a possible forum for worker protest, but one in which the workers are greatly disadvantaged, far more than they are in the cane field itself. The court is a much more amenable forum for employers. In theory, the courts provide an opportunity to contest the exercise of power by employers, but only by those able to marshall evidence and witnesses that the judge finds persuasive. Only a few attempt to do so, and they rarely succeed.

Many of the alcohol and drug offenses involve illegal manufacturing and selling by newcomers. The police are engaged in extensive spying operations to support the antidrug policy, as indicated in Cases 1893.4 and 1893.5, although they were only successful in one of these cases. As Cases 1893.2 and 1893.5 indicate, the court considered evidence from police surveillance operations carefully. The cases suggest that the Chinese were particularly targeted for surveillance. Drug cases and gambling cases both reflect reformist concerns—about temperance and the need to protect workers from unscrupulous gamblers. There are several cases of conflicts between members of different ethnic groups in workplaces and public areas that reveal the startling linguistic diversity of the population and the serious difficulties in communication that followed new waves of immigration.

Thus the courts are engaged in promoting a particular vision of social order developed by a community of longtime residents of Hilo steeped in the traditions of Christianity, New England morality, and modernist ideas of work and self-responsibility. They impinge most heavily on the strangers, the recent arrivals. But despite the courts' general pattern of producing decisions that support the established order, cases lacking compelling evidence do not produce convictions. Producing compelling evidence, of course, often means calling upon witnesses with credibility in the community, and the haole and Native Hawaiian elites clearly have more credibility than impoverished Asian newcomers unable to speak Hawaiian or English. This is a small town in which virtually all of the long-term residents are known to one another: only the imported sugar workers are strangers. Certain issues, such as assaults by workers on lunas, are far more serious to prosecutors and judges than others, such as violence by husbands against wives. The former challenge the power structure, whereas the latter reinforces it. Cases that challenge power relations, when brought by strangers, fare poorly in the absence of compelling evidence well formulated by someone who knows how the legal system works.

The 1900s

In 1903 the composition of the caseload changed dramatically again, since annexation to the United States eliminated the contract labor system and all the prosecutions it entailed. Workers were now employed under contracts not enforced by penal sanctions. Prosecutions focused instead on vagrancy, common nuisance, and other public order offenses. The caseload almost tripled to 1,032 cases. Drunkenness was the largest single category of offense (16 percent), followed by common nuisance (11 percent), debt collection (11 percent), assault and battery (8 percent), gambling (8 percent), and furious driving (8 percent). Five percent of the cases (forty-eight cases) were for vagrancy, and 2 percent (twenty-three cases) for disorderly conduct. Only nine were charged with adultery and thirteen with fornication, a total of 2 percent of the caseload. The court spent its time protecting the streets from fast riding of horses and public drunkenness and prosecuting vague "nuisances," along with eliminating pervasive gambling practices on the plantations and in town.

The number of Japanese defendants continued to be the largest, with 42 percent of all defendants, but it did not triple as the total caseload did. Japanese defendants are primarily charged with public order offenses (24 percent), public health and animal violations (16 percent) and gambling (11 percent). The Portuguese increased from thirty-three to 150, representing 15 percent of the caseload. Violence (20 percent) and drug and alcohol charges (21 percent) predominated. The most recent arrivals, from Puerto Rico, were not represented in the 1893 caseload but by 1903 were defendants in 120 cases, 12 percent of the total. Their most common offense was violence (26 percent). Among the old-timers, Native Hawaiians barely doubled in number, to only 13 percent of the total. Almost half are charged with drug/ alcohol violations (46 percent) and 17 percent with incidents of violence. The number of white defendants increased dramatically from seventeen to 101. Now almost as numerous in court as Hawaiians (10 percent) they are similarly charged mostly with drug and alcohol offenses (33 percent) and violence (14 percent). These figures suggest the expansion among Native Hawaiians and haoles of an urban underclass engaging in drinking and violence. The Chinese, only slightly more numerous in court now than ten years earlier, are only 8 percent of the defendant population. They are charged primarily with gambling (37 percent) and public order offenses (14 percent).

With the end of the contract labor system, the courts relied on vagrancy prosecutions to keep people at work, as indicated by Case 1903.1. The most recent newcomer group, the Puerto Ricans, faced particular discrimination and sometimes resorted to violence, as in Case 1903.2 and Case 1903.3. In Case 1903.2, the evidence seems inconclusive and contradictory, yet the worker is still found guilty, in contrast to some earlier cases in which ambiguous evidence produced an acquittal. In Case 1903.3, an apparently angry and desperate worker assaulted the nearest representative of authority, the store clerk, although he says his hands moved involuntarily and he did not strike willfully. Nevertheless, he is sentenced to one month of hard labor and fined court costs of $7.80. The court has become more interested in the control of workers and less in social reform or the protection of the Native

Hawaiians than in earlier times. The political power of the missionary/ planters is waning in favor of the larger commercial agents who increasingly came to dominate the politics and the economics of Hawai'i in the early twentieth century.

A series of photos taken of convicted prisoners admitted to the Hilo prison in 1903 provides another source of insight into the processes of the criminal courts. Each prisoner is described in minute detail, including moles, tatoos, and earlobe confirmations, as well as pictured in the accompanying book, that is in the Lyman House Memorial Museum. These photos, and the brief descriptions of the cases that brought these people to court, reveal the extraordinary diversity of the population of Hilo at the time. The faces of many of the prisoners indicate desperation and despair. The Native Hawaiian defendants appear far more composed in these photos than do the Puerto Ricans and the Japanese, the most recent arrivals in this complex, shifting borderland (see figures 15–21).

There is not a sharp break between the time the missionaries controlled the administration of justice and the time when it was largely in the hands of planters and businessmen. Instead, as the detailed biographies indicate, the missionaries became the planters, bringing their values of industry and profit into this new arena. At midcentury, when the support from the ABCFM was withdrawn, some missionaries worried about how their children would be able to stay and find work. The expansion of the plantations proved fortuitous, offering new opportunities for business and profit among those who felt at home in Hawai'i and had, through the experience of mission work, acquired a combination of paternalistic concern and disdain toward the Hawaiians that enabled them to imagine that the vast displacements suffered by the Hawaiian population as a result of the acquisition of land and the importation of labor would ultimately benefit the Hawaiian people. By the end of the century, however, many of the missionary descendant/planters were being displaced by a new, more commerce-oriented business class engaged in building railroads and consolidating plantations into a far more profitable enterprise. Some of these were still missionary descendants, such as Lorrin Thurston. Annexation proved an enormous boon to these businessmen.

As the new courts developed in Hilo, the legally trained New Englanders staffed them and created the practices by which they functioned. During the entire sixty-year period, the judges of the District Court and the Circuit Courts were either New Englanders or mission-educated Hawaiians. The smaller, rural courts typically had Hawaiian judges, but in the important courts of the port town, it was the New Englanders, Austin, Hitchcock, Lyman, and Severance, who had a major role in shaping the new legal institutions and determining their customs and practices. Two Christian, mission-educated Hawaiians also played critical roles in the Hilo court, Hapai and Joseph Nāwahī, an attorney discussed in chapter 7. Although there were significant differences among these individuals, they shared a background in Protestant Christianity and a commitment to maintaining marriages and containing sexuality, as we will see in chapter 8.

The Criminalization of Everyday Life

Legal intervention during this period tended to redefine some everyday activities and recreations as crimes. The parallels between the criminalization of everyday life in rural England and Ireland in the early years of capitalism (Thompson 1967) and the similar processes taking place in British colonial Africa in the late nineteenth century and in other parts of Africa and Oceania in the late nineteenth and early twentieth centuries (Cooper 1989) suggest that this process is directly connected with the effort to produce a "free" labor force: a labor force sufficiently disconnected from the land to be available as wage labor. Yet, although some of the new regulations facilitated a steady and punctual labor supply, others were related only indirectly to labor force participation. Efforts to control sexual practices, drinking, and festivals were typically framed in a discourse of disorder and immorality rather than the need to work. These prohibitions were designed to engender a new kind of person managed by self-restraint and internal control.

It was not simply the demand for disciplined labor that fueled the criminalization of everyday life. Instead, a distinctive theory of the potential social disorder of subordinate groups unconstrained by the control of masters or chiefs drove government officials to prosecute energetically the everyday practices of Hawaiian commoners and strangers. The images of child-like Hawaiians, dangerous Chinese, and Japanese and Filipino workers in need of authority justified subjecting them to special levels of surveillance and control. Newcomer laborers were seen as threats to public safety and public health. Their growing ranks within the courts and prisons simply confirmed these worries. Discourses of labor control were parallel to those of social order but different: an unreliable labor force rather than social disruption.

Throughout this period, the courts disproportionately prosecuted low-status outsiders. These were people who lacked local connections and were unfamiliar with the institutions and practices in their new location. In the Circuit Court from 1852 to 1985 as well as in the District Court from 1853 to 1903, the courts served as a frontline system for changing the culture of these outsiders to conform to the patterns of old-timer groups. But after the first decade or so, each newcomer group largely disappeared from the criminal caseload. Although many historical factors account for the rise and fall of caseloads for each group, the general pattern holds for both District Court (chart 6.5) and the longer time span of Circuit Court (chart 6.6). In the District Court, haoles are overrepresented in 1853, whereas in the 1860s,

15

16

17

18

15. This man was sentenced for adultery in the Hilo district court March 3, 1903. He was 53 years old and had a Native Hawaiian name. According to the case record, the woman was also Hawaiian by name. The incident took place twelve miles out of Hilo. A complainant took the police to the house where the man and woman had been living together for at least a year, her husband sleeping at another house. The woman claimed they lived in separate rooms and had never slept together. The man was fined $50.00 and court costs of $3.20; the woman was fined $25.00 and costs. The description in the prison record book says the man was is 5 ft. 4½ inches tall, nose large, hair black and grey, and a scar on the outside of right buttock, 134 lbs., among other details. Courtesy of the Lyman House Memorial Museum Photo Collection.

16. This woman was also sentenced for adultery on March 2, 1903. She is described only as Hawaiian. Courtesy of the Lyman House Memorial Museum Photo Collection.

17. Sentenced May 15, 1903, this man is described as 31, 5 ft. 5½ inches tall, "body quite hairy of a reddish color." In the court case records, he was charged with possession of a deadly weapon, a loaded revolver, and was fined $10 or three weeks hard labor and $1.00 court costs. Courtesy of the Lyman House Memorial Museum Photo Collection.

18. This 34-year-old man was charged with ass. [assault?] to commit murder. The physical description includes a scar on the right side, five inches from navel, indicating that these descriptions were written after a full examination of the body. His name indicates that he was Korean. Courtesy of the Lyman House Memorial Museum Photo Collection.

19

20

21

19. Identified in the description as Japanese, this man was sentenced September 21, 1903, as a disorderly person. According to the court records, he was a disorderly person for one month and especially on September 18. He said, through an interpreter, "I don't like to work. I like to sit down all of the time." He pleaded guilty and was sentenced to four months at hard labor and court costs of $1.00. In the prison description he is 31 years old, 5 ft. 2 inches tall, 118 lbs., "eyes light brown with a wild look." The description concludes: "He has an insane look about him." A person with a very similar name, possibly the same man, was charged with insanity on March 3, 1903, but the case was nolle pressed. Courtesy of the Lyman House Memorial Museum Photo Collection.

20. This young man, aged 15, was from Puerto Rico and was sentenced December 15, 1903, for vagrancy. He was five feet tall and weighed 113 lbs. According to court records, he changed his plea from not guilty to guilty and was sentenced to one month at hard labor. Courtesy of the Lyman House Memorial Museum Photo Collection.

21. This man, aged 29, was committed to the Grand Jury on December 30, 1903, for larceny, first degree, along with his brother. Bail was fixed at $300.00. He was 5 ft. 3 inches tall, 114 lbs., and described as Portuguese. He and his two brothers were sentenced the same day, all for larceny. Courtesy of the Lyman House Memorial Museum Photo Collection.

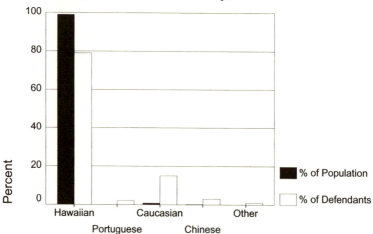

Ethnicity

Population = 24,450 - 1853 Census Hawai'i Island

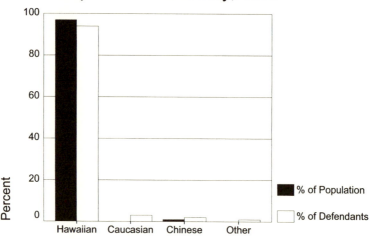

Ethnicity

Population = 19,808 - 1866 Census Hawai'i Island

Chart 6.5. Comparison of Ethnicity of Defendants and Population, Hilo District Court, 1853–1903

Comparison of Ethnicity, 1873

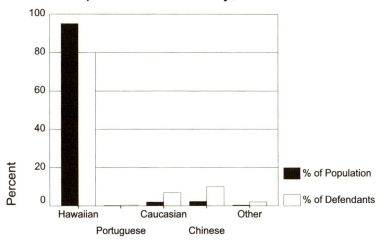

Population = 16,001 - 1872 Census Hawai'i Island

Comparison of Ethnicity, 1883

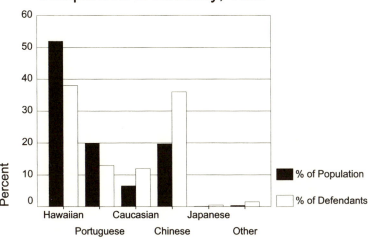

Population = 24,991 - 1884 Census Hawai'i Island

Chart 6.5. (*cont.*)

Comparison of Ethnicity, 1893

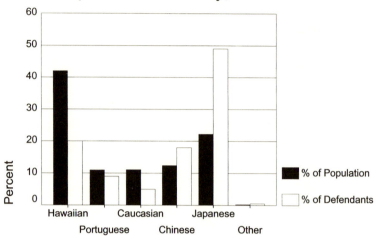

Ethnicity

Population = 26,754 - 1890 Census Hawai'i Island

Comparison of Ethnicity, 1903

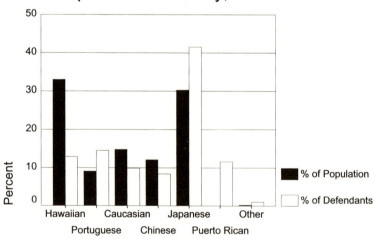

Ethnicity

Population = 33,285 - 1896 Census Hawai'i Island

Chart 6.5. (*cont.*)

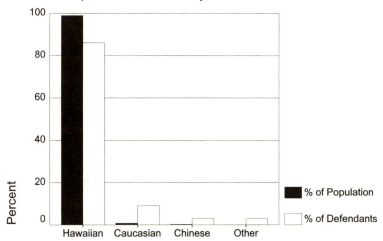

Population = 24,450 - 1853 Census Hawai'i Island

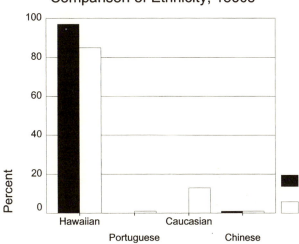

Population = 19,808 - 1866 Census Hawai'i Island

Chart 6.6. Comparison of Ethnicity of Defendants and Population, Hilo Circuit Court, 1852–1985

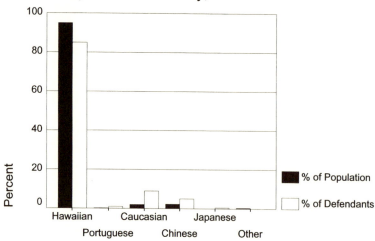

Population = 16,001 1872 Census Hawai'i Island

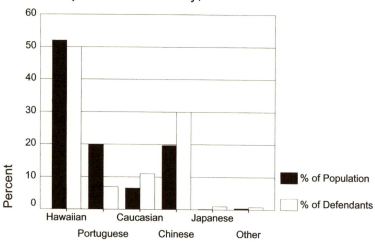

Population = 24,991 - 1884 Census Hawai'i Island

Chart 6.6. (*cont.*)

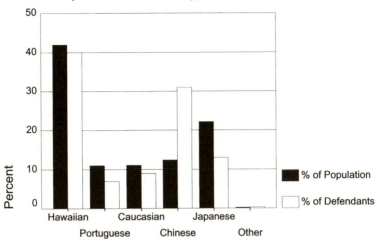

Comparison of Ethnicity, 1890 - 1892

Ethnicity

Population = 26,754 - 1890 Census Hawai'i Island

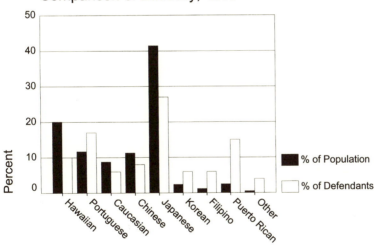

Comparison of Ethnicity, 1905

Ethnicity

1910 Census, Defendants = 48

Chart 6.6. (*cont.*)

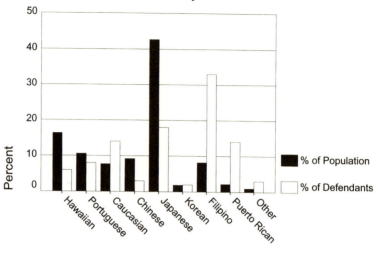

Chart: Comparison of Ethnicity, 1915

Percent (y-axis, 0 to 50)

Ethnicities (x-axis): Hawaiian, Portuguese, Caucasian, Chinese, Japanese, Korean, Filipino, Puerto Rican, Other

Legend: ■ % of Population   □ % of Defendants

Ethnicity

1920 Census, Defendants = 66

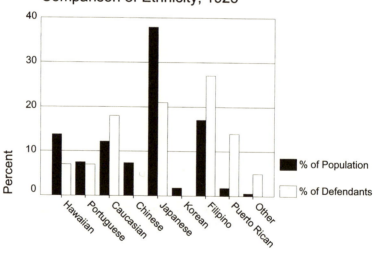

Chart: Comparison of Ethnicity, 1925

Percent (y-axis, 0 to 40)

Ethnicities (x-axis): Hawaiian, Portuguese, Caucasian, Chinese, Japanese, Korean, Filipino, Puerto Rican, Other

Legend: ■ % of Population   □ % of Defendants

Ethnicity

1930 Census, Defendants = 56

Chart 6.6. (*cont.*)

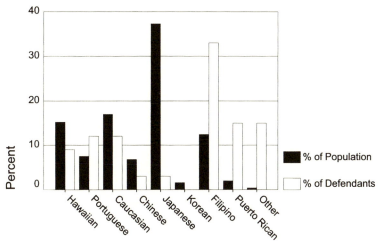

Comparison of Ethnicity, 1935

1940 Census, Defendants = 34

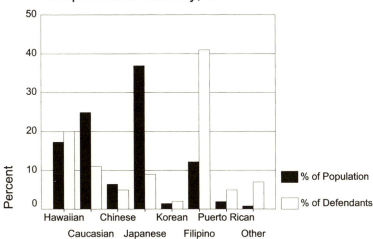

Comparison of Ethnicity, 1945

1950 Census, Defendants = 115

Chart 6.6. (*cont.*)

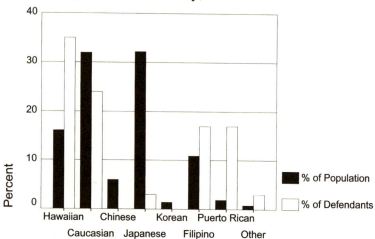

1960 Census, Defendants = 29

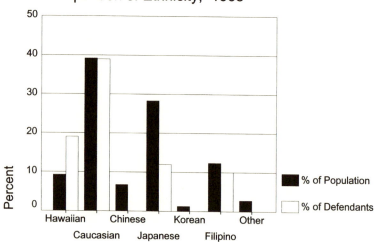

1970 Census - Self-reported Ethnicity, Defendants = 58

Chart 6.6. (*cont.*)

Comparison of Ethnicity, 1975

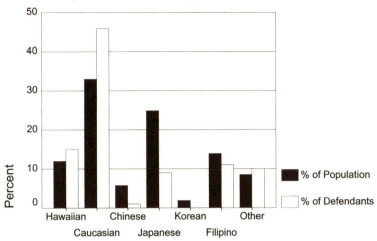

Ethnicity

1980 Census - Self-reported Ethnicity, Defendants = 188

Comparison of Ethnicity, 1985

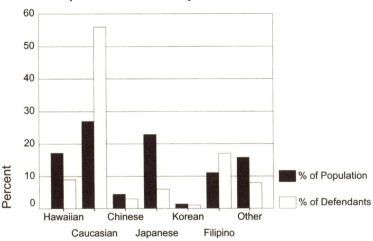

Ethnicity

1985 Dept. of Health Survey, Defendants = 200 sample only

Chart 6.6. (*cont.*)

1870s, and 1880s the Chinese are disproportionately defendants. In the 1890s and 1900s the Japanese and Puerto Ricans are in criminal court far more than their proportion of the population. The Circuit Court data indicate the same pattern in the nineteenth century but extend into the twentieth. From the 1910s to the 1940s Filipinos are overrepresented, and in the 1960s, 1970s, and 1980s, a period of rapid migration of whites from the continental United States and the emergence of considerable drug production and selling, the haoles are in court in larger proportions than in the general population. Obviously, a wide range of factors in addition to newcomer status explains these changes over the late nineteenth and twentieth centuries. Being a stranger can only explain one part of shifting prosecutorial strategies and defendant behavior.

Given this general pattern, however, it is less surprising that newcomers are disproportionately in court than that they disappear so quickly from court dockets. Two decades after new immigration from a particular nation ends, immigrants from that country are typically underrepresented in court. The Native Hawaiians were always underrepresented in comparison to their numbers. Do groups disappear from the dockets because the fear of criminal prosecution deters them from engaging in illegal practices such as drinking, sex outside of marriage, violence, drug use, and gambling? Or do they disappear because they no longer appear disruptive and their lifestyle no longer seems threatening? Although there are clearly some changes in the frequency of criminalized behavior, it seems unlikely that this is the entire explanation, considering the pervasiveness of the prohibited activities.

Many of the newcomers returned home, perhaps including those who could not adjust to the new order: 38 percent of Chinese immigrants between 1852 and 1887 returned, as did 55 percent of Japanese who came between 1885 and 1924, 16 percent of Koreans between 1903 and 1910, and 36 percent of Filipinos who came between 1909 and 1931 (Takaki 1989: 169).[62] Of the 17,500 Portuguese brought to Hawai'i, about 14,000 emigrated to the mainland, and of the 8,000 Spanish, few remained on the islands (Beechert 1985: 146). But rates of return dropped off over time. Until 1894, 75 percent of immigrants returned to Japan, but only 25 percent of subsequent immigrants went back (Beechert 1985: 131–132). Large numbers left the plantation for better opportunities in the towns after their contracts were finished, and many migrated to the United States.

But as the single male immigrants found wives and married, many were also able to create families and communities. The presence of wives allowed men to be fathers as well as workers while providing them with additional income, domestic comforts, and a female social network. Some brought wives along, some imported them later, and some enticed them away from local men. Hawaiian men rarely married foreign women; the pattern seems to be largely the other way. A sharp gender disparity marked the island of

Hawai'i throughout the second half of the nineteenth century, considerably worsening during the post-1876 years of labor immigration. The 1853 census indicates that women were only 47 percent of the total of Native Hawaiians, but only 34 of the 257 foreigners on the island were women. As the post-1876 migration of sugar plantation workers swelled the population, a great many more foreign men moved into competition with Hawaiian men for access to Hawaiian women. The 1890 census of the island of Hawai'i reports almost twice as many men (17,647) as women (9,107). The gender disparity was far greater among the foreign-born (21 percent women) than the Native Hawaiian population (47 percent women). American men numbered 210 and American women 78, while the disproportion of men was even greater among the British, Germans, and French. In 1890 there were 3,215 Chinese males and only 90 Chinese females, and 4,820 Japanese males and 1,119 Japanese females. In 1900 the census reported a population of Japanese women still only 28 percent that of Japanese men (Mengel 1997: 28). By the time the gender ratio reached parity for the Japanese population in the 1920s, their participation in court was quite low. The Portuguese, imported in family units because they were considered racially desirable laborers, similarly had relatively low crime rates (see chapter 5).

The creation of families paralleled the establishment of other community institutions such as churches and stores, institutions that provided leaders and translators. Plantations invited missionaries for the workers. Plantation villages in the Hilo area typically have a central street lined with stores and churches of various denominations: Mormon, Catholic, Protestant, and Buddhist. After the 1909 strike, many Buddhist temples formed on plantations (Beechert 1985: 197). Plantation housing was finally improved in the 1920s as plantations tried to produce an indigenous labor force and create the conditions of community that would hold the workers there instead of simply importing more. By this time, there was on the plantations a substantial Hawai'i-born population that had been educated in the public schools (Beechert 1985: 212), many of whom were U.S. citizens.

Workers also developed their own forms of organizing work by the end of the nineteenth century, providing a form of ordering separate from that of the luna and labor contract. Penal contract work was increasingly confined to new immigrant workers (Beechert 1985: 112). A majority of the workers who had completed their contracts chose to stay on, usually as free day laborers who could choose their employment (Beechert 1985: 325). By 1898 more than half the work force was free day labor (Beechert 1993: 55). The shortage of labor enabled the workers to form independent contracting companies in the period after 1875. Self-appointed leaders contracted with the planters with crews of perhaps eight to seventeen workers and took responsibility for dividing up the work and the money earned according to their own rules (Beechert 1985: 325). This system continued into the annexation

22. Plantation house, 1904. Photo of plantation house in Mill Village, Pepe'ekeo (north of Hilo), is taken from insurance valuation forms prepared sometime early in the twentieth century. The house was built in 1904 and is described with the following characteristics: no interior finish, lighting and plumbing poor, one story of ten feet height, general condition poor. It is valued at one thousand dollars. The names of the residents are all Japanese. From the Archives of the Hawaiian Sugar Planters Association, Honolulu.

period. Under this system, the worker was removed from the supervision of lunas, the source of most of the abuse in the fields (Beechert 1993: 53). Chinese and Japanese workers shifted extensively to independent contracting, leaving the most burdensome jobs for the newest arrivals (Beechert 1985: 235). Thus, three distinct forms of labor coexisted: indentured labor under penal compulsion, free day labor able to withdraw or be fired at any time, and a self-organized gang labor system contracting specific services, almost always ethnically distinct (Beechert 1985: 325).

Other forms of work organization developed in the early twentieth century, modeled on American labor unions. A nascent labor union movement, at first primarily Japanese, lead to strikes in 1903, 1904, 1905, 1909, 1920, and 1924 (Beechert 1985: 161–176). The union movement expanded from its Japanese base to incorporate Filipino workers by 1920, and by the 1940s began to achieve some signal successes. And the linguistic diversity of the immigrant population, often the source of conflict in the early days, was replaced by a linguistic patois called pidgin or Hawaiian Creole English, based on English, Hawaiian, and other languages, by which workers and lunas could talk to each other.

These emerging institutions of work and community life encapsulated and insulated activities defined as criminal from the observation and awareness of the dominant groups (see Takaki, 1983; Murayama 1988). These new communities developed institutions to conceal the criminalized practices, to shield them from the surveillance of the law. Prostitutes moved into brothels, gamblers into organized houses, drinkers into licensed establishments and private places. The police were paid off. Sellers of alcohol acquired licenses and others learned how to avoid police spies. There was an intricate network of gamblers who moved up and down the Hāmākua coast at the end of the nineteenth century, tolerated by plantation managers and the police and court system. A system of brothels persisted in Hilo into the 1940s, when a new-comer county attorney and judge embarked on a clean-up campaign.[63] Many became sophisticated at escaping the new regulations.

In effect, plural legal orders rooted in a developing community life emerged, which diminished the importance of the courts as sanctioning and control systems. As newcomer strangers learned to hide a criminalized practice, folding it into existing structures, the political pressures to stamp it out weakened, particularly when the offense was an issue of lifestyle such as opium consumption. Groups that initially seemed dangerous and undis-ciplined gradually became normalized and assumed a place in the racialized plantation hierarchy. The crime statistics that had provided evidence for their criminal tendencies began to decline as lawbreaking activities became more encapsulated and invisible. Prosecution diminished and the evidence of crim-inality declined. Indeed, in reading through the newspaper clippings col-lected by Severance covering the last quarter of the nineteenth century, the general lack of fear of newcomer populations after the first decade of immi-gration is striking. Pervasive racism, which deeply shaped the understand-ings that the white group held of other groups and of themselves, was foun-ded on notions of essentialized difference in labor capacities rather than on enduring fear. The system of control exerted by legal institutions was re-placed, over time, by new forms of incorporation and control such as fami-lies, schools, churches, and the class system, systems that maintained order but enforced social boundaries through housing, work, and a racial ideology of difference.

Clearly, the law is central to the control of economically powerless new-comer groups, part of the violence of the incorporation process. But what is surprising is the law's relatively quick move away from that role. The law has limited capacity to produce conforming and disciplined subjects. Over time the school, the church, the market, the plantation housing structure, racialized plantation identities, the community hall, and the family are far more effective. The law is a blunt instrument deployed against apparently threatening populations only as the leading edge of systems of surveillance and control. Its effects are less to change behavior than to declare and institute new normative orders, to act temporarily until more subtle and effective forms of control emerge, rooted in the community and workplace. Perhaps its most important role is to enunciate the cultural principles of the new social order. It is, in the end, the law's productive rather than its repressive power that is important to this cultural transformation.

7

PROTEST AND THE LAW

ON THE HILO SUGAR PLANTATIONS

H OW DID THE PRESENCE of the legal system redefine power relationships in nineteenth-century Hilo? The courts helped the planters to control their imported workers by enforcing the labor contract, suppressing violent resistance, and penalizing those who deserted their assigned plantation or who failed to work. The Masters and Servants legislation defined the terms of the contract between employers and employees and included some protection for workers against their employers (see chapter 4). In the 1850 legislation, for example, the victim of any master guilty of cruelty, misuse, or violation of any of the terms of the contract of the bound laborer "may make complaint to any district or police justice, who shall summon the parties before him, examine into, hear and determine the complaint; and if the complaint shall be sustained, such person shall be discharged from all obligations of service, and the master shall be fined a sum, not less than five nor exceeding one hundred dollars, and in default of the payment thereof, be imprisoned at hard labor until the same is paid."[1] Virtually the same text was included in the Compiled Laws of 1884.

In practice, however, contract laborers very rarely took their masters to court for contract violations or cruelty, whereas masters frequently took workers to court for desertion or refusal to work. Nevertheless, the law represented workers' only protection from the market. Fragile as the law proved in practice, it was one of the few mechanisms that regulated the enormous power of planters. Moreover, groups differed in their success: as chapter 6 indicated, Native Hawaiian and Portuguese workers were occasionally successful; Chinese, Japanese, or Puerto Rican workers far less so. After the abolition of the contract labor system in 1900, a union movement emerged employing legal tactics of strikes and collective bargaining. The new systems of pro-union regulations emanating from the mainland in the 1930s strengthened the movement, and by the 1940s a unionized workforce did have some legal protection against the employers (Beechert 1985).[2]

In the nineteenth century, decisions in the Hilo District Court provided critical support for the plantation labor system. Of the 320 workers charged with desertion or refusal of work, 97 percent were found guilty. Overall, district court defendants were found guilty in only 86 percent of the cases. A higher proportion of whites and Portuguese were found not guilty (20 percent and 15 percent respectively) than of Chinese, Hawaiian, or Japanese (3 percent, 3 percent, and 1 percent), but the number found not guilty was very small for all groups (chart 7.1). Very few workers took their bosses to court for violence, and in only one case did the worker win, yet in every case I recorded in which a worker was accused of using violence against his boss, the worker was convicted.

The ability to present evidence was critical. As chapter 6 showed, judges were very attentive to evidence and refused to convict if the evidence was unclear. Even police sting operations designed to catch people selling and making liquor failed when the evidence was not convincing. Yet plantation workers and the poor were less able to collect witnesses, to concoct a winning strategy, and to present a convincing case than the town's attorneys, most of whom spent their lives in Hilo and had relatives or childhood friends among the other attorneys and judges in town. Access to legal expertise was critical in putting together evidence that would be convincing to the court.

The workers in court for desertion or attacking their bosses in the fields moved from an environment in which their razor-sharp cane knives, strength, and allies among conationals speaking the same language advantaged them into one in which the rules and language were utterly unfamiliar. Those few able to hire lawyers did vastly better than the rest. A third of those with lawyers were found not guilty in contrast to only 3 percent of those without lawyers (chart 7.2). But only 11 work defendants out of 352 for which there

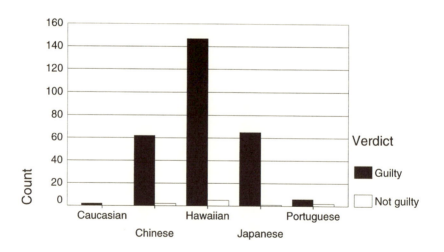

Chart 7.1. Work Cases: Verdict by Ethnicity, Hilo District Court, 1853–1903

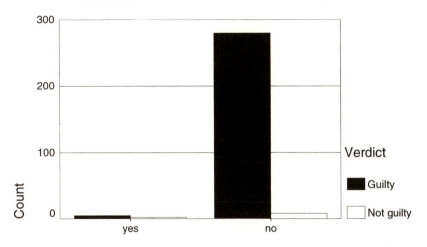

Chart 7.2. Work Cases: Verdict by Lawyer, Hilo District Court, 1853–1903

is information had lawyers—a dismal 3 percent. Again, work defendants were worse off than other defendants: 10 percent of defendants overall had lawyers. And lawyers in desertion of labor cases were not equally distributed by ethnicity. Fourteen percent of white defendants (one), 17 percent of Portuguese defendants (three), 4 percent of Hawaiian defendants (seven), and none of the Chinese or Japanese defendants had lawyers. Thus, those who had some knowledge of how to use the courts or could hire someone who did fared better than those to whom this institution was alien. Recent arrivals almost never came with these advantages.

Although the contract provided protections for workers, very few turned to the courts for help. The social and cultural linkages between the judges and planters and their shared understandings about labor, race, hierarchy, and Christian morality made it more likely that they would understand the planters' position than the workers'. Defendants' lack of legal consciousness and legal knowledge along with language differences, the absence of lawyers, and a lack of understanding of the court process disadvantaged them in court. In order to go to court and complain at all, a worker had to commit the crime of abandoning work. White workers were more likely to try the courts because they were more often literate, more aware of their rights through nascent labor union movements in Europe, and less burdened by the racism of the court and community in Hilo.

Once in a great while a worker was successful. On February 5, 1883, a

Portuguese worker represented by the attorney Joseph Nāwahī was acquitted
when he said he had gone to get medicine from the doctor for his wife. The
plaintiff, a Portuguese manager, threatened to appeal to Circuit Court.[3] On
this occasion, a white defendant who had a good reason for refusing to work
and who was represented by an attorney won the case. Another worker,
unrepresented, was acquitted of abandoning work the same day. Two months
later, a worker represented by D. H. Hitchcock was acquitted and two others
had the suit withdrawn. All these workers were Portuguese and were employed by W. G. Irwin and Co. It is possible that the Hilo judicial elite was
critical of the way Irwin was treating its workers, since another Portuguese
worker at a different company who refused to work because his boss swore
at him was ordered back to work and required to pay court costs. W. G.
Irwin was also sued by several Portuguese workers on November 9, 1883,
for not looking after them by not giving them enough food as stated in their
labor contract. Such suits of contract labor violations for failure to provide
food and housing are extremely rare. The fragmentary court records indicate
only that the company denied the suit and that the lawyer for the plaintiffs,
Ed Kekoa, asked to terminate the suit and pay the costs. It is not clear if the
workers won this case.

But the vast majority of workers who appeared in court were simply required to return to work regardless of illness, injury, or inadequate food and
housing. Workers were most likely to succeed in confronting their employers
in court when they were able to mobilize outside political support, when
they had a sense of rights, when they had an attorney, and when they were
white. This chapter describes two cases of worker resistance to lunas that
ended up in court at about the same time on adjacent plantations along the
Hāmākua coast. The differences in the two cases reveal the importance
of worker legal consciousness, literacy, nationality, and access to outside
sources of support. For outsiders to the social system of Hilo and to the
cultural system of the law, the courts held out little hope and a great deal of
control.

Protest on the Hakalau Plantation

On January 22, 1883, forty-eight cases, all with Chinese defendants, appeared in the Hilo District Court minute book with the charges of abandoning work, obstructing justice, or assault and battery. The plaintiff in most of
the cases was the Hakalau plantation and the prosecutor was Sheriff Severance. Perched on a steep hillside crossed by deep gulches and forced to load
harvested sugar by cables stretching down steep cliffs to ships moored outside the pounding surf, the Hakalau plantation faced constant difficulties and
challenges (Hakalau Plantation Records, U. H. Hilo). A newspaper story

based on a letter written by Severance to Marshal Parke (his brother-in-law) describes the incident as a strike by thirty-six "Chinamen," six of whom assaulted their luna, William Smith.[4] According to the newspaper story, warrants were issued for the arrest of the six, but as the police were taking them away, a group of Chinese attacked them, and despite the efforts of many on the plantation, were able to rescue the six and retreat to a large building. The Hakalau manager, Morrison, telephoned Luther Severance, and the neighboring plantations of Austin and Hitchcock for help. The next day Morrison moved in on the building. But the Chinese, alarmed, had left their building, and forty started for Hilo "intending to deliver themselves up to the authorities." They met the police under Severance on the road, who took them to Hilo and locked them up. Police on the plantation arrested ten others. The next day the ringleaders were brought before the court. According to the newspaper, six were convicted of escaping from the police while under arrest, seven for interfering with the police, and the balance ordered to return to the plantation. The story concludes that no one was killed or seriously hurt because of the discretion of Mr. Morrison in not permitting his men to use firearms and because of the availability of the telephone.

The court records present a slightly different story. Although most were convicted and imprisoned or ordered back to work, not all were found guilty. Two men charged with assault and battery on a public officer were represented by the attorney Joseph Nāwahī, and after a trial they were found not guilty. In the court records, the plantation was the plaintiff in the first twenty-six cases. The defendants, all with Chinese names, were identified by a number supplied by the plantation.[5] None of these defendants had a lawyer. All pleaded guilty and were ordered back to work and required to pay the costs of court—in effect a fine. Six other defendants had the suit withdrawn but still had to pay court costs. Of the fifteen charged with obstructing and perverting justice, three were nolle prossed and twelve pleaded guilty, receiving sentences from one to three months hard labor and fines from two dollars to five dollars. (Wages at this period were approximately one dollar a day or less. But these fines were usually paid by the plantation and converted into additional days of labor for the workers.)[6] None of these fifteen had an attorney.

Eight were charged with assault and battery or assault with a dangerous weapon. Of these, two were found not guilty after they pleaded not guilty and had a trial in which they were represented by Nāwahī, five were nolle prossed by the sheriff and discharged, and one was charged with assault with a dangerous weapon (a cane knife) and found guilty after a trial. He may have been represented by Nāwahī, but the court records are unclear. Apparently, having legal representation made some difference in the outcome.

Joseph Nāwahī was a politically prominent Native Hawaiian from Hilo, frequently in court as an attorney for the defense in the second half of the

nineteenth century. Although he was mission-educated and close to the Lymans and an active member of the Haili Church, he spoke out on behalf of
Native Hawaiians and, as the haole elite in Hilo became more pro-annexa-
tionist, he increasingly opposed them. He boycotted the Haili Church in
1890 when the trustees refused to let Wilcox, a supporter of the monarchy,
speak there.[7] According to his biography, written by John Sheldon in Hawaiian and translated by Puakea Nogelmeier, Nāwahī was born in Puna in 1842.
He attended Hilo Boarding School, living in the Lyman household for some
time about 1853, then went to advanced training in the mission schools of
Lāhaināluna and the Royal Children's School in Honolulu to learn English.
He returned to teach at Hilo Boarding School, served as assistant principle
under Lyman and then acting principle for a year. He grew up with Rufus
Lyman, who was about his age and a lifetime friend. Rufus Lyman himself
began his career as assistant overseer on Austin's Onomea Plantation in the
1860s (Martin, Lyman, Bond, and Damon 1979: 144).

Nāwahī taught himself law, was certified to practice in both the District
Court and the Supreme Court, and in 1872 began a long career in the legislature, which continued until 1892. He served many times in the House of
Representatives and spoke eloquently against the Reciprocity Treaty in 1876,
saying it would lead to annexation. It was he who introduced the proposal to
require Chinese laborers to come with women (see p. 133). In 1892 he was
named minister of foreign affairs in Lili'uokalani's cabinet and resigned
from his seat in the legislature, but two days later the cabinet was disbanded,
and he raced back to Hilo to get his name on the ballot. D. H. Hitchcock,
also a frequent representative from Hilo, ran against him, but Nāwahī succeeded in getting reelected by a daring crossing of the channels between the
islands in a small boat. He was a member of the educated, Christian Native
Hawaiian elite and close to the missionary community until the politics of
sovereignty drove them apart. His wife 'A'ima A'ii was a member of the
elite Hawaiian-Chinese community in Hilo and also a member of the Haili
Church (Kai 1976: 19). Nāwahī defended the two men charged with assault
and battery who were acquitted.

It is not clear whether Nāwahī defended the man charged with assault
with a cane knife; there is no indication of defense activity in the records. He
pleaded not guilty but was convicted. A Chinese interpreter was present at
the trial. The victim of the assault with a cane knife was William Smith, a
luna at Hakalau. Smith testified that "this Chinese" chased him, threatening
to cut him with the cane knife. Morrison interfered and grabbed the hand
holding the cane knife, only two feet from Smith. Smith testified that he did
not know why the Chinese worker threatened to cut him with a knife, and
said, "This Chinese is not one of my Chinese laborers; he is from somewhere else." On cross-examination, Smith said that he did not speak to the
man, but thought that his face looked really angry and noted that he spat.

23. Mrs. Emma ʻAiʻma Nāwahī. From *Autobiography of Joseph Nāwahī*, in Hawaiian, in Lyman House Memorial Museum Library. Courtesy of the Lyman House Memorial Museum Photo Collection.

Morrison testified that he did know this Chinese, that there had been a fight between two Chinese and their luna and that they were beaten up. That luna spoke to Smith and Smith spoke to Morrison, so Morrison went up to where the Chinese were. "I spoke to them saying that we should go down, makai [toward the sea]. The other Chinese man quit work. I ordered the Chinese to put down the knife. He did not put down that knife. He came at me and then at Smith with that cane knife so I blocked him. Just like what Smith said this was a fearful thing, what the Chinese did that evening." The defense had no witnesses, and the text of the trial indicates that the defendant did not speak. He was fined twenty dollars and sent to jail at hard labor for one month.

The penalty is severe—one month's wages plus one month in jail, yet the man had threatened his boss with a knife. From the perspective of formal legality, the defendants were well treated. The man convicted of assault with a cane knife did receive a formal trial, possibly with an attorney who was not himself a planter. The group of workers was not attacked by the plantation manager but rather brought to trial in town. All the defendants were given a hearing before Hapai, a man closely connected to Severance and the plantation and old-timer interests but not himself a planter. Judge Hapai may

24. Hon. Joseph K. Nāwahī. From *Autobiography of Joseph Nāwahī*, in Hawaiian, in Lyman House Memorial Museum Library. Courtesy of the Lyman House Memorial Museum Photo Collection.

even have spoken some Chinese, although there is no evidence on this point. Two men were found not guilty and several were not prosecuted. The presence of a defense attorney was of considerable importance. Lawyers sometimes opposed planter's interests as Joseph Nāwahī did in this case, although most of the lawyers, including D. H. and E. G. Hitchcock, were part of the plantation elite.

Thus the law regulated planter power to some extent, sometimes replacing brute force and regulating the exercise of that force. But the protections the law offered were diminished in practice by the intimate connections between judges and planters in the local social system and the workers' ignorance of how the law worked. The sugar workers were strangers to the people in town and to their system of law. In the fields they were on more familiar terrain. The newspaper story indicates that the fight in the fields was part of a larger collective labor action. The Chinese workers were clearly organized and working together. In the court, however, the battle was of procedure, evidence, and laws understood only through an interpreter. It does not appear that the Chinese were able to use the unfamiliar legal setting to further their cause.

The Norwegians in Pāpaʻikou

The second example of worker resistance again highlights the close-knit character of Hilo elites. In 1881, in an effort to bring more white workers to the islands, five hundred Norwegians were brought to Hawaiʻi on three-year contracts, the largest single group of which (sixty-three) ended up at the Hitchcocks' Pāpaʻikou plantation, just down the coast from Hakalau (Grip 1884). Conflict quickly arose over the living conditions, the food, and the promise that wives would be provided with food. Apparently this stipulation was included in the Norwegian version of the contract but not the English one. Although most other plantations coped with the misunderstanding by providing food for the women, the Hitchcocks refused. The Norwegians also complained about the harsh and overbearing foremen, who customarily administered kickings and beatings, and the numerous subtractions from pay for various infractions (Davis and Davis 1962: 17–19). They were aware of the higher wages for skilled workers in Hawaiʻi as well as the higher wages paid in California, yet they were locked into three-year contracts on the plantation at relatively low wages.

In October 1881 a number of Norwegians struck the Pāpaʻikou plantation and were brought before the court in Hilo (Davis and Davis 1962: 19). When they refused to return to work, fifty-seven were ordered to jail. Because the jail could only accommodate forty and already had fifteen residents, the sentence was not carried out. The men eventually returned to work. Abraham Fornander, for the kingdom, and A. Glade, consul for Sweden, Norway, and Germany, investigated the situation, the former reporting that there were no grounds for dissatisfaction. Norwegians on other plantations also resisted the conditions and terms of work, feeling that they had been tricked into signing contracts, that the labor laws of Hawaiʻi gave them little protection, and that their consul was of no help. Many wrote letters of complaint to newspapers in Norway and the United States, some of which were reprinted in Norwegian-language newspapers in the United States. European newspapers were soon running headlines about "slave labor conditions in the Sandwich Islands," part of an explosion of unfavorable publicity on the mainland and in Europe (Beechert 1993: 50).

On February 1, 1882, thirty-nine men from the Pāpaʻikou plantation wrote a letter of complaint titled "The Hawaiian Hades," which was published in the Chicago *Scandinavia* and republished on May 11, 1882, in the *San Francisco Chronicle*, an ardent critic of Hawaiʻi's contract labor system and an opponent of the Reciprocity Treaty. The letter described the brutal treatment and meager food the Norwegians received and said that they had told Hitchcock they would sue him if he did not fulfill the contract. He replied, the letter continued, that it would be useless to sue because they had no money and would lose, "which we afterwards, to our cost, found too true" (Davis and Davis 1962: 22). The complaints included being arrested for refusing to work more than ten hours and being fined $3.90 each, which was deducted from their wages, "and the Judge adding that we were obliged to work for our owner whenever he wanted, which clearly violated the contract, but what could we do against the cruel planter and a corrupt Judge? One became insane, but was still brought before this pliable Judge and fined money enough to amount to six month's wages, but was at last sent to the asylum in Honolulu" (Davis and Davis 1962: 22–23).

The letter listed a series of contract violations including extending the contract for the days a worker was ill. The workers said that at last, because of all these "atrocities," they went to the Hilo courthouse and sued Mr. Hitchcock for nonfulfillment of contract. The hearing lasted two days, with sixty immigrants assembled at the courthouse, but they lost and had to pay a fine of five dollars. The letter writers attribute their defeat to a poor interpreter and "the all-powerful influence of Hitchcock." The trial was attended by Consul Glade and Marshal W. C. Parke (Luther Severance's brother-in-law). Glade was unable to understand their language and ignored their complaints, telling them to be submissive.

A short time after the discussion with Consul Glade, Marshal Parke prevailed on Hitchcock to send two people from the group to Hilo to bring the case before a "tribunal," although it is not clear which tribunal they meant. The two engaged a lawyer, who determined that the group should be suing the Bureau of Immigration instead of Hitchcock, because its name rather than Hitchcock's was on the labor contract they had signed. So the group decided to leave Hitchcock's plantation, since they had no contract with him. On October 17 1881, seventy-seven men started for Hilo with two hundred dollars to hire an attorney to conduct their case. When they arrived in town they were arrested for having left the plantation and the same kind of a trial as before was repeated. Apparently they were again convicted of refusal to work.

As a last resort, they appealed their case to the Supreme Court in Honolulu, held in the middle of January 1882. Despite the assistance of Marshal Parke and a lawyer, they again lost the case and all their money. They concluded that it was useless to sue Mr. Hitchcock, saying that "[we] have resigned ourselves to our fate" (Davis and Davis 1962: 24).

Meanwhile, the government of Norway had sent the Swede Johan Anton Wolff Grip to investigate the conditions of the workers as a result of their complaints. In October 1882 he arrived in Hilo with Mr. Cleghorn, inspector general of immigrants of the kingdom, and was told by Sheriff Severance that fifty of Mr. Hitchcock's sixty Norwegians at Pāpa'ikou were in jail for refusing to work. After a day of investigation, forty-nine still refused to return to work. Grip and Cleghorn took half back to Honolulu with them because the Hilo jail was too small. Grip was unable to persuade the government of Hawai'i to reduce the terms of the Norwegians' contracts, so he attempted to disperse the Pāpa'ikou men to other plantations. D. H. Hitchcock refused to let the workers go at once, but agreed to let ten leave for other plantations every month. However, when those on O'ahu had finished their sentence working on the roads, they again refused to work on the Hitchcock plantation. After some negotiation by Mr. Grip, they agreed to stay five or six more months if Hitchcock would release them a year early. Grip concluded his report with the observation that the problem was that the Norwegians were predominantly artisans and townsmen with skills that would earn them significantly more in the Hawaiian economy than the plantation paid (Grip 1884). A large number canceled their contracts by buying them out and others absconded to San Francisco (Grip 1884).

Thus the Norwegians, when confronted with the harsh regimen of plantation life, its relatively low wages, and its practices of fines for multiple small infractions, resisted and complained, although there is general agreement that the conditions they faced were no more severe than those other groups faced (Davis and Davis 1962). Unlike others, this group quickly resorted to lawsuits, organizing, strikes, and letters of protest to government representatives and newspapers. They had a marked sense of their rights and an inclination to carry their battles to the terrain of the law, in contrast with the Chinese workers in the previous case. On the other hand, as they moved into the legal arena, they confronted the power structure of Hilo, in which the judge, plantation owner, and even Marshal Parke and Sheriff Severance were all part of a close-knit, long-established social world of shared understandings about identities and kinds of workers. They apparently benefitted, however, from tensions between Severance and Hitchcock, to which Hitchcock alludes in his personal letters and which Isabella Bird reveals (see chapter 6), and they were also supported, it appears, by Marshal Parke.

The workers failed in court, just as the Chinese workers did, but their approach to the law was strikingly different. They understood themselves as having rights and saw the law as an ally. With the added support of a representative from their government, some were able to negotiate an early release from their contracts, although only after serving time in prison. Ultimately they voted with their feet. Five years after their arrival, out of the 613 men, women, and children who had come from Norway, only fifty-two were left on the plantations (Beechert 1985: 87).[8] The planters viewed the Norwegian experiment as a disaster and the workers as troublemakers. They soon went back to getting the cheapest labor they could, including labor from China, instead of bringing these more independent, legally conscious workers (Davis and Davis 1962: 33).

Racism and national identity were both important here. Because this small group of workers was white, they may have received better treatment from the courts. Their importation was part of a policy of bringing in "citizen" labor that would strengthen the country rather than the "coolie" labor that, it was assumed, would not. The Norwegians certainly had more support from their home government than many other governments provided their workers. Japan and Portugal, like Norway, were concerned about the conditions of their workers in Hawai'i, while the British refused to allow any of their subjects to work in Hawai'i because of its dismal protection of labor. Chinese workers suffered from the weakness of the government of China at the time. Moreover, the Norwegian workers, like the Portuguese workers, came from a country with the beginnings of a labor union movement. They were largely urban people and at least some were literate. And they thought of using the courts and the media to protest.

These two stories illustrate the possibilities and limitations of the legal system for the protection of workers. In neither case did the law do the workers much good, but in conjunction with public opinion and government representatives, it produced a marginal benefit for those willing and able to use it. Some of the Hitchcocks' workers did, after all, get one year reduced from their contracts, although they suffered imprisonment at hard labor, while others were able to move to different plantations. In contrast, the protesters at Hakalau were almost all fined and imprisoned and gained nothing. The support of the home nation was also very important. For example, in response to the 1889 lynching of a prominent Japanese store owner named Goto by five haole lunas and one Native Hawaiian, the Japanese government actively worked to bring the assailants to trial. They were convicted of manslaughter but appealed and escaped the islands while the case was on appeal (Circuit Court Case #2579, December 1889; *Daily Commercial Advertiser*, January 16, 1890, p. 2; Beechert 1985: 115; Kubota, 1985; Kaya 1988; Okihiro 1991: 35). Defendants varied greatly in their political resources as well as their consciousness of rights and legal entitlement, variations that affected how they fared in court.

Law and Resistance

These cases, along with the cases in the previous chapter, suggest how law reshapes the terrain of power. As law regulates the workplace, community, and family life, it conveys an aspirational description of social relationships and moral behavior. In place of the raw coercion of the marketplace or the violence of the fields, it seeks to regulate employer/employee relationships, to protect workers from the unbridled impact of capitalism. Yet the texts of the law must be made socially real: enacted, implemented, imposed. As this chapter and the last indicate, there were enormous hurdles to getting into the court, building a case, and being heard. A small, close-knit group controlled the court and policing system; a group more sympathetic to Christian moral reform and Native Hawaiians than to immigrant newcomers, particularly if they were neither white nor Christian. To use the possibilities law offers required knowledge of process and strategy. Litigants had to learn to speak the language of law and frame their complaints in these terms. They were better off if they could hire an attorney, mobilize political support outside the courts, and phrase their claims in terms of rights and entitlements. It helped to be white. The white elite preferred and desired European workers, who they thought would make good citizens, and they hoped that the Asian workers would leave as soon as their contracts were completed. It is likely that Europeans' complaints were treated more seriously as a result, and most of the defendants acquitted in labor cases were white.

But there were significant changes in workers' relationships with the legal system over time. During the initial period, violence, drinking, gambling, and refusal to work—actions defined by dominant groups as dangerous or repugnant—thrust newcomers into the legal arena as defendants. But these actions were one of the few means stranger workers had to recuperate a complex social self, defined not just as a worker but also as a friend, neighbor, or citizen of another country, outside the regime that resolutely insisted on seeing them only as workers. The criminalized activities represented a social space outside the realm of plantation surveillance and control.[9] To drink, gamble, ride horses too fast, or have sex outside marriage were forms of resistance to disciplinary power that provoked its penalties but also spiced the pleasure of the activities. Engaging in practices defined as illegal was not necessarily a conscious form of resistance or one with a particular political agenda, but an inchoate way of insisting on a self and a social order other than that of dominant groups.

But as immigrants married and acquired family authority and connections, they were able to reconstitute a social self outside the workplace in other ways. They became fathers, mothers, community leaders, and leaders of contract work groups. And in a generation or less, immigrants who stayed in Hawai'i began to learn about the law.[10] As their children were educated in Hawai'i, they began to appropriate the power of law and its discourses for other purposes: in union movements, electoral politics, and for entrance into government jobs, the judiciary, and the law firms.[11] The successful union movement of the early twentieth century was lead by a coalition of immigrants and their children who used legal strategies to improve the conditions of labor on the plantation under the protection of the mainland union regulations (Beechert 1985). The grandchildren and great-grandchildren of the immigrant workers, particularly those of Japanese ancestry, are now prominent within the Hawaiian judiciary and bar. Thus inchoate resistance through criminal behavior gradually mutated into deliberate, political resistance using the discourse of the law itself. This process continues into the present, as

contemporary political movements work within the law as well as mobiliz-
ing political support outside the law. Prime examples of these strategies are
the Hawaiian sovereignty movement and the movement against gender violence (see Trask 1993; Hasager and Friedman 1994; Merry 1995; Merry
1997).

Taking a historical perspective radically changes the analysis of the way
the law shapes relations of power. The people subjected to the control of the
law in one generation mobilized the law in the next generation. The inchoate
resistance of the newcomers gave way to the more intentional resistance of a
new group of intellectuals descended from and shaped by the experiences of
their parents and grandparents. Historical transformations redistribute the
knowledge and skills required to appropriate legality in protest movements
as well as in individual court proceedings. From a historical perspective,
resistance through criminalized practices is the cauldron of a more articulated and deliberate form of resistance: some of those who undergo its
fire learn the system and resist from the inside through its discourses and
procedures.

But this is a form of resistance that depends on incorporation of those
opposed to the power structure and the transformation of their approaches.
Resistance occurs within the order created by law rather than outside of it.
But resistance within law is available only to already disciplined subjects. As
resistance moves inside the law instead of outside of it, the law itself, as a
privileged arena of contest over power, is strengthened. It consumes resources that would otherwise be devoted to political organization or to political violence and disruption. Once the game is played inside the courts, whatever the outcome, the hegemony of the game itself is strengthened.

This is a game different from physical violence or the violence of the
market. Fragile as the law proved in practice as a protection for workers, it
was a barrier between the workers and the labor demands of the employers.
It was an alternative to settling all problems with cane knives and lunas'
whips or lynching on a telephone pole, the fate of the activist Goto. And
over the long run, the law provided a discourse of rights and entitlement that
provided the opportunity for at least some of the immigrant and colonized
groups to assert more powerful positions in the emerging social order of the
twentieth century.

8

SEXUALITY, MARRIAGE,

AND THE MANAGEMENT OF THE BODY

URING THE 1850s and 1860s the Hilo courts, along with the courts of other parts of the kingdom, were full of cases concerning sexual conduct, particularly adultery and fornication. These cases represented between one fourth and two thirds of all cases in Honolulu, Kaua'i, the island of Hawai'i overall, and Hilo in the period from the 1830s to 1850s, as table 8.1 indicates. But prosecutions for offenses of sexual behavior declined precipitously both in Hilo and islandwide in the 1870s. By 1886 only 5 percent of the island of Hawai'i's arrests concerned sexual behavior. The same drop is apparent in the Hilo District Court, even as the population grew (see chart 8.1 and chart 8.2).[1] Of the 128 cases of adultery and fornication in the sample of Hilo District Court cases between 1853 and 1903, most (81 percent) were adultery rather than fornication, almost entirely charged against a man and a woman together (93 percent). Adultery is defined as sexual intercourse when one or both parties are married; fornication when neither is married. Only 7 percent of the 128 cases (nine cases) had lawyers, in comparison with 10 percent overall. A mere seven were found not guilty. Of those cases with a disposition in the record, 91 percent were found guilty in comparison to 86 percent overall. Those with lawyers were less likely to be found guilty, as in the desertion of work cases.

The vast majority of defendants were Hawaiian (82 percent), with a small minority Japanese (9 percent). From 1853 until 1893 all but two of the adultery and fornication defendants were Hawaiians, but in 1903 there were only two Hawaiian defendants out of twenty-two (chart 8.3). The rest consisted of eleven Japanese, one haole, one Chinese, five Portuguese, and three Puerto Rican defendants. Clearly, the prosecution of adultery and fornication was directed toward the Hawaiian population rather than the burgeoning group of imported laborers: it remained part of the national project of constituting a civilized citizenry from the Native Hawaiian population. Asian workers were not included in this national vision. In order to explain why sexual behavior was such a central concern of the courts in the middle of the century and why it faded from view toward century's end, it is necessary to return to the early years of Hawaiian/haole relationships. Whereas the previous chapter described law's place in the inequalities resulting from labor importation,

TABLE 8.1

Statistics on Adultery and Prostitution Cases in Nineteenth-Century Hawai'i

1838 (from all islands, apparently)

Offense	No. of Persons Convicted	Percentage of Caseload
Adultery	246	52
Lewdness	81	17
Theft	48	10
Riot	32	7
Falsewitness	30	6
Seduction	18	4
Mutiny	15	3
Manslaughter	4	1
Total	474	100

Offenses connected with sexual behavior: 73 percent

Source: Kanoa [attrib.] 1839, cited in Sahlins 1985: 23–24n.

1844–1845 (Cases in Honolulu District Court Minute Books, Jan. 1, 1844–1845)

Offense	Number Tried	Percentage of Caseload
MORALS OFFENSES		
Adultery	83	54
Husband-wife, "being afraid," abandonment	24	16
Prostitution/pimping	20	13
Sabbath violations	17	11
Gambling	7	5
Impersonating a God	1	1
Total	152	100
PUBLIC ORDER OFFENSES		
Theft	98	47
Insults, Swearing, Black Magic, False acc, Trickery	42	20
Assault	23	11
Rioting/Fighting/Brawls	16	8
Killing Animals/Injuring Animals/Tying on Street	11	5
Riding Furiously/Secretly Riding	7	3
Drunkeness/Selling, Making Liquor	6	3
Rape	3	1

TABLE 8.1 (*cont.*)

1844–1845 (Cases in Honolulu District Court Minute Books, Jan. 1, 1844–1845)

Offense	Number Tried	Percentage of Caseload
Breaking and Entering	2	1
Failure of Duty	1	0.4
Counterfeit Money	1	0.4
Total	210	100

Of total number of cases (362), 23 percent are adultery, 6 percent are prostitution, or altogether 29 percent are concerned with sexual offenses.

Source: Matsuda 1988a: 29.

1846–1947 (Cases in Kauaʻi District Courts, April 1, 1846–April 1, 1847)

Offenses	No. Tried in District Court	Percentage of Caseload
Fornication	140	63
Stealing	34	15
Working on Sabbath	21	10
Fighting and Brawling	10	5
Miscellaneous	16	7
Total	221	100

Offenses connected with sexual behavior: 63 percent

Source: Report of H. Sea to Attorney General, Archives of Hawaiʻi, quoted in Sahlins 1985: 24n.

1851 (Island of Hawaii, April 1, 1851 to Dec. 31, 1852)

Offense	Number of Crimes Committed	Percentage of Crimes Reported
Adultery	280	23
Fornication	80	7
Unnatural connection	64	5
Unlawful cohabitation	60	5
Carnal abuse	30	3
Affray	107	9
Violating the Sabbath	74	6
Drinking awa	31	3
Drunk	96	8
Fraud	20	2
Aiding crime	6	0.5
Stealing	60	5
Malicious mischief	120	10
Perjury	4	0.3

CHAPTER 8

TABLE 8.1 (*cont.*)

1851 (Island of Hawaii, April 1, 1851 to Dec. 31, 1852)

Offense	Number of Crimes Committed	Percentage of Crimes Reported
Subornation of perjury	2	0.1
Heedless riding of horses	10	0.8
Cruelty to Animals	6	0.5
False Arrest	4	0.3
Rioting	10	0.8
Disturbing peace of the night	20	2
Truancy	6	0.5
Gambling	4	0.3
Distilling intoxicating liquor	6	0.5
Vagrancy	3	0.3
Profanity	5	0.4
Unlawful opening of letters	2	0.1
Prostitution	8	0.7
Abetting to commit a crime	10	0.8
Planting awa	11	0.9
Malicious injury	20	2
Staying ashore without permission of the collector of customs	27	2
Anaana	1	0.1
Public worship	1	0.1
Contempt	3	0.3
Gross cheat	1	0.1
Arson	1	0.1
Total	1,193	
Total connected with sexuality	522	44
Total prostitution of sexuality	8	2

Source: Letter to Keoni Ana, Minister of the Interior, from George L. Kapeau, Governor of Hawai'i, Dec. 1, 1852, trans. by H. Hart, State Archives of Hawai'i, Interior Dept.—Misc. Box 6.

1853 Hilo Minute Books, Hilo Police Court (Total number of cases with charges 124)

Offense	No. of Cases in Court	Percentage of Caseload
Adultery	39	32
Accessory to adultery	1	1
Prostitution	0	
Fornication	8	7
Pimping	1	1

TABLE 8.1 (*cont.*)

1853 Hilo Minute Books, Hilo Police Court (Total number of cases with charges 124)

Offense	No. of Cases in Court	Percentage of Caseload
Keep Disorderly house	1	1
Lascivious Conduct	2	2
Lewdness	1	1
Common nuisance—lewd	2	2
Total number of cases with charges listed: 124		
Total number concerning sexuality: 55		44

Note: In this year, according to marriage records of Titus Coan, there were 110 marriages; in 1852, 75; in 1854, 94. Linnekin 1990: 134.

this one examines the place of law in the colonizing relationship between whites and Native Hawaiians.

The long history of conflict between Hawaiians and the American missionaries over the meaning of sexuality and marriage stretches back to the 1820s. Establishing a new order of sexual conduct was a fundamental part of the mission project: missionaries sought to constrain desire and to cabin sexuality within marriage. This was linked to the wider project of promoting

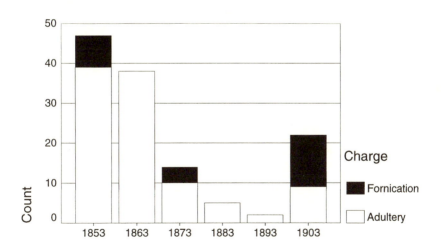

Chart 8.1. Adultery and Fornication Cases, Hilo District Court, 1853–1903

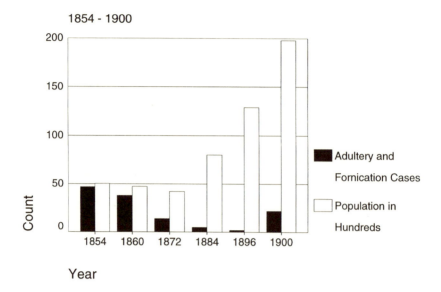

Chart 8.2. Comparison of Adultery and Fornication Cases and Hilo Population, 1854–1900

industry, thrift, punctuality, and responsibility concerning debts. Ironically, the missionaries opposed the merchants and mercantile capitalism, but their moral reforms prefigured the values of industrial capitalism as they promoted self-governance, self-restraint, and the enduring, property-owning family. The redefinition of sexuality and marriage predated Hawaiians' significant involvement in plantation agriculture yet it prepared the way for the creation of the modern subject engaged in wage labor and capitalist farming.

The battle over sexuality began with a fight against the sailors and prostitution but it was soon eclipsed by struggles to establish and police a new form of marriage. The 1820s were marked by confrontations between missionaries and whalemen over prostitution, but adultery rather than prostitution occupied the attention of the courts in subsequent years. The earliest court figures, from 1838, show no cases of prostitution at all. Even in Honolulu in 1844 and 1845, the major port during the peak of the whaling years when thousands of sailors romped through the town each season, adultery cases (eighty-three) were four times more frequent in the District Court than prostitution cases (twenty) (Matsuda 1988a: 28). In 1851 the governor of the island of Hawai'i reported that there were on the entire island 360 cases of adultery and fornication and only eight of prostitution. Of the fifty-five cases concerning sexuality heard in the Hilo Police Court in 1853, none were for charges of prostitution, one was for pimping, and one for keeping a disor-

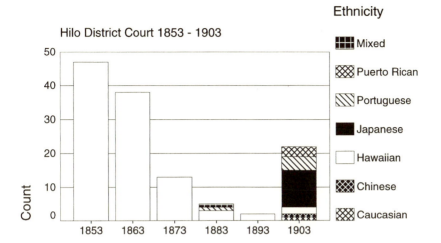

Chart 8.3. Ethnicity of Defendants, Adultery/Fornication Cases, Hilo District Court, 1853–1903

derly house, even though the town was now open to merchant trade and visited regularly by whalers. In the disorderly house case, only the Hawaiian owners, not the foreign clients, were punished (see table 8.1). The first prosecution for prostitution in Hilo I recorded was in 1903. Disorderly houses were prosecuted once in 1853 and once in 1903.

The mission's conception of permissible and prohibited sexual activity differed sharply from that of Hawaiian society in the 1820s. Missionaries considered sex a dangerous, destructive, and negative force (see Rubin 1993 [1984]).[2] Virtually all sexual acts outside marriage fell into the category of prohibited activity. Desire itself was potentially sinful. For example, Armstrong, a missionary from Pennsylvania who came in 1832 (himself the father of ten children), says in his answer to the questions posed to the missionaries by Wyllie in 1846 about the state of the kingdom that by far the most ruinous form of vice was licentiousness, which was particularly prevalent among unmarried people. He blames this vice on idleness, living in small miserable houses without partitions, the debased state of moral feelings, and "the licentious conduct of many foreigners who tempt Hawaiian females to the commission of crime, by money and other enticing articles. In the year 1846, 164 cases of adultery were brought before the courts in Honolulu; and it has often been said that a large portion of the money taken in the shops of this town—say three-fourths—is the wages of licentiousness" (Kingdom of Hawai'i 1846: 32–33). The means of containing licentiousness was prosecution and punishment. Yet adultery convictions provided the bald facts that validated charges of licentiousness. Along with stronger laws and punishments, Armstrong recommends restraints for people going from remote areas to seaports: "Multitudes resort to these places for the most trivial reasons, fall into temptation, become diseased and go back to their homes, only to scatter death around them and be a curse to their friends. Much licentiousness too is practiced on small vessels going to and from these central towns" (Kingdom of Hawai'i 1846: 32–33).

Here, Armstrong merges prostitution and adultery as instances of the same moral flaw—licentiousness. But they were very different. Prostitution as a market transaction emerged only after seamen started to arrive in the islands in significant numbers. Early transactions were probably reciprocal: sexual favors given in exchange for cloth, iron, mirrors, scissors, and beads (Kamakau 1961: 95, 100; Ralston 1989), paralleling earlier practices of reciprocal exchange of sexual favors for gifts. At some point early in the century, prostitution became a matter of buying and selling. Adultery and fornication, on the other hand, usually involved Hawaiian men and women living together who had not formally married before a clergyman. But in the Christian imagination of the early nineteenth century, both were instances of sex outside marriage: pleasure that escaped the bounds of duty and procreation. It was this domain of sensuality that the new moral order sought to contain in the name of "civilization."

Sexuality was divided into approved and prohibited spheres in Hawaiian society as well, but according to a different cultural logic. It was not generally viewed as dangerous or destructive although it was recognized as politically prickly. Permissible sexual activities and partners depended on rank, age, birth order, and marital status. Adultery was constrained for high-ranking ali'i, particularly women, based on conceptions of mana, or sacred power. Kapu systems protected others from the power of mana, and sexuality restrictions guaranteed that children would have high rank and possess mana. Hawaiian kinship was generally tolerant of sexual contacts outside of marriage, although promiscuity was disapproved because it muddied the clarity of a child's genealogy (Matsuda 1988a: 27) and was held in contempt by the majority (Handy and Pukui 1972: 162). Sexuality was regarded as natural and not a source of guilt or shame, marriages were relatively easily arranged, contracted, and dissolved, and periods of free sexual contact were not unusual in a person's life, although these conditions varied a great deal by rank (Malo 1951; Linnekin 1990; Handy and Pukui 1972; Ralston 1989).

The contact zone of nineteenth-century Hawai'i juxtaposed two fundamentally different ideas of the body and sexual expression. In the chiefly Hawaiian system, the body of high-ranking people was sacred and embodied

the fertility of the kingdom. The height and corpulence of many aliʻi be-
spoke their power and their wealth. Their bodies could not be touched by
inferiors, nor could inferiors wear their clothes or even cast a shadow on
their persons ('Iʻī 1959; see chapter 2). Clothes were thrown away, even
secretly into the sea, rather than being passed down the hierarchy (Sinclair
1995). The kapus of some of the aliʻi required that subordinates uncover
their bodies in their presence: Kamehameha had to take off his malo in front
of the sacred aliʻi Keōpūolani, for example (Kamakau 1961: 208–209). Un-
covering the shoulder or the body was required in front of other tabu chiefs
and chiefesses as well, depending on their personal kapu status. The body
was symbolic of rank and particular restrictions on touching and looking
marked a person's position in the hierarchy.

In contrast, the missionaries' concerns were not genealogies and distinctions of rank but covered bodies and contained desires. The body within the
Christian discourse of "civilization" was resolutely private and potentially
disruptive: it was to be covered, its effusions contained, its emotions subdued and checked, and its exterior cleaned. It also marked status, but in a
different way. Covering, privacy, and control over emotional and sexual expression expressed status. Social rank depended on firm self-governance of
the erotic, the denial of pleasure, and restraint in eating, drinking, and even
laughter. The body was a source of danger, requiring constant vigilance and
self-control.

An incident from the 1820s reveals the clash between these meanings of
sacredness and the body in the early years of Christian conversion. During
the 1820s, Hoapili, the powerful chief of Maui and an early convert, labored
energetically to construct the new sexual order. The missionaries insisted
that the law applied to everyone regardless of rank. Yet spiritual power and
social virtue had been based on rank and birth rather than religious faith
and degree of "civilization." Kamakau describes Kamehameha III before
Kaʻahumanu's death working at hard labor to pay for his sin of adultery: he
built a fence for the missionary Hiram Bingham to punish himself (Kamakau
1961: 334–335). Kamakau observes that this was strange in view of the
saying, "The body of the king is sacred!" The sacred king doing hard labor
in penance for his sexual transgressions represents a juxtaposition of two
fundamentally different conceptions of sacred power. In one case it was
earned through submission to a set of rules of morality applied universally
and in the other it was conferred through blood and ancestry and recognized
by kapus designed to protect lesser beings from the mana of the king. The
king's body as sacred contrasted with the king's body as subjected to a
universal discipline of desire in order to be civilized.

The management of sexuality was integral to the civilizing process (Elias
1994). Along with changing conceptions of the management of bodily
functions such as eating, defecation, and aggression came new ideas about

sexual activities (ibid.). All of these physical activities were newly regulated, moved "behind the scenes," and subjected to different conceptions of shame and repugnance. The management of sexuality, its movement into the se- cluded sphere of the family and its restriction to enduring marriages, became both a signifier of civilization and a central target of the new systems of discipline and control. For the American missionaries, containing and con- trolling the body and keeping its functions private were signs of religious morality and virtue, whereas bodily display awakened horror and repug- nance. For example, early missionary writers reported with horror that Ha- waiians, whose skill in swimming and surfing was a constant source of amazement and awe to visitors, swam naked. The Kailua missionaries Thurston and Bishop were appalled that soon after they arrived, two high chiefesses, returning from a swim in the ocean, stopped to visit the mission- ary house completely naked (Cheever 1856: 93). Missionary reports from the 1840s constantly complained about the lack of partitions in Hawaiian houses, which prevented privacy for sexual activities, and they bemoaned the early sexual experiences of young children (Kingdom of Hawai'i 1846).

There were two aspects to the transformation of sexuality sought by the missionaries. The first involved changes in the management of the body, the second the redefinition of the family. Using knives and forks instead of fin- gers, eating at tables instead of on mats, and avoiding activities that involved mixed-gender nakedness such as swimming and surfing were key features of the new management of the body. Privacy of bodily functions was also im- portant: separate sleeping areas, covered bodies, and concealed defecation were stressed. Differences in standards of privacy in sexual relations led to ongoing demands for partitions in houses and greater concealment of sexual acts. New standards of sobriety and the containment of emotion discouraged the dramatic displays of wailing and self-mutilation accompanying the death of prominent ali'i.

The second aspect involved changes in the nature of marriage. Christian marriage was envisioned as an enduring, religiously sanctioned, and perma- nent relationship in which the husband exercised authority over and pro- tected the wife. Sexual activity was restricted to marriage and divorce be- came virtually impossible. Since property ownership and its transmission through inheritance were core features of this type of family, it can be con- sidered a bourgeois family (see Collier, Maurer, and Suarez-Navaz 1995). This form of family is constituted by the liberal state.[3] The interior space is defined as a space of liberty outside the law but the exterior is regulated by laws about marriage, divorce, property rights, and inheritance (Fitzpatrick 1992: 180; W. Brown 1995). Internal governance is vested in the husband over the wife and in the father over the children. The state constitutes this private space but cedes its authority inside the space to the father/husband (Fitzpatrick 1992: 180).

Thus, the body was a fundamental terrain of struggle in the cultural transformation of the Hawaiian people. The fight over sexuality was really about
the disciplining of the body in the name of civilization, decency, and decorum. As we saw in chapter 5, Hawaiians were infantilized, in part over
issues about the management of the body. The Hawaiians transgressed
those behavioral rules that were used to differentiate children from adults in
Europe.

Hawaiian Conceptions of Sexuality and Marriage
in the Early Nineteenth Century

Understanding Hawaiian kinship in this period requires piecing together the
scarce, partial, and often Christian-influenced writings that are available.[4] I
have attempted to sort out the complexity of views toward permissible and
prohibited sexual relations and marriage, but make no claim that this is a
definitive study. Its purpose is primarily to indicate the contrasts between the
cultural logic of Hawaiian understandings of sexual relations and marriage
and missionary views, since missionaries advised the government as it instituted the new legal regime governing marriage and sexual relations. Unfortunately, many of the contemporary sources shared the Christian view of the
sinful nature of all sexual relations outside of marriage and could see marriage institutions only where they resembled their own. I rely on recent ethnographic research based on the detailed records of land tenure preserved in
the Māhele books from the 1840s, analyzed in Linnekin (1990) and Sahlins
(1992), and the excellent account of Hawaiian kinship in the remote region
of Ka'ū based on ethnographic observation in the 1930s, including interviews with elderly Hawaiians related to Mary Kawena Pukui (Handy and
Pukui 1972).

The meanings of sexuality and marriage varied enormously by rank. There
were clearly rules within maka'āinana communities; the existence of the
rural community depended on extensive reciprocity with serious penalties of
exclusion for those who failed to abide by the rules of the community and
the responsibilities of membership, including adherence to its sexual codes
of conduct (Handy and Pukui 1972: 107). Among maka'āinana who were
not first-born children (hiapo) or favorites (punahele), with special training
and tasks, marriage was entered into easily and ended relatively easily, not
marked with much formality at its inception (Ellis 1969; Handy and Pukui
1972; Linnekin 1990: 121). A young man spoke to his parents or grandparents about the woman he wanted for a wife, and they approached her
parents, or the girl's elders could approach the boy's. If she and the elders
agreed, he would move to her household and contribute to their support in a
relationship called noho pū ("just settling in") (Handy and Pukui 1972: 44,

107). It was the larger kin group, the 'ohana, rather than the husband/wife unit, that was the basis for production, exchange, and tribute payment, under the direction of the haku, or elder male, of the senior branch of the whole 'ohana (Handy and Pukui 1972: 6). An unhappy marriage could be easily broken by going elsewhere or by refusing to live together, and both partners would in time find other husbands and wives, although Handy and Pukui say that marriages were generally permanent and husbands and wives were very affectionate to each other (ibid.: 110).

Reports from the 1820s present a similar vision of marriage. A visitor in 1819 reports that marriage can be broken by mutual consent or at the will of either party (Freycinet 1978: 76). In his account of kinship based on his 1822 tour of the islands, the English missionary Ellis notes that marriage contracts are usually concluded by the parents or relations of both parties without gifts to her family or dowry. Ceremonies are few: the bridegroom casts a piece of tapa over the bride in the presence of her parents or relations and there is general feasting. The marriage tie is loose and the husband can dismiss his wife on any occasion (Ellis 1969: 434–435). Yet if a man steals another's wife, the husband is entitled to take the property of that man in vengeance if he can muster a large enough following (Kamakau 1961: 191). If the thief is a chief, everything could be taken in exchange for the woman. Polygamy was permitted whenever the husband had the means to feed several wives, and women occasionally took more than one husband (Freycinet 1978: 76). Ellis says this was allowed among all ranks but practiced only by chiefs, but Handy and Pukui describe a more widespread pattern of co-husbands and co-wives.

Hawaiians were initiated into sex early and continued to be sexually active during their lives, although particularly during the period of courtship before more permanent unions (Handy and Pukui 1972: 161). Linnekin quotes a Hawaiian testifying in court in 1854: "In the old days, before the custom of marriage became general, it was moe aku, moe mai [sleep there, sleep here]" (Linnekin 1990: 121). According to Malo, "in ancient times indiscriminate sexual relations between unmarried persons (moe o na mea kaawale), fornication, keeping a lover (moe ipo), hired prostitution (moe kookuli), bigamy, polyandry, whoredom (moe hookamakama), sodomy (moe aikane) and masturbation were not considered wrong, nor were foeticide and idol worship regarded as evils" (Malo 1951: 74). Unmarried people had considerable sexual freedom, but promiscuity and adultery for married people were not considered acceptable (Handy and Pukui 1972: 133, 162). Malo says that it was wrong to change one's husband or wife frequently or to keep shifting from place to place. Thus frequent and shifting sexual partners was condemned among married people, but divorce and remarriage were relatively easy for those without significant rank or social position.[5]

For the young, for junior siblings who could not move into leadership positions, and for most Hawaiian commoners, cohabitation was the norm. This was the pattern for the vast majority of the Hawaiian population, in which women were free to leave when they wished (Linnekin 1990: 58). It was the birth of children that held relationships together: births were marked by extensive ceremonies and, according to Kamakau, "sealed" the relationship between the families. They also secured the family's continuity and succession on the land, as grandchildren were seen as replacing grandparents. Thus the more enduring commoner marriages created household groups within and between ahupua'a (Linnekin 1990: 125).

In Sahlins's study of an Oʻahu valley in the early nineteenth century using Māhele records, he finds that the kin unit was a loose collection of affinal and consanguineal relatives joined by common descent from grandparents and ascent from a shared child, even an adopted child (Sahlins 1992: 192–206). The first-born child was typically the favorite, punahele, adopted by the grandparents and the focus of the kin group as well as endowed with rights to land, whereas younger siblings often had to go off in search of lands and affines. At least for a time, they lived lives of pleasure and little work. Marriage was frequently endogamous and local, a means of pulling the kin group together, but kin were also united through shared ancestry of a grandchild. Sahlins's account suggests that marriage practices varied with access to land, such that those without access to land were more likely to wander among kin and between the natal places of both the man and the woman than those who had it.

The organizing principle was the sibling tie, with senior siblings exercising authority and care over younger siblings, a general Polynesian pattern (Ortner 1981; Gailey 1987). Both kinship and rank were reckoned bilaterally. Although a person might leave his local kin group for marriage, this was often only temporary. Despite considerable mobility in the short term, over the long run a set of cross-sex siblings constituted the core of the family unit, with dependents attached to them. Pukui and Handy call the bilateral local household group the ʻohana, the true family, distinguished from unrelated dependents and helpers (Handy and Pukui 1972: 5). As Linnekin notes, given the fragile and ephemeral nature of marriage, affines were "structurally extraneous members of the household," people who could always return to their natal kin group and the land where they belonged (Linnekin 1990: 145).

Chiefly marriage, in contrast with makaʻāinana marriage, was politically important: it was a matter of alliances, political expedience, family influence, and rank. Among the reigning family, brothers and sisters married to protect and preserve their high rank (Ellis 1969: 434–435; Sahlins 1992). The first-born children of distinguished families had formal, binding engagements, hoʻopalau, marked by the exchange of gifts (Handy and Pukui 1972: 105). Kamakau's history of the ruling chiefs of Hawaiʻi reveals vividly the sexual politics of rule: the importance of strategic marriages, the constant threats of usurping junior siblings, the significance of affines in building support, and the critical significance of genealogy to claims to power (Kamakau 1961). Both men and women of the chiefly class could have more than one husband or wife. Although chiefly women had liaisons and secondary unions, they could not do so with impunity, especially if they had high kapu rank or politically important relatives (Linnekin 1990: 60). Boys dedicated to the kahuna class were also kept tabu and pure, and boys who were to take up some branch of learning were guarded from "defilement" (Kamakau 1961: 235).

Ali'i women's sexuality was particularly jealously guarded and their sexual liaisons frequently had serious political repercussions, sometimes resulting in death to the person guilty of adultery.[6] The sexual behavior of high-ranking women was closely controlled.[7] Rank apparently governed sexual access, entitling ali'i to sexual favors from maka'āinana while punishing maka'āinana males who had sex with ali'i women. Comments from visitors suggest that sexual relations by maka'āinana men with chiefly women were punished very severely. A French visitor to the islands in 1819 observed: "A commoner convicted of adultery with a chief's wife is punished, depending on the rank of the offended husband, by having one or both eyes put out. But the accomplice, it seems is immune to public vengeance. Men do not die of this horrible punishment, but if one had not seen the victims, it would be hard to believe that anyone could survive it" (Freycinet 1978: 89). Restrictions by rank applied to high-ranking males as well. Kamakau tells the story of a tabu chief of O'ahu, Kahahana, who made love to lesser chiefesses and lost his kapu of Fire, Heat, and Extraordinary Heat and was called Walia ("is degraded") (Kamakau 1961: 128). On the other hand, Malo notes that the wives of country people were sometimes appropriated by men about court and "even the men were sometimes separated from their country wives by the women of the court" but people did not resist much because they feared the king might take sides against them (Malo 1951: 64). Many left the country and preferred to live with the chiefs since life around the court was indolent and slack.

Few of the people about court lived in marriage, Malo says, and the great majority had no legitimate relations with women, since sodomy and other unnatural vices, fornication, and hired prostitution were common (Malo 1951: 65). He uses the term *aikāne*, which means male friends as well as the sexual act between them. His term *unnatural vices* refers to ho'o kā maka, "a "bestial form of vice" in which "man confronted man" (Malo 1951: 67 n. 6), and "hired prostitution," moe ho'okuli ho'okuli, to shut one's mouth with a bribe (ibid.: 67n. 7). Here the Christian lens on Hawaiian practices is obvious. Malo's account suggests a broader range of acceptable sexual practices than that of the missionaries (see Morris 1990). Kamakau also observes

that in the "old days" chiefs engaged in homosexuality, even putting away
their wives (Kamakau 1961: 234). He says that taking of many women as
wives was a cause of trouble as well as women taking too many husbands,
and that some women went off with whatever husband they pleased. Parents
and friends assisted so long as they could get a man or woman to take a
wealthy person as mate (Kamakau 1961: 235). This comment suggests a
practice similar to the Tonga practice in which a low-ranking person mated
with a higher ranking one in exchange for gifts (Gailey 1987: 156). Thus
women might engage in sex in exchange for goods and favors, but this was
not market-based prostitution.

Sexual forms of recreation within Hawaiian society contributed to missionary views of Hawaiians' licentiousness. Malo describes, for example, the
practice of 'ume, a pastime very popular with married Hawaiian maka'āinana (Malo 1951: 214–215). The people sat in a circle and the president
touched the 'ume stick to a man and a woman who were sent out and "en-
joyed themselves together." The husband would not be jealous of or offended by his own wife if she went with another man, nor the wife angry
with her own husband if he went out to enjoy another woman. A man might
indicate his choice to the wand bearer and put into his hands something of
value to be given to a woman as inducement, perhaps to be passed on to her
husband in return for his compliance (Malo 1951: 215 n.7). The woman
might refuse. "During the nights while this game was being played the man
consorted with the woman that pleased him, and the woman with the man
that pleased her; and when daylight came the husband returned to his own
wife and the wife to her own husband" (Malo 1951: 214). "Owing to these
practices, the affections of the woman were often transferred to the man, her
partner, and the affections of the man to the woman who was his partner; so
that the man would not return to his former wife, nor the woman to her
former husband" (Malo 1951: 214). The ali'i had a similar game, called kilu,
also a great favorite and played in the same enclosure but restricted to
individuals of rank. It led to a kiss or sex or the gift of some possession (Malo 1951: 216). Thus even playful sex did not cross lines of rank
indiscriminately.

The Hawaiian cultural logic for restraining the sexuality of women of rank
was fundamentally different from that of the missionaries. Prohibitions on
sexual contact with high-ranking women joined with other systems that
maintained the distinctions and separations of rank. A sexual kapu paralleled
kapus on other kinds of contact such as touching, eating together, and wearing another person's clothes. Preventing sexual access to a person's body
was a way of symbolically marking his/her rank and separation from others
of lesser rank. Unconstrained sexuality was immoral not because it was plea-
surable but because it violated the restrictions and distinctions of rank. Re-
stricting contact with high-ranking people, those who possessed great mana,

served to protect subordinates as well. Thus sexuality was controlled only
for those with mana, not for makaʻāinana. Whereas the New England Congregationalists sought to contain sexuality within the sphere of procreation
as a way of establishing self-governance, chiefly Hawaiians controlled sexuality to preserve the mana of their rank and avoid contamination from
low-ranking descent lines. When the missionaries condemned adultery and
fornication, they built on ideas of sexual restriction that were familiar to
Hawaiian aliʻi, but the cultural logic was fundamentally different. For the
makaʻāinana in particular, these changes were jarring and sharp. It is clear
that Hawaiian society was not a place of unrestricted sexuality but one in
which the shape of restrictions depended on rank and position rather than
gender and marriage.

Missionary Conceptions of the Body, Sexuality, and Adultery

Missionary conceptions of the body in Hawaiʻi were similar to those shared
by missionaries in many other parts of the world at the same time. Reed
(1997), for examples, reports a very similar discourse in Papua New Guinea,
in which notions of licentiousness were used to account for low fertility rates
among the people of the Massim. Many of the early encounters between
Europeans and Hawaiians were shaped by different logics of the body and
its display. Sex was the core sphere of conflict but not the only one. These
groups also differed in ideas about covering the body and concealing its
physical functions. For example, in 1833, soon after her arrival in Hilo,
Sarah Lyman wrote a letter to her sister in Royalton, Vermont, describing the
people she encountered (Martin et al. 1979: 57). She complains that the men
wear malos and the women leave their breasts naked and they have not the
least sense of shame about them. They also do their "duties" by the side of
the road—"They seem to think no more about it than the dumb beasts." She
is dismayed that little boys and girls have as much intercourse as they please
and nothing is kept private from children. "Whole families sleep in one
apartment, and on the same mat; this is perhaps one of the greatest evils
existing. The more I become acquainted with the people the more I feel the
importance of labouring to elevate them." A lack of privacy in dress, elimination, and sex evokes a language of bestiality and the need for civilization.
In her journal for 1832 Sarah Lyman comments on the condition of the
people:

> The majority of them are more filthy than the swine. Their houses are wretched
> hovels and the abode of vermin, and the inhabitants covered with sores from
> head to foot. Some are afflicted with boils, some with sore eyes and a variety of
> diseases unheard of in our country, arising no doubt from a want of cleanliness.
> My heart is pained within me when I enter these abodes of wretchedness. But

the awful stupidity which every where prevails among the people is enough to call forth the sympathies and prayers of all who have an interest at the throne of grace. Like brutes they live, like brutes they die.

(Martin et al. 1979: 45)

Moral uncleanness and physical lack of cleanliness and sanitation are equated in this account, a trend that continues as the decline of population is attributed to both licentiousness and unclean, dark houses.

Lyman's dismay extends also to surfing, "the source of much iniquity" (Martin et al. 1979: 64), and the lack of control Hawaiian parents exercise over their children. In 1834 she writes that very few have children of their own but almost all have adopted children over whom they have very little control and "if told it is their duty to watch over and correct these children for their faults, they immediately reply, that if they do so the children will leave them" (ibid.: 64). The native teachers she finds indolent and the children at first very wild, "running around the school house during school hours like so many goats" (ibid.: 71). These attitudes are widely shared by her contemporaries among the mission community (Piercy 1992). In 1835 Lyman opines that "[a] want of paternal government is a great barrier to the children" (Martin et al. 1979: 74). She writes to her sister in Vermont in 1835:

Could we see these children well disciplined at home we should have high hopes respecting them, but the influence exerted upon them by their parents and guardians is of a dreadful nature, and so paralises [sic] our efforts, that we often feel discouraged but we are not without hope that we do some little good. Their intellects are bright, but their minds are so dissipated, that they do not make rapid improvements in learning.

(Martin et al. 1979: 81)

In 1835 she complains that the natives spend so much time adorning their hair with flowers and making necklaces that will not last (Martin et al. 1979: 75). From the perspective of property accumulation and moral virtue, it is foolish to spend time on a task that does not produce permanent wealth.

A travel account of a visit about 1843 written by Rev. Henry Cheever—a noted minister, author, leader of reform movements such as abolition and temperance in New England—conveys the biblical basis for the prohibition of adultery along with a flavor of the way the missionaries viewed the Hawaiian recalcitrance in the face of these new regulations (Cheever 1856). On observing the decorum and seriousness of a church service on the island of Hawai'i, Cheever remarks:

You can only hope with trembling for the best of them, so liable are they to yield to temptation, and fall into the Hawaiian sin. Almost all of the suspensions [from church membership] have been on account of adultery, and the illicit intercourse

of the unmarried, some of them under circumstances painfully polluting. The
people are as yet but half-reclaimed savages; much further advanced in Christianity than civilization; perhaps, indeed, as far Christianized as they can be until
their habits of living, sleeping, working, and dressing are more civilized.

(Cheever 1856: 175)

While noting that it is church members who are foremost in leaving the
ways of "barbarism" and adopting the ways of "civilization," Rev. Cheever
nevertheless despairs of their slow progress. His critique links the Hawaiian
people to nature because of the way they eat and handle their bodily functions.

But they are not weaned at once; nor can they be in one generation. And living,
as they generally do, on a highly nutritious, gross food, without habits of self-
restraint; knowing no limit to the indulgence of any appetite by satiety; still
going, when away from foreigners, half naked in the bronze of nature, or with
the barest apology for clothing; generally without apartments in their houses; all
sleeping together on mats, and not abashed at bathing, or the performance of the
common offices of nature before each other, is it to be wondered at that adultery
and illicit intercourse are frequent?

(Cheever 1856: 176–177)

He notes, however, that through the rigor of the laws, the vigilance of magistrates and constables, and the discipline and restraints of the church, there is
probably no more licentiousness here than there is in England, France, or
America (Cheever 1856: 177). In the Bible, the adulterer and adulteress were
to be put to death, indicating the lengths to which the divine law
went in order to preserve the sacredness and inviolate character of marriage
(Cheever 1856: 179). He bemoans the laxity with which divorces are obtained from state legislatures in America: "a wide and dangerous departure
from the good old Puritan and English usage; and it is an evil that ought to
be steadfastly resisted by all the virtuous, both as proving, and itself provok-
ing the depravation of public morals" (Cheever 1856: 182). Moreover, there
is an intimate linkage between family order and the order of the state: "The
family compact is too important a bond of union to the State, for the State to
render it unstable by a readiness in yielding to petitions for divorce. Marriage is made by it a loose cloak for lechery and grossness, instead of a
permanent bond and mortgage for purity" (Cheever 1856: 182). To the missionary writers, much of the Hawaiian management of sexuality and the
body seemed repugnant. Cheever describes the nighttime circle parties rather
differently than Malo does, for example: "on moonlight nights, they used to
form rings in the open air, and shamelessly prosecute their abominable orgies with shouts and dancing. Modesty was a feeling quite unknown, or, if it
ever had existed, the sex at that time seemed utterly devoid of it" (Cheever

1856: 93). Cheever links this evidence of licentiousness and a lack of female modesty with the abhorrent practice of infanticide, allegedly done to preserve the beauty and pleasures of the mothers and free them from the burdens of children. And even those children not killed were cared for very poorly, he says (Cheever 1856: 93). Here again erotic pleasure and a failure to mother were seen as inextricably joined and a cause of infant death. The campaign against adultery was a pro-motherhood movement as well as an antisex one. Complaints about parental and particularly maternal indifference to children were common.[8]

By the late 1830s the precipitous population decline of the Hawaiian population was increasingly a subject of concern (see Malo 1839). The missionaries blamed the problem on licentious mothers who were not interested in bearing and raising children.[9] In his responses to the government's questions in 1846, one missionary complained that women are not "keepers at home, but, wandering about, fall into the society of the profligate, and, as is often the case, become tempters of others" (Green in Kingdom of Hawai'i 1846: 31). Bishop agrees that licentiousness is a prominent vice, although it used to be worse: "During the first years of my residence on these islands, it was shocking to witness the entire want of decency, both of feeling and action, among all classes" (Kingdom of Hawai'i 1846: 33–35). The problem is idleness, he thinks: women and children have scarcely any employment and women are "given to gossiping or absolute idleness, and the latter [children] of both sexes are left to grow up untaught in all kinds of work." Children are permitted to run at large and there is little family discipline or family instruction.

William Richards, writing to the commander of a U.S. exploring expedition in 1841, said "there was nothing among the Hawaiians that was worthy, or that could even bear the name of domestic happiness in a civilized community" (Sahlins and Barrere 1973: 32–33). There were some instances of domestic attachment, some showed grief at the death of their companions, and there was sometimes evidence of attachment between parents and children, but these were rare and a kind of "instinctive affection, which even all the force of heathenism could not eradicate" (ibid.: 33). He claimed that parents, especially females, were not willing to have children and would commit them to the care of others, especially if they were numerous (ibid.).

In 1848 the mission community chronicled their accomplishments over the years since 1820 for the supporters back home, revealing again how central containing desire and reformulating marriage was to the mission project. The creation of a law-governed family is the crowning accomplishment. In its general letter on the state of the mission to Rufus Anderson, June 2, 1848, Thurston, Hitchcock, Paris, and Comee note that the people now wear clothes, whereas before even high chiefs would swim naked and walk from house to beach naked.[10] In 1820 none of the relations of domes-

tic and social life were regarded as sacred and binding, but both men and
women could have as many partners as they wished. A man could have as
many as he could feed, a woman as many as she could entertain, and both
could turn their spouses out as suited their convenience and pleasure. There
was no such thing as conjugal affection, no domestic concord, and no such
thing as parental authority.

> There were no stated laws which defined the duties of parents towards children
> and of children towards parents; they regarded parental authority if they were
> quite at leisure to do so, and only so far as suited their convenience. No obliga-
> tions were felt on the part of parents to take care of their children, nor on the
> part of children to obey their parents, and they often destroyed their children
> before or after birth in order to be released from the trouble of taking care of
> them. Such are a few of the facts which belonged to the generation of 1820. The
> present generation are in a different position in these respects. . . . Then there
> was no law; nothing to regulate society. Now all the natural social and domestic
> relations are respected—the duties of each in some measure respected, and regu-
> lated by good and wholesome laws; and a neglect to perform the duties attached
> to these various relations is punishable by fine, imprisonment, or other disabil-
> ities. Parents and children, husbands and wives, masters and servants, are recog-
> nized in laws and on any delinquency in the performance of the duties of their
> respective relations, they are answerable to the laws of the land.[11]

The control of sexuality outside marriage was deeply important to the
missionaries and their sponsors in their own lives as well. The American
Board of Commissioners of Foreign Missions, which sponsored and supported, albeit at a bare subsistence level, the missionary enterprise, insisted
that all missionary men marry before they were sent into the field. This
restriction recognized natural sexual desires and established the boundaries
within which they could be expressed. Isolated mission families typically
produced large numbers of offspring, yet found that the Hawaiian playmates
of their children held unacceptable ideas about sexuality. Many restricted
their children from contact with Hawaiian children, from whom they might
learn different attitudes toward sexuality. Thus the imagining of the licentious nature of the Hawaiian doomed the mission wife to a highly circumscribed life of raising and training her children protected from the influence
of those she had come to live with and "save" (Grimshaw 1989). Many
families sent their young children back to the United States to be educated,
and a few attempted to raise their children in Hawai'i without contact with
Hawaiian children. Lucy Thurston, for example, constructed a high wall
around her house and prevented her children from having any contact with
the Hawaiian children outside. Her daughter remarked, on leaving Hawai'i,
at her surprise at how much people in other places laughed (Grimshaw 1989;
Piercy 1992).

The missionaries were engaged in creating a new world in a far-off land, and one of the major evils was lust. Their vision of a new world depended on the creation of a Christian form of marriage and the suppression of sexual desire outside marriage, which was defined as sinful.

In their advocacy of the criminal regulation of adultery, missionaries drew heavily on the way adultery was understood in biblical texts. For example, Cheever quotes Scripture (without a specific source) on the subject of who might remarry after adultery, noting that the adulterer should not remarry: "whosoever shall put away his wife, except it be for fornication, and shall marry another, committeth adultery; and whoso marrieth her that is put away, doth commit adultery" (Cheever 1856: 178). Moreover, he notes that in the Judaic law, the penalty for adultery was death. A high standard that prohibits remarriage for adulterers sets a good example, he argues, and further, he notes that some Hawaiians have actually "committed crime" in order to be released by divorce to marry someone else (Cheever 1856: 82).

Prohibitions against adultery and fornication enacted in Hawai'i in 1827 and 1829 stem directly from ideas about adultery held in New England. In eighteenth-century Massachusetts, the Bible was considered the basis for both public and private conduct, the only proper foundation for a state or a church and the appropriate source of public law (Ohlson 1937: 353). Because the Bible demanded the death penalty for adultery, early legislation in many of the colonies incorporated this penalty, although it is doubtful how often it was carried out (ibid.). Although Massachusetts eliminated the death penalty for adultery in 1694, it still provided for severe and humiliating punishments such as insignia worn by the offender (ibid.: 358). The Massachusetts statute from 1784, Chap. 40, reads as follows:

An Act Against Adultery, Polygamy, and Lewdness. Whereas chastity of behavior, and the due observance of the marriage covenant, are highly conducive to the peace, good order and welfare of the community, and the violation of them productive of great evils to individuals and the public;

Be it therefore enacted by the Senate and House of Representatives in General Court assembled and by the authority of the same, That if any man or woman shall commit adultery, and be thereof convicted, every person so convicted shall be set upon the gallows with a rope about his or her neck, and the other cast over the gallows, for the space of one hour, be publickly whipped, not exceeding thirty-nine stripes, be imprisoned or fined, and bound to the good behavior; all or any of these punishments, according to the aggravation of the offence.

(Ohlson 1937: 534n.)

By the end of the eighteenth century Vermont and Massachusetts both imposed a penalty of thirty-nine stripes for adultery (Ohlson 1937: 364–365).

The missionaries brought this conception of the sinfulness and seriousness of adultery with them to Hawai'i. They followed the biblical definition of adultery, which includes mere looking at a woman with desire, so that adultery can include thoughts, words, or deeds (Ohlson 1937: 339; Ching 1980: 3). According to the seventh commandment (which the missionaries were fond of quoting), adultery includes every kind of unlawful sensual indulgence, whether in thought or in deed (Ohlson 1937: 339).

Transforming family relationships into the model of the bourgeois family with enduring husband/wife bonds and exclusive sexual relationships was not easy. There are hints of resistance. The missionaries constantly bemoaned the inability of the "Hawaiian," as the people were called in the essentializing singular, to follow the path of correct conduct and to achieve conversion in the heart as well as on the surface of behavior.

The Battle against Prostitution, 1820–1830

The first attempt to change the sexual behavior of Hawaiian women was an attack on prostitution with European seamen. This endeavor earned the missionaries the undying hostility of the small but growing mercantile community and the visiting shipping community while failing to eliminate the sex trade. The campaign was supported by those ali'i associated with the American missionaries, such as Ka'ahumanu and Hoapili, whereas other ali'i more closely tied to the merchant community and sympathetic to the British, such as Boki and Kekūanao'a, not only tolerated the sex trade but probably profited from it.[12] In the early nineteenth century, maka'āinana women flocked to the European ships and port towns in large numbers to partake in the lucrative trade in sexual services.[13] This was one of the few ways that maka'āinana could acquire foreign goods since the ali'i controlled other forms of trade. It was a form of defiance by commoner women and men of tabus through which chiefs and priests organized trade with Europeans (Sahlins 1992: 34, 53). The conception of commodified sex emerged relatively quickly. In the early 1800s 'I'ī reports:

> Many Hawaiian women boarded the ships coming to port here. They did not think that such associations were wrong, for there was no education in those days. The husbands and parents, not knowing that it would bring trouble, permitted such association with foreign men because of a desire for clothing, mirrors, scissors, knives, iron hoops from which to fashion fishhooks, and nails. Some women, most of them wives of foreign residents, were seen wearing men's shirts and beaver hats on their heads. They thought such costumes were becoming to them.
>
> (I'ī 1959: 87)

As demands for cash payment of taxes and cash incomes increased while the productivity of agriculture became ever more tenuous, women flocked to the port towns during the whaling season in greater numbers. For example, the *Sandwich Island News*, March 10, 1847, reported (quoted in Linnekin 1990: 186):

> All the women come to Lahaina for it. Some put to them the question, What brings you here? They reply, we came to sell.—What have you to sell? They reply, We sell ourselves. . . . Not a native vessel comes into this harbor . . . that is not crowded with native women from the other islands, so that hundreds and thousands are semi-annually gathered into these places by government helps. . . . After a few weeks . . . they are carried back . . . their persons all filled with diseases.

In 1847 the government newspaper estimated that eighteen thousand ships assembled at the chief Hawaiian ports yearly, with an average stay of three to four weeks (Greer 1968: 6). By a conservative estimate, twelve thousand sailors arrived in the season in 1847, each spending ten dollars in cash, thus pouring $120,000 into the economy, of which nine-tenths went to prostitutes and grog shops and most of that to prostitutes (Greer 1968: 7). Even in remote Hilo, in 1846 four men-of-war, thirty-four trading schooners, and sixty-seven whaleships put into port (Kingdom of Hawai'i 1846: 18).

As early as 1825 the missionaries persuaded the chiefs to put a kapu on women going out to ships, eliciting riots and complaints by sailors and their captains. Although the ali'i backed the missionaries, the foreign residents continued to complain about the missionaries and the laws they promoted. The missionaries, on the other hand, constantly bemoaned the evil influences of visiting Europeans, upper-class captains and explorers who failed to restrain their charges and set a good example, as well as the lower-class sailors themselves. In an 1841 letter to her sister, for example, Sarah Lyman says that whale ships are in ports to get recruits and that "in the main, they are an abandoned, hopeless class. *They drink in iniquity like water* and *their feet are swift to do evil.* Licentiousness and drunkenness are their besetting sins, and most of them are profane in the extreme" (Martin et al. 1979: 113; emphasis in original). Two years later, she writes that they have as many as five ships in harbor at the same time and sometimes entertain masters and officers only to find that they are "guilty of open immorality among the people. The natives say, that foreigners deceive the missionaries, that we do not know who we entertain at our houses" (ibid.: 118).

Thus, as lines of social class were increasingly defined by sexual behavior in the Victorian period, the Victorian assault on sexual desire was imported into Hawai'i (see Foucault 1996). In Hawaiian waters, this was primarily a struggle to reform the morality of lower-class white men and to protect Christian converts from their immoral influences. The battle over prostitution was largely a struggle among Europeans over the meaning and constraints of sexuality as sexual conduct became a central mark of social class position (see Walkowitz 1980; Stoler 1995; Foucault 1996).

Clearly, the motivations and desires of women traveling to the port towns to acquire cash and goods were quite different from those of women having sexual relations outside of formal marriage or leaving one partner for another. Yet in the civilizing process as it was envisioned in Hawai'i, these activities were lumped together as manifestations of unrestrained desire. By the 1830s the dangers of uncontained eroticism appeared ever more clearly to rest in the fragility of marriage rather than in the booming sex trade. But this had always been the primary concern of the civilizing mission.

Sahlins's analysis of the behavior of Hawaiian women at the arrival of Captain Cook in 1778 bears a similarity to the views of the missionaries. He argues that women swarmed over the English ships eager for sex with the English men because their mana or attractiveness awakened the love and desire of the women (Sahlins 1985: 6, 26, 31). Yet his analysis merges love, desire, and commodified sex into an undifferentiated whole. Treating these different activities as if they were the same ignores the complexities of sexual behavior, just as the notion of licentiousness deployed by the missionaries failed to capture the detailed rules of acceptable and inappropriate sexual encounters in Hawaiian kinship systems. The missionaries lumped all sexual activity outside marriage together as a manifestation of lust, whereas Sahlins implies that the women's behavior was motivated by love and desire rather than pragmatic wishes for gifts of European goods elicited by well-known systems of exchanging gifts for sexual favors (see Kamakau 1961: 95–100). Indeed, perhaps the fantasy of the sexually desirable European male whom Polynesian maidens find irresistible is an even more powerful European myth than the notion that Polynesians must inevitably wish to deify Europeans (see Obeyesekere 1992; Sahlins 1995).

The Campaign against Adultery, 1830–1860

"The Kingdom Is Sick"

During the 1830s to 1850s the mō'ī and ali'i joined the American missionaries in energetic efforts to prosecute adultery and fornication. The ali'i's willingness to prosecute adultery was probably based on both religious and practical considerations. The Christian ali'i sought salvation for themselves and their people through the promised eternal life and benefits of civilization. At the same time, the twin problems of extensive foreign debts and catastrophic population decline required both more labor from maka'āinana and better rates of childbirth and child survival. Prosecuting adultery might check population decline and strengthen the nation through more stable families and improved parental care. Yet redefining the family failed to ameliorate the basic causes of population decline: introduced diseases, rampaging cattle populations destroying gardens and grass for thatching houses, and increasing tax burdens on the farming population.

The new system of marriage and sexuality represented a greater change for the maka'āinana, particularly junior siblings without access to land, than for the ali'i and elder siblings whose sexual interactions were already more restricted. However, for all ranks the new regime was based on a fundamentally different cultural logic and conception of marriage as a permanent, monogamous, and property-owning and -producing unit under the control of the husband.

By the 1830s leaders of the kingdom such as David Malo worried that the decline in population was a fatal blow to the nation itself. In his 1839 article he says, "the kingdom is sick,—it is reduced to a skeleton, and is near to death; yea, the whole Hawaiian nation is near to a close" (Malo 1839: 130). Although introduced diseases clearly led to massive depopulation, there was a great deal of debate about what other factors were producing the inexorable shrinkage of the Hawaiian population, a pattern that was not reversed until the end of the century. It is possible that the difficulty of acquiring land and of paying the taxes once that land was available discouraged marriage and childbearing. Malo says, enigmatically, that in the past mothers put their children to death thinking that "they should prematurely become old women without having gained property," and that a child was frequently destroyed because its father had no property or the mother feared the father would leave her and seek another wife, or because neither had a connection with the chief and therefore a source of support, so the relatives of the parents destroyed the child (Malo 1839:123–124). Malo is apparently referring to abortion as well as infanticide in this passage. Thus it appears that in the past, security of support was seen as a precondition for childbearing. The difficulty of providing adequate support for a family in the 1830s and 1840s may, therefore, have discouraged the maka'āinana from marrying and having children. In 1846 one missionary reports that as many as one quarter of the people regard holding land as a burden and avoid taking it up until they are married and have families, thus escaping for a time the great tax on landholders (Kingdom of Hawai'i 1846: 12). The American-influenced ali'i apparently accepted the missionary view that changing marriage and sexual practices would stem the decline in population.

The labor of convicted adulterers also buttressed the labor supply available to the chiefs and aided in the construction of roads. Hoapili, on Maui, was particularly energetic in adultery convictions. In 1843 Henry Cheever marveled at a road built across a vast lava field on Maui, smooth and straight and stretching for miles across the rough and broken rocks, constructed with crowbars and hands (Cheever 1856). Describing the road to Hāna, Cheever observes:

> Yet it is a way not devoid of interest and novelty, especially that part of it which runs to Kahikinui and Kaupo; for it is a road built by the crime of adultery, some years ago, when the laws relating to that and other crimes were first enacted, under the administration of the celebrated chief Hoapili; in whom was the first example of a Christian marriage.
>
> It is altogether the noblest and best Hawaiian work I have anywhere seen. It is carried directly over a large, verdureless tract, inundated and heaved up by an eruption from the giant crater of Haleakala; and when it is considered that it was made by convicts, without sledge-hammers, or crow-bars, or any other instrument, but the human hands, and their stone, and the Hawaiian Oo, it is certainly worthy of great admiration. It is as great a work for Hawaiians as digging the Erie Canal to Americans. A Yankee engineer, to stand on either side of that vast field (and yet by reason of its pits, and ravines, and blown-up hills, and dislocations, not a field) of blackened lava, would be confounded and put to his wit's end to know where to begin and carry a road. . . .
>
> Straight over such a tract the crime of adultery, under the energetic management of Hoapili, has built a commodious road from Honolulu to Kaupo. Like the old man in "The Rime of the Ancient Mariner," we almost "blessed it unawares," as our mules safely trotted or cantered by moonlight over the path it had made. . . . It is made by running two parallel walls about twenty feet apart, then partially McAdamizing the space between, and covering it with grass or stubble. For fifteen or twenty miles it runs almost like a railroad, only turning a little now and then to avoid some gigantic boulder, or forced into a zigzag to get over some precipitous ravine, which it would seem as if some impetuous after-stream of devouring fire from the mountain, had ploughed and eaten through till it reached the sea.
>
> (Cheever n.d.)

Other commentators noted that adulterers built most of the road system of Hawai'i during the mid nineteenth century. A French visitor in Kailua in the 1830s found a twenty-five-mile road almost finished, "thanks to the amorous propensities of the Hawaiians" (Piercy 1992: 79).

Redefining Marriage and Adultery in the Law

As early as 1825 the mō'ī and ali'i announced laws to redefine marriage (Silverman 1983). Three laws passed in 1827 outlaw murder, theft, and adultery, specifying imprisonment in irons as the punishment for adultery. In 1827 a missionary writing from the island of Hawai'i said that "The rulers of this district have declared that, in future, marriages shall not be accounted valid, unless solemnized by a minister of the Gospel. Offenders are punished by being made to work on a public road."[14] Ka'ahumanu, the regent, soon extended this provision to all of the islands. Her statement of the new regulations indicates a recognition that this is a shift from previous practices:

> If a man and woman are agreed to live together as man and wife, and there is nothing in the way to render it illegal, then let them marry in accordance with the word of God.
>
> But those persons who are united according to the former customs of this country, and are still living together . . . their union is hereby confirmed anew in the same manner as those who are married.
>
> But from the present time all persons are prohibited from uniting together according to the former customs, it is proper to marry.
>
> (Quoted in Schmitt and Strombel 1966: 267)

By declaring all cohabiting pairs married, Ka'ahumanu prevented Europeans from settling with local women who would bear them children, which the Europeans would then desert and fail to recognize. She diminished the population of illegitimate mixed-race children so common and so problematic in colonial situations (see Stoler 1989; 1997). Many foreign residents preferred the more temporary and unofficial liaisons found throughout the colonial world, with brown women serving as "keeps" or concubines of white men only until white women were available. Missionaries frowned on these relationships not because of racial differences but because they failed to restrict sex to the marriage bed.

In March 1830 Ka'ahumanu went on a circuit of the islands to encourage people to learn to read and write and to instruct land agents to take care of the teachers, to use the resources of the chief's land to maintain the teachers, and not to overburden the people. At the same time she pronounced certain laws orally (Kamakau 1961: 298–299). These include a law about adultery and prostitution: "Adultery (moekolohe) is prohibited, also prostitution (ho'okamakama); a man must not persuade away another's wife or a woman another's husband. Each is to have but one husband or one wife, and all must [from this time] be legally married, but those who were married before the word of God became known are to be regarded as legally married" (Kamakau 1961: 298–299).

Apparently no formal written document was produced from the 1830 pronouncements. An 1869 paternity suit provides extensive testimony from people living in Honolulu in 1830 that Ka'ahumanu had pronounced a law defining marriage, which established that cohabiters were considered married, and specifying who might and might not marry (Pierce 1869). The affidavits claim that there was no law of marriage until about 1830, when it was made by the decree of Ka'ahumanu titled Of Marriage and Divorce.

This law was re-enacted on November 12, 1840, and included in the Laws of 1842 (Chapter X). This law attributes its origin to Ka'ahumanu and incorporates the text from the 1830 edicts (Thurston 1904: 45). It declares plural marriages illegal and prohibits foreigners from marrying unless they declare an oath of allegiance to the government, assert their intention to remain, and prove they have lived in the islands two years. To be married, one must receive the written agreement to the marriage from the governor. Divorce is possible under very restricted conditions.[15] If a couple quarrels and hits one another, they should be punished for assault, but if the woman is in special danger from her husband's assaults, he should be confined in irons. If either attempts to kill his/her spouse and the judges conclude that the person's life is in danger, then the innocent person can divorce the other and marry again, although the guilty person may not (Laws of 1842, Chapter X, secs. 2, 4, 5, 7, 8 in Thurston 1904: 49–50).

The "Law against Lewdness," No Ka Moe Kolohe, proclaimed on September 21, 1829, reiterated the definition of Christian marriage, prohibited adultery, and permitted divorce for the spouse of an adulterer. The missionaries, following biblical doctrine, persuaded the ali'i that if a person commits adultery and is divorced, he or she cannot marry again until the partner dies, although the partner can marry again (Silverman 1983).[16] This provision remained in effect until 1866 (Schmitt and Strombel 1966: 270). Penalties were severe in the 1829 law. Offenders were fined three pigs to be given to the cuckolded partner and three pigs or equivalent value in work or other goods to the royal governor, with a portion for the king. A fine of five dollars for the king, five dollars for the governor, and five dollars for the injured spouse could be substituted. Both men and women were fined equally, but for the ali'i, fines were up to two hundred dollars. For all offenders, fines increased with repetition of the offense. Failure to pay the fine was punishable by imprisonment in irons for twelve or eighteen months (McGregor-Alegado 1980).

Penalties remained severe in the 1841 version of this law, which set the fine for the guilty party at thirty dollars, half to the cuckolded partner and half to the government, or eight months of hard labor (Chapter XXXIV of the 1842 Laws, the Law Respecting Lewdness). Fornication between unmarried people was a fifteen dollar fine or four months hard labor, or a mere three dollars if they married (sec. 8). The fine for a man having sex with a prostitute was five dollars and for the woman, four months hard labor in prison (sec. 10). The law also prohibited all lewd conversation, seductive language, libidinous solicitations, lascivious conduct leading to lewdness, and all licentious talking among the young by fines between two dollars and ten dollars (sec. 16) (Thurston 1904: 96–101).[17]

The Hawaiian word *moe kolohe*, literally "mischievous sleeping" (Silverman 1983: 67), includes adultery, fornication, lewdness, and sometimes turning to prostitution, although there is a separate word for prostitution itself. The missionaries who invented the term seem to have defined the prohibited forms of sexuality, or moe kolohe, according to the expansive notions of sinful sex found in the Bible. Indeed, careful studies of the translations of the Bible into Hawaiian indicate that the term *moe kolohe* was used as the translation for all sexual offenses: adultery, fornication, lewdness, incest, prostitution, and criminal intercourse (Ching 1980; Nakamura 1980: 3–40).

Moe kolohe was a new category invented by the missionary advisors to the government. It is more reflective of American categories of sexual behavior than Hawaiian. In a letter written from Lāhaināluna, the missionary high school, by its principal, Rev. Lorrin Andrews, on December 2, 1835, and reprinted in the *Missionary Herald*, Andrews explains the origin of the term *moe kolohe* (October 1836: 390–391). Andrews was one of the missionaries sufficiently versed in the Hawaiian language to contribute to the translation of the Bible into Hawaiian. His choice of terms for the law was clearly made after he had grappled with similar linguistic problems in deciding how to translate terms such as adultery and fornication in the Bible. In an article titled, "Unthinking Character of the People," Andrews offers the following observation on the thinking styles of the Hawaiian people:

> Certain things in their language evinces [*sic*] the same thing, viz., the great want of abstract and general terms. Thus, to *break* as a plate is *waha*; to break as a rope is *moku*; to break as a stick is *hai*; but there is no word for the general term. So it is in innumerable instances. Every thing is specific and of particular application. So in moral subjects. In translating the seventh commandment, it was found they had about twenty ways of committing adultery, and of course as many specific names; and to select any one of them would be to forbid the crime in that one form and tacitly permit it in all the other cases. It was necessary therefore to express the idea in another way, viz., "Thou shalt not sleep mischievously." They have no word answering to our word color, they cannot ask, "what color is it?" They can only ask, is it black, red, blue etc. but have no general term. They have no term answering to our word *number* & etc. The whole language shows that they never have been a thinking people. Their habits and manners show that everything is considered individually. The property of a husband and wife are perfectly distinct. Hoapili and his wife have two perfectly distinct establishments. They rarely eat together. No man ever uses his wife's book, and vice versa; and so with a slate and other property; each must have one of his own.

Indeed, the lumping of all sexuality outside marriage reflects Euro-American Christian categories rather than Hawaiian distinctions.

In this passage, directed to potential donors back home, the missionaries attempt to explain why, ten years after their remarkably successful conversion of the ruling chiefs, they had failed to transform the bodily deportment and the self-discipline of feeling of the Hawaiian people. In order to justify their lack of success, they offer a more negative picture of Hawaiians as inherently licentious, idle, and intellectually incapable. This image contrasts sharply with statements about their industry and their intellectual capacity of the early 1820s and their characterization as noble warriors in Captain Cook's time. A new rhetoric about the "nature" of Hawaiian people and their innate habits of thought naturalized and fixed difference and explained resistance to change.

Thus the government redefined marriage, divorce, and parenting through law. Marriages had to be registered and had to conform to the conditions established by the state. Divorce became a lengthy legal proceeding rather than a simple separation. With the concept of moe kolohe, the government targeted the surrender to all forms of desire. As convictions for adultery and fornication mounted, the foreigners developed the theory that Hawaiians were incapable of governing their sexual desires and therefore were childlike. In a few short years, this theory grew into a conviction that those incapable of governing themselves were also incapable of governing a nation.

Prosecuting Adultery and Fornication

Court caseloads reveal the extent of prosecutions for adultery and fornication during the 1830s to 1850s (see table 8.1). Prosecution was facilitated by a network of constables who received a portion of the fine for apprehending a culprit in the act. In the 1829 law a portion of the fine goes to the governor and king. In 1840 the law specified that police officers were paid by receiving one-fourth of the fine if they seized a man who was tried and convicted (Schmitt 1967: 359). Although Schmitt says that at the insistence of the British Commission, this practice was discontinued in 1843 and officers were paid $3.50 a month, and in 1847 $6.00 a month, the practice of paying constables was not uniformly adopted in all areas for quite some time. The statutes did not require constables to be paid until 1878. In the 1846 *Answers to Questions*, the missionary on Moloka'i, H. R. Hitchcock, complained about the system of constables paid by the fines of those they arrest. Although his concern is with the way these people prey on others, he is also distressed by their failure to engage in productive work. He complains about the large number of officers, or māka'is, appointed to detect crime by the governor. Instead of the sixteen who might be needed, they are saddled with seventy to eighty, who are all relieved from working on labor tax days even though they are all young men capable of a good day's work. This situation, he says, keeps society in a broil because these spies get nothing for their office unless they detect and convict what they call lawehalas, and part of the spoil is divided among them. They look at any disturbance, no matter how trifling or private, and drag the people before the courts. "Many and many a formerly industrious, good citizen has become a nuisance instead of a blessing to society, by no other means than being appointed a luna under the government" (Kingdom of Hawai'i 1846: 40).

The texts of the adultery cases in the Hilo District Court describe constables chasing couples into the fields and peering through the thatch of houses at night trying to catch "known moekolohes" and other offenders in the act. Church officials sometimes help to catch offenders. Some of the cases were initiated by disgruntled husbands who prosecuted the men who took their wives even if they no longer wanted them or had not lived with them for years, apparently simply to get some money from the men who took them. Because of the sharp gender imbalance, foreigners, especially Chinese and haole, often mated and married Hawaiian women, leaving a shortage of women for Hawaiian men.

Penalties were severe. As specified in the 1841 statute and revealed in court records from the 1850s and 1860s, men and women were typically fined thirty dollars or sentenced to eight months hard labor. This was an enormous penalty in a subsistence economy in which opportunities for earning cash were very limited.[18] Adultery fines represented about a half-year's wages for those fully engaged in the cash economy living near a port town. Clearly, many must have been forced to do hard labor instead. The accounts of road building indicate that this was probably a valuable source of labor for ali'i facing increasing debts, diminishing populations of maka'āinana on the lands, and incessant demands for repayment by foreign merchants.

An example of a typical case from the court minute books in Hilo from June 29, 1853, indicates that couples prosecuted for adultery were often engaged in open cohabitation known to many. Constables took an active role in detection and arrest. The defendants, a Hawaiian man and woman, pleaded not guilty to the charge of moe kolohe, but admitted they were in the house. The constable testified that he, Mokumaile, and Hāna Poi went to the defendant's house the previous night with a dark lantern. They entered the house and found the parties lying together. Witnesses testified that the defendants have long been reputed to be lovers. The husband and wife do not live together. Hāna Poi testified that the defendants were undressed when they were arrested. The defendants were found guilty and fined thirty dollars each or eight months in default of payment. The judge in this case wass S. L. Austin.

Several cases indicate that arrested couples lived together in a way that would have been accepted in earlier years. For example, on April 26, 1853, Kilioi and Kanowina were charged with adultery and pleaded not guilty. The woman's brother testified:

Kilioi and Kanowina have formed a situation of husband and wife according to
Hawaiian fashion. The woman and myself live in the same house. Kilioi visits
there often—he has always been trusted as one of the family. Last Saturday
Kilioi visited there and stayed over night. On going to bed the defendants lay in
different places apart from each other. In the morning when I awoke I saw the
defendants locked in each other's arms in the same bed. It was the woman that
left her place and went to where the man was. I did not see anything amiss
before that. The defendants were asleep locked in each others' embrace. It is a
long time that the defendants have been connected in this Hawaiian fashion.

The case record does not explain why the brother testified against his sister
unless he sought to break up the relationship. After considerable further testimony, including evidence that Kilioi had neglected his wife for some time,
the woman admitted she was guilty of adultery. The judge convicted them
and sentenced each to pay a fine of thirty dollars and in default of payment
to be imprisoned for eight months at hard labor. In this cash-poor town, in
which only a few hundred dollars were in circulation at all, such a fine
represented a staggering burden.

In 1866 the penalties were made unequal, with men receiving a larger fine
and longer sentence than women.[19] The debate in the legislature at the time
revealed concern that rich foreigners were enticing wives away from their
husbands. The large number of newspaper advertisements for wives who had
run away from their husbands provided further evidence of this problem.[20]
According to Harris, attorney general at the time,

What they wished to show was that a man's house was sacred and to bring to
justice those who went about invading their neighbors' houses for the purpose of
corrupting its women whilst the husband was absent at his work in the fields.
The family home for which a man worked must be protected by every possible means. The young girls of the Nation were its hope and unless they were
brought up virtuously the Kingdom must sink into the depths of the ocean.
(Supreme Court Reports 1924: 94)

The strength of the nation thus rested on the permanence of the nuclear
family and the enclosure of women within it.[21]

Although the courts devoted less attention to adultery and fornication after
1860, they became increasingly involved in forcing deserting wives to return
to their husbands. There were 181 cases of desertion by wives in the Hilo
District Court from 1852 to 1913.[22] This a significant number, although a
small fraction of the eleven hundred adultery cases that were handled during
the same period extrapolating from the sample data.[23] Prosecuting desertion
cases solidified the new form of bourgeois marriage. Formal marriage conferred on husbands the right to prevent their wives from traveling to visit
family or friends, even though such movement was common in Hawaiian

Adultery/Fornication Cases, 1853 - 1913

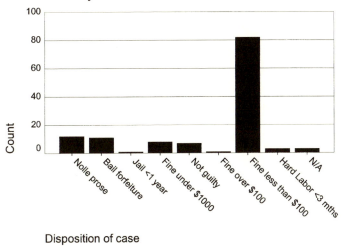

Disposition of case

Number = 128

Assault and Battery Cases, 1853 - 1913

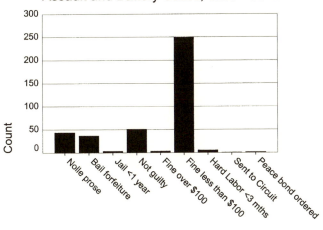

Disposition of case

Number - 427

Chart 8.4. Comparison of Dispositions: Adultery/Fornication, Assault/Battery, and Desertion of Husband Cases, Hilo District Court, 1853–1913

Desertion of Husband Cases, 1853 - 1913

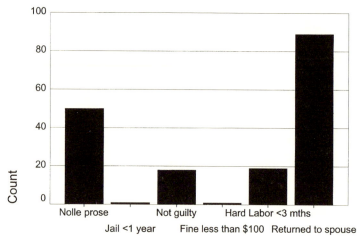

Disposition of case

Number = 181

Chart 8.4. (*cont.*)

kinship practices. Courts upheld these marriage obligations firmly. Wives were overwhelmingly returned to their husbands: 50 percent were returned to spouses, 10 percent were sent to hard labor, 28 percent were not prosecuted, and only 10 percent were found not guilty (see chart 8.4). Most of those not prosecuted had already returned to their husbands before the court hearing.

Frequent references to the marriage document in case records underscore the importance of formal marriage. The most common reason why women were not required to return was the absence of a marriage document rather than the acceptability of her reasons for being away. Women sometimes justified their desertion as the result of their husbands' failure to provide food or a house. Several of the women said that they and their husbands had no house to live in together so they moved back to their parents' houses. Occasionally a man built a house far outside of town and the woman resisted leaving her family to go there. Women often traveled to visit their families or live in a new place.

Fear of violence was another common reason women left their husbands. I counted how often violence, fear of violence, or insult and name calling were mentioned in court records. I also examined how many couples appeared in the court records at some other time with charges that the husband had assaulted his wife. These figures represent a minimum rather than a total number of cases involving violence, since the record often fails to give any details about the case. Violence was involved in at least 43 of the 181 desertion cases, 24 percent. This is more than twice the percentage of women found not guilty.[24] But the court rarely took violence into account as a reason to release a woman from the marriage. In all but three of thirty-seven cases with violence, the woman was sent back, punished, or the suit was withdrawn because she agreed to return. Preserving marriage was clearly valued well above protecting women from violence. As discussed in chapter 4, the 1842 law codes recognized fear of assault as a legitimate justification for leaving the marriage, but this protection was lost as the law became more American and less Hawaiian and emphasized more strongly the permanence and indissolubility of marriage.[25]

The men who appeared in court typically complained that their wives left them to travel and/or visit their families. Women sometimes said that their parents were sick and they needed to take care of them. But mobility was fundamental to Hawaiian kinship. Both commoners and chiefs traveled frequently to visit friends, go to town, or even change locations for fishing, farming, and trading. By contrast, men from the United States, Europe, and China had a conception of marriage more like that of the missionaries. Marriage was an enduring tie, the woman was under the authority of her husband, and she was expected to be obedient and subservient. Marriages of Hawaiian women with foreign men were common.[26] Given the shortage of women and the number of wealthy male foreigners in the islands, the courts' intervention helped men hang on to their wives against other claimants.[27] Thus foreigners appropriated not only land and water resources but also the reproductive power of Hawaiian women.[28]

Desertion prosecutions tied women more tightly to husbands and prevented them from moving around or changing husbands. It emphasized the marriage tie over ties to other relatives. In sum, the courts solidified marriage as the sole location for permissible sexual relations as well as a private sphere within which men exercised control and which women could not escape.

Conclusions

Between 1820 and 1900 the definition of the family was fundamentally transformed. Marriage became a more durable relationship and divorce became virtually impossible, introducing a new system of inequality (see Collier 1988) and increasing wives' vulnerability to violence. Violence and fear of violence were redefined as irrelevant to ending the relationship. Women who deserted in fear were returned to their husbands, sometimes with penalties. Women were expected to remain in the house performing domestic tasks rather than wandering more broadly visiting, farming, or keeping ties with other kin. As we saw in chapter 4, 1845 laws of coverture diminished married women's rights to property and disenfranchisement in 1850 displaced women from the sphere of politics and public office. The transformation in the family from the open ʻohana system to the circumscribed and contained bourgeois family with a private core protected from any public scrutiny made women far more vulnerable to gender violence than they had been before.

By the end of the nineteenth century, when Hawaiʻi was annexed to the United States as a colony, the project of transforming the Hawaiian family had apparently succeeded. The prosecutions of sexual offenses and violations of the marriage bed had diminished significantly, both absolutely and in comparison with other kinds of cases such as labor violations. It was generally accepted that marriage had to be certified by the state and divorce was difficult. At the same time, in more rural and isolated pockets of the islands, Hawaiian kinship practices that centered on the bilateral extended network of relatives, the ʻohana, persisted as subjugated knowledge, and siblingship and adoption remained important as well as marriage (Handy and Pukui 1972: 16–17; Langlas 1990; Linnekin 1990). By the middle of the twentieth century very few adultery cases were prosecuted and the law itself was coming under question. The 1985 Hawaii Penal Code no longer included adultery and fornication as crimes, and consensual heterosexual and homosexual conduct between competent persons in private was permitted.[29] By the late 1990s, by contrast, Massachusetts had not yet abandoned its adultery and fornication statutes although the subject was under debate.

These processes of refashioning the family and sexual subjectivity paralleled other efforts to constitute a nation according to European understandings of that entity (Anderson 1991). In the search for autonomy and the right to govern the nation, the aliʻi imposed stringent standards for sexual self-governance on the population and laid punishments on those who failed to conform. But the strategy backfired. As the numbers of adultery convictions piled up, foreigners thought they had hard evidence that this was a licentious population, unable to control its sexuality and incapable of self-governance. The childlike nature of the people was revealed. Those unable to govern themselves were obviously unable to govern a nation. In the class stratification system of the Victorian era, they were consigned to the bottom rungs of society along with prostitutes, the poor, and children as sexual self-control was increasingly linked to social power (see Foucault 1996).

Thus control over sexuality was an aspect of the search for sovereignty in European nationalist terms, but despite massive criminalization of the population, the campaign created a truth of licentiousness and lack of control that contributed to the redefinition of Hawaiians as childlike and incapable of self governance. This paved the way for the eventual takeover of the islands in a highly illegal act by the representatives of the U.S. government in 1893 at the point of a gun, this time mounted on an American warship in Honolulu harbor—the last gunboat to face an independent Hawaiian nation.

In a final ironic twist, the alleged eroticism of the Hawaiian people is fundamental to the current tourist trade (Trask 1993). The portrayal of sexualized Hawaiian women and men, scantily clad in scenes redolent of nature in a place far from the time and work discipline of industrial capitalism is the staple of tourist advertising. Thus the meanings and practices of sexuality that justified taking away sovereignty now create the cultural images that resell Hawai'i to the descendants of those people who denigrated Hawaiian sexual practices in the first place.

Clearly, there are deep connections between control over the body and control over the state; between the transformation of a gender order and the construction of modernity in such a way that a fragile and weak nation can make cultural claims to sovereignty on the terrain of European nationalism. These spheres that generally seem separate and separable are in historical practice intimately joined.

9

CONCLUSIONS

THE U.S. PROJECT of transforming Hawai'i was deeply ironic in several ways. The missionaries and lawyers who sought to help the Hawaiian people retain their sovereignty put into place legal and governmental institutions that depended on foreigners to run them. Those who had learned the practices of legal institutions in New England were necessary to make the new systems work. Moreover, these same institutions then facilitated the dispossession of maka'āinana, turning them into landless wage laborers. In another irony, the egalitarian beliefs of the missionaries prevented their creating a dual legal system for Hawaiians and whites. Anyone who could act "civilized" was welcome to participate in the new institutions of government and law. Although this promoted equality, it also speeded the cultural transformation of Native Hawaiians, since they too were subject to the new laws. As the "civilizing process" protected the sovereignty of the Hawaiian nation by allowing it to claim equal status in the world of empire, it also demanded from the Hawaiian people radical transformations in the management of sexuality and the body.

This instance of American colonialism differs from many of the British examples by its emphasis on incorporation rather than exclusion. Whereas many British colonies created dual legal systems and sought to construct boundaries between the colonizer and colonized, in Hawai'i ties of marriage and sociability cross-cut the Hawaiian/haole boundary. Throughout the nineteenth century, women of the Hawaiian royal family married elite haole men. As lines of class solidified at the end of the century with the rise of the plantations, the elite classes still included both Hawaiians and haoles. The Asian immigrants, however, were rigorously excluded from citizenship and political participation. Although many immigrants organized labor unions in the early twentieth century, it was only after the growth of a second generation entitled to citizenship that Asian descendants became full participants in the political and legal systems.

But incorporation depended on becoming "civilized." This demanded significant changes in gender, the family, and forms of bodily management. Much of the social change taking place in Hawai'i was dedicated to the idea of civilization, from changing names to riding horses to wrapping the body in clothes while swimming. Although civilization is no longer a dominant discourse, similar dramatic transformations are currently underway under the discursive umbrellas of development, modernization, and democracy.

In the nineteenth century, Hawai'i seemed at the periphery of emerging European and American nations. Yet it was at the center of an international crossroads of people and trade. Indeed, Honolulu in the early nineteenth century was far more of a cultural crossroads than the rural areas of New England that sent many of the Americans to Hawai'i. Understanding historical change in this contact zone has required the analysis of local, national, and global processes. Transnational movements such as commerce, evangelism, imperialism, faith in the rule of law, and capitalism shaped local change. Policies implemented in Hawai'i concerning land allocation, colonial legality, and capitalism were similar to those in other colonizing situations in the Pacific. Yet within these larger patterns there was serendipity and accident: people such as Lee and Austin who happened to arrive in Honolulu and people such as Ka'ahumanu who saw the new religion as a possibility and embraced its mana and palapala. Change was a product of choices made under the uncertain and changing conditions of a contact zone. Contemporary society is also characterized by places where competing cultural logics coexist and are appropriated by agents differentially situated to seize those which seem desirable or advantageous and combine them with others to produce new hybrids whose long-term consequences are unforeseeable. Ambivalent and ambiguous conditions marked the expansion of colonial projects, paralleling rather than contrasting with the conditions of much of the postcolonial world.

Rethinking Culture and History

Cultural meanings are central to historical change. While acknowledging the importance of political and economic forces, I argue that systems of meaning and the way they intersect with each other are fundamental to understanding the shape of social transformation. This is particularly true in situations where competing cultural logics coexist in the same social field. The decision to adopt new institutions such as the rule of law depended on congruent cultural logics, but once adopted, institutions such as the law had their own durability and immovability. Processes of historical change are incremental and uncertain rather than linear or inevitable. Competing cultural logics mesh at certain points and diverge at others, sending trajectories of change into directions often unanticipated or undesired by those instrumental in furthering them.

Cultural understandings explain why various groups and individuals acted as they did. Notions of moral reform, the creation of modern citizens out of the Native Hawaiian population, and the control of dangerous outsiders, particularly those with allegedly undesirable racial characteristics, shaped the implementation of the law in Hilo as elsewhere in Hawai'i. At the same time, the desire for a "civilized" identity contributed to the willingness of the ali'i and to a lesser extent the maka'āinana to adopt a new system of law and regulation, to study the new law books, and to participate as judges and litigants in the new courts. Competing cultural logics intersect in particular places at particular times. The ali'i needing to manage the contentious foreigners living in the port towns and arriving in whaleships were attracted to Christian ideas of law. Yet they initially found this form of law attractive also because it meshed with their own understandings of religion, authority, and law.

Concepts of cultural production and appropriation are valuable for describing the agentic and complex interactions between multiple social worlds characteristic of the contact zone. Understanding situations of historical change at the intersection of multiple groups requires a set of concepts derived from the analysis of societies assumed to have histories, complexity, and change. These concepts emphasize agency and the importance of producing new cultural meanings. In Hawai'i, the central act of appropriation was conversion to Christianity and the adoption of Anglo-American law and government. Appropriating Western law was a gesture toward civilizing the kingdom. The ali'i were seeking to navigate a new and complicated situation of power in a way that they imagined would strengthen their nation and preserve its autonomy. Ironically, the changes designed to create a civilized and sovereign nation had the effect of criminalizing the population and installing foreigners in key positions of government.

Transplanted systems of law are a widespread feature of the contemporary world as well as the colonial one, and understanding how this transplantation happens and what its implications are is a critical but understudied process. Reformist governments in Eastern Europe, for example, are now adopting segments of Western European law codes and practices, a practice followed years earlier by Attaturk in Turkey and numerous other governments in the name of reform (Hooker 1975). In the Hawaiian case, as in many others, the transplant was desired on the basis of a complex set of expectations made up of eagerness for Christianity, civilization, modernity, and moral reform, and the notion of ruling a society through law rather than alleged despotic power. Voluntary transplants are driven by a faith in the new world they will produce and a desire for the sense of personhood and power they evoke, now more often couched in the language of modernization, development, or nation-building than civilization. Those who import new systems of law often seek a new place in the global order even though this may require dramatic and even traumatic changes in the social life of the nation.

And it is often women who are changed. Women are often thought to carry on their backs, or in their wombs, the spirit of the nation and the core of its identity. Their commitment to family, to raising the next generation, to submission to a husband, sometimes embodies the moral virtue of the modern nation. And in the service of this identity, Hawaiian women, along with many other women, were pressed to define themselves as wives and mothers, domestically contained and voluminously clothed. Their allegedly unbridled sexual activity threatened to tear the nation apart much as recent talk of the loss of "family values," with its depiction of frightening rates of teen pregnancy and divorce, is linked to a fear of national weakness. Maintaining family order has long been defined as fundamental to the modern nation. At the same time, protecting women from a degraded status was a frequent justification for colonialism in Hawai'i as in other colonial situations (see Chatterjee 1989), redeployed now to legitimate modernization and development in sporadic attacks on gender violence, suttee, female genital mutilation, bridewealth, and other cultural practices.

Elites welcomed new cultural forms and structures, both because of strategic calculations about the capacity of these structures to provide sovereignty and because of cultural commitments to the civilizing process. The rapid adoption of Western names, dress, houses, religion, and writing by the ali'i was simultaneously driven by a recognition of the power inherent in these practices and by a desire to transform the self to conform to these images of the civilized person. Confronted with the image of the civilized person as one capable of commanding both resources and respect, many Hawaiians sought to refashion themselves without abandoning their commitment to Hawaiian traditions or selves. Instead, there was an expansion of consciousness, a multiplication of identities. The rule of law was central to this expansion, since it offered both the means to an enlightened government, as defined by the missionaries, and the sign of its accomplishment.

Law and Social Change

Law transforms through its texts, its performances, and its violence. Laws as texts embody cultural conceptions of persons and specify relationships and actions as legitimate or criminal. They may specify the proper business of women or declare that women should pay half as much tax as men. Texts are transferred from one society or nation to another in a process variously called transplantation, reception, or imposition. But texts are more readily transferred than the practices of interpreting and administering them. Practices of administering the law are often imported as well, but over time they adapt to local circumstances and local political agendas. As new laws are applied to particular situations through these practices, they create performances in courtrooms. Such performances allow authoritative judicial and prosecutorial figures to interpret everyday life in new ways. Decisions rendered by the courts are sedimented performances. When decisions lead to penalties, the meanings of performances are defined through the violence they have elicited (see Sarat and Kearns 1993).

As courts convict some and acquit others, they construct images of the kinds of people who are dangerous: those who possess degenerate characters, immoral drug habits, scurrilous gambling patterns, or irrational recreations such as cockfighting. By its silence, the law also oppositionally constructs the social identities of the virtuous and the respectable: those who do not appear in court. Defendants, plaintiffs, lawyers, judges, and the general public form the audience for these representations. Through convictions, social identities in the larger society are converted into a new register of truth, defined by the authority of the state and backed by its sanctioned violence. Identities are *refracted*, replicated but with new legitimacy and force. Through these processes, as Foucault (1980a, 1980b) points out, institutions construct knowledges that constitute power.

The social history of the introduction of Western law to Hawai'i reveals that criminal law was a fundamental strategy for changing the social life of newcomers, whether deserting seamen, immigrant sugar workers, or migratory marijuana growers from the mainland. The everyday activities of newcomer groups defined as dangerous or simply different were the targets of prosecution and conviction. But law as a direct sanctioning system was only the initial phase of a broader social transformation. Far more pervasive were the cultural effects of the new system of law. Legal performances in court and in the community enunciated a new normative order, a new system of identities and obligations. Men far more than women experienced the frontline system of control, but the same mechanism was adopted to redefine women as wives and mothers rather than active sexual persons or traveling kinsmen, as domestic rather than public persons. Reshaping gender and the family was essential to the colonizing project in Hawai'i: an enduring bourgeois marriage and stern husbandly authority over a submissive, domesticated wife were imagined as the basis of the modern nation.

The construction of some kinds of identity and the effacing of others is a fundamental aspect of the power of the law in the present as well as the past. Defining identities constitutes some as normal and others as deviant, some as citizens and some as aliens, some as having racial identities and others as unmarked racially, defined as the normal. The most fundamental distinction legal systems draw is that between the criminal and the noncriminal. Making this distinction with reference to particular persons is, of course, at the heart of the criminal process.

Newspaper writers, policy makers, opponents of immigration, welfare reformers, and many others cite crime statistics as evidence of the character of particular social groups. The chaotic, unsystematic, agentic, historically contingent process of criminalization, conviction, and counting defines some form of behavior as a crime, institutes social processes that persuade citizens to locate, prosecute, and punish those who engage in this behavior, and develops record-keeping systems that make it possible to count the instances of this form of interdicted behavior. This process produces a truth of bodies, a social knowledge of the extent of wrongdoing by particular groups, defined in terms of race, class, gender. In other words, a set of criminalized identities emerges, identities seen as dangerous, based on a secure knowledge of counting and reporting—forms filled out, boxes checked, tables rendered—a knowledge based not on experience or individual situation and circumstance but on numbers and kinds of bodies. Clearly, the collective knowledge under the Hawaiian government before 1825 was vastly different. In the absence of writing and record keeping, it was lodged in the minds of the chiefs, converted into narratives told and retold in ceremonial and social occasions as stories of wrongdoing, a differently produced and reproduced kind of knowledge. But as the modernist project of governance expanded in the nineteenth century, a new knowledge emerged, which targeted Native Hawaiians as sexually active and Asian immigrants as violent, opium-addicted, and given to gambling.

Ideas about dangerous persons in need of legal surveillance and control are created locally but circulate globally. In the nineteenth and twentieth centuries, systems of control moved transnationally along with ideologies of dangerous populations and their threats to social order. In the 1920s, for example, sociologists in Chicago began to ascribe urban problems such as prostitution, crime, suicide, and alcoholism to the breakdown of the social order of the village and the close-knit urban community. At about the same time, British colonial officials and anthropologists began to talk about the detribalization of Africans in town, torn from the fabric of their village society but not yet endowed with sufficient self-control to manage their own lives. Plantation managers in Hawai'i talked about the need for authority over their workers, who could not control themselves without a paternalistic hand. In Fiji, government officials worried about the tendency toward criminality of the Indian workers imported to harvest the cane, just as American planters in Hawai'i worried about the Filipino cane workers (Kelly 1994).

In each case, control was imagined in gendered terms as paternalistic authority exercised over a subordinated group imagined as feminine. The subordinated were envisioned as more emotional, less able to exercise self-control, less rational, and more in need of protection and care by a stern, fatherly hand than the elites who ran the plantations and colonial governments. White males were rarely if ever described as lacking in self-control, as needing authority, or as cast adrift in a moral void because they were detached from a close-knit community. It appears that white males were thought capable of controlling themselves.

Law and Resistance

In the process of historical transformation, law clearly embodies the desires and interests of groups in power. But the law also provides a powerful system of meaning-making based on ideas of rights and equality. It supports reformist humanism as well as capitalist transformation. Law was not just a mode of power for the dominant, but also an institution standing against the unbridled power of the market. It constrained the impact of the market on individuals and communities, although only through the mediation of local judges and attorneys and the capacities of individual litigants. For example, the incidents of worker resistance discussed in chapter 7 showed that the extent to which the law constrained planters' power depended on the laborers themselves: on their literacy, their knowledge of how to make claims and how to use government representatives, and the racial identities imposed on them by local elites. Thus the power of law to enforce particular social arrangements and structures is shaped by local social practices, interpretations, and the social location of officials.

Law creates structures of legitimation for relations of power that already exist, acting in a conservative fashion to support existing systems of power and control. At the same time, the language of law provides a critique of systems that fail to provide equal rights for all in a universalizing discourse as well as an arena in which to challenge subordination. Laborers use the law to resist their working conditions. Men use adultery laws to hold on to their wives, or at least to extract payment from the men who entice them away. Battered women see their husbands' violence as a crime rather than an attack they provoked. The law provides ways of rethinking relationships, ways that were taken up rather quickly by subordinated groups in Hawai'i as they framed their demands in terms of individualism and rights.

The law also creates a sphere of illegality, of prohibited activities, which inspire resistant behavior such as drinking, gambling, and violence. These activities become means of recuperating the self in a disciplined and alienated world, a way of asserting autonomy against state power. Yet in the long run the law incorporates resistance, defining the terms and the strategies within which resistance takes place and establishing itself as the fundamental terrain for challenges to the existing social order. These challenges redefine the balance of power within that order but do not contest the order itself. In Hawai'i, it was this incorporation that was the fundamentally transformative part of the colonizing process. Just as the ali'i of the 1820s accepted the missionaries because they desired the power of writing and its apparent wealth and mana, only to find themselves drawn into a new order of power in which they were increasingly marginalized, so the maka'āinana and later the imported sugar workers appropriated the law as an arena for their own claims to power and personhood despite the extent to which they themselves were subject to its control. Women, objects of surveillance and control when they deserted their husbands or had sex with other men, also mobilized the law in struggles against battering, both in the nineteenth century and in the present.

Clearly, the law is neither purely a tool for imposing the rule of dominant groups nor a weapon for resistance, but a site of power, defined by its texts, its practices, and its practitioners, available to those who are able to turn it to their purposes. The local context—the identity of judges, attorneys, and police officers—mediates critically between the law as authoritative text and the imposition of its power, thus defining the way law acts as a site of power.

The link between law and social change continues to be a central issue in the modern world. The United States, for example, continues to try to promote change in everyday social life through criminalization, whether diminishing drug use, controlling commodified sexuality, or reducing wife battering. Change occurs through a circular process in which the social meanings outside of law shape the statutes and pressure prosecutors, police, and judges to construct a particular defendant stream. Political processes that define a kind of person or a practice as dangerous or a social evil engender greater efforts by police and prosecutors to bring such cases to trial, and judges then take them more seriously. When plantation owners argued that they needed to control their indolent and potentially rebellious workers, for example, the officials in the courts cooperated by prosecuting and convicting large numbers of workers for failure to work. As the convictions mounted, planters were reinforced in their understanding that their laborers, defined in raced and gendered terms, required discipline. The prosecutions confirmed planters' beliefs that Hawaiians, Chinese, Norwegians, and Japanese were indolent and rebellious workers with, in some cases, dangerous violent tendencies. Prosecutions for adultery confirmed understandings of Hawaiians as licentious.

The political and economic transformation of Hilo was clearly reflected in its caseload, and as the community changed, so did the people whose activities were subject to legal surveillance. The interests and concerns of judges, sheriffs, prosecutors, police, and probation officers, changed as the hegemony of the Christian mission community gave way to the planter oligarchy, reflected in different patterns of arrest, prosecution, and conviction. These changes, in turn, produced new identities of the criminal and the law-abiding, the dangerous and the safe. Local political pressures and social anxieties shape patterns of arrests, prosecutions, and convictions, whose statistical outcomes confirm cultural understandings of identity.

The meanings produced by the law have force and power because they are institutionally embodied and speak with the authority of the state, taking on its legitimacy. Yet the law is constituted by individuals who don the authoritative roles provided by the state. These individuals can tailor and shape the pronouncements of the law within the space allotted by the structure.

The systems of meaning that inform court performances are both local and transnational phenomena. Pitman worried about the deserting seamen in Hilo, people already defined as problematic in his home environment in Massachusetts. S. L. Austin, arriving in Hilo fresh from New England, brought its ideas about morality and hierarchy with him. D. H. Hitchcock and Luther Severance, both mission products or married to missionary daughters, prosecuted adultery and desertion guided by their image of sexuality and marriage embedded in Protestant Christianity. Mission-educated G. W. A. Hapai, bearing the names of both his Chinese father and the first American president, spent much of his time convicting deserting workers, probably feeling closer affinity with the Christian elite of Hilo than with the newcomer Chinese laborers. In the twentieth century, Democratic reformers arriving from the mainland disrupted the virtually unchallenged power of Republican planters as they registered the second-generation plantation workers, now citizens, to vote and moved into positions such as judge and prosecutor. Some of these newcomers engineered moral cleanup campaigns of the brothels and cockfights of Hilo in the 1930s and 1940s. The accidents of person and place, as well as the large structural forces that bring particular persons to these places at various times, account for these processes of continuity and change.

The discourse of rights and the restraints on power incorporated within the law provide a rich resource for political movements. Not only does the law provide a language for resistance, but it also promises power in defense of rights. Rights have repeatedly been mobilized by subordinate groups to contest power within the legal arena itself. In recent years, the movement to criminalize and punish wife battering is a clear example, as is the extensive use of litigation and people's tribunals to condemn the U.S. takeover of Hawai'i. In the nineteenth century as in the present, law provides a vital terrain for struggles over nationhood and identity, including the place of women in the order of the family and the state and the civilizing of the body through the body of law.

APPENDIXES

A

CASES FROM HILO DISTRICT COURT

TITLED BY CHARGE

Some texts are shortened and paraphrased.

1853 Cases

1853. 1 Adultery

June 7, 1853

The King vs.
Waakahuli k [kane, male, Native Hawaiian]
Kaipo w [wahine, female, Native Hawaiian]

Defts plead not guilty

Paki, sworn says: Kaipo has been for some time in the habit of harboring moekolohes [people committing moekolohes—or fornicators]. Kaina put me to watch the house. I am a constable. Piena went with me. We stayed outside of the house for a long time listening. We heard whispering within the house and the usual noise that people make when in sexual intercourse. There was a hole through the house by which we could see inside of the house. Piena my companion went after a light. I caused the light to shine through the hole and it fell directly on the 2 defts who were in actual intercourse. The man was on top of the woman—as soon as they saw the light the man jumped off. Then we demanded an entrance. At last we gained an entrance and found that defts were the only persons in the house and we arrested them for adultery. Waakahuli lives on the same land as Kaipo who is the wife of John the Pilot. About as far as from here to the beach. I brought defts into the bay and we were met by Baranapa [variously spelled "Berenaba" "Baranaba"] who was angry with me for breaking some rules of the church in not bringing them before the church [illegible—could be something like: rather than . . . bringing them up in court]. He took us to Palo's [John the Pilot's?] house and there they arraigned the matter and told me to let the prisoners go and I did go and on last Saturday the woman's husband caused her to be arrested again on the same charge. So they are now here on John's information.

Piena sworn says in substance the same as the other witness.

Baranapa sworn says: I met the constables and defts coming to court on the 27th day of May last. Had some conversation with them, enquired if they had a church meeting. Constable said no. I then inquired into the case. Constable said he had seen them in actual intercourse, that he had demanded an entrance into the house, and the woman had admitted them—that he had found 2 defts there alone—that he had heard them whispering and talking while he was outside. I told him that what he was saying was inconsistent, that he could not see the parties inside of the house while he was outside and the door shut. Constable insisted that they were guilty of actual intercourse. I then gave him a lecture. Constable said after receiving lecture, "Well, what of it, let them go." I told him not to do so on my account. Constable said, "You are the church member of the whole of us, you are something like God to us. And as your opinion is against it I will go back." I told them again not to do so on my account and then left. I think that the seeing them through the crack in the door is an afterthought suggested by his conversation with me.

Adjourned for witnesses who are in Hilo.

[continued on June 8]

Kanola sworn says—I live at Kana near Kaipo's house and live in the same yard with Waakahuli. After defts had been arrested and let go again by the constable, Waakahuli told me that Kaipo was a curious woman. I asked him why. He said she wants me to continue to go and sleep with her at her own house until her husband comes back then to separate for fear of getting into trouble. It was told me in confidence. Sometime before this happened I had suspicions of defts being guilty of illicit intercourse. I saw the man leave his companions very often and go by stealth to where the woman seemed to be waiting for him. I have seen them playing together acting like lovers. On one such occasion I saw the man run away and hide himself among the coffee when other persons were approaching. My brother and I myself have reprimanded Waakahuli for going to the woman's house and for doing wrong generally. This reprimand has no effect. Every night he would be making for her house where he slept. On the night of the arrest, I heard the constable call out "haul in." [Paki was the constable.] I enquired "what is it." The constable answered, "I have just found Waakahuli and Kaipo together committing adultery." A few moments after the Constable lead Waakahuli down to my house and left him there till next morning. It is the general report among the neighbors that defts were in the habit of committing adultery.

Kanama sworn says—On the night of Monday after the defts had been brought to Hilo and discharged by the hoahanau [church member],

Waakahuli told me when we were in his house "I have great love for my woman." I asked him what woman. Deft said, "Kaipo. My love has increased for her and I [illegible] she has to stop so long in the bay." Defts have a reputation of being adulterers together. I heard the constable sing out "haul in" and saw him lead down Waakahuli from Kaipo's house to Kanola's house.

Kekelu sworn says—On Thursday of the week following that of the arrest and [one word—illeg] here to Hilo, I went up to settle a little business with John and on going back I called at Waakahuli's house. Waakahuli took me outside and engaged me in conversation, asked me where Kaipo was and where John was. He told me he had very great love indeed for Kaipo—that a plan was made up between them. He was to go to Hamakua and she was to follow him. It is the general report in the neighborhood that the Defts had been practicing adultery some time.

Defts are guilty and sentenced to pay a fine of $30 each or to be imprisoned for the space of 8 months at hard labor.

S. L. Austin
Dist. Justice of Hilo.

[Commentary: Clearly, local church members are important in supporting the new moral order, along with the courts. In this case, it appears that the constable is spying and trying to support the work of the church.]

1853.2 Assault and Battery

February 2, 1853

King vs.
Kuina K
Apakohuole K

Assault and battery on Acho on the 12th.

Defts. plead not guilty.

Summary of case:

Ai'i [probably Chinese] testifies defts committed an assault upon Acho: the Defts struck Acho with a stick.

Another witness, Namu, testified that he works on the Papaikou plantation (where the assault took place). On the day of the assault he was tending the furnace. He asked permission of Acho to leave. Acho asked Kuina to take Namu's place; Kuina refused saying his day's work was done. Namu says he told Acho not to make deft. work double; if he did he [referring to deft.] would "pound and hurt him." Acho said he didn't wish to fight and asked deft. Kuina if he wanted to. Deft. said "yes." Deft. struck Acho with a stick on the arm and back. Deft. dropped stick and they "went at it with their fists." Ai'i came and parted them. Deft. threatened to "kick the pair of them." Deft. struck Acho again and the two resumed the fight. The two were separated but the deft. turned and attacked the Chinaman again. The whole group of workmen at the mill surrounded the fighting pair saying ". . . let's help the boy, don't let the Chinaman hurt him." Apakohuole, a workman, came from the crowd and grabbed Acho by the hair, pulling him to the ground. "Here the fray ended."

Alohikia sworn says: "Substance the same as other witness."

Ahi testified that he didn't see the first of the fight but later saw Apakohuole take Acho by the hair and saw him later on the ground.

Kanekahi sworn for deft: Says he saw Kuina on the road heading for the sugar house. Witness saw Chinaman exit the sugar house with a stick in his hand. Acho came up to Kuina and struck him on the back which caused him to fall. Acho climbed on top of deft. and they began fighting on the ground. Kanekahi tried to stop the fight.

Kealo also testified it was the Chinaman who hit the deft. Kuina with the stick on the back and head and then in the face. Ai'i grabbed deft. by the hair and struck him in the mouth. Ai'i got the stick from Acho. The pair was then separated.

Apaapa sworn: Testified to the same facts as the other deft's witnesses did.

Judge notes that the complainant has a bruise across his back suggesting he was hit with the stick (on exhibit in court).

Defts. found guilty; Kuina is fined $10 and Apakohuole is sentenced to 20 days hard labor.

[Commentary: This case suggests that violence between workers and employers was a problem in the plantation business from its earliest days. In this case, the evidence favored the employer, showing that, as in many other cases, struggles over power begun in the fields through violence were ended in the courts, which supported the lunas against the rebellious workers.]

1853.3 Selling Liquor to Natives and Manufacturing Liquor

April 9, 1853

King vs. Aikon

Charged with violation of the 1st and 2nd sections of the 42nd. Chapt. of Penal Code. [Sec. 1—providing liquor to natives; sec. 2—manufacturing intoxicating liquor. Sec. 1 violations were subject to a fine not to exceed $200 or 2 years hard labor—so it was in jurisdiction of district and police courts. Sec. 2 violations were subject to a fine of up to $500 or 2 years imprisonment at hard labor.]

William Barnes testified that he's an employee of the deft. Deft. keeps an eating house and a bowling alley. Deft. also makes beer. "Another Chinaman makes beer sometimes." Witness says he wanted to make beer and also Sampson, but deft. would only allow the other Chinaman to do it. Witness goes on to say they use hops, water, and molasses and that the brew made from this is not strong enough within 24 hours to cause intoxication. Witness never saw anyone drunk on it.

John Nomore, sworn: Testifies he was a former employee of this place and tended bar. Deft. told him not to sell Kanakas any beer because it was against the law. He says he would refuse to serve anyone beer who appeared to be intoxicated. He left Aikon's employ two weeks ago and hasn't been back.

A. Penny testified that he was a boarder at deft's house. He says he has seen people there "three sheets in the wind." Penny says when there are intoxicated people, the establishment generally sends them on their way so the house won't be implicated. This man says the brew is strong enough to be intoxicating. He has also seen beer given to natives by Mr. Barnes. But he never saw deft. give beer to natives.

Maikuma testified he's had beer at the Chinaman's but it was Mikaele who sold it to him yesterday. (Deft. had refused to sell him beer). A foreigner gave him beer. Witness says he was drunk yesterday on beer he got at the deft's house. Mikaele is the bowling alley gamekeeper. It was Mikaele who sold the witness the beer but without the deft's knowledge. Witness said he never knew of anybody who'd gotten drunk at deft's house. Goes on to say he'd gotten drinks from elsewhere yesterday, including some brandy. (The liquor belonged to William's master.) Reiterated that deft. refused him beer—it was Mikaele the gamekeeper who sold it to him.

William Smith [who appears as a defendant twice in 1853 for beating his wife] says he was drinking at the deft's yesterday. He, Maikuna, Mikaele, and Wiliama were playing cards for beer. It was Mikaele who got the beer. Mikaele was in charge of the house at the time in deft's absence. W.S. testified they were drunk before they got the beer from Mikaele. They "got beer nowhere else that day." The beer came from a keg in the bar.

Wiliama testified he was with Smith and Maikuna that day and that they got drunk on the beer Mikaele sold them and also they consumed 5 pitchers of beer during dinner.

Wm. Parrish, sworn: Testified he's drunk at the defts' establishment but a few glasses of the beer do not intoxicate. He has never felt affected by the beer there.

Mikaele is sworn and testifies he's Aikon's bowling alley keeper and tends bar sometimes. M. says deft. knew of his selling beer. Mikaele sold beer to Maikuna and foreigners but the beer didn't get them drunk. Maikuna told witness he didn't get drunk there. Deft. had told Mikaele not to serve beer to the natives.

Charles Sampson testified that he saw Smith and Wiliama yesterday afternoon at deft's place and they were drunk. Witness says deft. refused to sell them any beer. Sampson saw Mikaele give Maikuna beer on a previous occasion. Sampson adds he had never seen anyone drunk there except for "two men that came there."

Dr. Sanger testified he'd bought beer at Aikon's. Mr. Barnes sold it to him. From his experience (two glasses) he says the beer would intoxicate. He's also seen others get beer there.

The Court ruled: "Held that deft. is brought under the first section by Mikaele selling beer to natives although deft. had told him not to do so. Fined for this offense $10. Under second section, deft. is found guilty and sentenced to pay a fine of $500 and in default of payment imprisonment at hard labor for the space of one year."

[Commentary: Clearly, the court takes providing liquor very seriously during this period. In Pitman's letters, he constantly struggles to keep out rum and comments on the relative quiet of the town as a result. Here a hefty fine is imposed in order to punish the maker of alcohol.]

1853.4 Drunkenness on Potato

January 4, 1853

King vs.
Kawika K.
Kahau W.
Paumano K
Kalnaakeli W.
Kainapau K
Kalalualani W.
Hulu W.
Kaaka W.

Charge of getting drunk on potato [probably beer]

Defts all plead guilty

The offence was committed in the night after 9 o'clock at night—Defts were making a good deal of noise. Three of defts have been fined before for the same offense. Kawika, Kaaka, and Kainapau having been fined before are fined in the sum of $6 each. And Kahau, Paumano, Kaualani and Hulu are fined $3.00 each and in default of payment—imprisonment until paid.

S.L. Austin
Dist. Justice

[Commentary: Thus, the court makes a distinction between a repeat offender and a first-time offender. The repeat fines are fairly significant given the overall availability of cash at this time.]

1863 Cases

1863.1 Damages for Criminal Connection with Wife

January 17, 1863

Charley Kamahina vs. Akana Liilii

"To recover $100 damages for criminal connection with his wife while he was at sea."

Deft. admits that Keanu was his mistress but says she was living separately from her husband for some time. The plaintiff admits he hadn't lived with his wife for four years, but argues that "deft. in keeping his wife for so long" has caused him damage.

"As deft. acknowledges the committing of the deed, no witness for pltf. examined." [noted by Judge Hitchcock].

Hoaai [perhaps the judge in the 1848 complaint against Pitman] testified for deft. that Keanu and pltf. were married but began to quarrel [witness is a neighbor of pltf.]. The wife sought help once from Hoaai during a quarrel with the pltf. Pltf., not having a home, lives with his wife's father. Adds that pltf. hasn't "been fined for adultery."

The Court is adjourned until Monday.

Keahi [perhaps D. H. Hitchcock's landlord in 1857] testifies that deft. "had been fined for adultery with the plaintiff's wife." Says pltf. isn't entitled to damages of $100, "$40 would cover it."

Kuahau says he "knows the facts in this case." He says that perhaps $45 would cover all the damage."

Kepio testified for the defense. Says that pltf and wife got along early in the marriage but started to fight. Keanu quarreled with pltf. because he'd been after Kapela. The couple lived with her father. "All her pono was from her father."

Pltf. went to sea; didn't provide for his wife. Then the wife went to the deft; the deft. didn't come after her. Since pltf's return "he's done nothing for his wife." Her father takes care of her. Doesn't believe pltf. deserves any damages.

Papa: Wife's father testifies that the pltf. hasn't supported his wife since he went to sea. He, Papa, has supported her. Says pltf. had another woman and left his wife first. "His wife did not go to the Chinaman for a long time after." She went to him "of her own will."

Kaohimaunu: Deft. gave $30 to "the house of Kapela, his mistress."

Hooaii: Deft. lived with Kepela and "was commonly [illeg.]." "This was before Akana committed adultery with her." Says there's no cause for damages.

"The judgement is rendered for the pltf. in the sum of $5.00 plus $5.25 court costs. Paid by deft. judgement and costs of $3.00.
$8 paid by pltf.

D. H. Hitchcock

[Commentary: Akana was one of the early sugar masters in Hilo. Chinese sugar masters married Hawaiian women, often high ranking ones. This case seems to be a contest over women played out in court. The Hawaiian pltf. probably found the Chinese's affluence irresistible and sought through the court to pursue damages. The low judgment by the court likely reflects its appreciation of the underlying motives of the suit.]

1863.2 Desertion of Work

April 25, 1863

Haalele Hana—Desertion of Work

Pauka Co. vs. Maiwela k [k= male]
Kalili k
Kaaipahi k [the judge has lined out this name]
Kipe k
Lonoheana k

"Plead that they did not exactly refuse to work but said if Keoni Ko did not give them better fish they would [refuse]."

Ordered to go back to work, pay costs $1 each. $6 paid by Keoni Ko.
D. H. Hitchcock

[Commentary: In this case, the workers use the courts to lodge a complaint against their working conditions. The court apparently did not respond to their complaint. The luna, Keoni, probably has a "Hawaiianized" Chinese name.]

1863.3 Assault and Battery

January 30, 1863

King vs. G. Waller
Assault and battery on Akino

Pleads not guilty.

Akino testified that he was eating last Wednesday when the deft. came in and told him to get back to the house and swore at him. Deft. pulled him out of the house, tearing his shirt, telling him that "the men do steal the sugar there."

Awako testified that deft. grabbed Akino "violently" tearing his shirt and "telling him to go off right away."

Kanua testified that he witnessed the deft. calling to the Chinaman. The Chinaman told deft. to wait until he had finished his meal. He went out to the lanai [porch], where they spoke to one another. Deft. grabbed him and his shirt was torn.

Kaino: testified he was not present at the time.

Akino was recalled and testified that he had received no injury.

Deft. discharged.
D. H. Hitchcock

[Commentary: In this case, the violence of the probably white luna, resulting in torn clothes but no bodily injury, was dismissed by the court.]

1863.4 Desertion of Work

January 30, 1863

Zucker and Waller vs.
Akino
Awako

Haalele Hana [judge makes note "join gen'l issue"]

Kamu testified that defts. left work yesterday and are not at work today.
Kanui testified that the defts. "came into the bay" yesterday to Hoopii and "have been there two days."

Defts. ordered to work and pay court costs of $2.00 each. D. H. Hitchcock

[Commentary: This is a routine desertion of work case, except that in the previous case, on the same day, Akina and Awako charged their luna with assault and battery. Pairing these two cases suggests that the workers fared less well than their luna.]

1873 CASES

1873.1 Desertion of Work

January 15, 1873

Jones & Kaina vs.
Laamea
Hoopii
Ku

E. G. Hitchcock for defense. Plea of not guilty

Jurisdiction of this court denied in Civil cases. Motion overruled.
Moved that as the justice is a partner in a ranch of which the plaintiffs are part owners, that he is incompetent to sit in the case.
Overruled. Exceptions taken to the ruling.

Wainilani S.

D. H. Hitchcock, Judge

[Commentary: Again, the close connections between the judicial staff and the plantations is notable.]

1873.2 Desertion of Work

November 21, 1873

Thos. Spencer vs. Daniela

Charged with Haalele Hana. Says he only left yesterday for food.

B. Macy, sworn: On Monday he was not in the gang and I found he was in the wood-cutting gang. Tuesday I sent him to Waiki's gang. On Wednesday morning I heard he had gone into Kunaha's gang. On Wednesday and Thursday I could not find him in the gang anywhere. No one has a right to stop without leave even for food.

Imprisoned at hard labor for two months and pay costs.

[Commentary: In general, first offenses receive an order to return to work and a court costs (fine) of about $5.00, roughly a half month's pay. Second offenses typically receive one month jail time plus costs.]

1873.3 Assault and Battery

December 8, 1873

Rex vs.
B. Macy

Assault and Battery on one Daniela ma kala 4th December at Amauulu [a plantation just north of Hilo].

E. G. Hitchcock for defense.

Daniela, sworn: I live at Amauulu and know the prisoner, was there on the 4th. I took up some of Spencer's [owner of the plantation; took over Pitman's lands when he returned to Boston] cattle on cause of trespass in my food and went up to Amauulu. Prisoner was outside and I told him that their cattle had been in this food. I wanted him to do something about it. He told me to go to work and I said yes as soon as we settle this matter. He then jumped for me and struck me and caught me by the throat and kicked me. Spencer was near. No other parties were near us. After that the prisoner's father-in-law came and took him off. He hurt me a good deal and the blood ran from my nose. Kamaka and Hoakimo came up when we were fighting.

Cross exam: I fell down when he assaulted me and he kicked me.

Kamaka, sworn: Knows about this assault. Saw prisoner strike Daniela at Amauulu and knock him down, last Thursday. He then caught him by the throat and kicked him in the neck. I got my tools and then left. I did not see Spencer there. When I left they were still fighting.

Cross exam: Am no relation of Daniela's.

Hoakimo, sworn: Lives at Amauulu and saw this assault on Thursday last. I was at work near there and I went after some nails. I heard a noise and saw Daniela down and Macy pound him. Do not know about the commencement. Spencer came up after. I and Kanaka saw it.

Crown rests.

Thos. Spencer, sworn for defense: There was a trouble between Macy and Daniela. Heard Macy tell him to go to work. Daniela replied in Native. The order was given 3 or 4 times. There upon Macy shoved him to go to work. Then the man struck him in the face and there was a scuffle. No one was near at that time.

Disp: Fined $10 costs $3.40.

Note appeal to Circuit Court; papers sent up.

D. H. Hitchcock
Police Justice

APPEAL

December 15, 1873

Notes on appeal from 1873 Third Circuit Court minute book: This appeal was heard in Hilo Circuit Court on Dec. 15th, 1873. L. Severance is listed as Sheriff for Crown; E. G. Hitchcock is defense attorney. F. S. Lyman is presiding judge.

Evidence:

Daniela, sworn: I live and work at Amauulu—know this foreigner, Beny [deft]. I was at Amauulu one Tuesday, to see Captain Spencer about his cattle trespassing in my food. Thursday morning I went again, early in the morning, as the cattle had trespassed again. I saw Macy about it—he went and saw Spencer about it and returned—we talked a little, and he assaulted me, struck me throwing me down, then kicked me on the head, then kicked me twice on my neck, while I was down. Kamaka, Hoakimoa, Spencer and Bill a half-white, were there; it was at the veranda of store at Spencer's plantation. Kaaihue, Macy's brother-in-law, pulled off Macy from me.

Cross: Kamaka was there all the time, also Hoakimoa, at work; I am certain they were there all the time of the trouble. Bila [Bill] and Spencer were a little distance off, but in sight. I first saw Kamaka by the trash house, a few fathoms from us, and while I was down on the floor in one room of the store house, I saw Kamaka come into the next room for nails. I also saw Hoakimoa at the trash house with Kamaka, and he came with Kamaka for nails when Kaaihue released me. I saw Hoakimoa standing near. Macy struck me first. I did not strike at him and miss, before he struck me. I saw the wife of Ahoan at the stream washing when Macy was striking me; when Macy had been to see Spencer, he came back, and told me to go to work. I wished to talk about trespass—but he immediately struck me on the nose; brought blood—I then took hold of him, and he seized me, and we both fell over into the room—he then kicked me on the head, and twice on neck, and also kept striking me—he only struck me once in veranda before we fell; the most of striking was in the house, after we had fallen. Tuesday, Spencer had given me the day to mend the fence of my food. I did so, and Thursday, came to Macy, the Overseer, as the cattle had trespassed again; no one came into the room where Macy was beating me, but Kaaihue, who came and stopped him. Spencer, Bila, Hoakimoa, and Kamaka, could see into the room where we were. Hoakimoa and Kamaka were standing on the veranda when we fell.

Kamaka, sworn: I am a workman of Spencer, at Amauulu, I know Macy—saw the fight between Macy and Daniela, at the store of plantation; saw Macy strike Daniela on nose, drew blood. When Macy seized him by throat, and threw him down—kicked and struck him: I was not far off, at trash house, did not see Spencer there, nor Bila, when I first came here. Hoakimoa was there: it was in the morning. Macy struck first: do not know the cause of the fight.

Cross: I was outside of the house when I first saw the assault, in veranda of store, as I was coming from trash house; the first I saw, Macy struck Daniela on the nose—I was coming to the veranda alone—did not see Spencer, or Bila, or Kaaihue. Hoakimoa came after me, some distance off, when Macy struck Daniela—I came and stood near veranda, a little while, but took my things and went away before they were separated. Macy struck Daniela, and then seized him immediately by the neck, and threw him down into the room—Daniela fell down, Macy held him down with one hand, kicked him once and struck him repeatedly on head with fist. I then went away. Hoakimoa came as I was going away. I have not told anyone that I was paid to testify in this case. I did not see Spencer, Bila, Kaaihue, or Ahoan's wife there.

Hoakimoa, sworn: I live at Amauulu—I know Macy—I saw the affray between Macy and Daniela—I did not see the beginning. Kamaka and I had our work with Reinhardt at trash house. Kamaka was sent for tools—afterwards I was sent to the store for some things. Kamaka was coming away. I heard a noise in the house, looked in and saw Macy striking Daniela, who was on his back on the floor. Spencer was coming, also Bila, and Kaaihue came and separated them. Macy had no shirt on. Daniela said he should prosecute Macy.

Cross: It was broad daylight when this happened. I was not present when the fight began—I did not see the beginning—the first I saw, Daniela was on floor in the store, and Macy struck him once with fist, then Kaaihue separated them—Spencer, and Bila came also. Kamaka was just going away when I got to store. When I first went to work at trash house, Spencer was standing by store. Bila was not there then; afterwards Spencer went to the ditch, and came to the store again, as I was coming from the trash house for nails: Kaaihue was coming from his house, at the same time I came—he called out to Macy to stop and pulled him away.

Prosecutor rests case.

Defense:

T. Spencer, sworn: December 4th in the morning, I was in my yard—saw the scuffle between Macy and Daniela, on the veranda of the store. I saw it all—they stood on the veranda—I heard Macy tell Daniela to go to work, three or four times, but the man persisted in remaining—talking in a loud voice to Macy. Macy put both hands on Daniela's chest, trying to push him along, telling him to go to work—there was no blow struck, and no attempt to do a forcible act—it was simply an attempt by Macy to push him along, to go to work; and when Daniela had gone backwards a few steps he struck at Macy—then they clinched, and fell down—Macy had his shirt torn off, and Daniela got the worst of it: there were no other men near, within 15 or 20 feet: there were men across the yard. The first man who came was the constable, the luna of the grub house. I told him to stop—he went onto the veranda—Daniela and Macy both fell into the door of the doctor's shop. I am the owner of Amauulu plantation, and manager also; men have to come to me about any trouble. Daniela had been to me twice before this, about trespass. I had given him nails, and a day to mend his fence: this morning of the trouble, Daniela had not been to me. Kamaka was not near during any of this affair of Macy and Daniela. I was particular to look about me, to see what evidence there was in the case; did not see Reinhardt at the time. Hoakimoa came from the trash house at the close of the fight, and I stopped him—and when it was over, he went along. I think there were some women at the bridge near the boiling house, about 100 feet from the store: could see from there to the veranda of store: should not think they could see into the house: this must have been 15 or 20 minutes past six o'clock A.M.

Cross: Have had Daniela at work some time—heard Macy and Daniela talking—do not know what they said or were talking about, not knowing much native. I heard Macy tell Daniela to go to work, in English—the rest of their talk was in native. Macy pushed Daniela with both hands on his chest, not in a rough way—they were both excited and spoke loud.

Kaawaihau, w [wahine, woman] sworn: Know of this fight between Macy and Daniela. I was at the flume of the plantation—saw Macy and Daniela on veranda of store—heard Macy tell Daniela twice, to go to work, pushing him with his hands: then Daniela struck Macy—then Macy struck Daniela, and Daniela clinched Macy, and they fell, Daniela under, into the doctor's room of the store—I was only a few rods off, and could see well. Macy did not strike Daniela at first—only pushed him—Spencer, and Bila were standing outside: no one else that I saw. Did not see Kamaka there nor Hoakimoa—I could see plainly, and no one could be there without my seeing. I saw Kaaihue run there and go into the room, at the close of the fight. Daniela was the first to strike.

Cross: I saw Macy push Daniela with one hand, telling him to go to work: did not hear what Daniela said—do not know the cause of the trouble.

Bila, sworn: Know Daniela and Macy—know of their trouble. I was present and saw them fight. I stood nearby and they fought in veranda of store: it was morning, between six and seven A.M. I heard Macy tell Keola to go to work, two or three times. Keola [Daniela's Hawaiian name] did not go—talked about his food—Macy pushed Keola to go to work—did not strike: both were excited—then Daniela struck Macy in face: then Macy struck Daniela, and they went into a regular fight, falling down into the door of the doctor's room—Daniela underneath. Kaaihue came and separated them. I could not see inside of the room. I stood there near by, with Spencer, from the beginning to the end of the fight. Kaawihau w. was at the flume and Kaaihue came to separate them—did not see anyone else near—Kamaka was not in sight—he came to the house for nails, after the fight was all over—he was not there during the fight. I know Hoakimoa, a workman at Amauulu—I did not see him there: he came at the close of the fight, after Macy and Daniela had fallen into the room: I should have seen him if he had come before. The veranda of store could be seen from where Kaawihau w. was, at the flume.

Kaaihue, sworn: I live at Amauulu, as overseer of the food. I know of this case—I was in my house when this fight began—my wife called to me that Macy and a man were fighting. I looked out of the window and saw Macy and a man striking each other, in the veranda of the store. I ran to the place, and found Macy and Daniela on the floor in the doctor's room, fighting—I separated them: no one else was here in the room—Spencer was standing outside. Kaawihau, w.[wahine, woman], was at the flume—I did not see Hoakimoa there, nor Kumahoa.

Kumahoa, sworn: I live at Amauulu—I know Daniela, and Macy—I was at Amauulu Dec. 4th in the morning. I went early in the morning to Macy, and asked him about work, then went to wake up the men, and saw Daniela come from mauka [toward the mountain] and soon heard the call that Macy and Daniela were fighting. I went down to the place—the fight was done. Daniela had gone—Kamaka went too and arrived there just before me.

Defense rests case—Argued.

B. Macy found guilty—Fined $10 and costs ($7.55)

[Commentary: Note that this fight follows soon after Daniela receives a heavy sentence for Haalele Hana, which may have enraged him since, he says, he had only left work in search of food. Subsequent to this case, Daniela continued to have problems with Spencer. In August 1876 he is charged with arson on Spencer's property. A witness had earlier testified that Daniela told him that if Spencer charged Daniela again for desertion of service, he would burn his house. Spencer did bring Daniela up again on these charges, and the houses subsequently burned down. In this case, Daniela is protesting cattle on his cropland, parallel to the situation in 1848 in which Pitman's cattle crossed farmland. In this case, Daniela succeeds in prosecuting his assailant, however, even though Macy is represented by an attorney, E. G. Hitchcock. It appears from the court record that Macy is white, married to a Native Hawaiian, and Daniela is Native Hawaiian. The prosecutor, defense attorney, and judge are all white. Nevertheless, both courts find Macy guilty and give him the same fine. There are some linguistic issues in the text, since Spencer does not understand enough "native" to follow what is happening, but it seems the others do. This is a case in which a relatively subordinate person uses the courts against a superior—Macy is a luna—and wins.]

1873.4 Furnishing Liquor to Native Hawaiians

December 23, 1873

Rex vs.
Kaaukai

Furnishing intoxicating liquor to native Hawaiians at Pepekeo, Hilo, on the 21st of December. (Same being . . . [illeg] potatoe beer)
E. G. Hitchcock, atty for pltff.

Plea of not guilty

Pilipo, sworn: Knows deft. I live at Kulaineano and am a native born Hawaiian. On Sabbath last went to this prisoner's house. We ate potatoes. Drank potatoe—it was sour potatoe. It was in a bowl. I drank two bowlsful and it made me drunk. There were a great many there. Kaluai and Wahineai also were there and they drank also. It was morning. Maloko and Makaikuana were there and that was all.

Cross exam: It was just after sunrise that we went there. Kaaukai came that morning and got me to go to his house. It is a long way to my house, as far as to Kulalau. I and the other two witnesses went with Kaaukai to his house. We ate right away after getting there. Those two women were there. He gave me two bowlsful first. Then the others. It was intoxicating. All hands were drunk. I returned before noon.

Kaluai, sworn: Am a native Hawaiian and live at Onomea. Knows prisoner and was at his home on Sabbath last and drank sour potatoes there and got two bowlsful. I was drunk from drinking the potatoes. Pilipo was there and got drunk too, on this potatoe. It was Pepekeo. Kaluuhonu, Maloko, and another woman—Apaapa—Mehuiai—Pilipo—[names illegible]—Kaaukai told us to go there. We went together. I and Wahiwai and Pilipo, Kaluuhonu (we four) went together. It was about 8 o'clock when we got there. I and Pilipo went away at noon—Kaluhonu went away before—Kaaukai gave me this potatoe beer. It was in his house. He first gave the potatoe to Pilipo. It was red potatoe beer. All hands drank the beer except prisoner's wife. Kaaukai told us to go and get the beer on the Saturday before.

Wahiwai, sworn: Am a native. Knows Kaaukai. Was at his house that Sabbath. He called us that morning to go to his house to drink sour potatoe beer. I drank two bowlsful and it made me drunk. There was present Kaaukai, Pilipo, Kaluhonu, Kuapuni, Maloko—another woman—Wahiwai, and Kaluai, Apaapa. It was early morning and we stayed until noon. Kaaukai went to my house and told me to come to his house. I and Kaluai, Kaluhonu and Pilipo all went with Kaaukai to his house. Apaapa came there afterwards. It was just after sunrise that we went down to his house.

Crown rests.

Maloko (w), sworn: Lives at Kakuilauania. Knows dft. He lives some ways off. I was at his house on Saturday eve and was taken sick and stopped there till Sabbath evening. No sour potatoe was drunk there at all that day. Pilipo nor any other man was there on that Sabbath day. Kaaukai is a kahuhipi and he goes off with the hipis ["kahu" is a caretaker and "hipi" is the Hilo name for taro mounds, thus, he is a taro farmer]. His cattle are shut up over the Sabbath. This man's wife is my "aikane" [friend]. There were no bowls or drinks taken at Kaaukai's home that day at all.

Cross exam: Kaaukai was there that day all day.

Discharged.

[Commentary: The judge clearly believed the defense more than the prosecution in this case, although the reasoning is unclear. The plaintiff even had E. G. Hitchcock as an attorney. It appears that the prosecution witnesses were attempting to entrap the defendant.]

1873.5 Haalele Hana

December 11, 1873

Thomas Spencer vs.
Jokepa Kea

Haalele Hana (Desertion of Work)

E. G. Hitchcock for pltff.
D. H. Hitchcock for deft.
Deft pleads that he did not go to work, as he was ordered to by the Police Judge Sisson, a few days since; on account of sickness and being unable to work.

Evidence:

J. C. Long, sworn: That deft. has been bro't up twice for Haalele Hana—that he plead sickness, the 1st time; but was ordered back to work a day or two after, was again arrested and bro't bundled up like a sick man.

Kalaau, sworn: That he arrested deft. found him lying sick and bro't him on a horse, very slowly, as he c'd not walk—being the second arrest.
Pltf. admits that deft has been subject to venereal disease for a long time; and that had he known deft. was really sick, w'd not have had him arrested.

Defendant discharged.

F. S. Lyman Circuit judge
acting for police judge, as per Sec. 937—Civil Code
(deft. apparently works for Judge at the time)

[Commentary: This case illustrates the close interconnections between attorneys—here they are brothers—judges, and plantation owners. Nevertheless, the defendant's excuse of illness is accepted.]

1873.6 Threat of Murder

May 27, 1873

Rex vs.
Bila Kaikona
Chas. Malay
John Fifi

Charged with threatening to kill one Ano, a Chinaman.
Plea of not guilty

F. H. Harris, sworn: Yesterday morning these three men came to Kawiki [plantation] and talked with me about Ano owing them. I told them that I'd pay the amount due of Ano. Bila Kaikona turned to me and said "God Damn the Chinaman, suppose I no get the money I kill him." He repeated it twice. At 2 o'clock I got to Paukaa. I sent for these men and the Chinaman. They came. Bila was a [illeg]. He had a jack knife open and walked out to the Chinaman and said "God damn Chinaman give me my money." I stepped up to Bila and asked him for the knife. Finally he gave me the knife. The Chinaman denied owing either of them any money. Fifi said what the hell that Chinaman lie for—I pound him tonight. Charley Malay then turned to the Chinaman and said, "if you don't give us our money you no sleep to night—we go up and pound you." Bila Kaikona then went up to the Chinaman and asked him for the money and said he'd pound him if he did not. Bila said if I sent them to the magistrate he'd set fire to the house. Ling and Akono heard this and ten men.

Ling, sworn: Evidence the same as Harris.

Ordered to give bonds in the sum of $100 each for one month.

[Commentary: This is one of many cases that reveal the extent of conflict along ethnic lines among the workers on the plantations. It also makes clear that violence and the courts are alternative approaches to justice. Going to court inspires the worker Bila to threaten to burn the house. Here the court imposes an order quite different than that provided by the workers threatening violence if their debt is not paid—it punishes those who threaten rather than awarding them the money they feel is owed.]

1873.7 Failing to Work

August 27, 1873

S. L. Austin vs.
Wahalau

To recover damages for non-fulfillment of his contract in reference to working properly being lazy and not doing a fair days work. Damages placed at $2.50 for one day's work.
Deft. joins "Gen'l Issue"

Contract produced in court and admitted by deft.

E.G. Hitchcock for ptf.

J. H. Wanahi for dft.

Pinao, sworn: Lives at Onomea, Hilo, Hawai. Knows Wahalau well. Saw him on Monday last at Onomea at work with other workmen. There were 63 men at work at that place that day. They had a stint [of] work given them to hoe. They had one row given them for their day's work. They had (two men) given them together two rows and then two men only did 1 [and] 1/4 row. Others had the same stint and finished. One man is put on one side [of] the row and the other on the other side. Both are about equally strong. Perhaps Pilikia is the strongest man of the two. Yesterday he had the same work—4 men had 5 rows given them yesterday and he got through his whole stint which was more than he had he day before. He got through before 3 o'clock. Ptf. demanded of Wahalau $2.50 for damages for not working as he should work.

Cross exam: He worked till 6 o'clock. When I got there at 3 o'clock, I stopped with him till 6 o'clock and he did as much between 3 and 6 as he had done before all day. The luna told him when they got through that he should only count them 1/2 day each. There were perhaps 20 who did not finish their work that day.

Kekoi, sworn: This man did 1/4 rows in the same place and got through at 1 o'clock and 6 min. I asked the Luna who had a watch and he told me. This man worked very easily all day on Monday and not industriously as yesterday. His evidence is the same as Pinao's.

Cross exam: The Luna nui [head luna] told them that those men who had come late he would not count but half a day. Dft. was one of them that came late. First they had 3 rows given to 2 men and afterwards they had it reduced to two rows.

R. A. Lyman, sworn: If a man does not do a fair day's work he is the cause of damage to his master, between $2 and $3 is a fair estimate of damage for non-fulfillment of a day's work.

Suit withdrawn.

D. H. Hitchcock
P. J. [Police Justice]

[Commentary: This case reveals the use of the law to institute a notion of time served rather than work accomplished as the fundamental principle of the new disciplinary order of the plantation. The worker had apparently worked at various rates during the two days although he accomplished similar amounts. Lyman supports the plantation owner, Austin, for whom he works, and the judge and attorney for Austin are both Hitchcock brothers. Nevertheless, the suit is withdrawn and the defendant found not guilty.]

1873.8 Selling Opium without a License

October 28, 1873

King v. Lauiona (Pake [Chinese])

The defendant is charged with selling opium without a license at Paukaa, Hilo, Hawaii on Oct. 23, 1873.

Pleads not guilty

Maluliana, sworn: I know the prisoner and know of his selling opium on the 22nd of this month at Paukaa. I bought .50 cents worth of him. Kekino gave me the money to buy it with. Kekino went with me and when Lau Yong [Lauiona must be his Hawaiian name] was weighing it out Kahuhu came in and saw me pay for it. I have bought opium of him several times this month.

Cross exam: I am here to testify in this case. The prisoner lives at Paukaa. I bought the opium at about 5 o'clock P.M.

Kekino, sworn: I know the prisoner. I live and work at Paukaa. I went to the prisoner's house on the 22nd with Maluliana to get opium. When the prisoner was weighing out the opium Kahuhu came in and saw Mahuliana pay for it. We all then left the house. I should think it was about 5 o'clock P.M. I had got through work.

Cross exam: A policemen sent me to get the opium. It was the first time I ever bought opium of the prisoner.

Kahuhu, sworn: I live at Paukaa and know the prisoner. I went to his house while on my way to bathe and saw the prisoner Maluliana and Kekino. The prisoner was weighing out opium. I saw Mahuliana pay him .50 cents.

Crown rests.

Nu Lou [illeg.] sworn: I live with Apana at Puuepaku. I know the prisoner. I worked for Apana last week at Kaiwiki from Monday till Friday in company with the prisoner and Achong. I was at work with the prisoner last Wednesday and came back home about 5 or 5 1/2 o'clock P.M. We all went home to Apana's, did not stop any where. Lau Yong did not stop any where.

Cross-exam. On Wednesday, I was at work at Kaiwiki about 1.5 miles back of the mill.

Achong, sworn: I live with Apana at Puuepaku. I worked last Wednesday at Kaiwiki with Lau Yong and [illeg.]. We got through work about 5 o'clock. We all went home together to Apana's. We did not stop at Paukaa.

Apana, sworn: I live at Puuepaku and know the prisoner he is in my employ. He lives at my house in Puuepaku. Lau Yong, [illeg.], and Achong worked together last Wednesday on Kaiwiki. I saw Lau Yong when he got home just before dark on Wednesday evening.

Prisoner discharged.

J. P. Sisson
P. J.

[Commentary: In this case, a policeman set up a Chinese worker to be caught selling opium. The prisoner was discharged on the basis of contrary evidence from other witnesses. Practices of spying to make convictions appear throughout the period from the 1870s to the 1890s, but they are not always successful.]

1873. 9 Threatening Language

November 15, 1873

King v. Akowai (Hawaiian male)

Using threatening language to one Kahaleohu on the 5th.

Kahaleohu, sworn: Knows Akowai. He is a laborer there and I am a luna. He works in my gang and when I was at work there on the 5th I told him to do some work and he sat down and I ordered him to work and he told me "Kulikuli, you Nika" [Shut up you nigger] and he ran towards me with his hoe uplifted and said "Aole au mina mina Kouola, ina make oe iau Kiula" [I don't care about my life if you kill me] and waved his hoe on me. He did not strike me. He used other threatening language towards me at that time. He has done the same thing before. It was at Onomea in Hilo.

Mama, sworn: Evidence the same.

Sent to imprisonment at hard labor 15 days and pay costs $3.20

[Commentary: This is another example of the legal support of authorities and the way struggles over power become displaced from the violence of the field to the courtroom.]

1883 Cases

Translated by Esther Mookini

1883.1 $200 Damages for Seizure, Detaining and Restraining Illegally

June 9, 1883

King Lau (Pake [Chinese]) v. L. Severance, Kaailaau, and Joe Puni
Claim damages $200 from the three of them because of seizure, detaining, and restraining him illegally and rolling the body of the plaintiff in the road and the bag of clothes on June 3, 1883 in Hilo, Hawaii.

Plea: Denies the accuracy of this entanglement

W. C. Jones, Ed Kekoa, and D. B. Wahine, lawyers for the plaintiff.
Joseph Nawahi, lawyer for the defendants.

W. C. Jones requested that the suit be corrected at a place that states June 3 when this wrongdoing was done. The correct date is June 5, 1883 after the arguments on both sides.
The court agreed to change the date from 3 to 5 and the entanglement to proceed.

Witnesses:

King Lau (Pake) sworn: I saw Joe Puni, Kaailaau, and L. Severance one day just passed. I met with Joe Puni and Kaailaau on the road. I was on the road gong to Puueo, returning from Kahalau. Kaailaau took my bag. Joe Puni grabbed me and turned my body around. This man hauled me and I was carried to the coffee house where I met L. Severance. [I was taken] mountainward, they opened my bag, turned it [inside out], didn't find opium inside, told me to go. This was on Tuesday 5 June 1883. At the time my bag was opened it was then that L. Severance opened and turned out the things that were inside. I was afraid then that I would lose $600. They had no warrant to seize me, etc.

Cross-examine: I did not want to claim damages in dollars. I want to stop those police. I want $200 damages from L. Severance, $200 from Kaailaau, $200 from Joe Puni, total $600.

H. Akana, sworn: The bag was opened and what was inside was turned out. I was there at that time. There was no opium found inside [the bag]. It was Severance who said to open the bag.
Plaintiff's side rests.

Motion by the defense: Terminate this entanglement. Reasons: because of the testimony of witnesses of the plaintiff that $600 was the amount he claimed that this act done to him amounted to but this court has no power to judge claims for damages more than $200.

The motion was agreed upon.
The plaintiff dropped [the case]. The side that dropped must pay costs of the court as follows:

Warrant of arrest	1.00
Execution	1.00
Court postponement	0.25
Two sworn witnesses	0.20
One pay to witness	0.25
Decision	1.00
	3.70
Less paid to one witness	0.25
	3.45

King Lau appealed to Hon. F.S. Lyman court, June 19, 1883. The plaintiff dropped the case—did not pay costs in 10 days.

G. W. A. Hapai

P. J. Hilo

[Commentary: In this case, the plaintiff lost on what seems to be a technicality, since his original claim was for $200 and he said he was not inter-
ested in the money but in stopping the police. Other cases from 1883 and
1893 indicate that the police were engaged in spying to detect opium and
liquor selling violations, as they had earlier engaged in spying to detect
adultery and fornication. Yet this case also indicates that a Chinese resident,
probably a long-term resident based on his name, did use the court to assert
his sense of his rights not to be stopped and searched by the police. The case
indicates, however, that in this context the plaintiff had not fully mastered
the discourses and practices of the court and was therefore unable to use it to
resist police surveillance.]

1883.2 Deserting Husband

June 5, 1883

King v. Manoa (female)
Deserting her husband Hukiki without cause. She refused to return and live
with him for three weeks just passed, until June 4, 1883.
Plea: Not guilty.

Reasons:

   1. She was not provided with food and clothing.
   2. He entertained men in the house and drank awa [Hawaiian intoxicating
beverage]
   3. One man stayed in their house and she was afraid and was defiled, etc., etc.

The wife agreed to return to live with her husband. The court instructed and
ordered them to return and live together and pay costs of court.

[Commentary: Like almost all desertion cases, the woman is required to
return to her husband regardless of the provocation that drove her away.
Here her fear of sexual violation is discussed in rather oblique ways.]

1883.3 For Bad Things

September 12, 1883

King v. Ah Sew
For bad things

Sheriff L. Severance made the charge. Later Rev. A. O.Forbes explained the nature of the things done by the defendant to the young girl. The court then instructed the accused not to do that again and pointed to the law regarding this wrongdoing and dismissed him for the time under the knowledge that if he should do it again then the law would be carried out against him.

Plea: Not guilty.
Decision: The court instructed [the accused] and terminated this entanglement.

[Commentary: This case obscures the nature of the offense, which is presumably some sexual violation of the young girl, not only concealed in obscure language but also not sufficiently serious to warrant a conviction for the first offense. The language is quite different from that of the Hawaiian woman in 1893, Case 1893.3, which describes the sexual behavior far more directly. These differences reveal also the shifting discourses about sexuality between haole and Hawaiian society in the late nineteenth century.]

1883.4 Fighting and Causing Injury

September 7, 1883

King v. Kamahikiea
Fighting and Causing Injury to Kaipoula (f.) his wife.

Severance, Sheriff, requests this entanglement be terminated. He said that in his interrogation of the witnesses this argument between the husband and wife was over the money from the sale of their land. The woman has the money according to the husband. The wife tried to strangle her husband, the husband tore the wife's dress. That is all.

Decision: The entanglement is terminated with the instruction of the court to both parties to live in peace with each other and stop being against each other.

1883.5 Refuse to Work

May 22, 1883

J. Austin and Co. assigns of Board of Immigration v. Bento [not identified by ethnicity]

Refuse to work

Plea: Not guilty

J. Austin for plaintiff.
Ed Kekoa and D. B. Wahine, lawyers for the defense.

[Trial is not translated.]
Decision: Defendant is right and the plaintiff dropped and will pay costs of court.

[Commentary: Although I do not have the text of the trial, this decision indicates that sometimes workers who refused to work, particularly if they were represented by lawyers, were not convicted.]

1883. 6 Desertion of Husband

June 25, 1883

King v. Kekuko (f)

Deserted, without cause, Joe Flores, her husband to whom she was married and their place to sleep, etc, etc., etc. and being stubborn by not staying with him on 24 and 25 of June 1883 in Hilo. Plea: not guilty

Joe Flores, sworn: Kekuko, the defendant is my wife. Yesterday morning I alone went down to Waiakea. I found her in Kalepolepo. Kalopi gave me the key to the house. I returned to the house. The children came home and I fed them all. I waited until 7 P.M., went to search for her in Kalepolepo, was told she returned. I went back, she was not at our house. She did not return until dawn.
This morning Poohina told me Kekuko was at their house. I went there and urged her to return to our house. She did not.

Cross examine: When I went down to Waiakea I left her staying in the house. I said to her she was a lazy wife who didn't wash or iron my clothes and the children's clothes, who didn't sew or keep the house in order. She just went about doing whatever she wanted to do. I said to her she was a messy woman.
Poohina (f), sworn. Last night at 7 P.M. Kekuko came to our house. I asked what is it? Kekuko answered, a man of Waiakea told her that Keo Pukiki [Hawaiian for Joe Flores, who was Portuguese] was going to break her neck

and step on her back and so ran to us because she was afraid of Keo Pukiki, that is what she said. She stayed at our house and slept the night. I pointed out Keo Pukiki and Kekuko.

Mamakauu, sworn. When I met them all I returned to my house my wife told me that Kekuko was at our cook house, asked what were we to do, my wife said that she was scared because of what Keo Pukiki said, that he would break her neck. I told my wife to go and tell Kekuko that she return to their house, to her husband. After that I went to the cook house, then returned, then at dawn I went to work.

Haolenamuole, sworn. I know Keo Pukiki and Kekuko. I don't know anything regarding this entanglement but the times before, they were always fighting. My house is close to their house. Keo Pukiki came to my house to ask for Kekuko. I said that I didn't see her and she wasn't at my house. I saw Keo Pukiki washing clothes one time and they were fighting. Keo showed me the dirty clothes. I did not hear them shouting in their house yesterday morning.

J. H. Nihoa, sworn. Keo Pukiki came to our house last night in Kalepolepo. He asked about Kekuko. I said that she returned and that was the end and Keo Pukiki went.

Joe Liilii, sworn. I was upland and when I returned my parents were not at home. I waited until Keo Pukiki returned. He asked me "didn't Mama return?" I said no, Mama did not return at all to our house until dawn. Papa fed me.

Cross examine: Mama went to milk cows yesterday morning.

The plaintiff side rests.

Defense witnesses:

Kekuko (f) sworn: At 6 A.M. yesterday I went up to milk cows. When I was done I took the milk and went home. When I got to the house Keo was angry at me. He threw all the clothes out of the dresser and scolded me as a lazy wife, dirty woman, who doesn't wash, iron or sew clothes. He said to me if yesterday was a day free of kapu [any day but Sunday] he would have broken my neck and let my blood flow. I didn't answer. At 10 A.M. he went down seaward to Waiakea. At 11 A.M. I went down with Kalopi to Waiakea to meet Keo at Kalepolepo. He came back and we, Kalopi and I, went to their house in Waiakea. Some women visitors who were staying with Kalopi's mother told me that Keo told them he would break my neck. When I heard what Keo was going to do to me in the upland [home] that he would break my neck I was scared that he would do something bad to me. At 5:30 P.M. I went back to our house. I saw Kaoihana; the policeman, and told him to stay there and that I was going inside the house and if Keo treats me badly then I would call him to save me. Kaoihana said to me that it would be best for me to go somewhere else, that night. Therefore I went to Mamakauu's place to stay the night because I was afraid of what Keo said, what

Keo said earlier, that I was lazy, didn't wash, iron or sew his and the children's clothes. This is a lie. The truth is I wash, iron and sew his clothes as well as for the children whenever I find the time since Keo gives me much work to do. He sends me to do work not fit for women to do, that is, to milk cows, go up for taro, cook and put them in a bowl. That is what Keo demands of me while he went down to Waiakea. And so I did not clean the house because I had to do all those other things Keo sent me out to do. Cross examine: I left Keo earlier because of the work Keo gave me just as I have said while Keo went out and had sexual affairs with an adulterous woman seaward of Waiakea. He always went to Waiakea every day. That is the reason for his bad behavior toward me.

Kalopi, sworn. I was at Keo's and Kekuko's house yesterday morning. I saw Keo remove the dirty clothes and I saw his anger toward Kekuko [calling her] a lazy, messy wife who did not wash, iron or sew clothes for Keo or the children. I know what Keo said to Kekuko, that he would break Kekuko's neck but I did not hear Keo say he was going to beat her up. Later Keo went seaward of Waiakea then later Kekuko and I went down [to Waiakea] and we found Keo in Kalepolepo, he was coming up so I gave him the key to the house. He went back and we, Kekuko and I, went down [to Waiakea]. I slept [at a place] seaward, did not return upland. The defense side rests.

By the court

I questioned Kekuko (f) if she would please stop their life of opposing each other and return to live in contentment and to look after the children, etc., etc. and Kekuko to stop being stubborn and to live together with Joe Flores. Decision: Kekuko (f) will be sent to prison at hard labor for 2 weeks and must pay costs of the court, $3.80

G. W. A. Hapai, P.I. Hilo

1893 CASES

1893.1 Assault and Battery

June 19, 1893

Provisional Government of Hawaiian Islands v. Nishida Aisuke Jap[anese] Assault and battery to the body of Geo. Chalmers in Wainaku, Hilo, Hawaii, June 16, 1893
G. W. Le Roy, sworn, interpreter in Japanese

The defendant pleaded not guilty.

Witnesses:

Geo. Chalmers, sworn. I am the deputy supervisor of Wainaku Plantation. The defendant is a Japanese male there. Last Friday June 16 I got into trouble with the defendant. He injured me with the handle of his hoe. The reason for this was that at 9 A.M. that morning the Japanese were working at a place under their boss R. Richardson. When I arrived there I knew he told this Japanese "work, don't just stand around and talk." This Japanese answered "I don't know why you're saying this to me." Later, this Japanese came to where I was standing, he was holding his hoe and told me "why did the boss say that to me?" I said "you know! Go and do your work. If you don't go to work I'll take you to Hilo. You pay $5.00." Then he said in a loud voice, "Hilo, Hilo, $5.00, $5.00." While he was backing up he fell down, got up and said again to me, "$5.00, $5.00." I told him again "if you don't go to work I'll take you to Hilo and you pay $5.00." Then he pushed me with the handle of his hoe which he was holding. I was standing in this place and he jabbed my chest. This is the injury and it is black and blue. He chased me with the handle of his hoe and hit my shoulders. He again pushed me with the handle of hoe and jabbed my thighs. Here is this injury. I did not punch him. I did not grab him.

R. R. Richardson, sworn. I am a work boss for the Japanese at Wainaku Plantation. Geo. Chalmers is the overseer. This Japanese, being accused, is on my work gang. On June 16, G. Chalmers got trouble from this Japanese. The following is what happened. I saw that this Japanese was just standing and talking and not working. When G. Chalmers arrived there at 9 A.M. I urged this Japanese saying, "if you work you go way ahead." He gave me a rude answer saying "why did you say that?" Then he left his work place and went with his hoe in his hand to where G. Chalmers was standing. He asked G. Chalmers why I had said that to him. Mr. G. Chalmers said to him "you know! Go back and do your work." This Japanese continued to talk to Mr. Chalmers. Mr. Chalmers said "if you don't go to work I'll take you to Hilo." Then this Japanese said "Hilo, Hilo." Then he backed away and slipped into the ditch and fell down. When he stood up he spoke again to G. Chalmers "take me to Hilo." Chalmers agreed to do so saying "you pay $5.00." Then the Japanese said "$5.00, $5.00." Then he pushed that handle of his hoe, jabbing the chest of G. Chalmers, then he chased him with the handle of his hoe, hitting the shoulders of Chalmers, then shoved the handle of the hoe again striking the thighs of Chalmers. Chalmers did not place his hand on this Japanese. Mr. Chalmers only said to this Japanese "I am going down to bring charges against you" and Chalmers came down [to Hilo].

Prosecution Rest

Defense witnesses: Gensanaka, Jap[anese], sworn. On June 16 at work, Chalmers came on horseback. He jumped down and said to this Japanese (Nishida), "$5.00." He kicked Nishida 4 or 5 times. Nishida fell down, holding on to his hoe.

Cross examine: the kicking was to Nishida's stomach and legs. I saw him kick many times.

Yokoyama Jap[anese], sworn. I was at work on June 16. I saw Chalmers come on horseback and talk to Nishida. He jumped down and kicked Nishida one time. I did not see which of his feet he used to kick but Nishida fell down when he was kicked. Chalmers held Nishida by the shoulders and kicked.

Meze, Jap[anese], sworn. On June 16 I heard Nishida and Chalmers say "$5.00." Afterwards Chalmers kicked Nishida and he fell down. I do not know how many times he kicked. I believe he kicked him once. Nishida did not injure Chalmers.

Yamato, Jap[anese], sworn. On June 16 I saw the things done by Chalmers and Nishida. They said "$5.00, $5.00." Later Chalmers jumped down from his horse and I saw him kick Nishida 2 or 3 times. Nishida fell down and Chalmers kicked him with his shoes.

Case rest

By the court: As I observed the witnesses on both sides regarding this entanglement I believe that the witnesses on the side of the defendant are not truthful. Therefore I have decided that the defendant is wrong.

Nishida Aisuke is fined $9.00 and costs of the court $4.90

G. W. A. Hapai

District Judge

So. Hilo

1893.2 Assault and Battery with a Deadly Weapon

June 28, 1893

Provisional Government of Hawaiian islands v. Jose de Reiso
P[Portuguese]
Assault and battery with a deadly weapon, a cane knife, on the body of Tanaka Ishida, Jap[anese] in Amauulu, Hilo, Hawaii on June 23, 1893. Case was deferred until today. The defendant pleaded not guilty.

Geo. H. Williams, Sheriff of Hawaii for prosecution
D. H. Hitchcock, Esqr., attorney for defendant
Joe Vierra, Esqr., sworn, Portuguese interpreter
G. W. Le Roy, Esqr., sworn, Japanese interpreter
Witnesses
Tanaka Ishida, Jap[anese] sworn. I live in Amauulu, Hilo. I work for Hilo Sugar Co. under a labor contract. I know the defendant. He is our boss. On June 23 he was our boss. Our work for that day was to cut cane. While I was sharpening my cane knife with a file, the boss was angry and called me. I

went close to him. He asked me for my cane knife which I was holding. I gave it to him. He took the cane knife, he snatched it, and swung it directly over my head as if to cut my head. I then placed my hand like this, on my head. This is the cut on my hand from the knife.

Cross examine:

When the boss called me to come I went to him. He said to me "very lazy." I said to him "what I do is more than what the Portuguese do." Then he grabbed my cane knife that I was holding, snatched it, took it away. He hit me directly on my head with the knife. I put my hand on my head and he cut my hand with this knife. The boss said to me, before he hit me with the knife: "you go away." He did not say that I gave the knife to him. I went to pile up sugar cane on the sled. The boss said to me to go and cut the cane and put them on the sled. Because my hand was cut by the knife I told the boss "my hand was cut by the knife." The boss did not have angry words at that time. My witnesses were standing nearby at this place piling up the sugar cane on to the sled. Yamane and that Portuguese were there too, looking after the sled.

Nakada Jap[anese], sworn. I am a contract laborer for Hilo Sugar Co. I know the defendant, he is our boss. I know Tanaka Ishida, we are on the same work gang. On June 23 I saw what went on between the Portuguese boss and Tanaka Ishida. Our work that day was to cut cane and pile them up on the sled. I was the first one to have known that the boss called out to T. Ishida to go to him. When T. Ishida went, the boss was very angry and called out in a loud voice. He grabbed T. Ishida's cane knife which he was holding on to. He snatched it and took it away. He raised this knife as if to bring it down to cut T. Ishida's head. T. Ishida protected [his head] with his hand and when the knife came straight down it cut his hand.

Cross examine:

I was a distance from the 2 of them at that time, [the distance] being like that of a large room. I was cutting cane on the sled at the time I heard the boss' loud voice. I stood up and looked. The first words of the boss to T. Ishida were "God damn son of a bitch." I heard the boss call T. Ishida 2 or 3 times to go to him. When T. Ishida went that was when the boss said: "god damn son of a bitch" in a loud voice. The words were angry. I did not hear what T. Ishida said to the boss. I heard T. Ishida say to the boss "all right." T. Ishida was holding the cane knife. The boss asked to give the knife to him. Here is how T. Ishida gave his knife to the boss. T. Ishida was holding the middle [part] of the knife and the base of the knife was to the boss. Then the boss grabbed the base of the knife and pulled on it and then he had the knife. He then raised the knife and brought it down as if to hit T. Ishida's head. It was then that T. Ishida protected his head with his hand and the knife came straight down and cut his hand. The boss then said "god damn, you go to the sled."

Dr. R. B. Williams M.D., sworn. I am a doctor. I no longer have a practice. My place of residence is in Hilo. Several days ago that Japanese (T. Ishida) came to me because of an injury he got, a cut on his hand. I looked at this cut. It was on top of the hand. It was 2/4 inches deep into the flesh. He got the cut from a sharp object, perhaps a knife. The cut looked like this. —< He did not get it from a direct cut since the cut has 3 corners. If the cut was a straight line then the sharp object that cut him would have struck him on a straight line. If he was struck in a lashing manner then he would have gotten a cut like this cut.

Cross examine:

If this was like a straight cut then he would have had gotten cut like this, the same way. If this was a slash from a knife then he would have gotten a cut like this. If one was holding the middle of the sharp knife and this knife was pulled by the handle by another then the one holding the knife would have gotten cut on the hand like this.

Shigeoka (Jap[anese]), sworn. I am a contract laborer at Hilo Sugar Co. I know Tanaka Ishida. Our work is like his. I know this Portuguese, he is our work boss. On June 23, we worked together with T. Ishida and this Portuguese was our boss. I know there was something between the Portuguese boss and T. Ishida that day. T. Ishida and I worked together at the same place. I heard the Portuguese boss call T. Ishida to go to him. When T. Ishida got there, in front of the boss, the boss grabbed the cane knife that T. Ishida was holding in his hand. He snatched it and took it away. The boss raised the knife and struck down, right on T. Ishida's head. T. Ishida shielded [his head] with his hand in front of his face. The knife came straight down and cut T. Ishida's hand. The boss said some words before he cut T. Ishida with the knife.

Cross examine: The boss first said to T. Ishida "god damn, lazy, you go [to the] sled." That's all the boss said and he cut T. Ishida with the knife, did not cut to the side, did not cut at any angle with the knife.

Prosecution Rest.

Defense Witnesses:

Joakim Rocha, P[ortuguese], sworn. On June 23 I was at the place spoken of here. The wrongful assault was done with a knife by Jose de Reiso, boss of that Japanese. My work was to take care of the sled. I was standing at the side of the sled and Jose de Reiso, the boss, was standing nearby at the side of the sled, watching the work of the men gathering the sugar cane and putting them on the sled. Then the boss said to the water carrying boy: "go and tell that Japanese (T. Ishida) to come here to load up the sugar cane and pile them on the sled." The water carrying boy went and spoke to that Japanese, T. Ishida. That Japanese came with his cane knife and stood in front of the boss. The boss asked him to give his cane knife to him. This Japanese gave the knife. This is how he gave it—this Japanese held that knife right in the middle, between the sharp tip of the knife and the base of the knife. Then he tossed it to the boss. The boss reached out for the base of the knife and got it. The boss showed that the knife was secure in his hand. He told this Japanese (T.I.) "go and pile up the sugar cane and load them up on the sled." Then this Japanese said "I can't, my hand was cut by the knife." He showed me and I saw his hand was really cut. The boss was not angry, the boss did not call him to come. The water carrying boy went and spoke to this Japanese because the boss ordered him to do so. The boss did not raise the knife to bring it down on the head of this Japanese. This Japanese did not raise his hand to protect [himself] from the knife coming down on his head. The boss said to this Japanese "you go to work on the sled."

Cross examine:

I was very near to the place at the time, as I was taking care of the sled. I heard distinctly the boss telling the water carrying boy to go and tell that Japanese to come. The boss called this Japanese to come to him. When this Japanese came in front of the boss and gave the knife to the boss, the boss took the knife from him. The boss gestured with the knife saying to that Japanese "go and pile the sugar cane and put them on the sled."

Case rest.

Based on my careful observation of the testimony on both sides regarding this entanglement and the testimony of Dr. R. B. Williams, M.D., the doctor, regarding the nature of the cut on Tanaka Ishida's hand, I have reliable cause to doubt the truth of this entanglement. Therefore I give the right of this doubt to the defendant. Jose de Reiso is dismissed, not guilty.

After making very clear to Tanaka Ishida, Nakada and Shigeoka about the law regarding giving false testimony they all were repentant before me. They said they told a lie. They told the truth that the boss did not raise the knife and tried to bring it down to cut T. Ishida's head when his hand was cut. Tanaka Ishida said his hand was cut by the knife the time when the boss pulled the knife away from his hand while he held on to the knife.

This court excuses them, will not arrest [them] for lying and instructed them not to do that.

G. W. A. Hapai
District Judge
So. Hilo

[Commentary: This case shows the careful attention to evidence as well as the tension and violence in the cane fields.]

1893.3 *Issuing Threats*

December 28, 1893

Provisional Government of Hawaiian Islands v. Kalupu (m).

Issuing threats against Kaluaikoko (f) his wife and being the source for her (Kaluaikoko) to be terrified and afraid that her physical body and life were in trouble, on the night of the 26th and dawn of the 27th of December 1893 in Alenoho, Hilo, Hawaii. This goes against Chapter XLVII, paragraphs 1, 2, 3 of the criminal code.

The defendant pleaded not guilty.

Geo. H. Williams, Sheriff of Hawaii prosecution
Kalapu, defended himself

Witnesses:
Kaluaikoko (f), sworn. Kalapu is my husband. Our place of residence is Alenoho. I swore out the warrant to the judge because I was afraid that Kalapu would cause trouble to my body and life since on the night of the 26th and dawn of the 27th of December he was very angry at me. The reason is as follows: while we were going to bed Kalapu ordered me to sleep with him. I agreed to what he wanted. There was sexual intercourse but he could not do his part (very soft) then he got angry and said that I was the one who weakened his genitals. I said I offered myself for you to make love and you did it and so it's your responsibility for being soft and incapable. Then Kalapu threatened me as follows:
I. Look out or I'll beat you up from now on. I'm not afraid of going to jail, I'm not afraid of murder.
II. I go to work, make money to buy liquor and get drunk. You think you're the only one for me.
Because of these words of Kalapu I became very frightened. I am in fear of him even now.
Cross examine: Between 9 and 10 P.M. he became angry at me and scolded me until 12 that night. After that Kalapu beat me up. Even before that I was injured. I sued and he was fined and went to work in jail. He was released from jail and returned to stay with me. A few days later this crime occurred again. The people in our house are myself, Kalapu and my small grandchildren, in our room. Umiloi and Kailianu were in their room near our room.
Umiloi, male, sworn. My wife, Kailianu, and I live in Kaluaikoko's house. It was there that we slept the night of the 26th until the dawn of the 27th of December. That night between 9 and 10 P.M. my wife and I were in our room. I heard Kalapu's loud voice in their room. He was angry and he said the following things to Kaluaikoko that I heard: "Take care or I'll beat you up from now on. I'm not afraid to be put in jail, I'm not afraid of murder. I go to work, make money, buy liquor, drink until drunk. You think to yourself

that I'm only one [man]." He said much more but these are the words I remember clearly.

Cross examine: our room is near Kaluaikoko's room. When you open one door it touches the other door. From 10 P.M. on they argued for a long time. If I was called to go and help I would have helped.

Kailianu (female), sworn. On the night of December 26th until dawn of the 27th I was in our room with my husband Umiloi. I heard Kalapu's loud voice coming from this room. Kalapu threatened Kaluaikoko as follows. Kaluaikoko, take care or I will beat you up from now on. I'm not afraid of being put in jail, I'm not afraid of murder. I go to work, make money, buy liquor, drink until drunk. You think to yourself that I'm only a single man.

Cross examine: I don't know why Kalapu was angry and said those words.

Prosecution Rest.

The defendant did not bring any witnesses.

Decision:

Kalapu (m) is held on $50.00 bond. He is confined for 6 months and pays costs of this court.

G. W. A. Hapai

District Judge

So. Hilo, Hawaii

1893.4 Selling Liquor without a License

Provisional Government of Hawaiian Islands v. Mrs. Mau Chong alias Ah Sam (Ch[inese])

Selling liquor without a license on 20 July 1893 in the town of Hilo, Hawaii.

The defendant pleaded not guilty.

Geo. H. Williams, Esqr. Sheriff of Hawaii for prosecution.

D. H. Hitchcock, Esqr. Attorney for defendant.

Ah Cho, sworn, to translate the Chinese language.

Witnesses:

Wong Gau (Ch[inese]), sworn. Yesterday morning between 8 and 10 A.M. I was in Waiolama in Mau Chong's house Wong Ling, Mrs. Mau Chong and another Chinese were there at the time. That house has 3 rooms—Wong Ling was in Mrs. Mau Chong's room. Benj. Brown was inside my room of that house at that time. I told Mrs. Mau Chong that I wanted to buy 6 bottles of wine. She said yes. I did not give her money at that time. I got the money later from Tin Pai. I got 2 half-dollars. I gave Mrs. Mau Chong the money and I got 2 bottles of wine. I returned 4 bottles of wine to Mrs. Mau Chong. I do not know where she got these bottles of wine. This wine was intoxicating. When I got these 2 bottles of wine I gave [them] to Benj. Brown. The door to the room that Benj. Brown was in was not shut.

Cross examine. I bought those bottles of wine from this woman. It was before Mau Chong was arrested. I brought suit against Mau Chong for selling 2 bottles of wine and the arrest and search warrants were issued for her. I said to the sheriff that Mau Chong sold me the wine, that Tin Pai gave $1.00 in 2 half-dollars, at 8 A.M. I did not see if these half-dollars were marked or not. I got those 2 half-dollars from Tin Pai. [Those were the half-dollars] I gave the woman (Mrs. Mau Chong) for the 2 bottles of wine. Those 2 bottles of wine that I bought are the things that I am bringing suit against Mau Chong. I first said to this woman (Mrs. Mau Chong) that I wanted to buy 6 bottles of wine. She said yes. She brought the 6 bottles of wine from my room and set them up on my table. At that time Benj. Brown was sitting on my bed inside the [mosquito] net. I told the woman to take back 4 of the 6 bottles of wine that she brought. I gave her these 4 bottles and I told this woman that later I would buy these 4 bottles of wine. I paid cash for 2 bottles of wine that [I] took. This was Wednesday night, July 19. I did not bring those 6 bottles of wine to this house. While Benj. Brown and I stayed inside this room the police arrived. He was sent to get Mau Chong. When Mau Chong came to the house the police arrived. He was sent to get Mau Chong. When Mau Chong came to the house the police arrested her. Then he searched her body for the 2 half-dollars that I paid her with for the 2 bottles of wine she sold me. Yesterday at 9 A.M. Benj. Brown left my room and came back here. I argued with Mr. and Mrs. Mau Chong earlier. Mau Chong said to me that if I did not want to stay in this house that I go somewhere else. I know Wong Ling. He was staying in our house. At the time I was buying those 2 bottles of wine from this woman, Wong Ling was eating rice in another room. I was sued earlier for the crime of stealing. I was dismissed, not guilty. I stayed in Mau Chong's house from April until now. I bought liquor earlier from Mau Chong in July, I forgot the day.

Benj. Brown, sworn. I am a policeman here in Hilo. Yesterday, July 20 between the hours of 7 and 9 A.M. I was at Mau Chong's house in Wong Gau's room. I was sitting on Wong Gau's bed, inside the mosquito net. Wong Gau brought food for me into the room. While I was sitting inside the mosquito net I could see the men pass by outside. I saw Wong Gau speak Chinese to this woman. Later I saw this woman go outside the house and come back with 3 bottles. She blew the dirt [off the bottles] then put these bottles down, went out again and returned with 3 new bottles and put those down. Wong Gau and this woman talked a short while and when they were done this woman returned. The door to the room I was in was shut. Later the door to this room was opened and when Wong Gau was standing at the door to the room this woman (Mrs. Mau Chong) came and stood outside the door. The space between the 2 of them and where I was sitting inside the mosquito net on the bed was from here to there—15 or 16 feet. I saw Wong Gau give this woman 2 half-dollars. This woman looked at these half-dollars and took [them] and Wong Gau returned 4 bottles to the woman. Only 2 bottles were left for him, Wong Gau.

Cross examine. After [the room was] searched, the door to the room I was in was shut. When the door was opened I saw Le Roy and others standing inside. When Wong Gau gave the 2 half-dollars to this woman, Wong Gau, was standing outside the door of this room. From the time Wong Gau gave those 2 half-dollars to this woman until the house was searched, perhaps 5 minutes had passed. The body of this woman was searched. I did not see the warrant for the search for liquor of Mau Chong. I have a search warrant to hold Mau Chong for something. Here are the 2 bottles of wine which were left for Wong Gau after he returned the 4 bottles of wine to this woman. This is intoxicating liquor. Here are the 2 bottles of wine which Wong Gau bought from this woman. Wong Gau gave [them] to me and I brought those here, upland, to [the sheriff's] office.

Prosecution Rest.

Defense witnesses:

Wong Ling (Ch[inese]), sworn. I live in Mau Chong's house seaward of Waiolama. I was there yesterday morning. Wong Gau and Mrs. Mau Chong were there also. Wednesday evening I saw Wong Gau when I returned to our house. He was holding a bag and there were some things inside this bag. Wong Gau put this bag down, opened the bag and brought out 6 bottles and set them up on the table and went inside the house. Wong Gau said "these are bottles of wine." Mau Ching and Mrs. Mau Chong, Wong Gau and I were there. It was dark at the time. Wong Gau said "there was liquor for dinner for them at another time." Wong Gau spoke again to Mrs. Mau Chong saying: "take the 6 bottles of wine back and look after them."

Mrs. Mau Chong refused, she did not want to look after them. Then Mau Chong told his wife (Mrs. Mau Chong) to take those 6 bottles of wine and put them in the kitchen. Mrs. Mau Chong agreed to do so. She took back those 6 bottles of wine and left them in the kitchen. Yesterday morning Wong Gau again spoke to Mrs. Mau Chong to go and get those 6 bottles of wine of hers and to bring them back to him. Mrs. Mau Chong went and got the 6 bottles of wine, brought them in and gave them to Wong Gau. Wong Gau said to Mrs. Mau Chong to bring his 2 bottles of wine. So then Mrs. Mau Chong brought [the 2 bottles] and 4 bottles of wine that she had looked after. After that Wong Gau gave Mrs. Mau Chong $1.00, payment for her looking after these bottles of wine. Mrs. Mau Chong refused, she did not take the dollar. After she refused Wong Gau, she did not take the money, the police came and searched the house. I did not witness Mrs. Mau Chong's body being searched since I went down to the house, below. One or more months passed while I stayed in Mau Chong's house. I did not see Mr. and Mrs. Mau Chong look after and sell wine or other kinds of liquor to anybody. I had seen Wong Gau frequently coming back with liquor bottles. I knew Wong Gau and Mr. and Mrs. Mau Chong had always argued before. Wong Gau was angry at the cries and shouting of the children. Mau Chong said "if the noise of my children deafens you, you can go and look for another place to stay." When Wong Gau gave the money to Mrs. Mau Chong she refused it, didn't take the money. When Wong Gau went and returned to the house, that was when the police searched the house. The police found 4 bottles of wine inside the kitchen. There was no other wine found in the search.

Cross examine: I frequently saw Wong Gau bring liquor to our house and leave it in his room where he would drink. He brought one bottle of liquor at a time and would do the same at another time. Wednesday evening was the first time I saw him bringing 6 bottles of liquor to our house. Whenever Wong Gau went out he would lock the door to his room and would take the key. Between 8 and 9 P.M. this past Wednesday night Wong Gau brought 6 bottles of wine in a bag into our house. It was not Mr. or Mrs. Mau Chong, it was not anyone else. The reason for my believing in this way is that Wong Gau spoke to Mrs. Mau Chong to return and look after the bottles of wine.

Mau Chong, Ch[inese], sworn. This past Wednesday I was with my wife and Wong Ling in our house between 8 and 9 P.M. That night Wong Gau came. He had a bag and some things in that bag. I asked: "what's in your bag?" Wong Gau said: "wine." He opened the bag and set up 6 bottles of wine on the table. I told him: "how is that you brought so many bottles of wine?" He said "tomorrow, Thursday, we cooks will have a party." He (Wong Gau) spoke to my wife, to take these bottles of wine and look after them. My wife refused. I said to my wife that she take them and leave them in the cook house. Those bottles of wine were taken and left in the cook house. On Thursday I went to work. Yesterday I went to work and a person came to get me to go back to the house. When I returned and arrived at my house I was arrested by the police for selling liquor. I was taken upland here. I have not looked after liquor in my house the past one or 2 months except during Chinese New Year. I often saw Wong Gau serve liquor in our house from one bottle. When he left it in his room he would drink there. One time he called me to come into his room to drink with him. I refused.

Cross examine:

If Wong Gau would go out he would lock his door with a key and would take the key.

G. W. Le Roy, sworn. I swore out Mau Chong's search warrant and affidavit for selling liquor. I searched but didn't find the "mark coin."

Defense Rest.

Rebuttal Evd.

Mr. Hardy, sworn. I am the Deputy Sheriff of Hawaii. On Wednesday evening, July 19th, I was here in the Sheriff's office with Mr. Williams, Le Roy, Tin Pai and Wong Gau. Between 7 and 8 P.M. Wong Gau was at the door, Tin Pai was behind him and Tin Pai entered. He was at the door and was in front as they entered. The 2 of them sat down until past 9 P.M. and then they left.

Cross examine:

I made out this search warrant and gave it to Tin Pai and he gave it to Le Roy. Wong Gau left at 9 P.M. that night.

Geo. W. Williams, sworn: This past Wednesday I sent for Wong Gau to come to my house, after 7 P.M. that night. He came. I left my house and went down to the Sheriff's office here. Wong Gau arrived at the sheriff's office. He stayed here until 9 P.M. then left. I returned and got to my house at 9:30 P.M.

Cross examine:

I believe the time was 9 P.M.

Case Rest

By the court: It is clear to me from the people who testified on both sides, that the statements of the defendant's witnesses are not true. Therefore I have decided the defendant is wrong.

Mrs. Mau Chong alias Ah Sam is fined $100.00 and

costs of court $3.70

For the appeal 1.10

Total $4.80

Notice of appeal for a new trial as the document is written:

Provisional Government v. Mrs. Mau Chong

Selling liquor without a license

Notice appeal

And now comes the defendant in the above-named case by her attorney D. H. Hitchcock, gives notice of appeal from the judgment of the District Court aforesaid in the above case to the January term of the Circuit Court, 4th Judicial Circuit, on the grounds that the judgment is against the law and evidence.

D. H. Hitchcock, attorney for defense

Hilo, July 21, 1893

1893.5 Selling Liquor without a License

Provisional Government of Hawaiian Islands v. Abay [Abe] Jap[anese]

Selling liquor without a license in Papaikou, Hilo, Hawaii in the month of March 1893, close to the 25th or 26th of that month, which goes against paragraph 23, chapter 44 of the Laws of 1882 which paragraph was amended to Chapter 3 of the Session Laws 1886.

G. W. Le Roy, sworn, interpreter, Japanese language

Defendant pleads not guilty.

Geo. H. Williams, Sheriff of Hawaii for prosecution

D. H. Hitchcock, attorney for defendant

Witnesses:

Ohara, Jap[anese], sworn. I know the defendant. This past March, 1893, I bought liquor from him 2 times, the 25th and 26th. On the 25th Abe sold me 2 bottles of liquor: wine and sake mixed, this is intoxicating. I paid Abe $1.30 for the 2 bottles. Tasaka and I went there and met Abe. We, Tasaka, Yamanaka, and I, came from Hilo and went there that day. At dawn we were near Suki's store. Yamanaka left us. At Yoshina's house we drank those bottles of liquor. We did not drink at Abe's house. Abe got the liquor from inside the doorway. Tasaka and I were there at that time and he saw me buying liquor from Abe. The time was 3:15 P.M. Abe brought the liquor out of the room and gave it to me at the door. The only people there at the time were myself, Tasaka and Abe. On the 26th Abe and I again bought a bottle of liquor from Abe, just like the liquor I bought on the 25th. I paid Abe 65 cents for this bottle of liquor. The people there at that time were myself, Tasaka, Abe and his wife. Yoshioka, Tasaka and I came from the house. I had the bottle of liquor and we drank it at a house of the man who died. I did not get his name. The people who drank that bottle of liquor were myself, Yamanaka, Tasaka, Inouye and some strangers who met Yamanaka in Papaikou and who came with him to the house of the deceased person. It was 6:30 P.M. that day that the bottle of liquor was bought. It was intoxicating liquor.

Cross examine: the government worked this way: [we] spied over the past months, before that we worked at the house of Okino. Before March 25th and 26th my work was to spy. I did not go to Pepekeo on March 19 and 20. I met Abe half a year ago while I was then staying in Okino's house. I saw Okita, I did not go with him to spy. We all left Hilo on 25 March and went to Papaikou, myself, Tasaka and Yamanaka. We met seaward of the fish counter of a Chinese. It was 12:30 P.M. at the time. I said to Tasaka and Yamanaka: "I'm going to Papaikou" and I urged the two of them to come with me. They agreed and we all went together. I did not tell them at that time the reason that was in my mind to go to Papaikou. We walked. We stayed right on the road, did not visit any place. When we arrived in Papaikou we separated: Yamanaka, Tasaka and I. Tasaka and I went straight to Abe's house. While we were on the road I did not tell my friends the reason why we were going to Papaikou. I did not tell the two of them we were going to spy. Yet, Tasaka knew we were going to spy. Yamanaka left us at the gate. After he left it was then I told Tasaka that we were going to spy when we got there. The reason for my telling Tasaka is that he is a spy. Yamanaka is not a spy. Abe's house is not as [you] enter the gate. There is a space from this gate to Abe's house. That house is like that at the corner. I was standing at the gate and Yamanaka said that he was going down to the house of ——— [blank in text]. When Yamanaka was gone I said to Tasaka "let's go and buy some liquor at Abe's house." We went and met Abe at his blacksmith's house. The room was opened and could be seen from the road. Abe was not shoeing a horse at this time. I greeted Abe and he returned the greeting. I asked him for liquor. Abe said: "how many [do you] want?" I said "2 bottles." It was 3:15 P.M. as I looked at my watch. I went inside Abe's blacksmith's house and stood right in the middle of the doorway. I said to Abe: "You give me wine." Wine and sake were mixed together in a bottle of liquor. Sake is stronger than wine. Before he gave me these bottles of liquor, Abe told me: "you'll get only wine in the Japanese houses, 50 cents a bottle," but he went on to say that the wine mixed with sake is his only for 65 cents for one bottle. I said "that is all right." He got and gave me 2 bottles of liquor. I stood at the door and Tasaka stood nearby, in back of me. At this time I paid Abe, $1.30 for these 2 bottles of liquor. I put the money from my hand into Abe's hand. I had some other money, $7.00. I got those bottles of liquor which were not wrapped with anything.

Tasaka and I went to the house of Yoshioka, seaward of the government road. That house of Yoshioka is the second house that I went into from the time we left Hilo that day. When I arrived at Yoshioka's house the people there were Yamanaka, Mrs. Yoshioka and also Tasaka. We all sat together at the table and drank from those bottles of liquor except the woman, she did not drink. Tasaka and I went into Abe's house at 3:15 P.M. Other Japanese people were entering the store, buying and leaving. At 3:30 P.M. Tasaka and I went to Yoshioka's house and drank liquor there. I looked at the watch at that time and told Tasaka and Yamanaka that we should drink the 2 bottles there until they were finished. At that time there was nothing remaining, nothing in those bottles of liquor to be taken to show the government. The reason for not having anything remaining of that liquor was that Sheriff Hitchcock taught me is that if you can show you saw the buying of the liquor then that is enough. After we drank those 2 bottles of liquor I went down toward the sea. Others in our group went also. I went down toward the sea then went up again toward the mountains to the Japanese tea house and ate. Later I went to the house of Inouye. That night I slept in Inouye's house. After we separated at Yoshioka's house I met Yamanaka again at Inouye's house that night. I slept with Yamanaka there that night. It was strong liquor and we were drunk yet I could walk straight. The bottles were left on top of the table with paper stoppers in those bottles. Liquor was in the cups from which we drank. When we were in Yoshioka's house that day I did not tell him about the place I got the liquor. I did not know when I got up in the morning the next day (March 26) since I did not look at the watch. The reason that I looked at the time for this buying of the liquor is that it is my work, as a spy to know the time when the wrongdoing was committed. When I was asleep the night of March 25 Inouye was up. At dawn (March 26) I got up and went to Furamoto's house. Afterwards I returned to Inouye's house and found Yamanaka. We both went to Furamoto's house, ate breakfast there, after eating I went to the gambling house seaward of the road where I gambled and lost $1.30. I did not come to bring suit for the crime of gambling. Afterwards, in the afternoon, the gambling started, at 6:20 as I looked at the watch. Yamanaka was also in the gambling house but he was only watching. I met with Tasaka that day March 26 at Muramoto, alias Furamoto's house at 6:30 P.M. Yamanaka and I went together from the gambling house to Muramoto's house. I did not speak to Tasaka earlier on March 25, he found me at Muramoto's house on the 26th. When I met Tasaka at Muramoto's house and I said to Tasaka "let's go again to buy liquor," Yamanaka was there but I could swear he heard those words I said to Tasaka, perhaps he did not. I was not drunk on wine that day. I slept at Inouye's house the night of March 26 and I returned to Hilo on March 27. In April, just past, I came to explain to the sheriff about this crime of buying liquor on the first day of that month [April]. Tasaka and I went to buy liquor from Abe on March 26. Yamanaka was staying at Muramoto's house. Tasaka and I returned with the bottle of wine and sake mixed, from Abe's place to Muramoto's house. We all drank this bottle of liquor, myself, Tasaka, Yamanaka, Inouye and 2 Japanese visitors. After drinking, everyone left. Tasaka and I went to Abe's house. We did not find him at his blacksmith shop. Abe's wife lit the fireplace. It was nighttime and there was some rain. I cannot be sure if Abe was sitting on the mat when his wife lit the lamp in the front room. I was not in the room when [I] first bought the liquor on that day, 25th. The last bottle of liquor was bought on the 26th. I said to Abe I want one bottle of liquor like the kind I bought earlier. He said all right, then he got one, brought it to me and gave it to me. I paid him 65 cents for this bottle of liquor, a half dollar, a dime and a nickel. Then Tasaka and I returned to Muramoto's house. It was 10 minutes before 7 P.M. Tasaka and I were inside Abe's room at the time I spoke to him (Abe) about a bottle of liquor. This bottle was not wrapped up. After we left Hilo on the 25th until I returned and was back in Hilo on the 27th of March. I did not get any other liquor except those 3 bottles of liquor I got from Abe. On the morning of March 27 I left Papaikou at 10 A.M. and went to Onomea. I did not see Yamanaka again. I did not return with Yamanaka, Tasaka was the one who returned with me to Hilo. When I went to Onomea I stayed there in a house of a woman. We talked, smoked. Afterwards I returned straight to Hilo that day. Tasaka was spying. I know Kono. His work is to bring liquor. I conversed with Kono that month about buying liquor.

Tasaka, Jap[anese], sworn. I know Abe. In March 1893 Ohara and I went to his house on the 25th and 26th. On the 25th Ohara and I were the ones who went there to buy liquor—sake. Ohara bought 2 bottles of liquor, $1.30 from Abe. I was there at the time. We came from Hilo that day—Yamanaka, Ohara and I. Yamanaka did not come along with us to Abe's place. He (Yamanaka) left us at the gate. It was 3:15 P.M. when we got to Abe's house, got the 2 bottles of liquor, left there and went to Yoshioka's house and joined Yamanaka in the house. Yoshioka's wife was there. We all drank from those bottles of liquor—myself, Ohara, Yamanaka and the woman. That day, March 25 when those bottles of liquor were bought, there were no other people there, only myself, Ohara and Abe at that time. On the 26th Ohara and I went again to Abe's place. It was almost night when we arrived there. Ohara said to Abe "I want one bottle of liquor." Abe went to get one bottle of liquor, wine and sake mixed. He gave it to Ohara and Ohara paid Abe 65 cents for the bottle. It was 6:30 P.M. at the time. Then we left. We went to Muramoto's house and we drank that bottle of liquor there, myself, Ohara, Yamanaka, and Mrs. Muramoto and 2 other people and Inouye, making a total of 8 of us, who drank that bottle of liquor. I went to Abe's house twice in the past month of March.

Cross examine: I left Hilo on March 25 and I returned here in Hilo on the evening of the 27th of that month. I slept all night of the 25th at Kono's house. We drank from those bottles of liquor on the 25th at the house of Yoshioka's woman. Yamanaka was there at that time. Afterwards we left. Ohara went seaward, Yamanaka went mountainward. I went to Kono's house. I saw the coffee house and there were Japanese below Osuke's place. Ohara and I were ahead to go and buy liquor in Papaikou near Abe's house. I knew why we were going to Papaikou, to get ready to buy liquor. Ohara and I did not talk about things regarding liquor. When we left Hilo and went to Papaikou I already knew about why 2 of us were going, which was to get ready to buy liquor while we spied before we went on 25 March. We only said we were going to Papaikou. The sheriff ordered the two of us to go and watch the buying of liquor everywhere. He said this past February when we went to Papaikou and Yamanaka passed by, Ohara said to me: "he's going to buy liquor at Abe's place." That was the first time I knew. We went to buy liquor from Abe. When we left Hilo it was then that I knew about us going on "spend day" [no work, spend money day?]. When we got to Papaikou and went to a place near Abe's house it was the first time that Ohara spoke to me, that we were going to buy liquor. From the start of our spying until we went to Papaikou on 25 March, if we were going to see friends and perhaps to spy on liquor, then I would have understood why we went, that is, to spy. Ohara and I met on 24 March. Before that day we did not speak to each other. On 25 March Yamanaka and I were standing at a Chinese fish stall seaward from here. Ohara came and spoke to the two of us, that we go to Papaikou, to "spend day" there. We agreed. At 12:30 P.M. I went to the Japanese hotel seaward of here. Ohara and Yamanaka came later and we met there and stayed a short while. At 1 P.M. we left the hotel and went straight to Papaikou, did not rest at any place along the way. When we arrived at Papaikou and got close to Abe's house Ohara then told me that he and I were to buy liquor from Abe. Yamanaka left us earlier at the gate and went on to Yoshioka's place. When Ohara and I went we found Abe in his black-smith's shop. We went to 2 different places to get liquor over those 2 days, not at the same house. On 25 March at the door to the room Abe gave Ohara 2 bottles of liquor. Abe gave Ohara the bottle of liquor on the 26th at the door of the watching room. The people in the room on the 25th were Abe, his wife and boy, Ohara and I. Ohara said to Abe "you give me sake." Abe agreed and went to get the liquor inside the doorway. He brought 2 bottles and gave them to Ohara. Ohara paid him $1.30. One of them said something but I forgot what, at this time. Abe said to Ohara, before he went to get the bottles of liquor, "you can get wine at the Japanese houses for 50 cents a bottle, my liquor is wine mixed with sake, therefore it is 65 cents a bottle." I witnessed the payment given to Abe and the kind of money used since I was standing behind Ohara at the time. The people who drank from the bottle of liquor were myself, Ohara, Yamanaka and the woman. It was 4:30 P.M. In the morning, the next day 26 March, I met with Ohara at Muramoto's house. Muramoto was dead. Inouye, Muramoto, Yamanaka, Ohara and I were there. I got there at 5:30 P.M. Ohara and Yamanaka arrived at 6 P.M. I again went with Ohara to Abe's place to buy liquor. It was 6:30 P.M. Ohara was the watch who would watch the time when the bottle of liquor was gotten. We left Abe's place and returned to Mrs. Muramoto's house where we drank from that bottle of liquor. It was 8 P.M. that night. We were myself, Ohara, Yamanaka, Inouye and Mrs. Muramoto. I slept at Kono's house that night. The next day, the 27th, I met Ohara. He said he was going to Onomea so we both went to Onomea, ate lunch at a house, and when we were done we returned directly to Hilo. We didn't bring any liquor from Onomea. We didn't get any liquor other than the 3 bottles of liquor we got from Abe. We had only the 3 bottles of liquor we drank on March 25 and 26. I did not go to gamble with Ohara folks those days. Only Ohara held on to those bottles of liquor, tucked in his clothes. The bottles were not wrapped. On March 23 I went to Papaikou to meet Kono, talked with him, and saw Masubara and talked with him. I saw Okita and talked with him.

May 16, 1893
Provisional Government of Hawaiian Islands v. Abay[Abe]Jap[anese]
Selling liquor without a license, etc.
Entanglement postponed for the rest of the witnesses today.
Defendant recalled.

Ohara: I don't remember. I went with Yamanaka, Toda and Suguchi from Hilo to Papaikou on a Saturday the past month of March. It was not on any other day in that month but I saw them (Toda and Suguchi).

Question by sheriff: I went to that gambling place in Papaikou. I returned and told the police about that gambling carried on there.

Defendant recalled: Tasaka: I did not go with Toda and Suguchi from Hilo to Papaikou on Saturdays during the month of March.

Yamanaka, Jap[anese]: I know Abe, Ohara and Tasaka. This past month of March on the 25th, 1893, I went with Ohara and Tasaka from Hilo to Papaikou. It was a Saturday. We left from the Chinese fish stall on the seaward side at 12:30 P.M. We visited the hotel on the seaward side and stayed a short time there. We left there at 1:00 P.M., went directly to Papaikou. We got a place near Shosuke's store, I heard Ohara and Tasaka say that they were going to buy liquor at Abe's place. They went down and I seaward at Yoshioka's house. I stayed there a while. When Ohara and Tasaka came I saw Ohara had 2 bottles of liquor, wine and sake. We, myself, Ohara, Tasaka and Yoshioka drank those bottles of liquor there. It was liquor. We did not bring any liquor from Hilo. My only baggage I had from Hilo was an umbrella. Ohara and I slept at Inouye's house that night, 25 March. On the night of the 26 I saw Tasaka, Ohara and Inouye at Muramoto's house. Ohara went to gamble on the 26th. That night we drank liquor at Muramoto's house, 2 women and 6 of us men. I saw Ohara bring liquor there. I don't know where he got the liquor, Japanese liquor mixed with wine, a liquor.

Cross examine: I met with Ohara and Tasaka at a Chinese fish counter, seaward from here. We left there at 12:30 P.M. I left from Yanahagara's place and met Tasaka at the fish counter. While we were there Ohara came, Ohara said let's go to Papaikou. We said all right. I did not know at the time why we were going to Papaikou. I went along with Ohara and Tasaka. They spied on the people selling liquor before that Saturday, March 25. That was in February. Tasaka and I spoke to each other before going to buy liquor. When we left that Chinese fish counter on the seaward side it was 12:30 P.M. I took my umbrella to Yanagahara's house, got the umbrella when I came and found Ohara and Tasaka. We came and visited the hotel on the seaward side, stayed there a short while, left there at 1:00 P.M. I don't remember going with Ohara and Tasaka to Papaikou on several Saturdays in March. I went with Ohara, Suguchi and Toda one day to Papaikou. I forgot the day, except I remember March 25. We did not drink wine that day when we went to Papaikou with Ohara, Suguchi and Toda. I don't remember when we left Hilo when we went there. I remember it was lunch time when we went. We did not have liquor when we went. The night of March 25, Saturday I slept at Inouye's house, slept there on the 26th. There are 2 Inouyes—one works at Onomea and the other at Papaikou. They are brothers. One of them has a house in Papaikou where I slept. When I got up on Sunday morning we went to Osuke's hotel at noon. I ate at Muramoto's house, stayed there until 6:30 P.M. I looked for a gaming house. Afterwards I returned to Mrs Muramoto's house, had dinner there at 7 P.M. I drank liquor. I did not drink liquor with Inouye, Toda and Ohara at Mrs. Muramoto's house except at another time in March, we, Ohara, Tasaka, Inouye and I drank liquor on the night of March 26. On the night of the 27th I was in Hilo and I slept that night. I did not drink liquor with Ohara, Toda, Inouye and Saguchi at house. On a day in March when we were near Osuke's store, we separated at the gate. I told Ohara and Tasaka that I was staying here and going down to Yoshioka's house. At that time I heard Ohara and Tasaka say they were going to buy liquor at Abe's place. I told them if that was so then "you two come down and I'll find Yoshioka's place." They agreed. I went down and they came. Ohara brought the bottles of liquor, they were not wrapped with something on the outside. There we all drank from these bottles of liquor. We poured the liquor with cups, it was warm, we drank.

Prosecution rest.

Defense witnesses: Suguchi, Jap[anese], sworn. I know Ohara, Tasaka and Yamanaka. On Saturday March 25, 1893 I met Ohara, Yamanaka and Toda in Hilo. We left Hilo town at 9 A.M. that day and went to Papaikou. We walked. Tasaka did not come with us that day. When we arrived at Paukaa Ohara and Yamanaka said they were going down toward the sea and would return, then we would go on to Papaikou. Toda and I stayed mountainward of the road. Ohara and Yamanaka went down to 30 minutes or so then they returned and we all left. We arrived at the tea house in Papaikou. It was 11:30 A.M. according to their clock. We ate there. We met Inouye there and when we finished eating we went to Yoshioka's house, stayed there until 2:30 P.M. We drank some liquor. He went and bought liquor in a tea pot and we drank. Tasaka was not there. We all sat there, Ohara and Yamanaka and I until 3 P.M. I did not go with Ohara and Yamanaka from Hilo to Papaikou at any other time in March except for the time when we went on the 25th of that month.

Cross examine: I don't work now. I worked in Papaikou earlier. The haole was bad in May. In April I worked in Mrs. Austin's garden, in March I did not work, I stayed here in front of the saloon. I went from Hilo to Papaikou twice in March, the first time on the 15th, I went alone and stayed in Inouye's house. The second time I went to Papaikou from Hilo was on the 25th. It was the day before the Sabbath. There were 4 of us going, myself, Ohara, Yamanaka and Toda. I met Ohara, Yamanaka and Toda at the house I was staying in, below the saloon. In the morning of 25 March Ohara said let's go to Papaikou. We all said yes and we left my place below the saloon at 9 A.M. I didn't have a watch to look at the time. We went as far as Paukaa. Ohara and Yamanaka went toward the sea, Toda and I stayed upland of the road. The 2 were gone for 30 minutes and when they returned we all went together. We arrived at the coffee shop in Papaikou, at 11:30 A.M., according to the time at the clock there. From this coffee shop we went straightway until we got to Yoshioka's house where we met Inouye Enodora there. Inouye Enodora stayed in Mrs. Yoshioka's house. All we did was talk at this house at this time. Ainsta Inouye was there. No other person came there. Tasaka was not there. We all drank liquor there, wine from Inouye Enadora. She went and brought it. She was gone about 15 minutes and returned with the wine. My labor contract ended January 1892. I've known Toda for more than a year. I know Ohara and Yamanaka.

Murai, Jap[anese] sworn. I work at the Malama Hale, hotel, in Hilo town at Waianuenue Street. I know Tasaka Jap[anese]. He was a resident there in my hotel (boarder), room and board. He began his stay in my hotel from February just past until this month. In March just past he stayed the entire month. I took care of the account for Tasaka in my book. This is my original account book. Here is Tasaka's account:

month of March 1893:

On the following days 1, 2, 3, 4, 5, 6 he ate 3 full meals. On the 7th he ate once, dropped him. On the days 8, 9, 10, 11, 12, 13, 14, 15, 16, 17, 18, 19 he ate 3 full meals. On the 20th he ate once and dropped him. On the following days, 21, 21, 22, 23, 24, 25, 26, 27, 28 he ate 3 full meals. On the 29th he ate twice and dropped him. On the 30 and 31 he ate 3 full meals. On the 25, 26, 27 Tasaka stayed in my hotel and ate 3 full meals.

Cross examine: this is my account book. Only I wrote this account of Tasaka in this book.

Asked to show all the things written in this book: the defense lawyer objected. He wanted to question the government side on only the above accounting of Tasaka, not the account of other people held in the book or other things written in the book. The 2 sides became involved in an argument so the court postponed [the case] until tomorrow, Wednesday, March 17, 1893, 10 A.M.

Wednesday, March 17, 1893, 10 A.M.: The defense lawyer's request. He objected yesterday to be questioned about all the things in the book that did not have relevance to Tasaka's account. It was returned to him and he was asked everything in the book which is written down below.

Cross examine. Here is Tasaka's account for the month of February, here is for the month of March, here is for the month of April, here is for the month of May. This account is Keroku's. Here is Tasaka's account for the month of February written in Japanese.

for the month of March written in Japanese;

for the month of April changed in the manner of March like this;

for the month of May changed in the manner of March like this.

Account of the people who stayed only for March in this manner, for the permanent people who are signed in, on this side, male, 11 people on this side, this is my original book of the accounts which I have entered in this book for every day. At one time I waited a while before entering [in the book] but no more than 3 days. This is Keroku's account, Tasaka owed me and paid me $4.00. In March Tasaka's account for the days 1, 2, 3, 4, 5, 6 was full for more than 3 days. On the 7th he had 2 more, on the 8th until the 19th it was full for more than 3 days on the 20th he had 2 more. From the 21st until the 28th it was full for more than 3 days. On the 29th he had one, on the 30th and 31st it was full for more than 3 days. If there were 2 more on one day then it would be counted as half day.

Muramoto Jap[anese], sworn. I did not know the Japanese, Tasaka before. There was not a Japanese by the name of Tasaka who came to my house in Papaikou.

Cross examine. At this time in February I came to Hilo and slept here one night. I returned to my place, I only heard some Japanese talking, one by the name of Tasaka. I did not see his face. My husband died this past February, on the 22nd. I did not see Tasaka there. I did not even know of the Japanese, Tasaka, who came to my house this past February and March. This is the first time I'm seeing Tasaka's face here before the court at this time. I am telling the truth, I never saw this Japanese, Tasaka, in my house.

Defense rest.

Prosecution recalled.

Murai: There are 3 books to take care of things in my hotel. One book for payment in dollars for things bought, one book where small things are recorded; laundry and debts, money; and this book where the boarder is charged. (Book mark A) I have seen this paper that was written. On one side of my book [I] have written Tasaka's account. This was written in the manner of a bill, written for the month of February from the 6th: wash dishes .50, cakes .10, board $7.00, total $7.60, paid $4.00, balance, $3.60. Month of March, washed 2 shirts .35, board $10.00, total $10.35. Month of April Tasaka took 3 shirts $1.60, board $10.00, total $10.80. I believe there is a mistake in the writing of this bill. Ohara came and paid $4.00 of Tasaka's debt. This page of my book was cut off and given to Ohara one day this past week.

Cross examine: Ohara did not pay me. Tasaka did not. This page on Tasaka's account was cut off and given to Ohara.

Prosecution recalled Ohara for rebuttal of the statements of his witnesses. The court agrees to the defense opposition.

Case rest.

After the lawyers on both sides were seated the decision was postponed until tomorrow, Thursday 18 March 1893, 10 A.M.

By the court: I observed thoughtfully and very carefully the statements from both sides regarding this entanglement. It is clear to me that Murai's testimony and his account book of his hotel relate to Tasaka, a boarder who always ate at his hotel, and that Tasaka is an important witness for the government side in this entanglement involving Abe. I know without a doubt that these are honest testimonies as well as those things written in his book. This court did not have a reason to doubt that book was handled unethically in order that the defendant would escape. Nothing has come before the court regarding this, therefore I have decided that the statements on the government side are not sufficient to find the defendant guilty based on Tasaka's statement which is not the truth. Therefore Abe is dismissed, not guilty.

G. W. A. Hapai
District Judge
So. Hilo

1903 CASES

1903.1 Vagrancy

March 24, 1903

Ter. of Hawaii vs.
Kageyama Hikataro

Vagrancy at Honomu, south Hilo, Island and Territory of Hawaii for one month passed.

Deputy Sheriff Overend for the Territory.

K. Takei, sworn as interpreter.

K. Takei, sworn: I am an interpreter. I know the defendant. I was an interpreter in his case of insanity and know he was discharged by the doctor. I have not seen him. He has not had work.

No cross exam.

Koolau, sworn: I am a police officer for South Hilo. I am acquainted with the defendant. He never did any work. He used to go around and beg for food from the Japanese. The Japanese reported to the head-luna and the head-luna reported to me. It was at Honomu. I arrested him.

No cross exam.

Prosecution rests.

No defense.

By the Court: Kageyama Hikataro. I sentence you to two months at hard labor and pay the costs of the court $1.20.

G. W. A. Hapai
District Magistrate
South Hilo, Hawaii

[Commentary: This defendant had been brought into court that same morning on charges of "investigation of insanity"—it was nolle prossed without any details. The vagrancy charge was successfully prosecuted next. Here the charge of insanity and vagrancy were both used to take marginal individuals off the streets. The defendant made no attempt to defend himself.]

1903.2 Assault and Battery

April 17, 1903

Ter. of Hawaii vs. Pablo P.R. [Puerto Rican]

Assault and battery. Continued from April 17. Case heard on April 20.

Captain Lake for the Territory

Joe Johnson sworn as interpreter.

A. Ford, sworn: My name is A. Ford. I reside at Honomu and I am a luna. I know the defendant. I am his luna. On April 13 I saw this man and ordered him to cut some cane. I told other men to work but this man did not work but go mad. He had a cane knife and he tried to cut me and if it was not for my rain coat he would have cut me. That is the stick he hit me with. (Stick offered as evidence.) This happened at Honomu, South Hilo, Hawaii. That mark on my head is the sore—he struck me with a stick.

No cross exam

Marion Rodrigues, sworn: My name is Marion Rodrigues and I live at Honomu. I saw this defendant outside of my house. I did not see anything. Yes, I saw this man strike the luna with that stick.

No cross exam.

Ramona Otis, sworn: My name is Ramona Otis and I live at Honomu. My work is house work. I know the defendant by sight. I know the luna by sight too. I have not seen more than that, that the defendant struck the luna with the stick.

No cross exam.

Bentura Cavalho, sworn: He was going to work last week Tuesday. When he got to a certain place there was a river and the luna told this man to go on. After the horse struck the defendant and he was falling, that was the time he drew his knife to defend himself and the luna ran back and called that this defendant wanted to cut him. Then the luna went and told the bookkeeper not to count his day. Then the luna called him a "God-damned-son of a birtch" [*sic*]. Then he took a small stick and struck him.

Cross exam: I was at Honomu on April 13. The luna ordered the man to cross the stream. No, I never saw that stick. Nobody told me to come. Because this man went to the bookkeeper. I was present when this man was with the bookkeeper. I only heard. He told me about it.

Hosena Hica, sworn: I don't know very much about this case. Only this that when we got to a river, the luna's horse got on the defendant.

Cross-exam: That is all I know about the case.

Pablo, defendant, sworn: We were all going to work and when we got to a river there were men who did not want to cross the river and I was one of them. The luna was coming on a horse and I defended myself with a knife. After the day was over I went to the luna to count my day but he would not. Then I went to him the second time and he said he would not put it down.

Cross exam: I was afraid to cross it. Nobody wanted to cross it. I did not see anybody cross it.

No arguments.

By the court:

Pablo, I know you are guilty, therefore I fine you $25 and costs of the court $3

G. W. A. Hapai
District Magistrate

1903.3 Assault and Battery

March 19, 1903

Territory of Hawaii vs.
Antonio de Jesus, P.R. [Puerto Rican]

Assault and Battery

(continued from March 17)

Deputy Sheriff Overend for the Territory

Joe Johnson, sworn, as interpreter

A. E. Minville, sworn: My name is A. E. Minville. I live at 8 Miles, Olaa,
District of South Hilo, Hilo, Hawaii. I know him by sight. He was employed
by the Olaa Sugar Co. On the 14th of March I opened up the store at 5 and
10 minutes afterwards he came and he said he was short $1.00. The defen-
dant came and said he was short and he insulted me and called me all kinds
of names. He slapped me on my face on the left side. The $1.00 he is
disputing was held back by the Olaa Sugar Company for his taxes. The
plantation holds back $1.00 for their poll taxes. Yes, that was all the trouble.
He did not give me a chance to explain to him.

Harry Doss, sworn: My name is Harry Doss. I live in the Portuguese Camp,
at Olaa. I know his face and he works on the plantation. He slapped A. E.
Minville across the [face] over the counter. He did not strike the defendant.

Cross-exam: He inquired what he had.

No cross exam.

Verginim de Cristo, sworn: I live at 9 Miles Olaa. I know the defendant. On
the 14th of this month I was in the store when he struck on the right of the
face of Minville. He came in and said he was short $1.00 and Mr. Minville
was busy with another fellow.

No cross exam.

Prosecution rests.

Defense

Albert Well, sworn: I can not tell what happened in the store. I was not present. My son was there.

No cross exam.

Laurenso Raulio, sworn: I don't know anything about it.

Antonio de Jesus, defendant, sworn: I went to Mr. Minville's store and told him I was $1.50 short. Afterward I told him that he began to call me names, "God damn, son of a bitch." Then I told him there is no use talking like that, he had better look in his books. He struck me and afterwards my hands struck him on the face. I did not strike him willfully.

Cross-exam: I never said it was $1.00. Yes, I did say $1.00 about. No, I did not strike him on the face. I did not strike him willfully.

Ramona Rodrigues, sworn: I don't know anything about this case.

By the Court:

Antonio de Jesus. I sentence you to one month at hard labor and costs of court $7.80.

G. W. A. Hapai
District Magistrate
South Hilo, Hawaii

[Commentary: In both of the cases with Puerto Rican defendants, the same interpreter, Joe Johnson, was present. The Japanese defendant also had an interpreter. None of the defendants had attorneys and all were found guilty. Clearly all were resisting the treatment of authorities in some ways, but in the forum of the court were unable to defend themselves, tell their side of the story, or present effective witnesses. Their inability to speak Hawaiian undermined their ability to mount a successful defense. In both the assault cases, the defendants say they were provoked and recognize that provocation constitutes some kind of defense. In the second case, the defendant says he was protecting himself, and in the third, he distances himself from the action by saying that his hands, as separate entities, did the deed. The Puerto Rican defendants were, in 1903, very recent arrivals, having come in a small group in 1901 and 1902 fleeing hurricane damage on Puerto Rico. Nordyke notes that in 1900 and 1901, 5,200 Puerto Ricans left their homes for Hawaii; 2,390 were male contract laborers on 3 year contracts, the others were

women and children. It is likely that this more African-appearing group experienced more racial discrimination than other groups.

The second two incidents are forms of resistance against authorities. Minville is listed as the manager of the Puerto Rican Store in Olaa and therefore
is the closest representative of the management and one of the few points at
which workers can register complaints.]

B

ACCOMPANYING TABLES

Tables for Chart 6.1
Circuit Court Cases, Hilo Region, 1852–1892

| | | | | | | | *Type of Crime* | | | | | | |
Decades	Violence	Sex	Property	Licenses	Family	Public Order	Adultery/ Prostitution	Gambling	Drugs/ Alcohol	Work	Public Health	Misc.	Total
1850s	12	2	24		1	12	46	1	11			6	115
1860s	37	11	62	3	3	40	72		34	14	1	8	285
1870s	84	15	124	12	10	48	94	13	122	50	4	19	595
1880s	183	28	247	14	15	71	59	41	351	49	13	61	1132
1890–2	44	3	81	8	6	34	25	8	103	7	2	33	354
Total	360	59	538	37	35	205	296	63	621	120	20	127	2481

Tables for Chart 6.1 (*cont.*)

Circuit Court Cases, Hilo Region, 1905–1985

Year of hearing	Violence	Sex	Property	Licenses	Family	Public Order	Adultery/ Prostitution	Gambling	Drugs/ Alcohol	Work	Public Health	Misc.	Total
1905	17	2	13			6	6	2	2				48
1915	22	7	24	1	3	5	1		3				66
1925	10	2	23		3	3	1		5		6	3	56
1935	13	5	10	2	1	2	1				1	2	37
1945	12	59	22			1	3		3	3	1	8	117
1955	6	9	11								1	2	29
1965	2	8	29			11	1		2		1	4	58
1975	19	6	97			10			37		2	17	188
1985	23	5	63		1	7		4	72		3	22	200
Total	124	103	292	3	8	45	13	6	124	3	15	58	799

Tables for Chart 6.2

Ethnicity of Defendant in Circuit Court, Hilo Region, 1852–1892

| | Ethnicity | | | | | | | |
Decades	Caucasian	Chinese	Hawaiian	Japanese	Portuguese	South Sea Islander	Other	Total
1850s	10	4	100				1	115
1860s	37	3	246		3			289
1870s	53	33	515	3	5			609
1880s	132	344	574	12	84	3	2	1151
1890–2	32	111	142	45	26			356
Total	264	495	1577	60	118	3	3	2520

Ethnicity of Defendant in Circuit Court, Hilo Region, 1905–1985

| | Ethnicity | | | | | | | | | | | |
Year of hearing	Caucasian	Chinese	Hawaiian	Japanese	Portuguese	Samoan	Filipino	Korean	Puerto Rican	Mixed	Other	Total
1905	3	4	5	13	8		3	3	7	1	1	48
1915	9	2	4	12	5		22	1	9	1	1	66
1925	10		4	12	4		15		8	1	2	56
1935	4	1	3	1	4		14	1	5	2	3	38
1945	6	6	25	10	7		48	2	6	1	7	118
1955	2		10	1	5		5		5		1	29
1965	17		11	7	6		6		11			58
1975	76	1	28	16	11		20		19	5	10	190
1985	91	5	21	13	27	5	36	2	1	9	4	214
Total	218	19	111	85	77	5	169	9	71	20	29	817

Tables for Chart 6.3

Ethnicity of Defendant by Type of Crime, Hilo District Court, 1853

| | | | | | Type of Crime | | | | | |
Ethnicity	Violence	Property	Public Order	Adultery/ Prostitution	Gambling	Drugs/ Alcohol	Work	Public Health	Misc.	Total
Caucasian	7	1				4	3	4		19
Chinese	1				2	1				4
Hawaiian	13	9	12	54		6	2	1	1	98
Portuguese	1			1						2
Mixed	1									1
Total	23	10	12	55	2	11	5	5	1	124

Ethnicity of Defendant by Type of Crime, Hilo District Court, 1863

| | | | | | Type of Crime | | | | | |
Ethnicity	Violence	Property	Public Order	Adultery/ Prostitution	Gambling	Drugs/ Alcohol	Work	Public Health	Misc.	Total
Caucasian	2								2	4
Chinese							1		1	2
Hawaiian	14	11		13	38	5	31	1	16	129
Samoan			1							1
Other									1	1
Total	16	11	1	13	38	5	32	1	20	137

Tables for Chart 6.3 (*cont.*)

Ethnicity of Defendant by Type of Crime, Hilo District Court, 1873

						Type of Crime						
Ethnicity	Violence	Property	Licenses	Family	Public Order	Adultery/ Prostitution	Gambling	Drugs/ Alcohol	Work	Public Health	Misc.	Total
Caucasian	1		1		1			6	2	1	4	16
Chinese	1	1					1	12	2	1	6	24
Hawaiian	21	12		4	3	14	9	21	90	7	12	193
Portuguese	1											1
Mixed									1			1
Other						1			1	2	1	5
Total	24	13	1	4	4	15	10	39	96	11	23	240

Ethnicity of Defendant by Type of Crime, Hilo District Court, 1883

							Type of Crime						
Ethnicity	Violence	Sex	Property	Licenses	Family	Public Order	Adultery/ Prostitution	Gambling	Drugs/ Alcohol	Work	Public Health	Misc.	Total
Caucasian	12		2		1	5			15	6	2	5	48
Chinese	8	1	9	1		5	1	1	20	70	7	23	145
Hawaiian	18		17		10	3	4		16	56	6	23	154
Japanese										2			2
Portuguese	8		4	1		3	2		6	18	3	8	53
Mixed			1				1					2	4
Other										2			2
Total	46	1	33	2	11	16	8	1	57	154	19	61	409

Tables for Chart 6.3 (*cont.*)

Ethnicity of Defendant by Type of Crime, Hilo District Court, 1893

											Public		
Ethnicity	Violence	Sex	Property	Licenses	Family	Public Order	Adultery/ Prostitution	Gambling	Drugs/ Alcohol	Work	Health	Misc.	Total
Caucasian	3		2			1			3		2	6	17
Chinese	5		5			5		4	33		4	12	68
Hawaiian	21		6		5	2	2	1	15		4	18	74
Japanese	7		8	3	1	8		28	19	83	16	12	185
Portuguese	6	1	2			4	1		2		5	12	33
Samoan	1								1				2
Total	43	1	23	3	6	20	3	33	73	83	31	60	379

Ethnicity of Defendant by Type of Crime, Hilo District Court, 1903

									Public		
Ethnicity	Violence	Sex	Property	Licenses	Public Order	Adultery/ Prostitution	Gambling	Drugs/ Alcohol	Health	Misc.	Total
Caucasian	14		5	1	13	1	1	33	5	25	98
Chinese	4		5	3	12	2	32	2	6	19	85
Hawaiian	22	2	8	1	20	4	3	61	3	5	129
Japanese	26	1	16	39	102	12	46	34	69	63	408
Portuguese	30	2	4	3	15	7	8	31	14	32	146
Korean					1					1	2
Puerto Rican	31		10		46	4	3	15	4	1	114
Mixed					1			3	1		5
Other	2		1		2						5
Total	129	5	49	47	212	30	93	179	102	146	992

NOTES

CHAPTER 1

1. Kipling 1921: 371–372. This poem was written just after the signing of the Treaty of Paris (December 10, 1898), formalizing peace between the United States and Spain at the end of the Spanish-American war, including the U.S. takeover of Cuba, the Philippines, and Puerto Rico. According to a 1914 commentary, "Both on selfish and unselfish grounds, it was imperative that, in spite of her Constitution, the United States should 'take up the White man's burden' of imperial responsibility and charge herself with the care of the semi-civilized islands that she had wrested from Spain" (Durand 1914: 229). This date is highly relevant to the situation in Hawai'i as well since it was shortly after this war that the United States agreed to annex the islands.

2. In his essay on Kipling, C. S. Lewis (1965) notes that a central concern in much of Kipling's writings is work and discipline. He focuses on the virtues of duty, of doing one's work rather than focusing on rights (p. 107). Achieving manhood requires licking and breaking the youth, "licking into shape" the cub, thus "making a man of him," to quote Kipling (ibid.). As Lewis points out, these virtues were extolled without much attention to the final ends of the work; discipline in work was an end in itself, a position that many find troubling.

3. Regardless of our discomfort with this poem and its title today, it was a commonplace phrase in the early part of the twentieth century (Orwell 1965: 83).

4. In his commentary on another Kipling poem, Durand explains the concept of "white man's country": "A country in which white men can live, do manual labor and rear families without physical degeneration. Countries where this is impossible—such as the East Indies, the Philippine Islands, India, etc., where the white man is an aristocrat and directs the labour of coloured men—have been called in contradistinction, 'Sahibs' country'" (Durand 1914: 212).

5. Keesing's study of resistance among the Kwaio suggests a model in which resistance does take place but adopts the forms and modes of the dominant group, such as the use of a written petition and large demands for monetary compensation (Keesing 1992).

6. Gramsci defines hegemony as that aspect of power founded on consent rather than coercion (Gramsci 1971; Simon 1991). After distinguishing between civil society, "the ensemble of organisms commonly called 'private'" and "political society" or "the State," Gramsci notes: "These two levels correspond on the one hand to the function of 'hegemony' which the dominant group exercises throughout society and on the other hand to that of 'direct domination'; or command exercised through the State and 'juridical' government. The functions in question are precisely organizational and connective. The intellectuals are the dominant group's 'deputies' exercising the subaltern functions of social hegemony and political government" (Gramsci 1971: 12). Gramsci's analysis emphasizes cultural transformation and acquiescence as a fundamental part of establishing rule. The spontaneous consent of the masses

produces hegemony whereas direct domination relies on the apparatus of coercive state power to "legally" enforce discipline on those who do not consent.

7. For example, rules of mannerly behavior in the fifteenth century concerning sharing a bed focused on relative rank: the person of higher rank should choose his side of the bed and the other should lie straight on it, and after a chat, say goodnight (Elias 1994: 132–138). There was no concern about nakedness, although people often slept naked at this time. By 1729 two people of the same sex were not to sleep in the same bed, and it was considered indecent to put your legs between those of another person of the same sex if forced to share a bed (p. 133). By 1774 there was concern about two people of opposite sex sleeping in the same room unless they were married, and if two of the same sex were forced to share a bed, this situation required "a strict and vigilant modesty" (p. 133).

8. He provides a vivid description of a famous and popular event during the festival of Midsummer Day in Paris in the sixteenth century, which involved burning alive one or two dozen cats (Elias 1994: 167). After a large crowd assembled, solemn music was played, an enormous pyre built with a scaffold above, from which was suspended a sack of cats. As the bag burned through the cats fell into the fire and died with great yowling, to the pleasure of the onlookers, who usually included the king and queen.

9. The enormous debate about Captain Cook's death in Hawai'i in 1779 turns on similar questions of interpretation. Sahlins (1985) argues that the Hawaiians interpreted Cook as a deity and that his murder when he returned at the wrong point in the ceremonial cycle was a ritual event dictated by the logic of cultural categories. Obeyesekere (1992) claims that the Hawaiians were capable of "practical rationality" and made decisions on the basis of pragmatic considerations rather than ritual meanings. The deification of Cook was a European myth, not a Polynesian one; Cook was installed as a high chief, not a god. Sahlins's rebuttal of Obeyesekere's book includes a detailed analysis of the rituals and an intensive examination of Hawaiian religious ideas, in which political and religious power are not sharply differentiated so deification as a deity and installation as a high chief are not necessarily distinct (Sahlins 1995). He argues that Obeyesekere's argument silences Hawaiian culture and reinterprets Hawaiians as Western bourgeois thinkers. This debate has sparked an enormous literature concerning this event and the broader question of how to interpret historical change (e.g., Friedman 1988; Hanlon et al. 1994; Parmentier 1994; Geertz 1995; Borovsky 1997).

Neither position examines how the meanings of these events unfold over time as participants endeavor to make sense of each other in the light of developing events and actions. Whether or not the Hawaiians thought Cook was a god at first, after he had spent some time in Hawai'i, fought over the theft of boats and other objects, raged against the chiefs, and revealed the power of his weapons, they must have reconsidered who he was and what forms of power he exercised. Although Sahlins clearly has ethnographic mastery of the situation, Obeyesekere's analysis is more open to the renegotiation of meaning over time. In Sahlins's account, the Hawaiians seem imprisoned within their own cultural categories, deploying Hawaiian cultural logic to make sense of the strangers initially, then retaining it doggedly. They seem to lack reflexivity and intelligent reanalysis. On the other hand, the concept of practical rationality Obeyesekere introduces brings its own difficulties. The eighteenth-century

Hawaiian ali'i are reconstituted as bourgeois rationalists, thinking in the disenchanted and instrumental terms of modernity. Yet they clearly shared a very different conception of the relationship between humans and the divine than Christianity does, as Sahlins points out (1995). It is critical to return agency and reflective, comparative analysis to the Hawaiians without stripping them of their own cultural logic. In this debate, Sahlins wins the battle with his careful attention to sources and detailed explication of Hawaiian concepts of divinity and chiefdom, but Obeyesekere wins the war with his identification of the ways in which anthropology, with its debates about whether "natives" think literally or commonsensically, is "an alienating discourse for those people whom we study" (Obeyesekere 1992: 142).

10. She notes that anthropologists tend to view "pure" cultures as more prestigious than less remote or isolated cultures, conferring differing levels of prestige on those who study these cultures as well (Jackson 1995: 19).

11. *Trobriand Cricket: An Ingenious Response to Colonialism.* Government of Papua New Guinea, 1975.

CHAPTER 2

1. "Hawaiians Compared with Other Polynesians." *The Friend* 23 (December 1, 1865): 89.

2. Although all agree that the population collapse was extreme, there is considerable debate about the size of the precontact population. Earlier estimates of three hundred thousand have recently been revised upward by archeological and archival research (Stannard 1989).

3. 'I'ī was born on O'ahu in 1800 and was brought to Honolulu in 1810, under his uncle Papa, an attendant of Kamehameha. When the missionaries arrived, he was sent to study under Hiram Bingham and became an assistant to Bingham and a teacher at his school. In 1841 he was made general superintendent of O'ahu schools and was an influential member of the court of Kamehameha III. In 1845 he became a member of the Privy Council; he was also appointed with four others to the Board of Land Commissioners. In 1852, as a member of the House of Nobles, he was selected to represent this body in drafting the Constitution of 1852. Judge William Lee represented the House of Representatives, and G. P. Judd the king. 'I'ī served in the House of Nobles from 1841 to 1854 and from 1858 to 1868. He served as a member of the House of Representatives during 1855. 'I'ī was associate justice of the Supreme Court 1846–1864, and resigned in 1864 to spend the end of his life in 'Ewa in the service of Christian ministry. According to his great grandson, he devoted his life to the furtherance of Christianity until his death in 1870 (Emory, preface to Ii 1959). 'I'ī wrote about Hawaiian society 1866 to 1870, inspired by Samuel M. Kamakau's newspaper articles. Kamakau, born in 1815, wrote articles on Hawaiian history in Hawaiian-language newspapers from 1842 until 1876. He studied at the mission school, Lāhaināluna, starting in 1832 and became the greatest Hawaiian historian (kame'eleihiwa, preface to Kamakau 1992 [1961]).

4. Sahlins describes five status groups in the Anahulu valley: (1) local elite of konohiki and government officials; (2) old kama'āina, people who have lived on the land and farmed it for two or more generations; (3) more recently arrived kama'āinas who came in under an earlier konohiki; (4) hoa'āina, tenants of the current konohiki;

and (5) 'ōhua, people such as affines who acquired rights to land through some connection to a local family. According to Māhele records from 1848, about half the landholders in this valley were old kama'āina (Sahlins 1992: 182).

5. Although this unit has been named the 'ohana, Sahlins prefers the term *mā* attached to the name of a leader to indicate that it refers to the collection of individuals centered around a big man. The term *kupuna kin* describes the sphere of "true" kin: "the bilateral group descended from common grandparents is a basic unit of Hawaiian thought and life, marked off by its solidarity, its internal ranking, and its role in the organization of practical existence from an otherwise diffuse and indefinite field of kinship" (Sahlins 1992: 197).

6. Malo grew up with Hawaiian traditions, came under the influence of William Richards at Lāhaināluna, and worked and studied there for many years starting in 1823. He became one of the first pupils at Lāhaināluna in 1831, when he was thirty-eight, and became very Christian, condemning ancient practices. He died in 1853 (Emerson, introduction to Malo 1951).

7. The journal was authored by Hiram Bingham, Daniel Chamberlain, Samuel Whitney, Samuel Ruggles, and Elisha Loomis (*Missionary Herald* 1821: 113).

CHAPTER 3

1. Sahlins argues that the first schools were simply grafted onto the ali'i system and attached to that hierarchy, with local konohiki taking on the functions of schoolteacher (Sahlins 1992: 91–92).

2. ABCFM 19.1, vol 2. Houghton Library, Harvard University. Chamberlain was born in Dover, Vermont in 1792, arrived in Hawai'i in 1823, worked as a superintendent, married in 1828, and died in 1849 at the age of fifty-six leaving eight children (Piercy 1992: 193–195).

3. February 22, 1827, to J. Evarts, ABCFM 19.1, vol. 2, no. 67. Houghton Library, Harvard University.

4. In a letter to J. Evarts, August 27, 1825, Levi Chamberlin notes that foreigners complain that learning palapala has made the Hawaiian people suspicious, in some cases more than they ought to be, especially of those to whom they are indebted. Moreover, writing has enabled the chiefs to transmit orders from one island to another with facility and to apprise one another of their wishes and designs (ABCFM 19.1, vol. 2, Houghton Library, Harvard University).

5. One of the sources on Honolulu events in the 1820s is the private journal of the American merchant Stephen Reynolds (King 1989).

6. In his introduction to Bingham's *Residence*, Terrence Barrow describes Bingham as an ardent advocate of the Calvinist Christianity of New England. He was born 1789 in Bennington, Vermont, was educated at Middlebury College and the Theological Seminary, Andover, Massachusetts, graduated from Andover in 1819, and was ordained that year in Goshen, Connecticut. He left Boston on October 23, 1819, on the *Thaddeus* in the first group of missionaries. He was the dominant figure in his group and became the dominant person in the mission until he left in 1840 (Bingham 1981: 1–5).

7. Reynolds says that on February 22, 1826, Captain Percival of the U.S. Navy ship *Dolphin*, then in port to enforce the collection of debts owed by the chiefs to the

American merchants, went to see "old Ka'ahumanu and talked about the Laws of the land, who first bro't them forward; with many questions the answers to which he wrote down. They told him Mr. Bingham was prime mover. Mr. B has always said he has never interfered" (King 1989: 124).

8. As early as 1825 the ali'i were interested in adopting a more comprehensive set of laws. They discussed this with Lord Byron, the British dignitary who returned the body of Liholiho and his queen to Hawai'i after their deaths in London on a state visit to King George IV. But which laws should they pass? (King 1989: xv). In a national council of the higher chiefs on June 6, 1825 (attended also by Lord Byron), British consul Charlton, two missionaries, and several American merchants discussed the need for new laws (Kuykendall 1938: 119–120). Kapi'olani spoke about her efforts to establish laws against robbery, murder, drunkenness, adultery, and child murder, which had been tolerably successful. Lord Byron, asked to speak, offered some hints about conducting their affairs but said the chiefs were the best judges of their people. He did propose trial by jury, which was adopted on his suggestion. Apparently it was expected that the British would send out a code of laws for the islands, but Byron made it clear that the king and chiefs were the best judges of what suited the people (Kuykendall 1938: 120). Indeed, while the royal party was in London in 1824, Boki had asked Mr. Canning, the British secretary of state for foreign affairs, for a code of laws for his country. Canning told him that the chiefs of the islands could frame their laws better than he (Bingham 1981: 260).

9. Susan Philips argues, for example, that written law provides the context for statements that judges make in American courts as they discuss guilty pleas (Philips 1998).

10. Letter from Hiram Bingham to Jeremiah Evarts, December 15, 1827, ABCFM 13, Houghton Library, Harvard University.

11. Stephen Reynolds describes this as a public oration as well. He writes on December 11, 1827, "Crier going about telling Old & Young to go tomorrow & hear the great law, to assemble under the Cocoa nut trees," and on December 14: "A Great Concourse of People collected under the Cocoa Nut Trees, where King, Boki, & all the Chiefs were present. The following were made laws for the present Thou Shalt not Kill. Thou Shalt not commit Adultery—Thou Shalt not Steal. Thus ended the great Meeting of the Chiefs" (King 1991).

12. It endured at least until the 1860s, when the traveler Isabella Bird (1882) remarked on it, although missionary influence began to decline during the 1840s and was considerably diminished by the 1860s (Daws 1967).

13. There are fleeting indications in the vast and largely self-congratulatory corpus of missionary letters, reports, and journals that some ali'i used the missionaries for their own advantage. For example, in a letter to J. Everts written May 7, 1825, Levi Chamberlin notes the Kailua mission is very costly because "the Chief of Kaiura [Kailua] though decidedly friendly to the objects of the mission and pleased with the residence of the missionaries there, has contributed scarcely nothing to their support, but on the contrary has seemed desirous of making as much money out of the two brethren as lay in his power" (ABCFM 19.1, vol. 2, Houghton Library, Harvard University).

14. According to Nelligan and Ball's sources, the chiefs originally sentenced the man to death after an investigation, but on the advice of the missionaries postponed the execution for three weeks and held a trial at which twelve Hawaiians again found him guilty and sentenced him to be hanged (Nelligan and Bell 1992: 120).

15. Bingham described one of these early murder trials in a letter to the ABCFM in Boston (ABCFM 19.1, vol. 5, #14, March 12, 1828, Houghton Library, Harvard University). On March 12, 1828, Bingham wrote that Ka'ahumanu nominated twelve men, among the most intelligent and trustworthy, to sit as a kind of jury to hear the case. The trial had taken place three days earlier, about six months after the offense. According to the evidence, the defendant was out cutting sandalwood and left the deceased, a man belonging to the same house, at home with the defendant's little child in the charge of an old woman. Just before the defendant's return, the child disturbed the deceased while he was preparing his food, so after asking the old woman to take care of it, he sprinkled water on the child. This offended the old woman, and a brief quarrel took place. The deceased was not blamed at all by the people. While the family were asleep the defendant returned and the old woman complained against the deceased, but soon all appeared quiet again. When all were asleep except for the defendant, he took a stick of sandalwood and hit the deceased twice on the leg and once on the side, breaking a leg and a rib. The deceased cried out and the old woman, awakening, spread the alarm of murder and went out to get help. In the meantime the defendant made several attempts to bind up the broken leg, but finding it badly broken and bleeding he abandoned the effort and ran away. He was taken into custody sometime before the death of the deceased to await his trial and execution in case the wounds should prove mortal. Bingham concluded that further than this he had not been informed and how the case would be decided was quite uncertain. "We have endeavored to explain to the prisoner the doctrines and duties of the gospel. We should leave him in the hands of God. Can you tell me what a New England jury would do in such a case?"

16. Hoapili was born in 1775, fought for Kamehameha, and died in 1840.

17. Levi Chamberlain to Jeremiah Everts, American Board of Commissioners of Foreign Missions, Honolulu, July 26, 1826, ABCFM 19.1, unit 6, Houghton Library Harvard University. Chamberlain was a leading member of the Mission who lived in Honolulu (Piercy 1992: 195).

CHAPTER 4

1. *The Friend* Nov. 1865: 82.

2. From a speech delivered May 31, 1857, at the Seamen's Chapel in Honolulu after Lee's death by Rev. S. C. Damon.

3. Since this was a proposed penal code, the chapters are not numbered nor is it paginated sequentially nor are the punishments filled in. The text is primarily concerned with defining and differentiating various crimes.

4. Frear notes that the punishments in the 1850 Criminal Code were virtually all fines and imprisonment, showing marked progress since 1840, and that whipping was kept only until 1872 for larceny for males only (Frear 1894: 18).

5. Letters from D. H. Hitchcock to brother Ed, Jan. 2 and June 22, 1858, Hawaiian Mission Children's Society Archives.

6. This information comes from a major tabulation of circuit court cases during the kingdom era, supervised by Jane Silverman, in the early 1980s, supported by the National Endowment for the Humanities, "The Social Role of the Courts in the Hawaiian Kingdom." I am grateful to Harry Ball and Jane Silverman for sharing the original data set with me.

7. In 1847 Marshal Henry Sea named fornication and thievery as the predominant evils of Honolulu, and his successor, Theophilus Metcalf, said the same in 1850 (Greer 1968). Of the 505 people fined in the city's police court from September 1, 1849, to April 1, 1850, nearly all were charged with these offenses (*Marshal's Report: Ending March 1850*, p. 9) March 31, 1850 Handwritten document in the Hawai'i State Archives, Miscellaneous.

8. Wyllie to Abell, January 28, 1846, FO and Ex., p. 10, Hawai'i State Archives.

9. "Report on Prisons," *Marshal's Report 1850.*

10. Anghie describes a similar process of change in the Spaniards' relations with the Indians in the sixteenth century. As Francisco de Vitoria sought to develop a theory about the legal relations between the Spanish and the Indians of the New World, he argued that the divine law articulated by the pope was replaced with a natural law system administered by sovereigns. Yet within this new system of law, in which the Indians were equal to the Spaniards, the Indians were obligated to allow the Spaniards freedom to travel, trade, and proselytize and any resistance justified war (Anghie 1996: 325–328).

11. The dual legal systems of Africa are the best-known ethnographic cases of the imposition of colonial European law and have been the focus of much of the work in the anthropology of law since the 1930s (see also Burman and Harrel-Bond 1979; Rouland 1994.) In addition to the classic studies by Gluckman, Evans-Pritchard, Rattray, and Schapera, more recent additions to this rich literature include Comaroff and Roberts 1981; Chanock 1985; Moore 1986; Comaroff and Comaroff 1991; and Roberts and Mann 1991.

12. Beginning in the early twentieth century, French colonies in Africa began a process of compilation and classification of customs, developing a synthesis of the various practices, an endeavor that persisted until the 1960s. At that point, newly independent African nations eager for national unity and economic development turned to European models of law that would facilitate economic change. The new leaders and their European advisors sometimes saw customary law as an obstacle to development (Rouland 1994: 312). Despite the protracted effort to produce law codes based on traditional law, these changes all tended to weaken "traditional" law (Rouland 1994: 307–308). After independence, in the majority of African states traditional law was abolished either by pro-Western states eager to move to a market economy or by socialist states who viewed it as linked to an archaic stage of production (Rouland 1994: 313).

13. Yet, as Brown points out with reference to Egypt, British colonial Africa has served too extensively as the model of law and imperialism, tending to emphasize processes of imposition and control rather than the ways in which national elites themselves imported legal systems, restructured them in their own way, and used them to resist imperial powers, and, equally important, the way the legal system in colonized places was shaped by the way it was used by litigants, by local judges, attorneys, etc. (Brown 1995). The language of imperialism and the focus on control and domination ignores this contest over the courts.

CHAPTER 5

1. They may bring particular intensity to their exercise of power, as did the local managers of rubber workers in Colombia (Taussig 1987) or the colonial elites Fanon (1963) describes in pre-war Algeria.

2. Hilo's 1853 population was 7,748 and its 1878 population only 4,231 (Schmitt 1968: 71), but the town grew rapidly to 7,988 in 1884, to 9,935 in 1890, and to 12,878 in 1896 (Kelly et al. 1981: 109).

3. *Planter's Monthly* 4 (1887): 499. In Hawai'i as a whole, the plantation labor force in 1887 was 12 percent Hawaiian, 26 percent Portuguese, 14 percent Japanese, 39 percent Chinese, 3 percent South Sea Islanders, and 5 percent other nationalities (ibid.).

4. *The Planter's Monthly* 8 (1889): 8:121–123.

5. In 1866 the French consul in Hawai'i was murdered by his Chinese cook, Asee, fanning the flames of fear even though Chinese merchants in Honolulu contributed to offering a reward for Asee's capture. In 1879 a group of Chinese workers attacked their luna with cane knives and in 1881 a Chinese employee murdered his employer (Lydon 1975: 59).

6. After their contracts were finished, thousands of Japanese workers left for the mainland and higher wages. By early 1907 forty thousand Japanese had left Hawai'i for the West Coast. The 1907 order prohibiting Japanese from Hawai'i from going to the mainland trapped many eager emigrants in Hawai'i (Takaki 1989: 148).

7. Takaki (1989) also uses the term *planter paternalism*, but without explicit attention to its gendered meaning.

8. Luther Severance, a prominent member of Hilo society, kept a scrapbook of newspaper clippings about Hilo covering the end of the nineteenth century. Many of the clippings are undated, presumably cut from Honolulu papers. This scrapbook is an invaluable resource on Hilo history. It is in the Lyman House Memorial Museum in Hilo, Hawai'i. Cited hereafter as Severance Scrapbook.

9. Hawaiian Kingdom, Finance Office, March 10, 1870, Hawaii State Archives; quoted in Kelly, Nakamura, and Barrere 1981: 87.

CHAPTER 6

1. These records are housed in the Hawai'i State Archives in Honolulu. The minute books from the District Court, technically a police court, have been preserved in a virtually complete set from Hilo from the 1850s until 1910, but subsequent records were destroyed. I recorded every case for each sample year until 1985. Out of a total of 436 cases I coded only 250. The work of coding was laboriously and carefully done by several research assistants: Marilyn Brown, Joy Adapon, and Erin Campbell. Since the Circuit Court covers the entire island of Hawai'i, I selected only those cases on the Hilo side of the island for analysis.

2. "The Social Role of the Courts in the Hawaiian Kingdom." National Endowment for the Humanities, Jane Silverman, Principal Investigator, Peter Nelligan, Assistant. This project was done in the early 1980s. I am grateful to Harry Ball and Jane Silverman for help in using these data and for sharing them with me.

3. The offenses were 20 percent drug and alcohol violations, 17 percent property violations, 14 percent acts of violence, 9 percent offenses against the public order, 9 percent refusal to work, and 8 percent adultery or prostitution. These figures combine District and Circuit Court cases from 1853 to 1903 but provide only Circuit Court data from that time until the 1980s. After 1913 the District Court minute books have disappeared. Moreover, the Circuit Court data from 1852 to 1892 are complete, whereas the other District and Circuit Court data are based on a decade sample.

4. Work offenses were only 4 percent of the cases in 1853, 23 percent in 1863, 40 percent by 1873, 38 percent by 1883, 22 percent by 1893, and none in 1903 after the abolition of the contract labor system following annexation.

5. Ninety-seven percent of the 1863 work defendants were Hawaiians, as were 95 percent of the 1873 defendants, but only 41 percent of the 1883 defendants. The proportion of Chinese defendants grew to 51 percent in the same year, after seven years of large-scale Chinese immigration. In 1893 100 percent of the defendants in work cases were Japanese, eight years after the extensive importation of Japanese laborers began. Public order offenses jumped from 5 percent of the 1893 caseload to 21 percent of the 1903 caseload as vagrancy violations took the place of labor contract violations.

6. Sixteen percent of charges over the whole period were for drug and alcohol violations, but these were only 9 percent of the 1853 caseload and 4 percent of the of the 1863 caseload. By 1873 they had grown to 16 percent of the caseload, 14 percent in 1883, 19 percent in 1893, and 17 percent in 1903.

7. In 1893 defendants were predominantly Chinese (45 percent), Japanese (26 percent), and Hawaiian (21 percent) as well as 4 percent haole and 3 percent Portuguese. The 1891 census of Hilo and its immediate coast reported 26 percent Portuguese, 27 percent Japanese, 12 percent Chinese, and 36 percent Natives, whites, and others (census from Luther Severance, Severance Scrapbook).

8. Chinese were only 1 percent, while the largest proportion of defendants were the Hawaiians (34 percent), Japanese (19 percent), haole (18 percent), Portuguese (17 percent), and Puerto Ricans (8 percent).

9. Gambling offenses grew from 2 percent in 1853, and none in 1863, 4 percent in 1873, none in 1883 to 9 percent in 1893 and 1903. In 1893, 85 percent of the defendants were Japanese. By 1903, after a period of renewed Chinese immigration, 50 percent of the defendants were Japanese, 34 percent were Chinese, 9 percent Portuguese, and 3 percent Puerto Rican.

10. Violence was 19 percent of all cases in 1853, 12 percent in 1863, 10 percent in 1873, 11 percent in 1883, 11 percent in 1893, and 13 percent in 1903.

11. They represented 30 percent of the cases in 1853, 13 percent in 1863, 4 percent in 1873, 26 percent in 1883, 7 percent in 1893, and 11 percent in 1903.

12. Eighty-five percent of all defendants were men: 89 percent in violence cases, 88 percent in drug and alcohol cases, and fully 98 percent in work cases. Only 5 percent of the defendants were female and they were primarily charged with alcohol, family, and violence offenses. Although 7 percent were male and female together, three-quarters of these defendants were accused of adultery or fornication.

13. His portrait, and that of his wife and son, now hang in the Peabody Essex Museum in Salem, Massachusetts.

14. Letter from D. H. Hitchcock to E. G. Hitchcock, January 1, 1861, in Mission Houses Museum Library, Collections of the Hawaiian Mission Children's Society, Honolulu (hereafter HMCS Archives).

15. Hill's social geography of Hilo in 1849 included the observation that the Chinese fill the gap between Europeans and Natives since the distance is too far for marriage being at all equal, although some are successful. Had there been mixed-race children born and educated, they could now marry. He noted that Coan insisted on newcomers being baptized and taught before they were allowed to marry Hawaiian women, and told a story of Coan trying to instruct a Chinese in church so he could

marry. Hill's theory was that the Native's mind is open to new ideas, but that of the Chinese is too rigid, narrowly defined (Hill 1856: 306).

16. From *Reminiscences of Honolulu Thirty-Five Years Ago.* Typescript, listed in card catalogue of Hawai'i State Archives as Saturday Press, 1881, by Henry Sheldon, pp. 27–28.

17. F.O. and Ex., November 1844, Hawai'i State Archives, Honolulu.

18. Interior Dept. Misc. April 1845, Hawai'i State Archives, Honolulu.

19. The letter continues: "The mode of Punishment is by passing a rope or line round the thumbs, fingers, or wrists and a post thus stretched up in the same manner as a man about to be flogged, and a stout stick is incerted [*sic*] in the two parts of the rope and twisted in the way of what is called a Spanish windlass thus compressing the parts to the post; the twisting is continued until the poor culprit promises to pay a bag of pulu or if she has it, or can get it, a rial, or as in the case of a woman last week until she faints away from excess of pain; the only answer returned on being asked why such punishment was inflicted was 'Ka! ua ukiuiki makou' [letters difficult to read]."

20. Interior File. June 29, 1845, Hawai'i State Archives, Honolulu.

21. Interior Dept. Misc., Hawai'i State Archives, Honolulu.

22. Interior Dept. Misc., March 1846, Hawai'i State Archives, Honolulu. Style and spelling as in original.

23. Hawai'i State Archives, Letter Book 1, Interior Dept. Letters, April 45–Nov. 46, p. 317.

24. R. C. Wyllie, Foreign Office Letter Book no. 15, pp. 101–102. Hawai'i State Archives, typed copy.

25. "Appointments by His Majesty the King," *The Polynesian*, January 29, 1848.

26. Letter, John Hoaai, District Judge here in Hilo, to His Highness, Keoni Ana, Minister of the Interior, Pu'u'eo, Hilo, February 10, 1848, trans. E. H. Hart, in Hawai'i State Archives, Honolulu.

27. Biographical information on S. L. Austin from Charles Wetmore, October 7, 1896, in HMCS Archives, handwritten.

28. Severance Scrapbook, p. 281, October 3, 1896, newspaper.

29. "Judge S. L. Austin," *The Friend* 54, 10 (October 1896).

30. "Sudden Death of Judge S. L. Austin." 281 of Severance Scrapbook, Lyman House Memorial Museum.

31. From D. H. Hitchcock, "Forty Years' Reminiscences of Life in Hilo, Hawaii," five articles in the *Hawaii Herald*, April 1, 1897, Severance Scrapbook, p. 211.

32. *Pacific Coast Commercial Record*, San Francisco, May 1, 1892, p. 12.

33. Letter to brother Rexford, Honolulu, March 9, 1857, HMCS Archives, Honolulu; From D. H. Hitchcock, "Forty Years' Reminiscences of Life in Hilo, Hawaii," *Hawaii Herald*, April 1, 1897, Severance Scrapbook, p. 211.

34. Letter to brother Ed, August 7, 1857, HMCS Archives. Hitchcock describes himself as an interpreter in a letter of September 10, 1857, HMCS Archives.

35. Letter to brothers Ed and Rexy, April 22, 1857, says that Judge Austin met them at the beach and they are taking their meals at his house (HMCS Archives.)

36. From D. H. Hitchcock, "Forty Years' Reminiscences of Life in Hilo, Hawaii," *Hawaii Herald*, April 1, 1897, Severance Scrapbook, p. 211.

37. Ibid.

38. Letter to brother Rexford, October 21, 1857, HMCS Archives.

39. Letter from Almeida E. Hitchcock to her sister, Hilo, June 3, 1857, in Lyman House Memorial Museum Library, *The Ancestry of and the Journal of Almeida Widger Hitchcock*, compiled by Nettie Chamberlain Lyman in the 1930s from missionary papers in the missionary archives of the Lyman Museum, Hilo.

40. Letter to brother Ed., January 2, 1858, HMCS Archives.

41. Letter to brother Ed, June 22, 1858, HMCS Archives.

42. Letters from D. H. Hitchcock to Ed and other family members in the HMCS Archives.

43. Humme 1986: 141; Description of Sugar Plantations, The Hawaiian Kingdom, Statistical and Commercial Directory and Tourist's Guide *1880–1881*.

44. *McKenney's Hawaiian Directory* (San Francisco: L. M. McKenney and Co., Publishers, 1884).

45. Letter from D. H. Hitchcock to brother Ed, November 30, 1894, in HMCS Archives.

46. Letter from D. H. Hitchcock to brother Ed, October 8, 1894, HMCS Archives.

47. Almeida Hitchcock's account of Hawaiian law written for her Michigan classmates reveals the late-nineteenth-century construction of Hawaiian law as despotic shared by other Anglo-Hawaiians, a vision that legitimated the new order. She says: "Kamehameha wielded a despotism as absolute probably as the islands ever knew" (Humme 1986: 143).

48. "He Died on Duty," *Hawaiian Gazette*, October 13, 1898, p. 2.

49. Hawaiian Kingdom, Finance Office, March 10, 1870, Hawaii State Archives; Kelly et al. 1981: 87.

50. "Judge Hitchcock's Will," *Star*, December 19, 1898.

51. "He Died on Duty," *Hawaiian Gazette*, October 13, 1898, p. 2.

52. The Archives of the Lyman House Memorial Museum in Hilo, Hawai'i have a genealogy of the Hapai family, from which this information is drawn, with the caveat on the bottom, "no guarantee of complete accuracy."

53. I am indebted to Winifred Lum for sharing her copy of the family genealogy with me.

54. "Judge Hapai Passes Away," *Hilo Tribune Herald*, no. 45, September 1, 1908.

55. Ruth Henderson, "Severances of Augusta," *Kennebec Journal*, April 2, 1969. In Lyman House Memorial Museum, Hilo.

56. Biography of Severance, Lyman House Memorial Museum, B-833 no. 1.

57. Henderson, "Severances of Augusta."

58. Lyman House Memorial Museum, Hilo. Severance File.

59. Photograph in the files of Lyman House Memorial Museum, Hilo.

60. *A Record of the Descendants of David Belden Lyman and Sarah Joiner Lyman of Hawaii, 1832–1933*, compiled by Ellen Goodale Lyman and Elsie Hart Wilcox, issued December 1933, Honolulu, Hawai'i, p. 39. Lyman House Memorial Museum and on file with the author.

61. *Hilo Record*, February 17, 1891, in Severance Scrapbook, p. 36. In this census, the town of Hilo itself had 2,550 inhabitants.

62. Rates of return of laborers: between 1852 and 1887, 26,000 Chinese arrived in the islands and 10,000, or 38 percent, went back to China; of 200,000 Japanese who came between 1885 and 1924, 110,000, or 55 percent, went back to Japan; between

1903 and 1910, 7,300 Koreans arrived and 1,200, or 16 percent, returned; and between 1909 and 1931, 112,800 Filipinos arrived, 18,600 went to the mainland, and 38,900, or 36 percent, went back to the Philippines (Takaki 1989: 169).

63. Interviews with Martin Pence, 1992 and 1993, Honolulu.

CHAPTER 7

1. Kingdom of Hawai'i 1850, An Act for the Government of Masters and Servants, sec. 28.

2. My previous work in New England towns convinced me that the law represents a language and a forum available to working-class people to contest both class and gender power, although they used it more often in conflicts with relative equals than with superiors (Merry 1990).

3. One of the Circuit Court judges at the time was F. S. Lyman, brother of Rufus Lyman and son of the missionary Lymans.

4. *Daily Commercial Pacific Advertiser*, January 30, 1883, p. 2.

5. It is likely that there were not forty-eight different defendants, since some of the defendants with the same number have different names. Some were probably charged with more than one offense and there may have been some confusion in the court about identities.

6. According to a prominent planter, wages of ordinary plantation laborer in the early history of the industry were five dollars or less per month, usually paid in goods, which gradually increased to ten dollars and thirteen dollars per month in 1876. Wages then went up to twenty and twenty-five dollars per month. By the 1890s plantations paid from thirteen to twenty dollars a month. The laborers were usually housed on the plantations in wooden houses. "On well-conducted plantations the rows of neatly whitewashed laborers' houses, surrounded with vegetable gardens, with here and there an attempt at a flower garden, present a conformable and homelike appearance. When the extent of the pasture land on the plantation permits, they are allowed to keep a cow or two and horses" (Baldwin 1894: 668).

7. "Hilo Happenings," *Daily Commercial Advertiser* 1890, in Severance Scrapbook, p. 32.

8. Davis and Davis (1962) say that there were fifty men and two women still on the plantations, of whom only four were still under contract.

9. I am indebted to Carol Greenhouse for this interpretation.

10. The Native Hawaiians similarly quickly acquired the skills and knowledge to use the law. As the Native Hawaiians became sophisticated participants in the legal system through law schools, such as those at which Hitchcock taught, through the distribution of law books, as indicated in Pitman's letters, and through widespread literacy, they began to use the courts themselves to seek redress and become active in politics (see also Matsuda 1988a). They developed a sophisticated legal consciousness and moved inside the law rather than remaining outside its discourses. Many became judges, attorneys, sheriffs, and constables in the nineteenth century.

11. As Fuchs points out, by the 1960s and 1970s Japanese Americans were dominant in political activities and state education at all levels. By 1975 the Asian American population had levels of educational attainment, employment, occupational distribution, median income, and home ownership above that of the haoles and had family

incomes far above those of locally born Filipinos, Hawaiians, Portuguese, and Puerto Ricans (Fuchs 1983: xv).

CHAPTER 8

1. Sexual offense cases dropped from 44 percent in 1853 to 28 percent in 1863, 2 percent in 1883, and 3 percent in 1903. The total number of cases of adultery and fornication dropped from 47 in 1853 to 38 in 1863, 14 in 1873, 5 in 1883, 2 in 1893, and 22 in 1903, even though caseloads grew steadily throughout the period.

2. Sex acts are, she argues, arrayed in a hierarchical system of value that places married, reproductive heterosexuals at the top, unmarried monogamous heterosexuals in couples below them, and far beneath, in the arena of bad, abnormal, unnatural sexuality transsexuals, transvestites, fetishists, sadomasochists, sex workers such as prostitutes, and cross-generational sexual actors. The stable lesbian and gay male couple is now verging on respectability, but the promiscuous gay man and the bar dyke are close to the line of stigmatized sexuality. She argues that the boundary between heterosexual, marital, monogamous, reproductive, noncommercial sex that takes place at home and that which involves pornography, sex toys, promiscuity, commercialism, masturbation, or takes place in public settings is a critical line that stands between cultural definitions of sexual order and chaos (Rubin 1993 [1984]: 14).

3. Fitzpatrick notes that modern law claims universal applicability but marks out a free, private realm of the family within which the subject engages in self-governance subject to the forms of self-discipline and policing embodied in the microtechnologies of power of the modern period (Fitzpatrick 1992: 180).

4. It is difficult to make firm statements about the nature of Hawaiian marriage practices in the period between 1778 and the late nineteenth century for three reasons. First, the sources are often Hawaiians who have been trained in missionary schools and consequently interpret Hawaiian kinship through the highly critical lens provided by the missionary intent on reformulating the Hawaiian approach to marriage and of sexuality. Second, marriage practices were themselves changing in a fairly significant way over time, in response to the pressure of missionaries and marriage and divorce laws enforced with varying levels of enthusiasm by the government. The family pattern of 1778 was probably quite different from that of 1820 when the first missionaries arrived and again probably quite different from 1845 when coverture was introduced. Third, it is clear that the speed with which new social forms and practices penetrated Hawaiian society differed greatly in urban and rural areas. While Honolulu, Lāhainā, and to a lesser extent Hilo were inundated with ships, foreigners, and new opportunities to marry and earn cash and goods for sexual work, rural areas remained, to highly variable degrees, less changed. Kʻaū on the island of Hawaiʻi was perhaps one of the most isolated. Thus an account of kinship from the 1930s by Pukui and Handy, writing in an anthropological tradition, is somewhat more representative of Hawaiian kinship of the earlier periods than studies of more urban areas. In addition to rural/urban differences, there was a major difference between the social lives of commoners and chiefs. The latter are far better described by visiting merchants, whalers, and missionaries than the former, and are more clearly presented in the accounts of missionized Hawaiians such as John Papa ʻIʻī and Samuel Kamakau. Jocelyn Linnekin, in her study of the changes in landholding by women following the

Māhele in 1848, relies on written sources as well as court documents produced during
the Māhele discussing land ownership and land division as the basis for her analysis
of the family at mid nineteenth century (Linnekin 1990). Sahlins's study of
Anahulu (1992) similarly relies on Māhele documents and statements of contemporary observers.

5. In addition to the common form of marriage, there was a more formal or ceremonial marriage, hoʻāo (Handy and Pukui 1972: 52). Kamakau describes hoʻāo as
"the binding form of Hawaiian marriage" (Kamakau 1961: 347). It could not be
dissolved and it involved ceremony and reciprocal exchanges between the families,
and children born to the couple sealed the relationship between the two families.
Kamakau, as a Christian convert, disapproved of the loose form of marriage. He said
it was a cause of trouble and brought on quarreling. But hoʻāo was the custom of the
chiefs, the first-born children of prominent people, and children who were family
favorites. Among the commoners, first-born children of prominent people and chosen
favorites were most likely to become family leaders and to have more enduring marriages. For these individuals, stable marriages were fundamental to the maintenance
of the local group, whereas junior siblings tended to wander more broadly (Sahlins
1992). Linnekin questions whether hoʻāo paʻa was a recognized social practice in
pre-Christian times, but if so, this indicates that some relationships were expected to
create a bond between families and were marked by feasting and exchanges, whereas
casual relationships were not.

6. ʻĪʻī tells a story of Kamehameha's sexual activities, which angered the husband
of the women who favored him. ʻĪʻī was born on Oʻahu in 1800 and was close to the
chiefs as well as a Christian convert. His stories, although revealing his respect for
Hawaiian history, are filtered through a Christian education (see chapter 4). He wrote
his articles in *Fragments* between 1866 and 1870, inspired by Samuel M. Kamakau's
newspaper articles (Ii 1959: Emory preface). Kamehameha, ʻĪʻī says, was attractive to
women, as was his younger brother, and the chiefesses gave them many gifts, but
they angered their uncle Kalaniʻōpuʻu when they had sexual relations with his wife
(ʻĪʻī 1959: 7). In 1809, Kanihonui, a nephew of Kamehameha, was put to death for
committing adultery with Kaʻahumanu (ʻĪʻī 1959: 51). Kamakau's interpretation of
this incident emphasizes its political ramifications (Kamakau 1961: 194). Kamehameha put his adopted son to death because he feared that if Kaʻahumanu had a
lover among the chiefs, it would lead her to rebel against his rule, drawing away her
relatives and leading to war. This story indicates that the sexual liaisons of the aliʻi
nui were politically charged, while the contrast between the two stories suggests
caution in interpreting what they mean.

7. For example, ʻĪʻī tells of an incident that happened when he was eight or nine
(about 1809). There were houses burned in Waimānalo, Oʻahu, and the overseer in
charge of the burning told the residents that it was so ordered by the royal court
because the people there had given shelter to the chiefess, Kūwahine, who ran away
from her husband Kalanimōku after associating wrongfully with someone. She was a
daughter of the Kaikioʻewa who raised Kamehameha III in his infancy. "She had run
away because she had been beaten for her offense and for other reasons, too, perhaps.
She had remained hidden for about four or five days before she was found. Here we
see the sadness that befell the people through the fault of the chiefs. The punishment
fell on others, though they were not to blame" (ʻĪʻī 1959: 29). Again, Kamakau puts a
different slant on the incident, noting that the thief was Kuakini and that Kalanimōku,

the war chief, loved his wife and took her loss hard (Kamakau 1961: 197). Kamehameha helped him to recover his wife by setting fire to all the houses of chiefs as
well as commoners and even to his own houses, warning people to have all property
removed from the houses first. As soon as Kūwahine was restored, the house burning
ceased. Here the incident seems a contest among powerful ali'i over a desirable
young woman.

8. Cheever tells a story that again reveals how different attitudes toward dress and
body covering contribute to European interpretations of Hawaiian childlikeness. He
tells the story of a marriage ceremony he witnessed in Kohala in which one of the
grooms appeared alone in the church. When the missionary asked him where his
bride was, he said she was at the church door putting on her frock. Cheever and the
missionary Bond found the moment very droll and amusing and long after "food for
fun." The bride had probably carried her dress and shoes for some miles, Cheever
says, since Hawaiians were not accustomed to wearing shoes and generally carried
them, putting them on only at the door of the church or the missionary's house
(Cheever 1856: 183–184). Differences in dress and notions of covering the body
produced a reaction of merry condescension on the part of these Americans toward
the Hawaiian converts.

9. Davin describes the emergence of a similar critique of mothers as a response to
population declines in early-twentieth-century Britain, which evoked an analogous
demand for training mothers rather than providing them the food, improved housing,
and better medical care they needed to reduce infant mortality (Davin 1997).

10. ABCFM Records, vol. 13, nos. 10–12, Houghton Library, Harvard University.

11. Ibid.

12. In his appendix to *Typee*, Herman Melville (1964) accuses Kekūanao'a of taking a cut from the prostitutes, based on his visit to Honolulu in the 1840s.

13. Linnekin notes that although women flocked to the ships of visiting Europeans
in the years after 1778 in large numbers to make alliances with the newcomers, only
the commoners provided sex, while chiefly women gave gifts (Linnekin 1990: 56).

14. James Ely, *Missionary Herald* 24 (September 1828): 275, quoted in Schmitt
and Strombel 1966: 267.

15. A woman may obtain permission to divorce from the governor if her husband
has left her and failed to communicate for four years or if he has been banished to
another island for four years or more. If either party's spouse is convicted of adultery
and if he or she has a good character, the person may divorce.

16. In 1840 one high chief, eager to remarry but frustrated by the constraint posed
by his still-living wife, took the logical step and poisoned her, thus freeing himself to
remarry. The Hawaiian king hanged the murderer, somewhat to the surprise of Hawaiians and some European visitors (Gutmanis 1974).

17. Chapter XXI of the laws of 1842 also defines parental duties. Parents should
direct the child and are not allowed commit the child to the care of another without
going before an officer and making their agreement in writing. This provision is
clearly directed to controlling the widespread practice of hānai or adoption. A parent
should instruct or punish a child if it is at fault. "They commit no crime by inflicting
pain on a mischievous child." But it is a crime to punish a child unmercifully, and a
parent who maltreats a child can be brought to trial and the child removed and given
to a good man, while the parent is fined to pay for care of the child.

18. Schmitt notes that in 1841 Native Hawaiian workers on the plantations were

paid 12½ cents a day (Schmitt 1967: 358). Three years later, Wyllie wrote that the average daily wage was 12½ cents, usually paid in goods (ibid.). According to Morgan, unskilled labor in 1844 earned from two to six dollars a month, with the highest pay near port towns. By 1853 or 1854 Hawaiians were hired for twenty-five cents a day and "free coolies" (Chinese workers not on contract) were available for eighteen cents a day (Morgan 1948, quoted in Schmitt 1967: 358). In the early 1850s imported Chinese contract laborers were paid thirty-six dollars a year in addition to food, housing, clothing, and transport (Lydon 1975: 15).

19. Territory v. Armstrong, 28 Haw. 88; Supreme Court of Hawaii Reports 1924: 92.

20. Supreme Court Reports 1924: 94.

21. In 1924 the Supreme Court upheld this distinction, arguing that the distinction of gender was rooted in nature (Territory v. Armstrong, 28 Haw. 88).

22. In order to look more closely at court cases involving the transformation of the family and gender relations, my research assistant Erin Campbell recorded every case in the Hilo District Court minute books between 1852 and 1913 that involved either wife battering or wife desertion, both of which were less common than adultery cases. We recorded 427 cases in which a man battered his wife.

23. In order to arrive at this figure from the ten-year samples, I multiplied the number for each sample year by ten.

24. The vast majority of desertion cases reporting violence occurred between 1878 and 1889: thirty-nine, or 91 percent of all the desertion cases in which violence appeared in the court records. Overall, however, only 46 percent (84) of all desertion cases appeared during this period, suggesting that it was a particularly tumultuous era. This was a period of significant social transformation in Hilo as the effects of the Reciprocity Treaty spurred the development of plantations and the importation of laborers and the growth of the town.

25. Of the 427 wife battering cases, the court found the violent husband not guilty 13 percent of the time and nolle prossed the case 11 percent of the time. Only two were sent to hard labor. Two thirds (63 percent) were convicted and received a fine of less than one hundred dollars, generally about six dollars, but this rate of conviction is considerably below that of the overall district court rate of 86 percent. Assault cases posed serious evidentiary problems. Assault cases required witnesses who saw the incident of violence. If they heard a fight but did not see the blow, their evidence received a good deal less weight. A woman's testimony alone that she had been battered was not sufficient for a conviction, by and large. The severity of violence was also of critical importance. A severely injured woman was far more persuasive than one who claimed to be afraid, who said her hair was pulled and she was knocked down, or that she had been punched. Use of weapons, which was quite rare, and serious injuries tended to increase the size of the fine and the likelihood of conviction. The closer the incident came to a mutual fight and moderately serious injuries with no eyewitnesses, the less likely a judge was to convict. The evidentiary issues for wife desertion cases, by comparison, were far easier. If she left, it was generally easy to find witnesses to her whereabouts. The only question was whether or not the couple was formally married. This issue did not always come up, but when it did there was recourse to judges and church officials who carried out marriages and kept records.

26. Statistics from *The Friend*, a Honolulu newspaper, from 1843 indicate that in Honolulu at that time there were 576 American or American-affiliated residents, of whom sixty-one had American wives and fifty-seven Native wives (Greer 1968: 4). An 1849 census of the islands indicates that there were 133 foreign men living with foreign wives in the kingdom and 343 living with Native wives, but there were only fifty-nine foreigners in Hilo altogether (Cheever 1856: 391).

27. Linnekin cites 1862 statistics on the declining native population from the *Polynesian* (August 2, 1862) that suggest that the death toll from disease was higher among girls and young women than men: the ratio of males to females under twenty increased from 109:100 in 1853 to 117:100 in 1860, after a devastating smallpox epidemic (Linnekin 1990:210). In 1872 the census reported a gender ratio in Hilo of 136:100, with a male population of 2,065 and a female population of 1,522 (Linnekin 1990: 211). The gender disparity was primarily among younger people rather than adults. In the 1850 census of the entire population, the male/female ratio among adults aged thirty-one to fifty-two was approximately even (Schmitt 1968: 43, cited in Linnekin 1990: 212). Hawaiian men were less often married than Hawaiian women. In the 1862 *Polynesian* article, the ratio of unmarried native men to unmarried native women was 123:100 in 1853 and 129:100 in 1860. Linnekin argues that the gender disparity in population is probably the result of different mortality rates among children, but acknowledges that this does not account for the married/unmarried contrast, which she thinks is related to the greater mobility of males, while women stayed behind on the land to inherit (Linnekin 1990: 212).

28. Many cases of wife desertion involved Hawaiian women married to foreign men. On November 1, 1887, for example, a Chinese husband took his Native Hawaiian wife to court for desertion. Apu (Chinese) charged Miala Apu (wahine [woman in Hawaiian]) with deserting her husband in Onomea, Hilo, October 30 1887. She denied her guilt. She agreed that she deserted her husband but said that she was afraid to talk to Apu because she feared he would beat her up and kill her. Apu testified that he did not say he would beat her up and kill her. "I told her that I would beat her up and hurt her for her talking sassy at me. At the time I told her that my work clothes were in a bad way and that she should sew my shirts. She said she would not do so." Keka testified: "I went to get Miala to return to her husband. She answered she would not return because of the suit." The court ordered the two of them to live together in peace. Miala refused and said she would not return to Apu and wanted a divorce. Judge G. W. A. Hapai sent Miala to jail at hard labor for one month along with a fine for the payment of court costs, $3.80. Preserving the marriage was more important than protecting the wife in this case. Hapai typically sought to preserve the marriage. This case was translated from the Hawaiian by Esther Mookini.

29. Hawaii Revised Statutes 12, 1985 Replacement: Supplemental Commentary on Chapter 707–715: 165–171.

REFERENCES

Abu-Lughod, Lila. 1993. *Writing Women's Worlds: Bedouin Stories*. Berkeley and Los Angeles: University of California Press.

Alexander, M. Jacqui, and Chandra Talpade Mohanty, eds. 1997. *Feminist Geneologies, Colonial Legacies, Democratic Futures*. New York: Routledge.

Anderson, Benedict. 1991 [1983]. *Imagined Communities*. Rev. ed. London: Verso.

Anderson, Rufus. 1866. *Kapiolani: Heroine of Hawaii*. From "Hours at Home" for May 1866. New York: Charles Scribner and Co.

Andrews, Lorin. 1836. "Letter from Lahainaluna." *Missionary Herald* (October): 390–391.

Anghie, Antony. 1996. "Francisco de Vitoria and the Colonial Origins of International Law." *Social and Legal Studies* 5: 321–336.

Anon. 1864. *From Chamber's Journal*: A Doomed People. *Eclectic Magazine* 64 (February): 250–256.

Anon. 1865. "Hawaiians Compared with Other Polynesians." *The Friend* 23 (December 1): 89.

Baldwin, H. P. 1894. "The Sugar Industry in Hawaii." *Overland Monthly* 25: 663–668.

Beechert, Edward D. 1985. *Working in Hawaii: A Labor History*. Honolulu: University of Hawaii Press.

———. 1993. "Patterns of Resistance and the Social Relations of Production in Hawaii." Pp. 45–69 in *Plantation Workers: Resistance and Accomodation*. Honolulu: University of Hawaii Press.

Bhabha, Homi. 1997. "Of Mimicry and Man: The Ambivalence of Colonial Discourse." Pp. 152–162 in *Tensions of Empire: Colonial Cultures in a Bourgeois World*, ed. Frederick Cooper and Ann Laura Stoler, Berkeley and Los Angeles: University of California Press.

———. 1998. "Anxiety in the Midst of Difference." *Polar: Political and Legal Anthropology Review* 21 (1): 123–37.

Bingham, Hiram. 1981 [1847]. *A Residence of Twenty-One Years in the Sandwich Islands*. Rutland, Vt.: Charles E. Tuttle Co.

Bird, Isabella L. 1882 [1875]. *Six Months among the Sandwich Islands*. Fifth ed. New York: G. P. Putnam's Sons.

Bishop, Sereno. 1893. "America in Hawaii: The Strategic Position of the Islands, and the History of American Diplomacy and Influence in Hawaiian Affairs." *The Review of Reviews* 7 (33): 180–185.

Blaisdell, Kekuni, and Noreen Mokuau. 1994. "*Kanaka Maoli*: Indigenous Hawaiians." Pp. 49–68 in *Hawai'i: Return to Nationhood*, ed. Ulla Hasager and Jonathan Friedman. Copenhagen: IWGIA Document no. 75.

Boelen, Jacobus. 1988. *A Merchant's Perspective: Captain Jacobus Boelen's Narrative of his Visit to Hawai'i in 1828*, translated, with an introduction and notes by Frank J. A. Boeze. Honolulu: Hawaiian Historical Society.

Borovsky, Robert. 1997. "Cook, Lono, Obeyesekere, and Sahlins." *Current Anthropology* 38: 255–282.

Bradley, Harold Whitman. 1968. *The American Frontier in Hawaii.* Gloucester, Mass.: Peter Smith. (Reissue of the 1943 edition.)

Brigham, John. 1996. *The Constitution of Interests: Beyond the Politics of Rights.* New York: New York University Press.

Brown, Nathan. 1995. "Law and Imperialism: Egypt in Comparative Perspective." *Law and Society Review* 29: 103–127.

Brown, Wendy. 1995. *States of Injury: Power and Freedom in Late Modernity.* Princeton, N.J.: Princeton University Press.

Buck, Elizabeth. 1993. *Paradise Remade: The Politics of Culture and History in Hawai'i.* Philadelphia: Temple University Press.

Burke, John G. 1972. "The Wild Man's Pedigree." Pp. 266–267 in *The Wild Man Within,* ed. Edward Dudley and Maximilian Novak. Pittsburgh: Pittsburgh University Press.

Burman, Sandra, and Barbara E. Harrell-Bond, eds. 1979. *The Imposition of Law.* New York: Academic Press.

Case, Suzanne Espenett. 1992. "Almeda Eliza Hitchcock (Moore)." Pp. 17–36 in *Called from Within: Early Women Lawyers of Hawai'i,* ed. Mari J. Matsuda. Honolulu: University of Hawai'i Press.

Chanock, Martin. 1985. *Law, Custom, and Social Order: The Colonial Experience in Malawi and Zambia.* Cambridge, Eng.: Cambridge University Press.

———. 1995. "Criminological Science and the Criminal Law in the Colonial Periphery: Perception, Fantasy, and Realities in South Africa 1900–1930." *Law and Social Inquiry* 20: 911–941.

Chatterjee, P. 1989. "Colonialism, Nationalism, and Colonized Women: The Contest in India." *American Ethnologist* 16: 622–633.

Cheever, Henry T. 1856. *The Island World of the Pacific.* New York: Harper and Brothers.

———. n.d. "Letters from the South Seas, 1842–44." Scrapbook of clippings from the *New York Evangelist.* American Antiquarian Society, Cheever Family Papers c.1800–c.1900, vol. 2.

Chinen, Jon J. 1958. *The Great Mahele: Hawaii's Land Division of 1848.* Honolulu: University of Hawaii Press.

Ching, Nadine. 1980. "Adultery and Fornication as Used in the Hawaiian and Tahitian Bibles." No. 4 in *Ka Unuhi: The Translator.* Department of Indo-Pacific Languages, University of Hawaii, Honolulu, vol. 1.

Classen, Constance, David Howes, and Anthony Synnott. 1994. *Aroma: The Cultural History of Smell.* London: Routledge.

Coan, T. M. 1879. "The Peopling of Hawaii." *The Nation* 29 (741): 170–171.

———. 1882. *Life in Hawaii: An Autobiographic Sketch of Mission Life and Labors (1835–1881).* New York: Anson D. F. Randolph & Company.

Cohn, Bernard S. 1996. *Colonialism and its Forms of Knowledge.* Princeton, N.J.: Princeton University Press.

Cole, Douglas, and Ira Chaikin. 1990. *An Iron Hand upon the People: The Law against the Potlatch on the Northwest Coast.* Vancouver/Toronto: Douglas & McIntyre; Seattle: University of Washington Press.

Collier, Jane Fishburne. 1988. *Marriage and Inequality in Classless Societies.* Stanford, Calif.: Stanford University Press.

Collier, Jane, William Maurer, and L. Suarez-Navaz. 1995. "Introduction to Special Issue on Sanctioned Identities." *Identities: Global Studies in Culture and Power* 2: 1–29.

Comaroff, Jean. 1997. "The Emperor's Old Clothes: Fashioning the Colonial Subject." Pp. 400–420 in *Situated Lives: Gender and Culture in Everyday Life*, ed. Louise Lamphere, Helena Ragone, and Patricia Zavella. New York: Routledge.

Comaroff, Jean and John L. Comaroff. 1986. "Christianity and Colonialism in South Africa." *American Ethnologist* 13:1–22.

———. 1991. *Of Revelation and Revolution: Christianity, Colonialism, and Consciousness in South Africa*, vol. 1. Chicago: University of Chicago Press.

Comaroff, John L. 1989. "Images of Empire, Contests of Conscience: Models of Colonial Domination in South Africa." *American Ethnologist* 16: 661–685.

———. 1995. "Ethnicity, Nationalism, and the Politics of Difference in an Age of Revolution." Pp. 243–276 in *Perspectives on Nationalism and War*, ed. John L. Comaroff and Paul C. Stern. Sydney: Gordon and Breach.

Comaroff, John L. and Jean Comaroff. 1992. *Ethnography and the Historical Imagination*. Boulder, Colo.: Westview.

———. 1997. *Of Revelation and Revolution: The Dialectics of Modernity on a South African Frontier*, vol. 2. Chicago: University of Chicago Press.

Comaroff, John L., and S. Roberts. 1981. *Rules and Processes: The Cultural Logic of Dispute in an African Context*. Chicago: University of Chicago Press.

Conley, John, and William O'Barr. 1990. *Rules vs. Relationships*. Chicago: University of Chicago Press.

Conrad, Agnes C., ed. 1975. "Hawaii in 1855." From *Borta ar bra, men hemme ar bast*, by C. Axel Egerstrom, translated from the Swedish by Caroline Bengston. *Hawaiian Journal of History* 9: 37–59.

Cook, J. 1894. "Boston Monday Lectures: Shall We Annex Hawaii?" *Our Day: Record and Review of Current Reform* 13: 124–132.

Cooper, Frederick. 1980. *From Slaves to Squatters: Plantation Labor and Agriculture in Zanzibar and Coastal Kenya, 1890–1925*. New Haven: Yale University Press.

———. 1987. "Contracts, Crime, and Agrarian Conflict: From Slave to Wage Labour on the East African Coast." Pp. 228–253 in *Law, Labour, and Crime: An Historical Perspective*, ed. Francis Snyder and Douglas Hay. London: Tavistock.

———. 1989. "From Free Labor to Family Allowances: Labor and African Society in Colonial Discourse." *American Ethnologist* 16: 745–765.

———. 1997. "The Dialectics of Decolonization: Nationalism and Labor Movements in Postwar French Africa." Pp. 406–435 in *Tensions of Empire: Colonial Cultures in a Bourgeois World*, ed. Frederick Cooper and Ann Laura Stoler. Berkeley and Los Angeles: University of California Press.

Cooper, Frederick, and Ann Laura Stoler, eds. 1997. *Tensions of Empire: Colonial Cultures in a Bourgeois World*. Berkeley and Los Angeles: University of California Press.

Cotterrell, Roger. 1995. *Law's Community*. Oxford: Oxford University Press.

Damon, S. C. 1857. The Biography of William Little Lee. Published by Request—Tribute. Text of a discourse delivered at Seamen's Chapel in Honolulu, May 31, 1857. *Tribute to the Memory of Hon. William L. Lee*. Honolulu: H. M. Whitney's Press.

Darian-Smith, Eve. 1995. "Law in Place: Legal Mediations of National Identity and State Territory in Europe." Pp. 27–44 in *Nationalism, Racism and the Rule of Law*, ed. Peter Fitzpatrick Aldershot: Dartmouth.

———. 1996. "Postcolonialism: A Brief Introduction." *Social and Legal Studies* 5: 291–301.

———. 1999. *Bridging Divides: The Channel Tunnel and English Legal Identities in the New Europe*. Berkeley and Los Angeles: University of California Press.

Davenport, William. 1969. "The Hawaiian Cultural Revolution: Some Political and Economic Considerations." *American Anthropologist* 71: 1–20.

Davin, Anna. 1997. "Imperialism and Motherhood." Pp. 87–151 in *Tensions of Empire: Colonial Cultures in a Bourgeois World*, ed. Frederick Cooper and Ann Laura Stoler. Berkeley and Los Angeles: University of California Press.

Davis, Eleanor H., and Carl D. Davis 1962. *Norwegian Labor in Hawaii—The Norse Immigrants*. Honolulu: Industrial Relations Center.

Daws, Gavan. 1967. "The Decline of Puritanism at Honolulu in the Ninteenth Century." *Hawaiian Journal of History* 1: 31–43.

———. 1968. *Shoal of Time: A History of the Hawaiian Islands*. Honolulu: University of Hawaii Press.

De Boeck, Filip. 1996. "Postcolonialism, Power and Identity: Local and Global Perspectives from Zaire." Pp. 75–107 in *Postcolonial Identities in Africa*, ed. Richard Werbner and Terence Ranger. London: Zed Books.

Doty. 1969. "Introduction." In *Polynesian Researches: Hawaii*, by William Ellis. New ed., enlarged and improved. Rutland, Vt.: Charles E. Tuttle Co.

Durand, Ralph. 1914. *A Handbook to the Poetry of Rudyard Kipling*. Garden City, N.Y.: Doubleday, Page, and Company.

Dutton, Meiric K. 1953. *William L. Lee: His Address at the Opening of the First Term of the Superior Court . . . Biographical Note by Meiric K. Dutton*. Honolulu: Loomis House Press.

Elias, Norbert. 1994 [1939]. *The Civilizing Process: The History of Manners and State Formation and Civilization*, trans. Edmund Jephcott. Oxford: Blackwell.

Ellis, William. 1969. *Polynesian Researches: Hawaii*. New ed., enlarged and improved. Rutland, Vt.: Charles E. Tuttle Co.

Escobar, Arturo. 1995. *Encountering Development: The Making and Unmaking of the Third World*. Princeton, N.J.: Princeton University Press.

Evans-Pritchard, E. E. 1940. *The Nuer*. Oxford: Oxford University Press.

Ewick, Patricia, and Susan Silbey. 1998. *The Common Place of Law*. Chicago: University of Chicago Press.

Fanon, Frantz. 1963. *Wretched of the Earth*. New York: Grove.

Ferguson, James. 1994. *The Anti-Politics Machine: Development, Depoliticization, and Bureaucratic Power in Lesotho*. Minneapolis: University of Minnesota Press.

Firth, Raymond. 1936. *We, the Tikopia*. New York: American Book Company.

Fitch, George H. 1888. "The Pygmy Kingdom of a Debauchee." *The Cosmopolitan* 4: 123–133.

Fitzpatrick, Peter. 1987. "Transformations of Law and Labour in Papua, New Guinea." Pp. 253–298 in *Law, Labour, and Crime: An Historical Perspective*, ed. Francis Snyder and Douglas Hay. London: Tavistock.

———. 1992. *The Mythology of Modern Law*. London: Routledge.

Foucault, Michel. 1979. *Discipline and Punish: The Birth of the Prison*. New York: Vintage.

———. 1980a. "Truth and Power." Pp. 109–126 in *Power/Knowledge: Selected Interviews and Other Writings 1972–1977*, ed. Colin Gordon. New York: Pantheon.

———. 1980b. "Two Lectures." Pp. 78–108 in *Power/Knowledge: Selected Interviews and Other Writings 1972–1977*, ed. Colin Gordon. New York: Pantheon.

———. 1991. "Governmentality." Pp. 87–105 in *The Foucault Effect: Studies in Governmentality*, ed. Graham Burchell, Colin Gordon, and Peter Miller. Chicago: University of Chicago Press.

———. 1996 [1980]. *The History of Sexuality, Vol. I*, trans. Robert Hurley. London: Penguin.

Frear, Walter F. 1894. "Evolution of the Hawaiian Judiciary." *Papers of the Hawaiian Historical Society* 7: 1–25.

Freycinet, Louis Claude de Saulses de. 1978. *Hawai'i in 1819: A Narrative Account by Louis Claude de Saulses de Freycinet*, trans. Ella L. Wiswell, notes and comments by Marion Kelly. Pacific Anthropological Records, No. 26. Department of Anthropology, Bernice Pauahi Bishop Museum, Honolulu, Hawai'i.

Friedman, Jonathan. 1988. "No History Is an Island: An Exchange between Jonathan Friedman and Marshall Sahlins." *Critique of Anthropology* 8: 7–39.

Fuchs, Lawrence H. 1961 [1983 preface]. *Hawaii Pono: An Ethnic and Political History*. Honolulu: Bess Press.

Gailey, Christine. 1987. *From Kinship to Kingship: Gender Hierarchy and State Formation in the Tongan Islands*. Austin, Tex.: University of Texas Press.

Geertz, Clifford. 1983. *Local Knowledge: Further Essays in Interpretive Anthropology*. New York: Basic Books.

———. 1995. "Culture War." *New York Review of Books* (November 30): 4–6.

Gellner, Ernest. 1983. *Nations and Nationalism*. Ithaca, N.Y.: Cornell University Press.

George, Milton C. 1948. *The Development of Hilo, Hawaii, TH, or A Slice Through Time at a Place Called Hilo*. Ann Arbor, Mich.: Edwards Letter Shop.

Gething, Judith. 1977. "Christianity and Coverture: Impact on the Legal Status of Women in Hawaii, 1820–1920." *Hawaiian Journal of History* 11: 188–220.

Glick, Clarence E. 1980. *Sojourners and Settlers: Chinese Migrants in Hawaii*. Honolulu: University Press of Hawaii.

Gluckman, Max. 1955. *The Judicial Process among the Barotse of Northern Rhodesia*. Manchester: Manchester University Press.

Godkin, E. L. 1893. "Hawaii." *The Nation* 56 (1441): 96.

Goldman, Irving. 1970. *Ancient Polynesian Society*. Chicago: University of Chicago Press.

Gordon, Colin. 1991. "Governmental Rationality: An Introduction." Pp. 1–53 in *The Foucault Effect: Studies in Governmentality*, ed. Graham Burchell, Colin Gordon, and Peter Miller. Chicago: University of Chicago Press.

Gould, Stephen Jay. 1996. *The Mismeasure of Man*. Rev. ed. New York: Norton.

Gramsci, Antonio. 1971. *Selections from the Prison Notebooks*, ed. and trans. Quintin Hoare and Geoffrey Nowell Smith. New York: International Publishers.

Greenhouse, Carol. 1986. *Praying for Justice*. Ithaca, N.Y.: Cornell University Press.

Greenhouse, Carol, Barbara Yngvesson, and David Engel. 1994. *Law and Community in Three American Towns*. Ithaca, N.Y.: Cornell University Press.

Greer, Richard. 1968. "A Sketch of Ke-Kua-Nohu, 1845–1850, with Notes of Other Times Before and After." *Hawaiian Journal of History* 2: 3–41.

Gribble, T. Graham. 1893. "American Annexation of Hawaii." *Engineering Magazine* 4: 898–905.

Griffin, Eldon. 1938. *Clippers and Consuls: American Consular and Commercial Relations with Eastern Asia, 1845–1860.* Ann Arbor, Mich.: Edwards Bros.

Grimshaw, Patricia. 1985. "New England Missionary Wives, Hawaiian Women, and 'The Cult of True Womanhood.'" *Hawaiian Journal of History* 19: 71–100.

————. 1989. *Paths of Duty: American Missionary Wives in Nineteenth-Century Hawaii.* Honolulu: University of Hawaii Press.

Grip, Johan Anton Wolff. 1884. "The Condition of the Swedish and Norwegian Laborers on the Hawaiian Islands. Report by Mr. A. Grip to the Minister of Foreign Affairs at Stockholm." *Honolulu Almanac and Directory, 1884*: 41–55.

Guha, Ranajit. 1997. *Dominance without Hegemony: History and Power in Colonial India.* Cambridge, Mass.: Harvard University Press.

Gulliver, P. H. 1963. *Social Control in an African Society.* London: Routledge and Kegan Paul.

Gutmanis, June. 1974. "The Law . . . Shall Punish All Men Who Commit Crime." *Hawaiian Journal of History* 8: 143–145.

Hall, Stuart, David Held, and Tony McGrew. 1992. "The Question of Cultural Identity." Pp. 274–325 in *Modernity and Its Futures.* Cambridge, Eng.: Polity Press.

Handy, E. S. Craighill, and Mary Kawena Pukui. 1972 [1958]. *The Polynesian Family System in Ka-'u, Hawai'i.* Rutland, Vt.: Charles E. Tuttle.

Hanlon, David, Lilikalā Kameʻeleihiwa, Nicholas Thomas, Valerio Valeri, and Ganath Obeyesekere. 1994. "Book Review Forum: Ganath Obeyesekere, The Apotheosis of Captain Cook." *Pacific Studies* 17: 103–155.

Harvey, David. 1989. *The Condition of Postmodernity.* Oxford: Blackwells.

Hasager, Ulla, and Jonathan Friedman, eds. 1994. *Hawaiʻi: Return to Nationhood.* Copenhagen: International Work Group for Indigenous Affairs, Document no. 75.

Hawaii Island (Hawaii). 1996. *County of Hawaii Data Book 1995.* Hilo: Department of Research and Development, County of Hawaii.

Higham, John. 1970 [1955]. *Strangers in the Land: Patterns of American Nativism, 1860–1925.* Reprint. New York: Atheneum.

Hill, S. S. 1856. *Travels in the Sandwich and Society Islands.* London: Chapman and Hall.

Hoffnung, A. 1893. "The Revolution in Hawaii." *(The Imperial and) Asiatic Quarterly Review (and Oriental and Colonial Record)* 15: 406–416.

Hooker M. B. 1975. *Legal Pluralism: An Introduction to Colonial and Neo-Colonial Laws.* Oxford: Clarendon Press.

Hoxie, Frederick E. 1989 [1984]. *A Final Promise: The Campaign to Assimilate the Indians, 1880–1920.* Cambridge, Eng.: Cambridge University Press.

Humme, June Hitchcock. 1986. "Almeida Hitchcock: First Woman Lawyer." *Hawaiian Journal of History* 20: 137–150.

Humphrey, S. J. n.d. *Titus Coan: Missionary and Explorer, 1801–1882.* From "American Heroes on Mission Fields," by permission of the American Tract Society. Archives of the American Antiquarian Society, Worcester, Massachusetts.

Hunt, Alan. 1992. "Foucault's Expulsion of Law: Toward a Retrieval." *Law and Social Inquiry* 17: 1–39.

————. 1995. "The Role of Law in the Civilizing Process and the Reform of Popular Culture." *Canadian Journal of Law and Society* 10: 5–29.

Hunt, Nancy Rose. 1997. "'Le bebe en brouse': European Women, African Birth Spacing, and Colonial Intervention in Breast Feeding in the Belgian Congo." Pp. 287–321 in *Tensions of Empire: Colonial Cultures in a Bourgeois World*, ed. Frederick Cooper and Ann Laura Stoler. Berkeley and Los Angeles: University of California Press.

Hutchinson, William R. 1987. *Errand to the World: American Protestant Thought and Foreign Missions*. Chicago: University of Chicago Press.

Ii, John Papa. 1959. *Fragments of Hawaiian History*, trans. Mary Kawena Pukui, ed. Dorothy B. Barrere. Honolulu: Bishop Museum Press.

Ingram, J. N. 1891. "The Hawaiians." *Chataugua Quarterly* 13: 755–758.

Jackson, Jean. 1995. "Culture, Genuine and Spurious: The Politics of Indianness in the Vaupes, Columbia." *American Ethnologist* 22: 3–28.

Johnson, Richard. 1986/87. "What Is Cultural Studies Anyway?" *Social Text* 12: 38–79.

Jolly, Margaret, and Martha Macintyre, eds. 1989. *Family and Gender in the Pacific: Domestic Contradictions and the Colonial Impact*. Cambridge, Eng.: Cambridge University Press.

Judd, Laura Fish. 1966. *Honolulu: Sketches of Life in the Hawaiian Islands from 1828 to 1861*, ed. Dale E. Morgan. Chicago: R. R. Donnelley and Sons.

Kai, Peggy. 1974. "Chinese Settlers in the Village of Hilo before 1852." *Hawaiian Journal of History* 8: 39.

————. 1976. *The Story of A'lai*. Privately printed. Ms. on file with author.

Kamakau, Samuel M. 1961. *Ruling Chiefs of Hawaii*. Honolulu: Kamehameha Schools Press.

————. 1991. *Na Mo'olelo a ka Po'e Kahiko: Tales and Traditions of the People of Old*, trans. Mary Kawena Pukui, ed. Dorothy B. Barrere. Honolulu: Bishop Museum Press.

Kame'eleihiwa, Lilikalā. 1992. *Native Land and Foreign Desires*. Honolulu: Bishop Museum Press.

Kaplan, Martha, and John D. Kelly. 1994. "Rethinking Resistance: Dialogics of 'Disaffection' in Colonial Fiji." *American Ethnologist* 21: 123–151.

Kaya, Fumiko. 1988. *Katsu Goto: The First Immigrant from Japan*. Published in Japan; English version in Hawaii State Archives, Honolulu.

Keesing, Roger M. 1992. *Custom and Confrontation: The Kwaio Struggle for Cultural Autonomy*. Chicago: University of Chicago Press.

Kelly, John D. 1994. *The Politics of Virtue*. Princeton, N.J.: Princeton University Press.

Kelly, Marion. 1980. "Land Tenure in Hawaii." *Amerasia Journal* 7:57–73.

Kelly, Marion, Barry Nakamura, and Dorothy B. Barrere. 1981. *Hilo Bay: A Chronological History*. Prepared for U.S. Army Corps of Engineers District, Honolulu. Typescript.

Kent, Noel J. 1983. *Hawaii: Islands under the Influence*. New York: Monthly Review Press.

Kidder, R. L. 1979. "Toward an Integrated Theory of Imposed Law." Pp. 289–306 in *The Imposition of Law*, ed. S. B. Burman and B. E. Harrell-Bond. New York: Academic Press.

King, Pauline N., ed. 1989. *Journal of Stephen Reynolds*, vol. 1, 1823–1829. Honolulu: Ku Pa'a, Inc.; Salem, Mass.: Peabody Museum of Salem.

Kingdom of Hawai'i. 1846. *Answers to Questions: Proposed by His Excellency R. C. Wyllie, His Hawaiian Majesty's Minister of Foreign Relations, and Addressed to All the Missionaries in the Hawaiian Islands, May 1846*. Prepared by R. C. Wyllie, Minister of Foreign Relations.

———. 1847. *Third Organic Act: An Act to Organize the Judiciary Department of the Hawaiian Islands*. 64 pp. in *Statute Laws of His Majesty Kamehameha III, King of the Hawaiian Islands, Passed by the Houses of Nobles and Representatives during the 22nd Year of His Reign and the Fifth Year of His Public Recognition*. Honolulu: Charles E. Hitchcock, Printer, Government Press.

———. 1850. *Penal Code of the Hawaiian Islands; Kanawai Hoopai Karaima no ko Hawaii Pae Aina*. Honolulu: Mea Pai Palapala a na Misionari (Henry M. Whitney, Government Press).

———. 1884. *Compiled Laws of the Hawaiian Kingdom*. Published by Authority. Honolulu: Hawaiian Gazette Office.

———. 1894. *Constitution and Laws of 1840: Hawaii's "Blue" Laws: A Practical Illustration of the Missionaries' Love for the Hawaiians*. Republished Honolulu: Holomua Publishing Company.

Kipling, Rudyard. 1921. *Rudyard Kipling's Verse, Inclusive Edition 1885–1918*. Garden City, N.Y.: Doubleday, Page, and Company.

Kirch, Patrick Vinton. 1985. *Feathered Gods and Fishhooks: An Introduction to Hawaiian Archeology and Prehistory*. Honolulu: University of Hawaii Press.

Kirch, Patrick V., and Marshall Sahlins. 1992. *Anahulu: The Anthropology of History in the Kingdom of Hawaii*. Chicago: University of Chicago Press.

Kubota, Gaylord C. 1985. "The Lynching of Katsu Goto." *Honolulu* (November): 6–8, 124–137.

Kuykendall, Ralph S. 1938. *The Hawaiian Kingdom*, vol. 1. Honolulu: University of Hawaii Press.

———. 1953. *The Hawaiian Kingdom: 1854–1874, Twenty Critical Years*, vol. 2. Honolulu: University of Hawaii Press.

———. 1967. *The Hawaiian Kingdom: 1874–1893, The Kakakaua Dynasty*, vol. 3. Honolulu: University of Hawaii Press.

Lam, Maivan. 1985. "The Imposition of Anglo-American Land Tenure Law on Hawaiians." *Journal of Legal Pluralism* 23: 103–129.

Lancaster, Roger. 1992. *Life Is Hard: Machismo, Danger, and the Intimacy of Power in Nicaragua*. Berkeley and Los Angeles: University of California Press.

Langlas, Charles. 1990. *The People of Kalāpana, 1823–1950: A Report of the Kalāpana Oral History Project*. Typescript on file with author.

Lazarus-Black, Mindie. 1994. *Legitimate Acts and Illegal Encounters: Law and Society in Antigua and Barbuda*. Washington, D.C.: Smithsonian Institution Press.

Lazarus-Black, Mindie, and Susan Hirsch, eds. 1994. *Contested States: Law, Hegemony, and Resistance*. New York: Routledge.

Leithead, A. Scott. 1974. "Hilo, Hawaii: Its Origins and the Pattern of Its Growth, 1778–1900." B.A. honors thesis, University of Hawaii, Department of History.

Levin, Stephanie Seto. 1968. "Overthrow of the Kapu System in Hawai'i." *Journal of the Polynesian Society* 77: 402–431.

Lewis, C. S. 1965 [1963]. "Kipling's World." Pp. 99–118 in *Kipling and the Critics*, ed. Elliot Gilbert. New York: New York University Press.

Lind, Andrew. 1955. *Hawaii's People*. Honolulu: University of Hawaii Press.

Linnekin, Jocelyn. 1990. *Sacred Queens and Women of Consequence: Rank, Gender, and Colonialism in the Hawaiian Islands*. Ann Arbor: University of Michigan Press.

———. 1991. "Structural History and Political Economy: The Contact Encounter in Hawai'i and Samoa." *History and Anthropology* 5: 205–232.

Lydgate, J. M. 1922. "Hilo Fifty Years Ago." *Thrum's Hawaiian Annual*: 101–108.

Lydon, Edward C. 1975. *The Anti-Chinese Movement in the Hawaiian Kingdom, 1852–1886*. San Francisco: R and E Research Associates.

Macrae, James. 1972 [1826]. *With Lord Byron at the Sandwich Islands in 1826: Being Extracts from the MS Diary of James Macrae, Scottish Botanist*. Hilo: Petroglyph Press.

Maine, Henry. 1917 [1871]. *Ancient Law*. Everyman's Library. London: J. M. Dent and Sons.

Malo, David. 1839. "On the Decrease of Population on the Hawaiian Islands," trans. L. Andrews. *Hawaiian Spectator* 2 (2): 16, 122–130.

———. 1951 [1898]. *Hawaiian Antiquities (Moolelo Hawaii)*, trans. Nathaniel B. Emerson. Bernice P. Bishop Museum, Special Publication 2, second edition. Honolulu: Bishop Museum Press.

Mamdani, Mahmood. 1996. *Citizen and Subject: Contemporary Africa and the Legacy of Late Colonialism*. Princeton, N.J.: Princeton University Press.

Manderson, Lenore, and Margaret Jolly, eds. 1997. *Sites of Desire, Economies of Pleasure: Sexualities in Asia and the Pacific*. Chicago: University of Chicago Press.

Martin, Margaret Greer, Nettie Hammond Lyman, Kathryn Lyman Bond, and Ethel M. Damon. 1979. *The Lymans of Hilo*. Hilo: Lyman House Memorial Museum.

Mather, Lynn, and Barbara Yngvesson. 1980/81. "Language, Audience, and the Transformation of Disputes." *Law and Society Review* 15: 775–822.

Matsuda, Mari J. 1988a. "Law and Culture in the District Court of Honolulu, 1844–1845: A Case Study of the Rise of Legal Consciousness." *American Journal of Legal History* 32: 16–41.

———. 1988b. "Native Custom and Official Law in Hawaii." *Law and Anthropology: Internationales Jahrbuch für Rechtsanthropologie* 3: 135–147.

Maurer, Bill. 1997. *Recharting the Caribbean: Land, Law, and Citizenship in the British Virgin Islands*. Ann Arbor: University of Michigan Press.

McClintock, Anne. 1995. *Imperial Leather: Race, Gender, and Sexuality in the Colonial Contest*. New York: Routledge.

McGregor-Alegado, Davianna. 1980. "A Translation and Analysis of *No Ka Moe Kolohe*, A Law of King Kauikeaouli Enacted on September 21, 1829." No. 7 in *Ka Unuhi: The Translator*. Department of Indo-Pacific Languages, University of Hawaii, Honolulu, vol. 1.

Mehta, Uday S. 1997. "Liberal Strategies of Exclusion." Pp. 59–87 in *Tensions of Empire: Colonial Cultures in a Bourgeois World*, ed. Frederick Cooper and Ann Laura Stoler. Berkeley and Los Angeles: University of California Press.

Melville, Herman. 1964 [1846]. *Typee: A Peep at Polynesian Life*. New York: New American Library.

Mengel, Laurie M. 1997. "*Issei* Women and Divorce in Hawai'i, 1885–1908." *Social Process in Hawai'i* 38: 16–40.

Merrill, George. 1868. "Hawaiian Civilization." *Overland Monthly* n.s. 1 (July): 69–81.

Merry, Sally Engle. 1981. *Urban Danger: Life in a Neighborhood of Strangers*. Philadelphia: Temple University Press.

———. 1988. "Legal Pluralism." *Law and Society Review* 22: 869–896.

———. 1990. *Getting Justice and Getting Even: Legal Consciousness among Working-Class Americans*. Chicago: University of Chicago Press.

———. 1991. "Law and Colonialism: Review Essay." *Law and Society Review* 25: 879–922.

———. 1995. "Gender Violence and Legally Engendered Selves." *Identities: Global Studies in Culture and Power* 2:49–73.

———. 1997. "Legal Vernacularization and Transnational Culture: The Ka Ho'okolokolonui Kanaka Maoli, Hawai'i 1993." Pp. 28–49 in *Human Rights, Culture and Context: Anthropological Perspectives*, ed. Richard Wilson. London: Pluto Press.

Messick, Brinkley. 1992. *The Calligraphic State: Textual Domination and History in a Muslim Society*. Berkeley and Los Angeles: University of California Press.

Miller, Char. 1989. "Rumors and the Language of Social Change in Early Nineteenth-Century Hawaii." *Pacific Studies* 12: 1–28.

Mintz, Sidney. 1985. *Sweetness and Power*. New York: Viking.

Mitchell, Timothy. 1988. *Colonising Egypt*. Cambridge, Eng.: Cambridge University Press.

———. 1990. "Everyday Metaphors of Power." *Theory and Society* 19: 545–577.

———. 1992. "Orientalism and the Exhibitionary Order." Pp. 289–318 in *Colonialism and Culture*, ed. Nicholas B. Dirks. Ann Arbor: University of Michigan Press.

Mookini, Esther T. 1994. "George Washington Akao Hapai, 1840–1908." *Kaulike: Newsletter of the Friends of the Judiciary History Center of Hawai'i* 6: 2–4.

Moore, Sally Falk. 1986. *Social Facts and Fabrications: Customary Law on Kilimanjaro, 1880–1980*. Cambridge, Eng.: Cambridge University Press.

Morgan, Lewis Henry. 1964 [1877]. *Ancient Society*. Cambridge, Mass.: Harvard University Press.

Morgan, Theodore. 1948. *Hawaii: A Century of Economic Change 1778–1876*. Cambridge, Mass.: Harvard University Press.

Morris, Robert J. 1990. "*Aikāne*: Accounts of Hawaiian Same-Sex Relationships in the Journals of Captain Cook's Third Voyage (1776–80)." *Journal of Homosexuality* 19: 21–54.

Murayama, Milton. 1988 [1959]. *All I Asking for Is My Body*. Reprint, Honolulu: University of Hawaii Press.

Nader, L. 1990. *Harmony Ideology: Justice and Control in a Zapotec Mountain Village*. Stanford, Calif.: Stanford University Press.

Nader, Laura, and Harry F. Todd, eds. 1978. *The DisputingProcess—Law in Ten Societies*. New York: Columbia University Press.

Nakamura, Cathleen N. 1980. "Legal Terms Regarding Marriage, Divorce, and Lewdness in 1841." No. 1 (pp. 1–50) in *Ka Unuhi: The Translator.* Department of Indo-Pacific Languages, University of Hawaii, Honolulu, vol. 1.

Native Hawaiians Study Commission. 1983. *Report on the Culture, Needs and Concerns of Native Hawaiians*, vol 2, *Claims of Conscience: A Dissenting Study*. Submitted to Committee on Energy and Natural Resources of the U.S. Senate and Committee on Interior and Insular Affairs of the U.S. House of Representatives.

Nelligan, P. J. 1983. *Social Change and Rape Law in Hawaii.* Ph.D. diss., Department of Sociology, University of Hawaii.

Nelligan, Peter J., and Harry V. Ball. 1992. "Ethnic Juries in Hawaii: 1825–1900." *Social Process in Hawaii* 34: 113–163.

Obeyesekere, Gananath. 1992. *The Apotheosis of Captain Cook: European Mythmaking in the Pacific.* Princeton, N.J.: Princeton University Press.

Ohlson, Winfield E. 1937. "Adultery: A Review." *Boston University Law Review* 17: 328–368, 533–620.

Okihiro, Gary. 1991. *Cane Fires.* Philadelphia: Temple University Press.

Oleson, Wm. Brewster. 1908. "Just Like a Hawaiian." *The Friend* (October): 80.

Ong, Aihwa, and Michael G. Peletz, eds. 1995. *Bewitching Women, Pious Men.* Berkeley and Los Angeles: University of California Press.

Ortner, Sherry. 1981. "Gender and Sexuality in Hierarchical Societies." Pp. 359–409 in *Sexual Meanings*, ed. Sherry Ortner and Harriet Whitehead. New York: Cambridge University Press.

Orwell, George. 1965 [1946]. "Rudyard Kipling." Pp. 74–88 in *Kipling and the Critics*, ed. Elliot Gilbert. New York: New York University Press.

Osorio, Jonathan Kamakawiwoʻole. 1996. "Determining Self: Identity, Nationhood and Constitutional Government in Hawaiʻi 1842–1887." Ph.D. diss. Department of History, University of Hawaiʻi, Mānoa.

Otto, Dianne. 1996. "Subalternity and International Law: The Problems of Global Community and the Incommensurability of Difference." *Social and Legal Studies* 5: 337–364.

Parker, Elizabeth. 1852. *The Sandwich Islands as They Are, Not as They Should Be.* San Francisco: Burgess, Gilbert and Still. (By a frontier journalist.)

Parker, Linda. 1989. *Native American Estate: The Struggle over Indian and Hawaiian Lands.* Honolulu: University of Hawaii Press.

Parmentier, Richard J. 1994. "Review of Ganath Obeyesekere, *The Apotheosis of Captain Cook.*" *The Contemporary Pacific* (spring): 238–240.

Philips, Susan U. 1998. *Ideology in the Language of Judges.* Oxford: Oxford University Press.

Phillips, Willard, and Samuel B. Walcott. 1844. *Report of the Penal Code of Massachusetts.* Boston: Dutton and Wentworth, State Printers.

Pierce, Henry E. 1869. *In the Matter of the Legitimacy of Henry E. Pierce, A Native of the Hawaiian or Sandwich Islands.* Honolulu: n.p. (Testimony, argument, and text of laws.)

Piercy, LaRue W. 1992. *Hawaii's Missionary Saga: Sacrifice and Godliness in Paradise.* Honolulu: Mutual Publishing.

Pitman, Almira. 1931. *After Fifty Years: An Appreciation, and a Record of a Unique Incident.* Norwood, USA: Plimpton Press. (Privately printed.)

Pratt, Mary Louise. 1992. *Imperial Eyes: Travel Writing and Transculturation.* New York: Routledge.

Pukui, Mary Kawena, and Samuel H. Elbert. 1964. *English-Hawaiian Dictionary.* Honolulu: University of Hawaii Press.

———. 1965 [1957]. *Hawaiian-English Dictionary.* Third ed. Honolulu: University of Hawaii Press.

Rafael, Vincente. 1988. *Contracting Colonialism: Translation and Christian Conversion in Tagalog Society under Early Spanish Rule.* Ithaca, N.Y.: Cornell University Press.

Ralston, Caroline. 1985. "Early Nineteenth-Century Polynesian Millenial Cults and the Case of Hawai'i." *Journal of the Polynesian Society* 94: 307–331.

———. 1989. "Changes in the Lives of Ordinary Women in Early Post-Contact Hawaii." Pp. 45–65 in *Family and Gender in the Pacific: Domestic Contradictions and the Colonial Impact,* ed. Margaret Jolly and Martha Macintyre. Cambridge, Eng.: Cambridge University Press.

Reed, Adam. 1997. "Contested Images and Common Strategies: Early Colonial Sexual Politics in the Massim." Pp. 48–72 in *Sites of Desire, Economies of Pleasure,* ed. Lenore Manderson and Margaret Jolly. Chicago: University of Chicago Press.

Report of the Minister of the Interior. 1847. Read before his Majesty to the Hawaiian Legislature, April 30th. Honolulu: C. E. Hitchcock, printer.

Riles, Annelise. 1999. "Infinity within the Brackets." *American Ethnologist* 25: 1–21.

Roberts, Richard, and Kristin Mann. 1991. "Law in Colonial Africa." Pp. 3–61 in *Law in Colonial Africa,* ed. Kristin Mann and Richard Roberts. Portsmouth, N.H.: Heinemann.

Rodriguez, Noelie Maria. 1988. "A Successful Feminist Shelter: A Case Study of the Family Crisis Shelter in Hawaii." *Journal of Applied Behavioral Science* 24: 235–250.

Rosen, Lawrence. 1989. *The Anthropology of Justice: Law as Culture in Islamic Society.* Cambridge, Eng.: Cambridge University Press.

Rothman, David J. 1971. *The Discovery of the Asylum: Social Order and Disorder in the New Republic.* Boston: Little Brown.

Rouland, Norbert. 1994. *Legal Anthropology,* trans. Philippe G. Planel. Stanford, Calif.: Stanford Univ. Press. (Originally published 1988 in French.)

Rubin, Gayle. 1993 [1984]. "Thinking Sex: Notes for a Radical Theory of the Politics of Sexuality." Pp. 3–45 in *The Gay and Lesbian Studies Reader,* ed. Henry Abelove, Michele Aina Barale, and David M. Halperin. New York: Routledge.

Sahlins, Marshall. 1958. *Social Stratification in Polynesia.* Seattle: University of Washington Press.

———. 1985. *Islands of History.* Chicago: University of Chicago Press.

———. 1992. *Historical Ethnography.* Vol. 1 of *Anahulu: The Anthropology of History in the Kingdom of Hawaii,* by Patrick Kirch and Marshall Sahlins. Chicago: University of Chicago Press.

———. 1995. *How "Natives" Think, About Captain Cook, for Example.* Chicago: University of Chicago Press.

Sahlins, Marshall, and Dorothy Barrere, eds. 1973. "William Richards on Hawaiian Culture and Political Conditions of the Hawaiian Islands in 1841." *Hawaiian Journal of History* 7: 18–41.

Said, Edward W. 1978. *Orientalism.* New York: Random House.

Santos, Boaventura de Sousa. 1995. *Toward a New Common Sense.* New York: Routledge.

Sarat, Austin, and William Felstiner. 1995. *Divorce Lawyers and Their Clients.* New York: Oxford University Press.

Sarat, Austin, and Thomas R. Kearns. 1993. "Beyond the Great Divide: Forms of

Legal Scholarship and Everyday Life." Pp. 21–63 in *Law and Everyday Life*. Ann Arbor: University of Michigan Press.

———, eds. 1992. *Law's Violence*. Ann Arbor, Mich.: University of Michigan Press.

Schmitt, Robert C. 1967. "Statistics on Income in Hawaii, 1825–1966." *Hawaii Historical Review* 2: 358–372.

———. 1968. *Demographic Statistics of Hawaii 1778–1965*. Honolulu: University of Hawaii Press.

Schmitt, Robert C., and Rose C. Strombel. 1966. "Marriage and Divorce in Hawaii before 1870." *Hawaii Historical Review* 2: 267–271.

Schouler, James. 1894. "A Review of the Hawaiian Controversy." *The Forum* 16 (February): 670–689.

Scott, James C. 1985. *Weapons of the Weak*. New Haven: Yale University Press.

———. 1990. *Domination and the Arts of Resistance: Hidden Transcripts*. New Haven: Yale University Press

Sharma, Miriam. 1980. "Pinoy in Paradise: Environment and Adaptation of Pilipinos in Hawaii, 1906–1946." *Amerasia Journal* 7: 91–117.

Sheldon, Henry. 1881. "Reminiscences of Honolulu 35 Years Ago." Saturday Press. State Archives, Honolulu. Typescript.

Sheldon, John G. 1988 [1909]. *The Biography of Joseph K. Nawahi*, trans. Marvin Puakea Nogelmeier. Hawaiian Historical Society. Typescript.

Sider, Gerald M. 1986. *Culture and Class in Anthropology and History*. Cambridge, Eng.: Cambridge University Press.

Silva, Noenoe K. 1997. "Kū'ē! Hawaiian Women's Resistance to the Annexation." *Social Process in Hawai'i* 38: 2–16.

Silverman, Jane. 1982. "Imposition of a Western Judicial System in the Hawaiian Monarchy." *Hawaiian Journal of History* 16: 48–65.

———. 1983. "To Marry Again." *Hawaiian Journal of History* 17: 64–75.

———. 1987. *Kaahumanu: Molder of Change*. Honolulu: Friends of the Judiciary History Center of Hawaii.

Simon, Roger. 1991. *Gramsci's Political Thought: An Introduction*. London: Lawrence and Wishart.

Sinclair, Marjorie. 1969. "Princess Nahienaena." *Hawaiian Journal of History* 3: 3–31.

———. 1995. *Nāhi'ena'ena: Sacred Daughter of Hawai'i, A Life Ensnared*. Honolulu: Mutual Publishing.

Stannard, David. 1989. *Before the Horror: The Population of Hawai'i on the Eve of Western Contact*. Honolulu: Social Sciences Research Institute and University of Hawai'i Press.

Starr, June. 1992. *Law as Metaphor: From Islamic Courts to the Palace of Justice*. Albany: SUNY Press.

Starr, June, and Jane F. Collier, eds. 1989. *History and Power: New Directions in the Study of Law*. Ithaca, N.Y.: Cornell University Press.

Stevens, John L. 1893. "II. A Plea for Annexation." *North American Review* 157 (December): 736–745.

Stoler, Ann Laura. 1985. *Capitalism and Confrontation in Sumatra's Plantation Belt, 1870–1979*. Ann Arbor: University of Michigan Press.

———. 1989. "Making Empire Respectable: The Politics of Race and Sexual Morality in 20th Century Colonial Cultures." *American Ethnologist* 16: 634–661.

———. 1991. "Carnal Knowledge and Imperial Power: Gender, Race, and Morality in Colonial Asia." Pp. 55–101 in *Gender at the Crossroads of Knowledge: Feminism in Anthropology in the Postmodern Era*, ed. Micaela di Leonardo. Berkeley and Los Angeles: University of California Press.

———. 1995. *Race and the Education of Desire: Foucault's History of Sexuality and the Colonial Order of Things*. Durham, N.C.: Duke University Press.

———. 1997. "Sexual Affronts and Racial Frontiers: European Identities and the Cultural Politics of Exclusion in Colonial Southeast Asia." Pp. 198–237 in *Tensions of Empire: Colonial Cultures in a Bourgeois World*, ed. Frederick Cooper and Ann Laura Stoler. Berkeley and Los Angeles: University of California Press.

Stoler, Ann Laura, and Frederick Cooper. 1997. "Between Metropole and Colony: Rethinking a Research Agenda." Pp. 1–58 in *Tensions of Empire: Colonial Cultures in a Bourgeois World*, ed. Frederick Cooper and Ann Laura Stoler. Berkeley and Los Angeles: University of California Press.

Sullivan, Louis R. 1923. "The Labor Crisis in Hawaii." *Asia Magazine* 23: 511–534.

Takaki, Ronald. 1983. *Pau Hana: Plantation Life and Labor in Hawaii, 1835–1920*. Honolulu: University of Hawaii Press.

———. 1989. *Strangers from a Different Shore: A History of Asian Americans*. Boston: Little, Brown.

Taussig, Michael. 1987. *Shamanism, Colonialism, and the Wild Man: A Study in Terror and Healing*. Chicago: University of Chicago Press.

Tennyson, Alfred. 1892. *The Works of Alfred Lord Tennyson*. New York: Grosset and Dunlap.

Thomas, Nicholas. 1994. *Colonialism's Culture: Anthropology, Travel, and Government*. Princeton, N.J.: Princeton University Press.

———. 1997. *In Oceania: Visions, Artifacts, Histories*. Durham, N.C.: Duke University Press.

Thompson, E. P. 1967. "Time, Work Discipline, and Industrial Capitalism." *Past and Present* 38: 56–97.

———. 1975. *Whigs and Hunters: The Origins of the Black Acts*. New York: Pantheon.

Thorne, Susan. 1997. "'The Conversion of Englishmen and the Conversion of the World Inseparable': Missionary Imperialism and the Language of Class in Early Industrial Britain." Pp. 238–263 in *Tensions of Empire: Colonial Cultures in a Bourgeois World*, ed. Frederick Cooper and Ann Laura Stoler. Berkeley and Los Angeles: University of California Press.

Thurston, Lorrin A. n.d. (circa 1897). *A Handbook on the Annexation of Hawaii*. Pamphlet.

———. 1898. "President Dole and the Hawaiian Question." *The Outlook* (February 5): 317–320.

———. ed. 1904. *The Fundamental Law of Hawaii*. Honolulu, T.H.: Hawaiian Gazette Co.

Trask, Haunani-Kay. 1987a. "The Birth of the Modern Hawaiian Movement: Kalama Valley, O'ahu." *Hawaiian Journal of History* 21: 126–153.

———. 1987b. "From a Native Daughter." Pp. 171–179 in *The American Indian and the Problem of History*, ed. Calvin Martin. New York: Oxford University Press.

————. 1993. *From a Native Daughter: Colonialism and Sovereignty in Hawai'i.* Monroe, Me.: Common Courage Press.

————. 1994. "*Kūpa'a 'Āina*: Native Hawaiian Nationalism in Hawai'i." Pp. 15–34 in *Hawai'i: Return to Nationhood*, ed. Ulla Hasager and Jonathan Friedman. Copenhagen: IWGIA Document no. 75.

Trask, Mililani B. 1994. "The Politics of Oppression." Pp. 71–91 in *Hawai'i: Return to Nationhood*, ed. Ulla Hasager and Jonathan Friedman. Copenhagen: IWGIA Document no. 75.

Turrill Collection of Letters, 1845–1860. 1957. *Hawaiian Historical Society Annual Report*, Sixty-Sixth Annual Report. Pp. 27–93. Honolulu: Hawaiian Historical Society.

Twain, Mark. 1990. *Mark Twain in Hawaii: Roughing It in the Sandwich Islands.* Honolulu: Mutual Publishing.

Walkowitz, Judith R. 1980. *Prostitution and Victorian Society: Women, Class, and the State.* Cambridge, Eng.: Cambridge University Press.

Webb, M. C. 1965. "The Abolition of the Taboo System in Hawai'i." *Journal of the Polynesian Society* 74:21–39.

Williston, Samuel. 1938. *William Richards.* Cambridge, Mass.: Privately printed. Harvard Law Library.

Wise, John H. 1933. "The History of Land Ownership in Hawaii." Pp. 77–91 in *Ancient Hawaiian Civilization: A Series of Lectures Delivered at the Kamehameha Schools by Handy, Emory, Bryan, Buck, Wise, and Others.* Honolulu: Kamehameha Schools.

Wolf, Eric. 1992 [1982]. *Europe and the People without History.* Berkeley and Los Angeles: University of California Press.

Wyllie, Robert. 1844. "Native Seamen." *The Friend*: 79.

Yngvesson, B. 1988. "Making Law at the Doorway: The Clerk, the Court, and the Construction of Community in a New England Town." *Law and Society Review* 22: 409–448.

————. 1993. *Virtuous Citizens, Disruptive Subjects: Order and Complaint in a New England Court.* New York: Routledge.

INDEX